Asine and the Argolid in the Late Helladic III Period

A socio-economic study

Birgitta L. Sjöberg

BAR International Series 1225
2004

Published in 2016 by
BAR Publishing, Oxford

BAR International Series 1225

Asine and the Argolid in the Late Helladic III Period

ISBN 978 1 84171 590 2

BAR Publishing is the trading name of British Archaeological Reports (Oxford) Ltd. British Archaeological Reports was first incorporated in 1974 to publish the BAR Series, International and British. In 1992 Hadrian Books Ltd became part of the BAR group. This volume was originally published by Archaeopress in conjunction with British Archaeological Reports (Oxford) Ltd / Hadrian Books Ltd, the Series principal publisher, in 2004. This present volume is published by BAR Publishing, 2016.

Printed in England

BAR
PUBLISHING

BAR titles are available from:

BAR Publishing
122 Banbury Rd, Oxford, OX2 7BP, UK
EMAIL info@barpublishing.com
PHONE +44 (0)1865 310431
FAX +44 (0)1865 316916
www.barpublishing.com

Acknowledgements

This book has evolved out of a doctoral thesis defended at the Department of Archaeology and Ancient History, Uppsala University, in 2001. The research was made possible thanks to financial support from the University. My work has also been supported by grants from the Friends of the Swedish Institute in Athens and from the A.W. Persson fund, grants which have been most welcome as they have helped defray costs for accessing important parts of the material upon which this work is based. There is often no good substitute to getting to know the archaeological record first hand; this is as true for research that to a considerable extent depends on the excavations, descriptions and analyses carried out by several generations of scholars as for other approaches.

In this connection it is most appropriate to thank the Nauplion Ephoria for permission to work at the Lionardo apotheke, Nauplion. It goes without saying that the material generated by the various excavations at Asine from the 1920s onward and now kept there and at Uppsala has been critical to my endeavours. The German Archaeological Institute at Athens gave me the permission to visit the store rooms at Tiryns, then supervised by Dr. G. Albers. Special thanks are due to Dr. A. Papadimitriou for all information concerning the pottery material excavated at Tiryns. I am also most grateful to Dr. S. Voutsaki for her permission to refer to her unpublished thesis (Cambridge 1992). The staff of the Swedish Institute at Athens has been a most valuable source of support as has the staff of the Nordic Library in Athens. My sincere thanks are similarly due to the librarians at the Dept. of Archaeology and Ancient History in Uppsala, for acting on and indeed anticipating so many of my needs.

During my work I have received much help and generous support from a large number of colleagues and friends. To begin with I would like to express my gratitude to my former tutor Prof. em. T. Linders and to my thesis adviser Prof. P. Hellström. Various parts of the text that follows has at one point or other benefited from constructive and most helpful criticism solicited from or volunteered by several persons. Whatever qualities this work may have thus owes a great deal to Dr. J. Bennet, Dr. C. Gillis, Prof. G. Nordquist, Prof. B. Santillo-Frizell and Prof. G. Walberg. I would also like to express my gratitude to Prof. H. Mommsen for all information concerning pottery analysis. The participants in the seminar of Classical Archaeology at Uppsala and the workshops on 'Trade and Production' held at the Swedish Institute at Athens have similarly provided important ideas and feedback during these years of research.

The numerous technicalities associated with producing a hard copy of my research findings have at times been little short of overwhelming. In this connection I would like to express a special thanks to Dr. B. Alroth for her expert help with the bibliography. I am also grateful to Mr. N. Tomkinson who revised my English, Chapters 1 to 7, and to Mrs. C. Risberg for reading the first round of proofs. My husband in addition to carrying out proof reading on parts of the manuscript also diligently laboured with the equally thankless tasks of formatting and layout. As a geographer, he will be pleased to note that the maps in Figs. 6-11 have been expertly drawn by my colleague Dr. A. Klynne. A special thank to my colleague Dr. A. Sundkvist for computer support in the final critical stage of the manuscript.

The map in Fig. 1 has been reproduced with the kind permission of Prof. J.L. Bintliff, while Fig. 2, which originates from K. Kilian, 'The emergence of *wanax* ideology in the Mycenaean palaces', *Oxford Journal of Archaeology*, vol. 7:3 , 1988, has been included with the permission of Blackwell Publishing Ltd. The first of the two maps in Fig. 5 was originally compiled and drawn by D.L Indge from information supplied by J. Lavery, in 'Some "new" Mycenaean roads at Mycenae, *BICS* 37, 1995. The permission granted by the ©Institute of Classical Studies, School of Advanced Study, University of London, to reproduce these maps here is gratefully acknowledged. The maps in Figs. 6-11 are based on a base map originally published by R. Hägg in *Die Gräber der Argolis in submykenischer, protogeometrischer und geometrischer Zeit*, 1. *Lage und Form der Gräber* (Boreas. Uppsala Studies in Ancient Mediterranean and Near Eastern Civilizations, 7:1) Uppsala 1974. The plans in Figs. 3 and 4 are taken from the publication O. Frödin and A. W. Persson, *Asine. Results of the Swedish excavations 1922-1930* , Stockholm, 1938.

CONTENTS

FIGURES

PART I

SETTING THE STAGE

CHAPTER 1
ECONOMY AND CENTRALISATION IN THE LATE HELLADIC ARGOLID

1.1 INTRODUCTION

Mycenaean society, it is commonly asserted, was characterised by centralised decision making over an integrated and culturally homogeneous region. In matters political and economic, the lords of the palaces, and in particular that of Mycenae held sway over a population subject to taxes in kind and corvée labour. Beyond his obligations to the Palace, the Late Helladic inhabitant of the area commanded little by way of resources to engage in anything but subsistence activities. Indeed, the average subject had no apparent reason to take part in trade or any other commercial activity on his or her own account. This was left to palatial control.

Such is the power of this long- prevailing view that, until recently, few thought of questioning the logic and implications of conceptions and models based on the above – here admittedly simplified – mode of reasoning. At its most simple, the argument revolves around the issue whether Mycenaean society was strongly centralised with redistributive traits or whether the power and homogenising influence of the centre, if any, did not quite reach into the far corners of everyday subsistence activities. If the latter view has anything to commend it, this will have far-reaching ramifications for our perception of the nature of life and society in the Mycenaean Argolid. If, on the other hand, this long-dominating view can be proved to be correct, we shall be on much firmer ground with respect to the inferences that we may legitimately make.

This study is an attempt to address that particular issue.[1] Its purpose is to evaluate, by examining the conceptual and theoretical foundation upon which the now predominant view is based, the claims made with respect to the nature and character of the economic system of Late Helladic society in the Argolid. Both various conceptual angles on the problem and recent findings in the literature will be drawn upon in order to find out whether or not it is warranted to challenge the images of a strictly hierarchical society projected by earlier work on the subject.
In order to do so, it is necessary to analyse the economy of Mycenaean society as a whole and not merely as an appendix to the palaces. This is especially so as the emerging critique of the dominant paradigm underlines the likelihood of lateral economic links co-existing with top-down, political control. Although some attempts to construct central- place models, or settlement hierarchies, have indeed been made, they are premised on the assumption that the palaces had control over the area. As this may be to overstate the case, a more open-ended approach will be employed here. Furthermore, to emphasise this point, the present study also sets out to analyse in more detail the role of Asine, a mid-tier settlement in the Argolid, with a view to establishing the vertical and horizontal linkages that this settlement may have had with the surrounding communities.

1.2 THE AEGEAN DEBATE ON ECONOMY AND CENTRALISATION

The received view

The debate on economic issues among Aegean archaeologists has for the most part taken second part to other concerns. Mycenaean studies are no exception in this regard. This state of affairs may possibly account for the fact that we often find a core set of ideas applied without much further ado. Indeed, it is not an infrequent occurrence that these ideas appear as assumptions – often implicit and perhaps unconscious – about the nature and character of the society examined. For the most part, this implies that the Mycenaean economy is characterised as a pre-market society. Market transactions, if they occurred at all, were clearly less important than the redistribution of resources and produce.

This in turn is premised on the view that Mycenaean society had the centralised political structures and institutions; paralleled by the imposing palatial structures that are still there for us to wonder at; necessary for the successful re-allocation of material means and goods between various parts and segments of society. Given the level of political centralisation, it is often assumed that society was homogenous in economical, political and cultural terms. These character traits, perhaps the most important of which is the uniformity across Late Helladic society, will in the following pages be referred to as the homogeneity thesis.

This particular manner of looking at the Aegean world of the Late Helladic era was made manifest already in the

[1] Sjöberg 2001 is an earlier version of the present study. Individual chapters, or parts thereof, have been published as Sjöberg 1995; 2002.

first, and most important works that followed the deciphering of the Linear B tablets. A review of the studies on economic, political and social issues in the Late Bronze Age yields several different ways of approaching these problems. Yet there are common traits in the models that we may designate as traditional and implicit. They are based on a view of Late Helladic society as being centralised and homogeneous; empirically, they are squarely focused on the palaces. This view, supported by several scholars, has dominated the debate, but, as will be demonstrated later, analyses based on the idea of a more decentralised and heterogeneous, Late Bronze Age society have recently been advanced. It is quite obvious that with increased access to textual material and other archaeological remains, the debate has become more sophisticated. Even so, the discussions on the economic aspects of the palatial administration of the Mycenaean economy, as such, are still, however, predominantly based on the twin ideas of centralisation and redistribution.[2]

How can we explain the strong emphasis on the centralised and redistributive character of the Mycenaean economy? The most obvious answer probably rests with the evidence collected by archaeology itself. At first glance, Mycenaean society displays all the components, including palace structure, administrative records embodied in Linear B material, tholos tombs and so forth, postulated by adherents of the received view. In short, the material evidence can be taken to imply a centralised Mycenaean world focused upon the palaces. Excavations have revealed monumental palatial structures with areas dedicated to the élite and storage facilities readily interpreted as basic features of economic centralisation. The redistributive side of the economy was further emphasised by the clay tablets: they mention commodities that seem to be flowing in and out of the palace centres. The Linear B material even brought forth evidence of the organisation of manpower under the supervision of the palaces and effectively outlined a redistributive system under centralised control. The contextual interpretation of the texts and the archaeological material thus resulted in a view of the Mycenaean world as centralised and redistributive.[3]

Already Finley observed that this society was centralised in nature and suggested that probably the palace economy comprised the entire economic system.[4] In line with the ideas put forward in Finley's article, several other major works based on Linear B texts have conveyed the message that Mycenaean society was predominantly redistributive in character. Typically, it has been stated that the palaces functioned as redistributive centres, and Linear B texts from both Pylos and Knossos, with the economic interests focused on persons belonging to the palatial élite, have been brought forward as evidence to this effect.[5] Renfrew, for instance, in an important work explicitly identified the palaces as redistributive centres with the entire economy, or certain areas of it, controlled by a central authority.[6] Other consequential contributions to a similar effect include articles by Killen, whose work focuses on the analysis of Linear B texts, in which an emphasis on the palaces as foci for a redistributive and centralised economy is made explicit.[7] That Late Helladic society was redistributive and centralised in character is also the view advanced by Palaima in several interesting and well-argued articles on Mycenaean sealing systems and textual evidence.[8]

These centralised traits are further emphasised by Bintliff and Kilian, who both, in their discussions on the settlement systems of the Argolid plain, accept the redistributive nature of the society and, as a consequence, interpret the archaeological material from the perspective of the centralised economy.[9] A quite recent contribution to this received view is presented by Snodgrass who defines exchange in the Bronze Age society as both reciprocal and redistributive and therefore not commercially oriented.[10] Also in I. Tournavitou's recently published and important study, *The Ivory Houses at Mycenae,* the same general traits of the Mycenaean world are emphasised.[11] Common to all these works, and several others not mentioned here, are thus their insistence on the Late Helladic society as centralised and highly stratified, with the palaces as economic, political and social nodes for a region or major parts thereof.

The emphasis on the centralised nature of Mycenaean society also resulted in another important conclusion, namely that the Mycenaean world should be regarded as a homogeneous entity in economic, political and cultural terms, with no significant regional variations. In the 1960s, the stances of scholars such as Desborough and Vermeule were based on an assumed hegemony over

[2] Furumark 1944, 262 regarded Argolis as the political and cultural centre of the Aegean world and the king of Mycenae as the overlord of a great realm; Finley 1957-58, 128-141. This article was to be followed by a flood of works discussing the economic structure of the Mycenaean world. To mention but a few of the more important ones, we may note the contributions by Chadwick 1976; Demakopoulou, 1995; Halstead 1988; 1992a; 1992b; Killen 1985; Kilian, 1987b; 1988a; Morris 1986; Renfrew 1972; Snodgrass 1991; Tournavitou 1995; Voutsaki 1992; 1997. I am most grateful to Dr. S. Voutsaki for her permission to refer to her unpublished thesis (Cambridge 1992).

[3] Halstead, 1996, 33; Kilian 1987b, 32; Morris 1986, 32; Renfrew 1972, 291-297, 462; Snodgrass 1991, 15-20; Tournavitou 1995, 285-298; Wright 1984, 27-28. Studies concerned with storage facilities and centralisation, although representing other geographical areas, include D'Altroy & Earle 1985; Earle & D'Altroy 1982; Moody 1987.

[4] Finley 1957-58, 134-135.

[5] Palmer 1965, 114; Ventris & Chadwick 1973, 110.

[6] Renfrew 1972, 296-297.

[7] Killen 1985.

[8] Palaima 1987; 1990.

[9] Bintliff 1977, 115-116, 134-138, 689-702; Kilian 1988a.

[10] Snodgrass 1991, 16.

[11] Tournavitou 1995.

much of the Aegean.[12] At that juncture, however, the dissenting voice of C.G. Thomas argued the importance of emphasising the plurality of the Mycenaean world and against the notion of an overlordship.[13] This argument was followed up in a later article with the proposal that regional variations continued throughout the period; this is exemplified by the diversity in the distribution of tholos tombs between the different regions.[14] Moreover, Thomas questioned the utility, indeed appropriateness, of phrases such as "the Mycenaean world" or "the Mycenaean Age" commonly applied to the Late Bronze Age. She argued that such a terminology 'calls to mind unity and concerted action or even hegemony' without much by way of evidence to support it.[15] Yet the view of the Mycenaean world as homogeneous in a variety of aspects is still more or less implicit in several works.[16] A trait prevalent in these works is their extrapolation of archaeological material, such as palaces, houses, artefacts and Linear B material, into the different Mycenaean regions without much consideration of the obvious discrepancies in the quantity and quality of material evidence or the contextual background.

Following upon the critique formulated by, for example Thomas, the received view has increasingly been challenged by scholars who have extended the research agenda to include not only material found in the palace grounds but also material found beyond the confines of the traditional sites of excavation. Interesting new ideas and hypotheses have now been applied to both Mainland material and other regions. As a consequence, the need for a re-evaluation of the nature of Mycenaean society in general and the palatial economy in particular has emerged as a second strand in the literature of the Late Bronze Age society.[17]

The emerging critique

That centralisation and redistribution ran like the main thread through a substantial part of the literature was observed by H. Morris, who in a thesis on the Mycenaean economy maintained that the favoured models do not always seem to be consciously formulated as theoretical frameworks. Instead, they appear as implicit models to characterise Mycenaean civilisation. Common to all of them, according to Morris, is the assumption that all the important aspects of society are concentrated in the élite.[18] The concept of markets is, she notes, occasionally mentioned, but the possible use of markets as important nodes for the distribution of goods during the Mycenaean period is not considered. Morris is of the opinion that most Aegean pre-historians reject the market system, on *a priori* grounds, as a mode of exchange; in fact, markets have not even been regarded as a secondary mode of exchange.[19]

In her study, Morris focuses not only on the palace at Pylos but also on the activities conducted at Nichoria and its interrelationship with the wider region. She thus breaks the prevailing mould and represents a new approach to the study of the Late Helladic economy and society. To the best of my knowledge, her study is the first one to approach the Mycenaean economy and society with a focus not only on the palace centre but also on a non-palatial site. Empirically, the analysis is based on a survey of architectural remains, Linear B texts, artefacts and so forth, and the archaeological data provide, according to Morris, mostly information on the central authority and its involvement in economic transactions. A critical assumption in her work is that the economic activities administered by the palace were those that were necessary to maintain political control. Other economic activities, such as production and distribution for consumption, were instead conducted on the local and regional levels. Morris concludes that her model emphasises not the political bases of the economy, but rather the ideological and social ones. It is also suggested that Mycenae and the other kingdoms, including Pylos, established reciprocal relationships and it is conceivable that Mycenae exerted an extended control over the international trade system.[20] In other words, also in this study, the homogeneous nature of the Late Bronze Age is taken for granted, although now with a considerable concession to the possibility of many activities being decentralised.

Further works in this critical vein include a model formulated by Halstead of the Late Bronze Age economy based on agriculture. Also this analysis accepts the redistributive and centralised nature of the economy. However, it does so in a much more nuanced manner, arguing that the non-palatial sites obviously played an important role in the agricultural sector without therefore being a link in the redistributive chain to the centres. That is, they were to some extent independent.[21] Exceptions include extraordinary situations, such as when 'independent late bronze age farmers with access to only marginal land will have been unable to secure long-term economic viability through agricultural or craft specialisation and so will have been dependent on the

[12] Desborough 1964, 218; Vermeule1964, 232.
[13] Thomas 1970.
[14] Thomas 1995.
[15] Thomas 1970, 184.
[16] Gates 1995, 296-297; Kardulias 1999, 189; Lewartowski 1989, 165.
[17] See for example Hooker 1976, 81, 134-135, who retains the idea of the homogeneity of the material culture but also claims that this does not necessarily imply unified political control; Bennet 1988a; 1988b; Dickinson 1982; Galaty & Parkinson 1999; Gillis 1997; Halstead 1988; Schallin, 1993, 188, discussed the role and position of the Cyclades at this particular point in time. The conclusion is that the Mycenaean presence is not overwhelming; Voutsaki 1992; 1998.

[18] Morris 1986, 8.
[19] Morris 1986, 32-33.
[20] Morris 1986, 1, 26, 186.
[21] Halstead 1992a, 63-74; 1992b, 114-115.

central redistributive authority for subsistence relief in times of shortage, presumably reciprocating with unskilled agricultural or craft labour'.[22] This interpretation of the agricultural economy points towards a more decentralised situation, in which the redistributive features, revealed by the archives, are limited to those which served the élite and the centrally controlled artisans, whereas distribution to other groups was limited to periods of shortage.

Halstead's model includes interaction and regular transactions, as evidenced by archival material, of products inside the palatial sector, and non-staples (taxes) as regular transactions between the non-palatial and the palatial sector. It is interesting to note the lack of regular transactions of goods. Rather, or so Halstead argues, the palace sponsored large-scale production, much of which was later redistributed to a specialised workforce. But the model also identifies a flow of products and services from the non-palatial to the palatial sector and, interestingly, these goods were not produced under palatial control. Further, non-staple commodities were contributed through taxation and there was also a need for seasonal agricultural labour at harvest times. The opposite flow, from the palatial to the non-palatial sector, included products from palace workshops and subsistence relief to farmers and some administrative, juridical and ritual services. The Linear B material, both at Pylos and Knossos, records toponyms, and the taxation was, according to Halstead, decentralised and organised by regional or local sub-centres.[23]

It is worth noting that Halstead proposes a model emphasising the decentralised nature of the agricultural economy. In addition, this sector of the economy is a well-defined one, in which regular redistributive transactions seem to have been used and where other transactional modes worked in parallel. Also this model presupposes that the Late Bronze Age world was homogeneous. It is suggested that the Mycenaean palaces of both mainland Greece and Crete should be treated as similar institutions.

Others are still more sceptical. A certain caution with respect to the strict acceptance of the centralised and homogeneous nature of Late Helladic society is advocated by, for example, Dickinson and Cavanagh and Mee.[24] Studies such as these, with a focus primarily on tomb material, have discussed the social aspects and their analyses have recognised regional variations, indicating a heterogeneous development. Dickinson noticed, for example, the obvious homogeneity in material culture in the LH IIIA2-IIIB periods, but also that the material development in the Argolid, and especially Mycenae, is considerably more advanced than at other centres and regions in the Peloponnese. Dickinson therefore asks whether the qualitative differences should not be perceptible in the social organisation and settlement distribution. He clearly has his doubts about imposing the social ramification, deduced from the Linear B evidence from Pylos, on the Argolid.[25]

Our knowledge of Late Helladic society has an important source of information in tombs, which may be viewed as exponents of economic, political and social diversity. Cavanagh and Mee observed both regional and chronological differences in the range of tomb types on an inter-regional level. On the bases on this observation, they argue that the tendency to stress the cultural homogeneity of Mycenaean Greece is over-simplistic.[26] Dickinson brings forward the theory that the various regions of the Peloponnese show differences in the distribution of different grave types. The tholos seems to have been relatively well represented in Messenia and, despite this it has generally been regarded as a royal tomb. The opposite is true of the chamber tomb, which has been stated as the tomb for the middle class, but appears instead, according to Dickinson, to display a degree of local variation.[27]

The differences between the two regions have recently also been pointed out in an article by Kopcke, who proposes that Mycenae had a much stronger position with international connections, than did Pylos, which was something of a backwater.[28] Regional differences are observed also by Thomas, who argues that the dispersed distribution of tholos tombs at Messenia points towards a situation with local élites constructing their own tholoi. This is in contrast to the situation at Mycenae, which is interpreted as a centralised power with a strong leader subduing leaders in local regions.[29] According to Thomas, the power of Mycenae was strong and is indeed attested to in the settlement pattern. The destructions did not interrupt the occupation of Mycenae where a continued use of the settlement can be observed, whereas most of the outlying settlements were destroyed. Also in this case, the situation is the reverse of that in Messenia, where Pylos was ruined and inhabited by few in the LH IIIC period, whereas Nichoria and other towns survived into the later periods.[30] For the Mycenaean world, Voutsaki in her important study suggests the existence of different political processes with no evidence of political unity. Indeed, the expansion of palaces was uneven across regions and, as a result, there were spatially

[22] Halstead 1992b, 115.

[23] Halstead 1992b, 115, 116, fig. 1. On non-staple commodities such as spices, hides, flax, wood, etc., as some kind of taxes, see Halstead 1992a, 59.

[24] Cavanagh & Mee 1990; 1998; Dickinson 1982; Mee & Cavanagh 1984.

[25] Dickinson 1982, 135-136.

[26] Cavanagh & Mee 1998, 134-135; Mee & Cavanagh 1984, 45, 50-54, 61-62; 1990, 238.

[27] Dickinson 1982.

[28] Kopcke 1995, 92-93.

[29] Thomas 1995, 354.

[30] Thomas 1970, 191-192.

differentiated outcomes.[31] That the debate on the Mycenaeaen world as homogeneous has not ended is shown by a recent contribution by W. Parkinson. In a most interesting article, he argues convincingly for approaching the palaces as individual systems by using only data that may be directly relevant to each system.[32]

To sum up, a survey of works on the Mycenaean economy reveals that discussions concerning problems in this field of research have relied on earlier theories and therefore have concentrated on the "view from the palace", as it were. It is also obvious that theories and hypotheses on contacts, trade and so forth have mostly been constructed and tested on material from major centres, that is, the palaces. Since the earliest works on the subject, following the decipherment of Linear B, the discussion among scholars specialising in the study of the Mycenaean economy has thus emphasised redistribution and centralisation as the main principles guiding Mycenaean economic activities. Excavations have similarly been concentrated on the palatial sites and have generated material which has influenced our perception of not only economic life, but, as will be seen below, also of the political and social aspects of society during the Late Helladic III period. The question remains, however, how all this came about.

1.3 SUBSTANTIVIST ORIGINS AND THE AEGEAN ECONOMY

No doubt, the favoured manner of reasoning behind the received view was reinforced by the theories formulated within the so-called substantivist paradigm of economic thinking. Associated primarily with Karl Polanyi, this school of thought emphasises the social embeddedness of most economic formations, a theme that incidentally has received renewed interest in the humanities and social studies recently. In his influential book, *The great transformation: the political and economic origins of our time*, [33] Karl Polanyi touched upon the concept of early economies and the foundation stone of what were to become theories on primitive and archaic economies was thereby laid. The theories concerning these early economies were to be developed in more detail in Polanyi's later works, in which he launched the debate on how we should interpret pre-modern economic transactions. The ideas concerning archaic economies were further elaborated in *Trade and market in the early empires*, where the concepts of formal and substantive economic discourse were first outlined.[34] In this article and his following works, the substantivist approach was strongly emphasised. The essence of the ideas presented by Polanyi was the senselessness of regarding prehistoric economies as operating along the lines of modern ones; to do so would be to commit oneself to undue formalism. On the contrary, Polanyi asserted, it would not be possible to apply modern economic terminology, such as "maximising" and "supply and demand", to early economies. Polanyi's aim was to demonstrate that, in the absence of markets the production and distribution of all kinds of goods were controlled through the social system.[35] The transformation and exchange of goods and also labour, land and services in primitive and archaic societies were administered in the main by two principles of behaviour: "reciprocity" and "redistribution". Polanyi saw these two behavioural principles as socio-economic transactional modes.[36]

The debate which followed upon the publication of Polanyi's seminal works on early economies seems to have been dominated by the substantivist school, that is, those who sided with Polanyi against the so-called formalists, who emphasised the universal nature of rational economic behaviour. The discussion among scholars is, however, becoming less polarised and the theories formulated by Polanyi seem to be undergoing revision, not only in the area of economic anthropology but also in other disciplines influenced by the substantivist theory.[37] One of the first attempts to deal more explicitly with the two paradigms instituted by Polanyi in Aegean prehistoric research is *Prehistoric production and exchange: the Aegean and eastern Mediterranean*, in which various problems concerning exchange and production during prehistory are discussed.[38] The articles in the volume all use the formalist approach more or less explicitly, and their authors try to explain prehistoric economic behaviour by using optimising theory. Two articles in particular, by A.B. Knapp and T. Earle, focus on the theoretical aspects and implications of the economic theories, as advanced by Polanyi.[39]

Another relevant and more recently published work is *Bronze Age trade in the Mediterranean*,[40] in which several articles address economic theory and economic models as applicable to the subject matter under review. For example, A. and S. Sherratt analyse the impact of economic theories on our understanding of the ancient economy, as formulated by Polanyi, Weber and other early researchers. Especially the impact of the substantivist theory on the discussions concerning exchange during the Late Bronze Age and the strong influence of the redistributive mode of exchange are

[31] Voutsaki 1992, 10.2.2; 1998, 42, 55.
[32] Parkinson 1999, 84-85.
[33] Polanyi 1944 (1957).
[34] Polanyi, 1957.

[35] Dalton 1975, 82.
[36] Dalton 1965, 3-4; Polanyi 1944 (1957), 47, 51-52; 1968a, 18-19.
[37] Cook 1966; Halperin 1985; von Reden 1995.
[38] Knapp & Stech 1985. The bibliography provides a good survey of research on the prehistory of the Aegean, especially as regards research during the 1970s and 1980s.
[39] Earle 1985; Knapp 1985.
[40] Gale 1991.

subjected to reconsideration by the authors.[41] Similarly, T. Earle in his contribution discusses the definition of redistribution as expounded by Polanyi but also as it has subsequently been applied by other authors. Earle believes that the term has been used much too widely and as a result we find many separate institutional forms lumped together under this heading.[42] Further, Douglass North, himself an advocate of the neo-institutionalist school of economic history, questions specifically the widely held view that a market must be a price-setting market and describes this as 'confusion that has been propagated by Karl Polanyi and many subsequent writers'.[43] According to North, 'any form of voluntary contractual exchange involves a market' and therefore Polanyi is rather off the mark as far as his description of the economic institutions of pre-modern societies is concerned.[44] In keeping with such a view, the phenomenon of markets in prehistoric context has recently been reconsidered by A. and S. Sherratt. They contend that markets existed also in Bronze Age economies and were subject to the forces of supply and demand. They do not deny that the objects involved were those that typically belonged to the élite rather than to peasants. In that sense, based, as they were, on palace centres and personal relationships with the rulers, Bronze Age economies were "redistributive", but they were also market economies, 'in that their allocative decisions were sensitive to market forces'.[45]

Similarly the concept of reciprocity has been the subject of much discussion and there does not seem to be any agreement of a definition.[46] Often, we meet with a generalised definition based on the assumption that reciprocity is not only an equal but also a simple mode of exchange. However, as pointed out by Sahlins, reciprocity need not be balanced and instead a whole class of exchanges may be included. Similarly, reciprocity takes many forms; there is the pure gift and at the other extreme we may find negative reciprocity.[47]

Also with respect to Aegean societies, recent research has thus increasingly challenged the prevailing views on the nature of Late Bronze Age society, thereby providing the basis for a new departure. It has been noted that the archives, while they are, of course, important, do not give a full picture of the economy owing to their fragmentary nature. The silence with respect to basic commodities, such as pottery, cereals, pulses and other crops, has been noted. Similarly, the lack of information concerning the acquisition of exotic raw materials, such as tin and ivory, not to speak of the silence concerning the craftsmen involved in activities connected with primary production or simple technology, has been pointed out.[48] A further significant observation is the fact that the Linear B tablets cover one year, or even less than a year, of palatial bookkeeping, namely the one prior to the destruction of the palace. An important consequence of this is that it is impossible to give an informed opinion as to whether this year was representative or not.[49] Further, the discrepancy in the size of the archives has been noted and the Linear B texts and their validity as empirical material in both the regional context and the inter-regional perspective is still a highly relevant problem.

1.4 RESEARCH ISSUES

Against the background of an emerging critique of long-held notions of centralisation and redistribution, the aim of the present study is thus to discuss the economy of a Late Helladic region. For this purpose, it seeks an answer to the question, which of the two above alternative conceptualisations is closer to the material record currently at our disposal? To do this requires that we address the following issues.

What type of material is at our disposal?

Can this be used to shed light on the economic issues in focus in the Aegean debate?

If so, what does it tell us about the economic system in place?

Are these findings consonant with the conceptualisations of the Late Helladic economy in the Argolid currently in favour?

Do they tip the balance in favour of any of them?

As is evident from this list of research questions, the focus is squarely on the issue of economic activities and related dimensions of social organisation. This obviously includes issues of political organisation, as any system other than the fully self-sufficient community presupposes an institutional framework within which contacts between communities can be carried out. This is not to imply that it needs to be integrated into one political system or realm; it is only to state that some sort of political organisation can be assumed to exist.

Thus, while earlier studies indicate that the regional variations concerning not only settlement patterns but also architectural and written features are too distinct for us to accept the region as a homogenous unity, we do not need to commit ourselves on *a priori* grounds

[41] A strong critique is presented by Sherratt, 1994, 343; Sherratt & Sherratt 1991.
[42] Earle 1977, 215.
[43] North 1981, 42.
[44] North 1981, 42; Polanyi 1968b, 308.
[45] Sherratt & Sherratt 1991, 376.
[46] Polanyi 1944 (1957), 47-49, 54-55, 61; Sahlins 1972, 188-189, follows in the footsteps of Polanyi and forwards the view of reciprocity as movements between two parties and as symmetry. Redistribution, on the other hand, is regarded as centricity. Snodgrass 1991, 16, also advocates that reciprocity is gift exchange; van Wees 1998, 13-49.
[47] Sahlins 1972, 190-191.

[48] Halstead 1992a, 60, 62; Tegyey 1988, 5.
[49] Halstead 1988; Morris 1986.

to any specific form of political governance. The assumption that the Argive plain during the Late Bronze Age period was to be found not within the realm of a Mycenaean empire or overlordship, but independently as concerned economic and political strategies can be accommodated with equal ease as the opposite view. To facilitate this work, however, it is assumed that the cultural koine identified earlier by several scholars is in fact a reality.[50] By taking a regional perspective the need to take a stand can be postponed for the time being; it will rather be an outcome of the discussion on how economic relations were organised. If the balance tips in favour of the received view, clearly the Argolid is more likely to have been under a centralised political control than need be the case if the emerging critique appears to be closer to the archaeological record.

[50] Mountjoy 1999, 15. The Mycenaean pottery koine began in LH IIIA1 and continued, with local variations, until the destruction, end of LH IIIB, when regional styles slowly emerged.

CHAPTER 2
ARGIVE SETTLEMENT PATTERNS

2.1 INTRODUCTION

Ever since the early excavations during the second half of the nineteenth century, the Argolid of the Late Helladic era has attracted considerable archaeological attention. Whether the attention was focused on the major palatial sites, such as Mycenae, or on minor settlements, this region in the north-eastern part of the Peloponnese has typically been taken as a natural point of reference. Usually defined to include the Argive plain and the surrounding foothills, the Argolid fulfils most of the stringent conditions required of homogeneous regions. This is as true as regards both topography and the activities of its inhabitants. There are also good reasons to believe that the region has often been functionally integrated – culturally, politically and economically. The rich archaeological record suggests that this has been the case for a considerable length of time.

For this reason, the approach adopted here is one which explicitly recognises the utility of taking a regional perspective. Accepting the Argolid not only as a readily identifiable territorial unit, but also as one that may well have been functionally integrated throughout the period in focus here, the Late Helladic era, we must be careful not to uncritically impose on it findings from other parts of the Peloponnese or further a field. Rather than a template, the latter should be thought of as particularly useful for comparative ends. However, accepting the Argolid as the relevant geographical unit of analysis does not necessarily imply that we impose on it, or assume on its part, a homogeneous character in most or all respects. Rather, in order to make some headway beyond the rather polarised positions implied by the debate detailed at some length in the first chapter it is useful to assess, as well as the homogenising and integrating factors, the extent to which the forces of spatial differentiation are at work. What is needed, then, is a framework that allows us to view the region as an integrated whole, yet one that simultaneously allows us to pick up local phenomena and processes that may serve to differentiate the various sub-regional units and settlements, both from each other and from the larger unit, the Argolid.

2.2 DISCUSSIONS ON ARGIVE SETTLEMENT PATTERNS

Against the above background, it is worth while to consider the two models presented by John Bintliff and Klaus Kilian.[1] Although now of some age, they remain the two most detailed studies that discuss settlement relations in the Argolid during the Late Helladic period. As will become evident below, these two models are distinguished by analytical finesse. The model proposed by Bintliff is based on voluminous material and is derived with attention to detail. Kilian's, on the other hand, is more general in character and not as detailed as the former. Focusing on the regional hierarchy of settlements, they both take the form of central-place models, long familiar from human geography and, increasingly over the past few decades, from anthropology and archaeology.

Although diverging in approach and complexity, these settlement models are of relevance to any study of the Argolid in which the inter-relationship between a settlement or excavation site and its neighbours is at issue. Empirically, the models are based on a discussion of archaeological material such as architecture, Linear B tablets and tomb material. Implicitly, they are both based on an economic model in which the redistributive character of the economy is accepted as the point of departure.

2.3 THE BINTLIFF MODEL

In his *Natural environment and human settlement in prehistoric Greece*, John Bintliff presented the first, more developed settlement model for the Argolid.[2] The model is based on an evaluation of archaeological material and natural resources, the former of which is composed of the palatial structures, tombs and also Linear B tablets. The palatial mansions, tholoi and the wanax and lawagetes together identify the upper level in the social hierarchy as well as in the settlement hierarchy. The tholos was the tomb reserved for the wanax at this level and the wanax is regarded by Bintliff as a king figure and also the organiser of the socio-economic system. The next level is represented by sites with one or several tholoi, a larger number of chamber tombs and palaces or mansions inhabited by higher-ranked officials such as the lawagetas, telestai and hequetai, all of whom were also buried in tholoi. These settlements should be regarded as major centres subordinate to the regional "supercentre" and "super-palace". The third level is characterised by the presence of a fair number of chamber tombs and a small-scale settlement of village or hamlet character

---

[1] Bintliff 1977; Kilian 1988a.

[2] Bintliff 1977.

(medium/ minor).
The Linear B material is considered as representative and typical of the Mycenaean civilisation. Bintliff looks upon the Mycenaean world as a homogeneous unit. Other important factors determining the location of settlements in prehistoric societies are brought up for discussion. Prehistoric settlements, even small hamlets, were located primarily with a view to securing food resources whereas defence considerations seem to be slightly less important, although examples of settlements that occupy defensible positions are given. These sites are either located close to a steep hill dominating arable or marine resources, as for example at Argos and Tiryns, or, as is the case with Midea and Mycenae, they possess an acropolis and a domestic complex below it. Furthermore, it is observed that the availability of fresh water is not a frequent priority in settlement location. Also trade and communication routes are shown to be of secondary importance as factors of location. As importantly, there were no significant movements of people or goods to justify specialist settlements to be established for their handling. Bintliff concludes that both the Minoan and Mycenaean civilisations were constructed upon the redistribution of local foodstuffs rather than commerce and mercenary service. He further notes that, even if the other factors are important for prehistoric sites, they obviously maintained close links with basic food production and should therefore be regarded as fundamentally agricultural, pastoral and piscatorial.[3]

Combined, these factors are used as indicators of different levels in a basic hierarchical model of settlements. According to Bintliff, three grades of settlements can be recognised in the Argolid. We find what are defined as major centres, followed by a second grade of sites and a third level of farms and hamlets and, finally, above the three grades are a small number of supercentres (*Fig. 1*).[4]

A non-graphical rendering of the hierarchy of central places suggested by Bintliff would look like this.

1. Supercentre

   Location: Centres for one or several regions.

   Characteristics: Tholoi and chamber tombs, palace construction, Linear B archives.

2. First-grade settlements

   Location: Separated by a distance of 1 hour with a lesser community at the midway point.

   One or two tholoi, numerous chamber tombs.

3 Second-grade settlements

   Location: On the border area between two major centres

   Characteristics: Small-scale settlement of village or hamlet character, possessing a fair number of chamber tombs.

4. Third-grade settlements

   Location: Farms and sub-hamlets occupying the interstices in the settlement system.

   Characteristics: Few chamber tombs or none at all.

Comments

Bintliff did not stop at this point but took his analysis further by offering different versions of the same map, but with varying statuses of the settlements. The resulting territorial ordering shows that the reconstruction of settlement systems is difficult. The result is several diverging maps with varying statuses for sites of unclear importance. However, the basic settlement model based on architectural features, types of tomb constructions, the Linear B texts and location factors such as arable land and fishing, is the one used as the point of reference in the present study. A closer examination of the different tiers of the settlement system shows that Mycenae dominates the upper level. According to Bintliff, the reason for the status of Mycenae as a supercentre is not to be found in locational factors such as defence and the convergence of important overland routes. Instead, it has to be explained by the relative location of the settlement, as Mycenae is located at equal distances from Nauplia and ancient Corinth. At this time, the latter was not an important settlement and military, judicial and probably religious and economic control was instead concentrated to the nodal point represented by Mycenae.[5]

On the next tier are Prosymna, Argos, Berbati, Dendra/Midea, Tiryns and Asine, all of which are denoted as major sites, whereas Nauplia, Kasarma, Malandreni, Profetis Elias, Phriphtiani, Skala and Lerna are sites with unclear statuses. Of special interest is the discussion concerning the status of Nauplia as the site has been designated as a third-level settlement, whereas in the table of inter-site distances Nauplia is assigned the higher status of a major/medium site.[6] Furthermore, depending on the criteria used, the settlement is treated either as an internal subsidiary of Tiryns, also a site with strong marine functions, or as a settlement with its own territory or hinterland. Indeed, the status of this particular settlement is difficult to evaluate, as we have a large chamber tomb cemetery, but so far no evidence of a tholos, a palace or even a domestic settlement. Even so, according to Bintliff the cemetery indicates that the site could have been a separate centre. The lack of a corresponding settlement is problematic, but on the other hand, the site has a well-protected bay and notable

[3] Bintliff 1977, 114-116, 136-138, 156-157, 288-289.
[4] Bintliff 1977, 136-138, 367, map 7, 690.
[5] Bintliff 1977, 138, 345-346.
[6] Bintliff 1977, 690-692, maps 1A, B and C.

fishing grounds and is therefore a good location for trade, fishing and farming, although a possible competitor in the neighbouring Tiryns is to be recognised.[7]

Another site of particular interest, owing to its significance for the present study, is Asine. Owing to being mentioned in the *Iliad* and the abundant occurrence of chamber tombs (although, as also noted by Bintliff, only few of these are excavated) the site is ranked as a site with major status. Obviously, Bintliff assumes that there have also been at least one tholos and a palace construction. Furthermore, the distance from other centres should be an argument for a high rank. Other factors are the marine location, here associated with both harbour facilities and fishing. Bintliff also suggests that the old plain east of the settlement would have been suitable for growing cereals and olives, while to the west a terraced basin of soils of particular fertility existed. The defence argument is not applied to Asine and it appears that Bintliff does not regard the Acropolis (Kastraki Hill) at Asine and the Lower Town beneath it as of interest in this discussion.[8]

As mentioned above, Bintliff adopts the central tenets of the substantivist school of thought, which emphasises the centralised and controlled economy, based on redistribution. He also argues that commerce and mercenary service were not essential to the Mycenaean world. Accordingly, foreign contacts, and with them cultural relations, were prevalent before the Late Helladic period and the economic significance of the contacts is therefore more visible in the earlier periods. It should be noted that he is further of the opinion that even intra-regional commerce is out of the question. This particular argument will be discussed in more detail later, when it will be noted that we have evidence of both external trade and also intra-regional contacts, set in the local context.

To conclude, for the Argolid, Bintliff identified one supercentre and several major centres. The position of Mycenae is discussed and he argues that the prosperity of the site emerges early but that the construction of local palaces and the number of tholoi until LH III may indicate that Mycenae was the head of a league of local princes and that no strict hierarchical order was in question. The situation had changed by LH IIIB when, according to Bintliff, tholoi were built only at Mycenae and also ceased to be in use at the local centres. This is a change that may be interpreted as the manifestation of the absolute power of Mycenae.[9] Bintliff's model projects a picture of centralisation and hierarchy. The palatial centre determines not only the economic but also the political and social characteristics; Mycenaean society is believed to be homogeneous in all these respects.

[7] Bintliff 1977, 308-311.
[8] Bintliff 1977, 312-315.
[9] Bintliff 1977, 346.

2.4 THE KILIAN MODEL

In the article entitled the 'The emergence of wanax ideology in the Mycenaean palaces', Klaus Kilian proposes a somewhat different settlement model for the Argolid during the LH IIIA and LH IIIB periods.[10] The prominent position of the wanax is in primary focus, but the implications of the social stratification for Mycenaean society, as such, are also discussed.

Using existing archaeological evidence as the point of departure, Kilian establishes the position of the wanax. Palace constructions, burial material and Linear B tablets are identified as an expression of social stratification, but also as personal propaganda. The deciphered tablets expose a picture of the wanax as the head of a hierarchical society, not only in military, political and religious affairs, but also economically. The position of the wanax is similarly reflected in the elaborate architectural design of the palace with megaron, throne and four-columned hearth, characteristic adjoining rooms, upper stories and frescos. It is possible as early as at the beginning of the Mycenaean period, or so Kilian asserts, to link socio-political leadership to the architectural evidence.[11] What is more, the palace has a further important function, as the economic organisation is concentrated in the palace and the wanax. The oikos of the wanax was the centre of the redistributive economy and workshops provided him with a surplus beyond the needs of his own household and its dependants.[12]

Kilian also brings up burial material for discussion. He is of the opinion that a high degree of social stratification becomes apparent at the beginning of LH IIIA, for example at the Argive Heraeum (Prosymna). He states that 'it might thus seem reasonable to link the treatment of the wanax in an ideological setting with the rigid observance of hierarchical status in burial grounds during the same period'.[13] These issues are also at fore in other articles and, by recourse to topographical and architectural analysis, it is possible, or so Kilian argues, to confirm a process of centralisation during LH IIIA. However, as compared with the development of centralisation in Messenia during the same period, the model for the Argolid is somewhat different. It is possible to trace also in the Argolid a parallel transition although here, unlike Messenia, we find a plurality of smaller kingdoms instead of a single large one (*Fig. 2*).[14] According to this model, the economic organisation of the Mycenaean world is concentrated in the palace, with the oikos of the wanax as the centre of a redistributive economy.[15]

[10] Kilian 1988a.
[11] Kilian 1988a, 291-296, 299; 1988b, 136.
[12] Kilian 1988a, 293.
[13] Kilian 1988a, 296.
[14] Kilian 1988a, 296, fig. 3; 1988b, 136.
[15] Kilian 1988a, 293.

Comments

Although Kilian may be right in asserting that 'by linking all the relevant archaeological evidence together we may thus begin to catch a glimpse of the historical implications associated with the rise of the centralised Mycenaean kingdoms',[16] his account assumes rather than demonstrates that it was in fact a centralised political structure. The article emphasises the importance of making use of the full range of factors, such as architecture, tombs and written documents, in reconstructing settlement systems. The categories of material drawn upon are logical, as they are the archaeological evidence best preserved. But the problem with the model is the lack of a more explicit and detailed discussion of the assumptions made in constructing it and ranking the settlements. Unfortunately, Kilian does not engage in a more detailed discussion concerning the archaeological material; neither are possible changes in the material evidence during the LH IIIA and IIIB explicitly addressed. Instead he suggests a more general approach to this kind of question.[17]

Compared with Messenia, where according to Kilian we find a more centralised system with Pylos as the dominating settlement, the model of the Argolid projects a picture of a more decentralised system with a plurality of kingdoms. It defines five centres on the Argive plain, namely Mycenae, Argos, Midea, Tiryns and Nauplia. The wanax ideology is itself said to be closely associated with the palace constructions and, according to the material survey presented, we have evidence of two palace complexes in the area, the one at Mycenae and the other at Tiryns. Unfortunately, the article does not discuss the criteria used when also Argos, Midea and Nauplia are defined as centres or nodes in this somewhat more decentralised system. This is especially so as the archaeological material diverges between these settlements. Neither of these had, at the time of the article, been associated with obvious palace remains, although in the case of Midea, thanks to recent excavations there, we have reason to believe that this may now change. Also the known tomb material shows a different pattern, as tholoi are not found at Argos and Nauplia and the frequency of identified chamber tombs fluctuates between the settlements.

To sum up, Kilian's model is that of a more decentralised settlement system for the Argolid, with a plurality of kingdoms. In this sense, the pattern differs from the one in Messenia, where there is a single kingdom with Pylos as the palatial node and undisputed centre. However, the economic system is still regarded as a redistributive with the economic organisation centred on the palaces and ultimately on the wanax.[18] In this sense, Kilian sides with the substantivist school. As far as the organisation of settlements and also the economic, political and social aspects of the tombs are concerned, he obviously regards the Mycenaean world as a homogeneous entity, including different regions.[19]

Finally, one may perhaps be forgiven the thought that the above two models in some sense reflect the cumulative nature of scientific endeavours. Yet the more recent of the two, Kilian's, makes no explicit reference to the efforts and insights embodied in Bintliff's exercise. This in itself is an opportunity foregone. This is not to suggest, however, that they are mutually incompatible. On the contrary, and as will be seen below, they have many things in common.

2.5 COMPARISON AND DISCUSSION OF THE SETTLEMENT PATTERNS

Most importantly, thanks to the presence of palace structures, tholoi, numerous chamber tombs and Linear B material, discussions on settlement hierarchies in the Argolid have as a rule regarded Mycenae and Tiryns as major sites. At lower levels have followed, with decreasing statuses, settlements represented by chamber tombs and other minor architectural finds, and a group of minor sites or scattered farmsteads, signified by pit graves and dispersed architectural remains and few other categories of finds.

A comparison of the proposed models thus yields a quite similar picture in which the settlements in the Argolid can be divided into three tiers. To the extent that they are made explicit, the criteria made use of by both Bintliff and Kilian are reasonably similar. Preserved architectural remains, presence of Linear B material and the tombs are the main indicators of the statuses of the individual settlements at the various levels. The first tier is characterised by palaces, storage facilities and workshops and in a few cases also by impressive houses, whereas the tomb material is composed of tholoi and larger chamber-tomb cemeteries. The next level is much less prominent as far as architectural remains are concerned. These settlements often lack large constructions, such as palaces and frequently no elaborate domestic architecture has been preserved. However, also chamber tombs are to be found in this group. The third level includes the scattered remains of habitation represented by occasional walls, burials and often cist or pit graves. This group is characterised by small hamlets and farmhouses.

Mycenae and Tiryns with their impressive palace constructions, including what have been interpreted as storage rooms,[20] tholoi and larger chamber-tomb cemeteries, are the dominating settlements representing the first level. The monumental palatial remains at Tiryns are well known, as the citadel area has been excavated, and our knowledge of the domestic habitation activities

[16] Kilian 1988a, 296.
[17] Kilian 1988a, 299.
[18] Kilian 1988a, 293.
[19] Kilian 1988a, 298-300.
[20] Kilian 1987b, 25, 27-28.

surrounding the palace area has, owing to recent excavations increased notably. The excavations at Mycenae have also been rewarding as concerns domestic architecture. We are here in possession of domestic architectural material from both inside and outside the citadel area. By virtue of its location, Bintliff even regards the settlement as a supercentre, that is, the uppermost level in the settlement system.

The settlement patterns arrived at by the two scholars agree on the statuses of Mycenae and Tiryns, whereas their interpretations of other settlements differ. While Bintliff identifies Argos, Berbati, Dendra/Midea and Prosymna with the first tier, Kilian includes Nauplia but excludes Berbati and Heraion from this level. At this juncture, it should be noted that at Midea a Linear B inscription has also been found[21] and this will serve to further underline the importance of this settlement. Second tier settlements defined by Bintliff include, for example, Nauplia, quite possibly Asine (although not on the map), Priphtiani/Monasteraki, Schoinochori and Fychtia. North of Mycenae is located a site with an obviously larger number of chamber tombs than most other sites but without a name. The structure of the second tier in the settlement system constructed by Kilian diverges slightly from this, as Prosymna, Berbati and Asine are identified as subcentres. These settlements are all mainly related to tomb finds but in some instances, as in the case of Asine, also to other architectural features. The third group consists of small sites or farmsteads only recognisable by their poor and simple cist or pit graves and scattered finds of walls and pottery. Larger building constructions have not been found, not even clusters of structures that could be identified as a settlement.[22]

A comparison of the two settlement hierarchies suggests that there are more similarities than differences in the interpretation and classification of the sites. We may observe that both systems show a plurality of territories with their respective major centres – with the interesting exception of Argos – symbolised by a tholos, a larger number of chamber tombs and in some cases impressive architectural features (although not always in the form of a palace and sometimes also domestic architecture). Both of the proposed settlement patterns differ in their structures from the pattern found, for example, in Messenia, where Pylos is the only major centre on account of its being the only one with a palace. Also, on a more fundamental level, the models devised by Bintliff and Kilian share several characteristic traits. Most importantly, both models assume rather than arrive at the basic features of the society they analyse. First-tier settlements, invariably those with palaces and tholoi, are assumed, not shown, to have had centralised economic power. It is also these settlements that are assumed to have more organised redistributive activities. Yet, as the so-called Aegean debate makes abundantly clear, no such simple assumptions can be proved; indeed, they are at times not warranted at all.

2.6 EXTENDING THE ANALYSIS

The attempts by Kilian and Bintliff to identify a hierarchy of settlements in the Argolid have been the only ones applied to this particular region, at this particular time. In the wider literature, however, a large and variegated range of settlement models exists. The arguably most common type of model is the one based on systems of markets (as was the case already with W. Christaller's original model of central places), closely followed by those that set out from political or administrative considerations.[23]

It is beyond the scope of the present work to detail developments within this particular field of inquiry. Suffice it to note that the essential difference between the two types of models, other than their focus on different aspects of social life, is the fact that the former is typically seen as capturing bottom-up processes (i.e., those that arise spontaneously as a result of everyday activities not governed by some political authority), the latter as a top-down phenomenon imposed for reasons of power or administrative convenience. Furthermore, while the latter focuses squarely on vertical links, the former emphasises the co-existence of lateral or horizontal links along with vertical.

Classified in this fashion, the models of both Kilian and Bintliff would appear to fall into the top-down category. For a variety of reasons, including the focus on political factors and the assumption that markets took second place to other modes of exchange, theirs are top-down constructs. This has important implications for our efforts here. Should we find, on the one hand, that the critique of the predominant school of thought is right, the models developed by Kilian and Bintliff will need to be amended accordingly. This implies, primarily, that lateral links must be taken seriously and that the criteria for establishing rank must be extended to include not only political factors but also economic ones derived from processes of exchange. Should, on the other hand, Kilian and Bintliff prove right in their assertion that Mycenaean society is best characterised as redistributive in the sense employed by Polanyi, we shall be able to bolster the strengths of their models by adding supporting evidence.
Also in this latter case, however, there would be a need to amend their models. For one thing, the models are not identical and are as such in part mutually exclusive. Thus, we would need to establish which of the two best reflects the archaeological and other material available. What is more, both models can be criticised for collapsing a long time span into one snapshot. Given the rather dramatic changes that took place on the Argive plain during the Late Helladic era, a synchronic perspective is probably less than fully ideal. Rather, what

[21] Walberg 1992a, 93.

[22] Bintliff 1977, 309, 690.

[23] Roberts 1996, 54-56.

is called for is a model or a series of models that introduces a measure of dynamism, identifying changes that occur throughout the period.

What this may entail can be illustrated by a market-place model of the variety pioneered by G. W. Skinner. In his seminal work on markets in traditional rural China, Skinner detected several tiers within the market system.[24] His study is based on fieldwork in Szechwan (Sichuan) in 1949-50 when interviews were made with emigrants, but also on published works and local documentation. Skinner follows in the footsteps of Christaller and Lösch where a central place can be typed according to its position in the interlocking spatial system and within this the economic functions are associated with a hierarchical level.[25] Although founded on another historical context and different type of sources it is believed that the model as a tool is of relevance for the present study, as it raises the possibility of capturing a differentiated market system.

Skinner identifies several levels of markets and of particular interest to note that he observed that peasants living in dispersed farmhouses or small clusters, such as hamlets, could participate in exchange below the lowest tier in his hierarchy of markets. The significance of this observation consists in the insight that scattered farms and nucleated villages could support a system of local markets, i.e. minor markets, specialising in the horizontal exchange of goods produced by peasants, and according to Skinner the importance of the minor market as an entry point for locally produced goods into the larger system was negligible. The market is simple to its character and many necessities are not constantly available and services and imports are not always found.

The next tier is the standard market which also met the trade needs of the peasant household and functioned as an outlet for local products. Products produced locally, but not consumed were traded, and products not produced, but consumed were acquired. The market was, and this may be the most essential point, not only the starting-point for the upward flow of locally produced products, but also the end of the downward flow of imported goods intended for local peasant consumption. The standard market is tied to the intermediate, or even a higher-level market, through the regular movement of goods and services. According to Skinner, the standard market could be dependent on several higher-level markets. The next higher level is defined as an intermediate market with vertical flows of goods and with an intermediary position in the market system. The market could have two areas to serve, a primary one that included nearby villages whose inhabitants attended the market regularly, and a second area that included villages farther away. The people not living nearby attended the market only occasionally and did so with a view to obtain goods hard to find at the local standard market, to attend festivals, and so forth. The situation was rather different as concerned the local élite, as they, possibly with the purpose of setting themselves apart from the peasantry, attended the intermediate market. Finally, the central market is characterised as strategically located at a central node of the transportation network. Facilities are constructed not only for the storage of imported items later to be distributed to the hinterland, but also for the collection of locally produced goods meant for export to other central markets.[26]

In effect, the model constructed by Skinner provides us with an alternative interpretation of a system with all the archaeological features otherwise associated with a redistributive system focused on the palaces of Late Bronze Age Greece. The difference, of course, is the underlying assumptions. Skinner's model assumes that market relations exist also at the local level and that there is a measure of specialisation in production that both necessitates and makes possible exchange between households within the local community and possibly with neighbouring points in the settlement system. As such, it is consonant with the main tenets of the emerging critique.

What is more, for reasons of economic viability, markets are integrated in a system of periodic markets. Periodic markets, as opposed to continuous or daily markets, are found in most traditional and agrarian societies. Indeed, the high degree of self-sufficiency of the average peasant household reduces the need of daily markets.[27] The benefits of periodicity rest with the ability of a set of local markets operating by turns to create an aggregate demand big enough to support the activities of individuals specialising as traders, a demand that no single market-place could generate on its own. At the market the peasant exchanges what he has for what he needs and that is not necessarily only ordinary commodities. Characteristic of these markets are the wandering craftsmen and artisans carrying their workshops with them. The workman could also be hired to work in village households. Sometimes also workshops could be located here. For the consumer the periodicity of markets was of importance, as it reduced the distance that must be travelled to obtain goods and services.[28]

The existence of a model such as that devised by Skinner can be used to consider assumptions on both sides of the divide in the Aegean debate. Skinner's model fills a void, in the sense that it can be used as a substitute for models that are not yet readily available. This is of considerable importance, as the outcome itself (i.e. with respect to the identified hierarchy of settlements) will not allow for discriminating between the two major strands of the

[24] Skinner 1964; 1976.
[25] Skinner 1964, 3-5.
[26] Skinner 1964, 6-9, 20-21, 25, 27.
[27] Skinner 1964, 10-11, 20-21.
[28] Skinner 1964, 10-11.

debate. This is so precisely because any model that uses Skinner as the point of departure is likely to arrive at a model that, at least superficially, has an outward appearance quite indistinguishable from those of the models devised by Kilian and Bintliff.

In short, the archaeological record, at least as now available to us, cannot be employed to differentiate between the two if only the final outcome, that is the structure of the models as such, is to be evaluated. The fact that the three models are based on different logics and very different assumptions as regards the existence of different modes of exchange, however, allows us to circumvent this problem. Storage facilities are likely to be of use to both a redistributive and a market-based system, or any combination of the two. Instead, the critical feature is the size of the storage facilities, large ones presumably being required for purposes of redistribution, and the context in which they are found. So is the existence of evidence that goods originating in one place turn up in another. Written evidence, such as the Linear B tablets, however, is likely to tip the balance in one of the two directions. As we have seen, most of those that have been subjected to careful analysis and interpretation fit well with the notion of redistribution, save perhaps for the fact that critical products are altogether missing from the records. Findings that should provide strong evidence for markets include, for example, means of exchange (currency of one sort or another) and mention of market-places.

As far as we know, no currency was in circulation in the Late Helladic period, but the occurrence of weights indicates that different commodities had different values and exchange rates, needing a scale for measuring, and some form of a price-setting market was obviously established. The majority of weights found in the Argolid have been found in early, Late Helladic tomb contexts[29] and indicates the need for measuring, and evidence of exchange already in the LH II and LH IIIA periods. Weights found in LH IIIB2 contexts have also been reported[30] and, as stated by Halstead, the occurrence of weights in both palace and settlement contexts are clear indications of exchange.[31] Also, Linear B tablets show the need to measure quantities of different products[32] and the need to calculate quantities later distributed to different categories of people or as payment for performed services. Halstead has also shown that exchange was the most probable form of transaction, as several commodities were produced only outside the palatial context. He also notes that there is empirical evidence to the effect that the palace actually bought some products.[33] A fragment of Linear B tablet found at Tiryns documents the price for alum as, amongst others things, wine and linen.[34] The term *tu-ru-pte-ri-ja,* alum, is found also on two tablets from Pylos, on which it is followed by the term *o-no*. Discussing this particular term, Killen observes that, in contrast to woollen cloth that may have been produced under the system of *ta-ra-si-ja*, linen may have been bought in exchange for various goods.[35]

All of this goes to prove that there are indeed possibilities of discriminating between models or favoured interpretative frameworks. However, it presupposes that support for the underlying assumptions will be systematically sought in the detailed archaeological record. This has several implications, not least with respect to where to place the emphasis in the analysis. As a result, however, it also implies that both the depth and the breadth of analysis should ideally be sought. This is not typically feasible for a project of this nature and trade-offs between the two will therefore be considered. More specifically, and in the interest of keeping it at an empirically manageable level, this will be done by an analysis of a village or minor urban settlement; this can then be extended to several settlements on the same or other tiers of the hierarchy should it be deemed desirable and feasible.

2.7 DEFINITIONS

Adam Smith may have argued that it was human nature to 'truck, barter, and exchange one thing for another',[36] but as not least the anthropological literature has taught us, this does not quite exhaust the range of types of exchange that can be identified. Indeed, also Polanyi's three modes of exchange – reciprocal, redistributive and market – have been found wanting in this respect. He associated redistribution with centralised and often large-scale bureaucratic systems distinguished by extensive, communal storage facilities. Thus, whereas reciprocity is assisted by a symmetrical pattern of organisation, redistribution is characterised by an elaborate organisation taking care of production and distribution of

[29] Dendra: tomb 10, LH IIA-LH IIA2; Mycenae: tomb 515, LH IIA-LH IIIA2; Prosymna: tombs XXVI, LH I; XLIV, LH I; XXV, LH I or LH II; II, no date; XLIII, LH III.

[30] Midea, room VII; Tiryns: tomb XVI; Prosymna: tomb XLIII; Argos: tombs XII, XVII.

[31] Halstead 1992a, 72.

[32] Sherratt & Sherratt 1991, 360; Ventris & Chadwick 1973, 50-51, 53-60.

[33] Halstead 1992a, 71.

[34] Godart, Killen & Olivier 1979, 452-453.

[35] Killen, 1988, 168, 180-183. *ta-ra-si-ja* signifies a system in which raw material is allocated from the palace to dependent/semi-dependent workers and returned to the palace in the from of an equivalent quantity of finished products. The tablet Un 1322 at Pylos records *o-no*, which may mean payment(s) given to a net-maker and a weaver. A parallel to this record is L 693 at Knossos, which contain the transaction term *qe-te-o*, which appears to serve as the correlative of *o-no*. Owing to these similarities it has been suggested that the two tablets have similar functions, i.e. the price payable for different commodities. Another interesting series of tablets referred to by Killen deal with the sale of slaves where the term *qi-ri-ja-to* "(he) bought" is mentioned. The definition of the *ta-ra-si-ja,* system is under debate; see for example Bech Gregersen 2000; Gillis 1997.

[36] Smith 1776 (1999), 117.

goods under the supervision of a central political authority. Market exchange included barter and sale and was dependent on money. A fourth mode only marginally mentioned by Polanyi is householding, based on autarky.[37] However, that redistribution need not to be equal with large-scale systems has been shown by C. Smith who in her study of markets in Guatemala uses the concept on a local marketplace level where products are sold by local producer-sellers. At the following level goods bulked elsewhere for redistribution are sold by local middlemen and the third is a kind of redistribution when specialised import goods, local or regional, are sold by professional long-distance traders. What she also finds is that the presence of many producer-sellers indicates a centre for local exchange, or for bulking of goods for upward redistribution to other market places where they could be sold. On the middle level goods are sold for local consumption or for redistribution down the hierarchy.[38]

The concept of reciprocity shows a complicated pattern of networks emerging. The social and symbolic meaning emphasises the importance of social integration, in which networks of friends and kinsmen are important. But the need to produce for exchange and subsistence is also critical, as exchange is really important in a situation of shortage. Therefore, a reciprocal exchange system does not exclude hoarding, conspicuously displayed wealth and investment. In cases in which reciprocity is highly centralised, redistribution may be prevalent and in such situations goods and services are moved to a centre from where they, or their equivalents, are dispersed. Also, reciprocity may be defined as either generalised or balanced, where the former is more flexible with extensive networks whereas the opposite is valid for the latter.[39] Generalised reciprocity is altruistic and consists of the pure gift. It may, for example, be aid given in times of need to neighbours and kinsmen. Balanced reciprocity is a direct exchange of the same type and amount of goods or services. It may also be less personal, more economic and may also involve transactions such as buying and selling. As shown by D. Perry, reciprocity is not limited to only the farming context, divorced from the market place. Instead, market-based reciprocity can also be identified.[40] Negative reciprocity is also discussed by Sahlins and according to him this is the most impersonal type of exchange and as such the one that most closely corresponds to the behavioural assumptions of formalists, that is, neo-classical economics. Those participating in this exchange try to maximise utility at the expense of the other.[41] In a prehistoric context, reciprocal exchange could therefore have worked on several levels and for different purposes.

In the interest of clarity, for the purposes of this thesis the following definitions will be adopted. Exchange is considered the broader category, covering most forms of inter-personal transfers of goods and services other than pure gifts, taxes and tributes. The term exchange is therefore restricted to include all transactions in which there is some immediate and clearly identifiable good or service – or money, should currency exist – given in return for some other good or service. This need not be in any sense an equal transaction but implies that it can be nominally negotiated by the parties to the transaction; as such, it is not simply unilaterally imposed (as are taxes and tributes) under the threat of force or otherwise. This is in fact equivalent to North's notion of a market already referred to above, and involves 'any form of voluntary contractual exchange'.[42]

In turn, exchange other than in the form of redistribution can be divided according to two criteria. One is whether or not money or some other medium of exchange is present. If such a medium is present, be it salt-bars, pelts, shells or money in a more modern sense, we have in some sense a monetized transaction. If not, we speak of barter transactions between two nominally equal parties. This would be the equivalent of Polanyi's market mode of exchange, only with the added proviso that price-setting markets do not presuppose money as Polanyi seemed to believe.[43] After all, and although clearly more cumbersome than in the presence of money, the price of a unit of olive oil can be expressed as X units of cloth, and that price is in some sense open to negotiation or rather to the forces of supply and demand. As a shown by van Wees reciprocity is in no way resistant to the law of supply and demand and can also be used to make a profit.[44] S. Voutsaki observes that although generosity and reciprocity are important this must not be taken to imply that components such as profit making or economic advantage are not found in primitive exchange. The forces of supply and demand are at work, although these market forces are not always working in the same way in all economic systems.[45]

As will be readily appreciated, the simplicity of the above, two-pronged typology conceals a much more messy reality. In fact, it only serves to highlight the importance of recognising that markets and trade should not be restricted to those instances in which money is present. In actual fact, both anthropology and economics point to a much wider range of forms of exchange than could be subsumed under the heading "market". Barter, for instance, is not only or even predominantly of the good-for-good variety. It may form part of elaborate barter chains in which the fact that exchanges do not take place simultaneously presupposes a measure of trust between the individuals or groups involved. Paradoxical

[37] Polanyi 1944 (1957), 47-52, 56, 68.
[38] Smith 1985, 313.
[39] van Wees 1998, 15-19, 21-25, 38.
[40] Perry 2000, 474-480.
[41] Sahlins 1972, 195.
[42] North 1981, 42.
[43] Polanyi 1944 (1957), 68.
[44] van Wees 1998, 36-37.
[45] Voutsaki 1995b, 11-12.

as it may seem, the classic barter of the good-for-good type may be less dependent on social conventions than is the typical transaction taking place in a modern spot market (modern currency, after all, is backed by powerful conventions; why else would we accept as payment paper notes with no intrinsic value?). The importance of this insight lies in the recognition that we may look at markets in quite a different, but not necessarily an incompatible, fashion. We need not endorse Grannovetter's original argument[46] in full to realise that at some level or other, all exchange is subject to its particular context, its social or institutional embeddedness. Thus, while the above typology focuses on the existence and nature of the medium of exchange, a case can also be made for a complementary typology which targets the extent to which and, if so, how exchange is subject to social conventions and other institutions that provide as well as a structure of incentives also mechanisms for co-ordination and transaction costs mitigation. For classificatory purposes, this can be conceived of as a number of points along a continuum from the ritualised and prescribed to the truely unregulated. By way of an example, it was noted above that reciprocity is not necessarily a category that precludes redistribution. Similarly, reciprocity may form part of market exchange.

As such, reciprocity can go hand in hand with types of behaviour more typically seen as part of economies in which market transactions are prevalent, including hoarding, stockpiling and investment. Reciprocity can, as has been shown earlier, be either generalised or balanced, that is, particularistic. In the following discussion reciprocity will be referred to as the giving and receiving of gifts and favours, with the purpose of creating either social or economic networks, or both. Although it may be nothing more sophisticated than an expectation that exchange is likely to be repeated, what such a definition adds to those usually employed is the possibility, indeed likelihood, that reciprocity as an exchange category can be influenced by or even based on supply and demand.

It is thus to be noted that, as also market exchange based on supply and demand can take on features of socially embedded transactions, the two categories of exchange are not mutually exclusive. Rather, any exchange may contain elements of both. This being the case, it is, on the one hand, next to impossible to separate the two, not only on grounds of logic but crucially also in practice. As such, it does not provide the sharp-edged, conceptual categories that one would like to wield in an attempt to cut through the empirical material. On the other hand, it allows for some flexibility in application when strict stringency is not needed or not even possible to achieve in the first place.

[46] E.g., as outlined in Granovetter 1985.

2.8 Chronological and geographical Scope of the study

The chronological limitations of the thesis consist of historical events. The earlier periods LH I/II will be discussed in some detail when necessary as we here have some of the archaeological evidence crucial for our understanding of the following LH III periods. As they can be regarded as the mature Mycenaean periods the LH IIIA and LH IIIB periods are focused on in more detail. Especially the LH IIIB period is of great interest, as during this period we find the culmination of palace architecture, objects of different categories and not least the Linear B material. The period is also of great importance in any discussion of economic structures as we are here dealing with the so-called, centralised, palace economy. The transformation to the LH IIIC initiated a new era dominated by the destruction of the palace centres in the end of the LH IIIB period. We may assume that the transformation of the economical and political system profoundly affected the entire society. These periods and the transition to the Submycenaean are represented at the village of Asine, as well as at other settlements on the Argive plain, and therefore provide an important opening for an analysis of structural change in a local and intra-regional perspective.

The geographical borders will be nearly the same as have been used in previous works in which settlement systems in the prehistoric Argolid have been on the agenda. The Argive Plain, in the Peloponnese, is a coastal plain of about 243 km^2, surrounded by mountains rising to 400-700 m. The plain was apparently shaped by three phases of soil instability, the first occurring in the Middle to Late Neolithic. Probably the most extensive environmental changes occurred during the EH II period, as the coastal zone was covered with flood-plain deposits. The final deposit seems to have taken place in the LH IIIB2 or early LH IIIC period and to have been caused by man-made diversion of a stream close to Tiryns. Alluviation associated with this work buried the Lower Town of Tiryns.[47]

The region, with its natural border of hills in the north, west and east and the coastline in the south, is well suited for an intra-regional study. The settlement of Asine is located in the south-eastern "appendix" of this geographically well-defined plain.[48] The location of the village on the coast will probably be of great importance in evaluating the status of the site in a regional settlement system. The proximity to water and harbour facilities gives any settlement important natural advantages in such a ranking.

[47] Finke 1988; van Andel & Zangger 1990, 145-147, fig. 7; Zangger 1993; 1994, 202-203, fig. 8.

[48] Finke 1988, 35; the map shows the extent of the Argive Plain.

CHAPTER 3
ESTABLISHING RANK:
THE ARCHAEOLOGY OF STATUS AND WEALTH AND OTHER EMPIRICAL CONSIDERATIONS

3.1 INTRODUCTION

In the previous chapter it was noted that although settlement hierarchies are useful in analysing the Argolid as a region, without recourse to traditional, archaeological material, they fall short of clearly indicating which of the two favoured interpretative frameworks is the more plausible. Indeed, also with access to this category of evidence it may prove difficult to differentiate between alternative interpretations. To mitigate this ambiguity, it is proposed that a contextual, archaeological approach should be used.

The rationale of this approach rests with the realisation that the same artefacts may be used in several ways and may signify different things across contexts.[1] For instance, the analysis of social hierarchies has depended on burial data from which the ranks of the deceased and related characteristics have been deduced. Critics, prominent among them I. Hodder, have pointed out that functional relationships and formal analysis are not enough to establish the characteristics and significance of the objects found.[2] To achieve this end, scholars should avail themselves of a broader perspective, allowing for the inclusion of the structure of ideas, beliefs and so forth. This implies that tombs are included in a general analysis in which not only other groups of archaeological evidence are considered, but other criteria such as the exchange systems and the settlement organisation are also taken into account. Hodder also proposes that analyses restricted to only one class of data are best avoided, as the relationship between patterns in life and in death are dependent on the cultural context. This analytical approach is not structuralist, the aim is rather to examine analytical techniques and to develop models and analogies.[3]

The perspective adopted in the present work follows these prescriptions in the sense of using several supplementary categories of data. Specifically, in addition to tombs also other groups of material remains must be analysed in detail. Furthermore, the importance of more detailed, chronological analyses is emphasised, as is the search for material that may shed light not only on one but also on a wider range of modes of exchange transaction. But the use of tomb material serves an additional purpose: to establish the relative rank of settlements. To do so, however, there is a need to identify concepts that are up to the task of capturing essential aspects of the diverse activities and livelihoods of the inhabitants of Late Helladic Argolid, while at the same time allowing for the use of a wide range of archaeological data. To this end, the concepts of status and wealth are introduced in the following pages.

3.2 STATUS AND WEALTH

Apparently the notion of a commodity is to be found already in the Aristotelian idea of value and since then many theories have been formulated.[4] The interest in measuring economic, political and social status and wealth in pre-industrial societies is well documented also in archaeology. It comes as no surprise that the concepts of status and wealth are widely used and applied to a great variety of archaeological contexts. As will be shown in the following pages their respective definitions are neither invariably clear and distinct nor is it always obvious whether the two concepts are being used synonymously or are considered to refer to different phenomena. Yet they represent universal phenomena that are therefore next to impossible to avoid when matters and materials archaeological are discussed. The following is a survey of some of the opinions that exist within this particular field of research.

Although often thought of as synonymous or at least closely related, G. Graziado and others have taken care to point out that the concepts of social status and wealth are not always to be equated.[5] By the same token, P.J. Ucko emphasises that it is not always simple to identify the poor and rich members of a society; there is no once-and-for-all ratio between status and wealth. Anthropological parallels support this fact and there is a low level of correlation between the amount and the quality of burial goods, on the one hand, and the overall level of material wealth on the other. Ethnographical material also shows that the display of exclusive, exotic or expensive goods does not always emphasise the status of a person.[6]
In fact, the difficulty of interpreting archaeological material as an indicator of wealth has frequently been

[1] Hazelgrove 1982, 81; Hodder, 1982, 152.
[2] Hodder 1982, 152.
[3] Hodder 1982, 152-153.
[4] Gregory 1994.
[5] Graziado 1991, 412.
[6] Ucko 1969, 266-267.

pointed out. C. Renfrew remarks that wealth is not always defined by the usefulness of the goods concerned. Gold, for example, is often considered desirable, even though it is not particularly useful for practical purposes. Furthermore, wealth can be both a social and an economic phenomenon.[7] A recent study by Pearson makes a similar observation with respect to status: it is often difficult to distinguish status achieved in life from ascribed status.[8] In a prehistoric context in particular, it may be difficult to distinguish between ascribed status (age, sex) and achieved status that is attained though personal advancement. Although the latter may take the form of, for example, economic prosperity or political or military influence, there is little to indicate that it earns its bearer fame in other spheres of activity. However, in the following study the two definitions will be applied to the empirical material in a Late Helladic context. It will then be hypothesised that ascribed status may be connected with female and child burials but also with male, whereas achieved status may be reflected in armour, jewellery, exclusive objects made of precious material and so forth.

The opposite view also has its advocates and the value of precious materials and objects as possible indicators of status and wealth has been underlined in studies not concerned with Aegean prehistory.[9] Earlier work in the area has predominantly been empirical in character, measuring either the quantity or the diversity of goods found in tomb contexts or employing a more impressionistic and subjective qualitative method of interpretation. A qualitative approach need not imply lack of stringency, however, especially if it is used more explicitly, as by Dickinson. He argues that items such as weapons, jewellery and objects of precious or unusual material are indicators of high or special status. He admits that this is an imprecise method but suggests that such an approach still has its value.[10] Cavanagh and Mee for their parts, are less sanguine and are of the opinion that it is dangerous to associate all burials with possible statuses. They question assumptions such as that items were symbolic messengers and ask how we can know whether a dagger or a seal was a symbol of middle or high rank or how we can know the value of, for example, amber, metals and so on, in the Mycenaean world?[11]

Voutsaki also rejects the possibility of using only quality as an indicator of status. According to her, it is difficult, owing to lack of information, to discuss and establish the economic value, in a strict sense, of objects used during the prehistoric period.[12] In her thesis Voutsaki makes extensive use of valuable objects found in tombs.[13] Furthermore, in a recent article she proposes that the value and prestige of an object are created not only by the labour at the moment of production but also during the circulation in a gift-exchange network.[14] Finally, as observed by van Wijngaarden, it should also be remembered that value is culturally constructed and accordingly we should approach it from its specific cultural context. Import goods, for example, could symbolise that the owner had the ability to acquire such objects. Also, the spatial distribution of goods and fluctuation in deposition among different contexts can indicate the extent to which these were avialable to different groups.[15]

An article by Smith also identifies further means, other than the specific functional categories of artefacts, of analysing wealth. Three useful examples are *quantity*, *diversity* and *origin*. According to Smith, it is reasonable to expect that wealthy households will tend to possess more material goods and consume more food than poor households do. One result is that rich households produce more refuse per day and this is of relevance in an archaeological context. Also, rich households show a greater variety or diversity of goods and this connection between wealth and diversity is of some significance from an archaeological point of view. Furthermore, the place of origin can also be used as a good wealth indicator, as goods of exotic origin tend to have a high value.[16] This type of goods may also have a ritual power that is transferred to the person who is in possession of the object. Being in possession then indicates the status of the person in question. Another observation is that wealthy households also tend to have wider geographical networks based on a similarity in lifestyle that permits easy reciprocity.[17] The long-distance, interaction systems constructed by these networks of social interaction can be expressed in household, material culture as a higher frequency of exotic goods and goods from farther away

The variables discussed by Smith are in no way exclusive to his study but are presented as possible designators also by other scholars. Prestige goods with a symbolic value could be, for example, decorated daggers, metal vessels, clay vases of high quality, etc.[18] Graziado employs the definition of wealth introduced by J. O'Shea who uses as symbolic designators artefact quantity, variety and especially exotic trade items and says that the disparities in wealth may be related to differences in rank.[19] Also Hazelgrove adopts the definition that artefacts belonging to this group required rare material, technical skill or a high labour input or were foreign trade goods.[20] As has been noted by S.

[7] Renfrew 1972, 370.
[8] Pearson 1999.
[9] To mention but a few, prestige is discussed by, e.g., Clark 1986, and more recently by Taffinder 1998.
[10] Dickinson 1983, 56.
[11] Cavanagh & Mee 1990, 56.
[12] Voutsaki 1995a, 56.
[13] Voutsaki 1992.
[14] Voutsaki 1997, 40.
[15] van Wijngaarden 1999, 4-5.
[16] Smith 1987, 319-320.
[17] Douglas & Isherwood 1980, 160; Smith 1987, 320.
[18] Graziado 1991, 405-406; Moody 1987, 237-236.
[19] Graziado 1991, 412; O'Shea 1981, 42, table 3.3.
[20] Haselgrove 1982, 82.

Shennan, the consumption of prestige goods was of significance for groups seeking to legitimate status. It is interesting to note that these objects are assumed to have an intrinsic value, which can be used when rank was to be established.[21]

Judging from the above, it is no possible to reach a consensus regarding how prestige objects are to be defined. Ethnographical material shows that there is not always an agreement between the objects deposited and the actual situation of wealth. However, several scholars agree that both quantity and quality can be regarded as measures of status and wealth. The same position will be adopted also in the following study, owing to the fact that there are quantitatively observable discrepancies in the number and quality of the objects deposited in the different periods. It is also believed that goods traded over long distances and of exotic origin, made of rare or exotic materials and showing high technological skill and low frequency were more valuable also in the context of a prehistoric economy. It will also be maintained that, owing to their quality, precious materials and objects are to be regarded as prestige goods and markers of social and economic status, as they were obviously not accessible to all members of the society. The absence or presence of these objects in tombs and settlement contexts can therefore be used as a measure of status or wealth.

To conclude, if a more qualitative and subjective approach is needed to discuss the physical remains, such a method will not be refused in the following study. I am aware that status may not in all situations have been reflected in valuable goods deposited at the moment when the specific burial took place, nor need status always have been retrieved in the goods deposited. However, owing to the difficulties of demonstrating this in the archaeological context, it will be assumed that the definitions of status and wealth in the case of Late Helladic society are synonymous. That is, objects made of precious material are assumed to indicate high social status and economic prosperity.

3.3 ARCHAEOLOGICAL INDICATORS OF STATUS

The discussion of the status of individual settlements to follow will necessarily confront questions of great importance for identifying the empirical evidence for status. This study sets out to survey such potential indicators. It does so with a view to establishing a wider range of tools for the assessment of status, to be applied to one particular archaeological setting, that of the Late Helladic Argolid. Here will be brought up for discussion the usefulness of conceivable variables, such as architecture, tombs and household possessions as measures of status.

The two variables that, independently of chronological or geographical focus, seem to have been most extensively used in examining status differentiation have been burial practices and architectural remains. The main argument for using architectural remains and burials as indicators of socio-economic and political inequality is the comparatively good access which we have to these archaeological groups of material remains. They are typically easy to recognise in the landscape as, for example in Late Helladic terms, we have preserved palace architecture, tholoi and chamber tombs. The first group is useful, as complex societies tend to manifest economic, political and social power through architecture. The noticeable variation in size and quality between houses indicates stratification and the occurrence of monumental architecture, for example, palaces, serves to underline the plausibility of such assumptions. Further evidence of centralisation and redistribution is also represented by the structures regarded as magazines and storage areas. The relevance of using storage facilities as a group of data reflecting the exchange system used has been discussed by, for example, T. Earle and T. D'Altroy.[22] Also the presence of workshops will be discussed in the presentation of the archaeological evidence.

Burials represent the second group used for measuring status. It is often rewarding to use this group, as tombs are likely to be well represented in the archaeological record and to supply the researcher with plentiful material information. For example, with reference to the Late Helladic period it is possible to find tombs ranging from the tholos type to simpler pit and cist graves. Thus, the architectural aspects of tombs have been used in discussing status in Late Helladic society.

Burials may also have grave goods that can be used as indicators of the status of the deceased. For example, ivory is an exclusive and precious material and the presence of ivory objects may perhaps be interpreted as an indicator of status on account to their uniqueness. Krzyszkowska does not exclude the possibility that the ivory objects in chamber tomb I:2 at Asine were heirlooms.[23] The proposal is attractive on account of the character of the material. The presence of amber in the area in the Late Bronze Age has been observed. The occurrence of amber is associated with a hierarchical social structure with local élites involved in the consumption of objects used as symbols of prestige and rank. Interesting is also suggestions made by Shennan that amber objects functioned as prestige goods as they are often found together with other items of a prestige and élite nature, and in tombs their presence has a social significance.[24]

[21] Shennan 1982, 38.

[22] Earle & D'Altroy 1982, 265-290.

[23] Krzyszkowska 1996, 86.

[24] Shennan 1982, 38. See also Waarsenburg 1995 on amber. In addition to what Smith 1987 designates as the contextual variable (burial form, orientation, grave goods) there is also the osteological variable to take into consideration. This category is most interesting as an indicator of the nutritional status of those

3.4 EMPIRICAL CONSIDERATIONS

The empirical research will primarily be based on the archaeological material from the Late Helladic Asine and published material representing other Argive sites. The material from Asine consists of both settlement and tomb material already published and hitherto unpublished, settlement material from the storerooms at Uppsala.[25] The Lower Town at Asine will be focused on in detail as this is the largest exposed section of the Late Helladic settlement. Frödin and Persson published their findings from the excavation of the area in a volume where we find a dating for the architectural remains, i.e. the houses. Furthermore, previous research concerning Late Helladic pottery has given us more details on the different sectors of the site during this broad period.[26] It is hoped that an examination of the pottery material stored at Uppsala will reveal more information concerning the dating of the houses located in the Lower Town. However, it is to be observed that my intention is here not to publish a catalogue of Late Helladic pottery from the Lower Town of Asine, but to give relevant references to significant deposits whereupon the stratigraphical analysis of the Lower Town will be based.

The discussion concerning the tomb material will comprise the hitherto published material. The eight excavated and subsequently published chamber tombs were all discovered during the campaign of the 1920s, but the total number of chamber tombs seems to have been fairly large, as it is reported that during the 1924 campaign 25 tombs were discovered.[27] A Greek team excavated some chamber tombs in the 1970s, but unfortunately they are still unpublished. To the very few published chamber tombs we may also add some earth cut and cist tombs as well.

The archaeological material will also include tomb and settlement material from the other Argive-plain settlements. We are in possession of different types of tomb evidence, and also domestic archaeological materials. Furthermore, as the purpose of the present study is to test whether storage facilities can be used as an auxiliary instrument to deduce the degree of economic centrality and control exercised by the palaces, these facilities will be discussed in detail. The presence of workshops will also be discussed.

The excavated material from Asine is dominated by pottery and, unfortunately, the status of it can for the most part be characterised as sherds. Whole items are very rare in settlement deposits and the following examination will therefore have to be based on sherd material. As at other settlements, unpainted pottery is the most common ware at Asine and this, combined with the lack of whole shapes, makes identification and dating problematic. This is particularly true of the identification of LH IIIC and Submycenaean material.

Another group of evidence used in the discussion is Linear B material from the Argive sites. This category is methodologically difficult to handle and its value as the mediator of information must be carefully evaluated. Here it is argued that any presumption that the textual evidence is a general instrument, which it would be possible to extrapolate to the whole Mycenaean world and especially to the economic aspects, is not valid. The Linear B evidence from the Argolid lays bare a completely different, archaeological context compared with Pylos and Knossos. This is so, as we have no evidence of archives and also owing to the chronological discrepancy. The discrepancy may be explained by the fact that the tablets were not fired to the same extent as those at the other palaces, that material was not noticed by the excavators at Mycenae and Tiryns or that excavations have been conducted at the wrong spots. All these arguments can of course, be used, but they do not seem entirely plausible. The discrepancy in the amount of material is enormous and we have to ask ourselves whether we can explain this only through factors such as those outlined here. Methodologically, the approach used in this study will therefore be one based on an acceptance of the textual evidence as valuable, together with the archaeological material, but the Argive tablets will be discussed in their own, unique, regional perspective. Some scholars have also accepted the tablets as representing the entire economy. However, as has previously been shown, this overall view of the Late Bronze Age economy is neither applied nor accepted by all. As noted, details are missing and therefore a full picture of the entire economy is not to be expected. For example, potters are hardly mentioned, although their products are to be seen everywhere in the archaeological material. Nor do we find any information about products such as pulses, tin and ivory and practically nothing about foreign trade.[28]

Finally, some words on the importance of anthropology in archaeology. It has been pointed out by Ucko that the use of ethnographical parallels 'is to widen the horizons of the interpreter' and thereby also to widen the approaches to archaeological interpretation.[29] The use of this material as a source of information in discussions

buried. A co-ordination of osteological material and grave goods may therefore be a rewarding option for the examination of status of the deceased. A recent article by Smith Kirkpatrick 1999 shows that differences in dental status lends support to the hypothesis that low status people exhibit higher rates of caries and ante-mortem tooth loss than do high status individuals.

[25] I would like to like to offer my thanks to the Dept. of Archaeology and Ancient History, Uppsala University for giving me permission to work with and publish the material from the storerooms at Uppsala, Sweden. I also wish to thank the Nauplion Ephoria for permission to work at the Lionardo apotheke, Nauplio, Greece.

[26] Frizell 1978; Santillo Frizell 1980; 1986.

[27] Frödin & Persson 1938, 151.

[28] Halstead 1988, 525-526; 1992b, 62, 64; Tegyey 1988, 5-6.

[29] Ucko 1969, 262.

concerning prehistoric societies has increased also among prehistorians working within the field of Aegean archaeology. The following study will also take this course and, as the point of departure for the reconstruction of a prehistoric settlement, the use of ethnographical parallels as a method of reconstructing prehistoric societies will be adopted. The value of non-European, ethnographical material as a source of information can, of course, be questioned. It can be argued that studies of non-Balkan settings are not a valuable source of information, as they describe cultural and geographical contexts and settings not paralleled in the Aegean region. In the present study, however, it is argued that there is no automatic similarity between the prehistoric Aegean and the descriptions of mostly early 19th century, rural life in the Balkans.

The latter are mainly ethnographic in a traditional way and seldom describe such aspects as economic transactions, trade, production, burial customs and so forth.

With these considerations in mind, in the following chapter settlement activity at Asine will be discussed. Subsequent chapters extend the geographical scope of the analysis to include the entire Argive Plain (Chapter 5) and to categories of material other than settlement remains, such as tombs (Chapter 6) and specifically those at Asine (Chapter 7). The final empirical chapter takes a look at the chamber tombs of the Argolid and the material contained therein (Chapter 8).

PART II

DOMESTIC ARCHITECTURE: EVIDENCE FOR ECONOMIC ACTIVITY

CHAPTER 4
SETTLEMENT ACTIVITY AT ASINE

4.1 INTRODUCTION

Any attempt to establish a chronological sequence for the Lower Town of Asine is likely to take on the appearance of a gigantic, uncompleted, jigsaw puzzle in which the pieces are distributed over a large area. The stratigraphy presented by the excavators had already been questioned by A. Furumark, who in an article in 1944[1] convincingly showed that House G was of a later date than the originally proposed. With this in mind the primary aim of this chapter will be to re-examine some of the material from different locations in the Lower Town. Each house will be studied in detail, in order to find out the layout, chronological order and possible function. Finally, the results of the survey of the Lower Town will be discussed with the material from other parts of the settlement, with the purpose of mapping out the chronology and the possible status of Asine through time.

The dating of the constructions unearthed during the early excavations meets with considerable problems. The pottery material from the latest period of the Late Bronze Age is not easy to classify, and the locations mentioned on the boxes of pottery are not easy to find on the excavation plan with the desired degree of precision. In spite of these problems, an attempt will be made to carry out a more detailed examination of the Late Helladic pottery found in the Lower Town. The results will be used in the stratigraphical discussion to reveal more details concerning the chronology of the houses in the Lower Town.

The material used for this purpose consists of both already published and unpublished pottery, deposited in the store-rooms at Uppsala. The original aim of the study was to give a full presentation of this material, but as the work has progressed it has become increasingly obvious that such a presentation would need, and indeed deserve, a study of its own. Therefore, in this study the pottery will be used only as a chronological reference. The latest excavations conducted at Asine have been concentrated in areas of the settlement other than the Lower Town and the publications are also more detailed as concerns the dating of the pottery. These publications are of considerable importance in discussing the chronology of the excavated part of the Late Helladic settlement.

4.2 THE QUALITY OF THE EXCAVATION DOCUMENTATION

The excavations in the Lower Town was published by Frödin & Persson in 1938, and in their publication we also find a dating for the Late Helladic architectural remains, that is, the houses. The publication is rewarding in many ways, but there are also some problems, primarily because the information is at times conflicting. For example, it is reported that the floor levels found in the houses of the prehistoric period were only occasionally clearly marked. However, to mention but one instance, House G is described in the final publication as having all floors on practically the same level.[2] In the field notes in *Diary* 8, the only references to floors are to those in room XXXII. Likewise the levels of the identified column bases reported on the excavation plan do not correspond to those on the plan in the report by Frödin and Persson in 1938. Furthermore, on different pages of this publication, different levels for the bases are mentioned.[3]

The diaries therefore play a crucial role in attempts to decipher the results. For example, *Diary* 8 has a set of very useful drawings that come in handy in identifying walls and so forth. Unfortunately, the floor levels are seldom reported and at times it is also very difficult to follow the descriptions of walls. We also know from the diaries that the walls found were not always documented on the plan. This is especially notable in the case of the Hellenistic and Geometric walls. Moreover, when locations outside the so-called megaron are described, the situation becomes even more complicated. In short, the information provided by the diaries reveals an excavation situation that is sometimes complicated, complex and confusing.

[1] Furumark 1944, 206, 210-211, figs. 3- 4.

[2] Frödin & Persson 1938, 66, 74-75.

[3] Frödin & Persson 1938, 66, 77.

4.3 METHODOLOGICAL COMMENTS

The archaeological material from the Lower Town is dominated by pottery. Whole items are, of course, generally very rare in settlement deposits and Late Helladic Asine is no exception in this regard. As at other settlements, unpainted pottery is the most common ware also at Asine and this, combined with the lack of whole shapes and even good profiles, makes identification and dating problematic. This is particularly true of the LH IIIC and Submycenaean material, where our knowledge of settlement material is still very poor. In his pioneering work on Submycenaean pottery, Styrenius[4] published material from burial contexts, but so far substantial studies of settlement material have been few. Apart from the work by Styrenius, the study by Santillo Frizell on the late material from Asine, and work by others on the LH IIIC and the Submycenaean/Early Iron Age material from Tiryns rank as major contributions to the studies of the settlement material.[5]

In the 1938 report by Frödin & Persson, levels are specified as above the sea-level (a.s.l.). On the original excavation map, different zero points are referred to, depending on which area was being excavated and drawn. The diaries also refer to levels as "above the floor-level" and "from the surface". According to *Diary* 8, on 14 April 1926, the zero point was moved from an unspecified point to the round column base located in room XXXII, House G. Obviously the figures used for the published plan in the final publication were converted from the excavation plan. Reasonably, there should be a correspondence between the meter levels referred to on the excavation plan and those found on the published plan. The southern column base in room XXXII was used as a point of correlation of the stratigraphical relations and it was found that the level of the base was 217 cm under the surface on the excavation plan and 6.98 m a.s.l. on the published one. It was expected that these levels would correspond in the sense that the measurements given would add up. However, when the other levels, on both the original and the published plans, were plotted out, it became obvious that the excavators had probably mixed several reported levels when transferring them from the excavation plan. As reference levels are not always compatible, it goes without saying that this adds to the difficulties in interpreting the plans.[6]

The final publication underlined the varying state of preservation of the walls, and this is easy to confirm from the original plan and also on photographs taken during the excavation.[7] The confusion concerning the height of the walls, while not surprising, is a problem. On the original plan, levels are noted, but these are measured at the tops of the walls, while the bottom levels are not given. Some help to mitigate this problem is to be found in the publication on the Large Section, where some of the walls belonging to the Late Helladic period are documented.[8] These walls are thought to give an indication of the heights of walls generally. We may observe that some walls seem to be c. 1 m, for example, Wall 74, that is, the west wall of the structure known as the upper Mycenaean house. The walls surrounding the megaron, room XXXII, House G, were probably approximately 0.30 m high.

Another problem is that explicit references to floor levels are very seldom given. An exception is room XXXII in House G, where the diary mentions three floors and where the first floor is aligned to a reference point, making it possible to identify a floor level. Fortunately, also some other floor-level references were found, such as the floor in room XXXIX. Still, there are disturbing gaps and all these unknowns or informational voids make an interpret-ation of the excavation plan fraught with uncertainty.

The difference between the original plan and the published one is interesting in its own right. Despite all question marks, I would like to suggest that the levels found on the original plans may be used in a discussion concerning the chronology and layout of the Late Helladic houses in the Lower Town. The problem here is to interpret the conflicting figures from the diaries, the plans and the final publication. Much of the general stratigraphical discussion will be based on the field notes and the original excavation plan. Although it must be said that old age and wear make them difficult to use (the figures are often difficult to read), the quality of the excavation plans as such is good.

[4] Styrenius 1967.

[5] Podzuweit 1978, 471-498; 1979, 412-440; 1981; 194-220; 1983, 359-402; 1988, 213-225; Papadimitrou 1988, 227-243. The publication of this important material from Tiryns will be very welcome. I am most grateful to Dr. A. Papadimitrou for all her information and for her kindness in showing me the material. I would also like to thank the German Archaeological Institute for giving me permission to visit the store-room at Tiryns. I also appreciate all the help received from Dr. G. Albers; Santillo Frizell 1986.

[6] Frödin & Persson 1938, fig. 77. A note on one of the original plans indicates the disagreement in the team concerning the excavation methods. Someone has emphasised, see original plan entitled "Lågstaden Söder I", that 'the levels are from the sea-level 13 m. above, and that is it!' (original in Swedish).

[7] Frödin & Persson 1938, 63-64, figs. 54-57.

[8] Frödin & Persson 1938, fig. 77.

4.4 DISCUSSION OF THE MATERIAL

In the present study, the examination is based on the remains of seven Late Helladic houses in the Lower Town at Asine (*Figs. 3-4*). According to the excavators, the houses in the Lower Town were in a fairly bad condition; this was primarily due to later building activity causing damage to the earlier constructions.[9] Some of the houses, including Houses F, L and W,[10] are preserved only as small units consisting of a few walls and a more penetrating analysis of function and status is in these cases not possible.

The present study will concentrate on Houses G, H, I and K, where the remaining walls and other installations seem to have been in a fairly good condition and therefore were more carefully documented on the architectural plan of the Lower Town, published in the excavation report.[11] According to the excavation report, three of the dwellings (G, I and K) are, dated to the LH IIIB period, while House H is dated to LH IIIC.[12] Furumark established that House G contained material of a later LH IIIC character and consequently also questioned the date originally given for House H.[13]

House F *(Fig. 3)*

Location: Lower Town. Sq. I-K13-14.
Date: Frödin & Persson 1938, period 5 = LH IIIA. New = LH IIIC.
Layout: The walls are differently oriented from the surrounding walls. They are on much the same level than the rest of the walls in this part of the excavation. Above Walls 47 and 51 runs Wall 58.
Walls: 47, 48, 49, 50, 51.
Floors: -
Stairs: -
Doors: -
Rooms: XXVI, XXVII.
Architectural details: -
Finds: -
Condition: Fragmentary unit.
References: Frödin & Persson 1938, 63, 74, 90, figs. 43, 53; Hiesel 1989, 176; Shear Mylonas 1968, 279-280.
Diary: 8.

Discussion: There are questions concerning the stratigraphy in this part of the excavation. The excavators dated the house to the LH IIIA period,[14] but the top levels mentioned on the original plan correspond to those of other walls, LH IIIC, in the eastern part of the excavation. Also, the top levels of the walls surrounding room XXVII are on the original plan reported as being at a higher level. It was observed in the final publication that Wall 58 was above Walls 47-51. The levels on the excavation plan show that the eastern part of Wall 58 may have been part of House F. Unfortunately, the chronological context cannot be verified by finds of pottery. However, the top levels of walls indicate a stratigraphical position belonging to a later date than LH IIIA. A date in LH IIIC, or even later, is more plausible.

Summary: Our knowledge of this part of the excavation is scanty. This is made worse by the fact that, so far, it has not been possible to trace the pottery material and make a connection with information provided by the excavation plan. Therefore we can only assume that the date proposed in Frödin & Persson is correct; given the parallels to the above cases, even this may be questioned. Be this as it may, the function of this part of the Lower Town should be connected with the surrounding buildings, where the domestic function is predominant.

House G (*Fig.* 3)

Location: Lower Town. Sq. E-K10-15.
Date: Frödin & Persson 1938, period 6 = LH IIIB. New = LH IIIC:Middle/Late /Transitional/Hellenistic.
Layout: Wall 58 runs partly above the walls of House F. The top levels mentioned and the orientation in this part of the excavation indicate that the western part of Wall 58 is not part of House G. Wall 69 was defined as belonging to the structure, but the top levels diverge much from the western part of the construction. For Wall 69 a Geometric connection cannot be ruled out. The diary comments that above Wall 56 runs a level of stones, whereas the part beneath is more straight. Close to and under the "upper Mycenaean wall", Wall 74, appeared a wall of unburned fine clay, Wall 61, probably mudbrick. Pieces were found also elsewhere during the excavation.
Walls: 52-69.
Floors: In the *Diary* 8 (27/3, 29/3, 12/4, 14/4), three floors in room XXXII are mentioned. The figures, however, diverge, as the upper lime floor is reported on two different levels, 210 cm and 220-230 cm. These figures may possibly be explained as measurements made at different times and points. The measurements for the base found in room XXXII and the connected floors are slightly confusing. The floor of room XXX was also in lime stucco and was repaired with flat stones in the middle, 220 cm below the surface level. According to Frödin & Persson the floor in room XXIX was probably situated on a somewhat higher level than the floor of room XXX. The levels on the plan verify this, as the upper stone on the uppermost level is 165 cm below the surface level and the walls here are not high.

[9] Frödin & Persson 1938, 104.
[10] Frödin & Persson 1938, 96, fig. 69. House W is located on Terrace III.
[11] Frödin & Persson 1938, figs. 43, 53, 58.
[12] Frödin & Persson 1938, 90.
[13] Furumark 1944, 206, 210-211, figs. 3-4.
[14] Frödin & Persson 1938, 90, fig. 53.

Stairs: Room XXX was connected with room XXIX by a stairway of three or four steps. The information in Frödin & Persson 1938, fig. 43, indicates that the slabs increased from 6.91 to 7.50 m above sea-level. However, the original plan shows that there was variation and irregularity as the first slab in room XXX was found on a level of 194 cm and the following ones 204, 188 and 165 cm below the surface level.
Doors: Wide doorway in Wall 58. Nothing preserved of a door but a line of rubble masonry along the north side of Wall 58, in room XXXII, may be explained as a support for a threshold. This arrangement is repeated on the west Wall 56 of room XXXII.
Rooms: XXVIII-XXXVI.
Architectural details: Two column bases found in room XXXII. The southern base is roughly circular and the northern is a triangular slab. On the published plan they are 6.90 and 6.96 respectively above sea-level. Both were sunk into the third, lower floor. Wall 56 was well constructed with a core of oblong stones that on both sides have low rubble constructions resembling benches or ledges. Wall 61 had a similar ledge or bench reported on the west side. A bench and a hearth are located in the north-eastern part of room XXXII, close to Wall 58. The diary reveals that in the south-eastern part of the room a fireplace was documented. Shear Mylonas suggests that rooms XXXIII and XXXIV were storage areas, as they are small and have no doorways. The small room in the south-eastern corner of the house, similar in design to room XLI in House I and room LI in House K, may perhaps also have been a storage area.
Finds: Room XXXII, square H14.
1. Jug with neck downward, LH IIIC; 2. Triple bowl, LH IIIC:M; 3. Kalathos, LH IIIC:M/L; 4. Stemmed goblet, LH IIIC:M; 5. Cup with three handles; 6. Bowl with two handles, LH IIIC:L; 7. Bowl with two handles, LH IIIC:M; 8. Amphora, LH IIIC:M.

Other finds of pottery:
1. Stirrup vase, fig. 207:2, LH IIIC:L; 2. Squat bowl, three feet, fig. 207:3, LH IIIC:M; 3. Cup, floor of room XXXII, LH IIIC:M, no. 3535 at Leonardion, Nauplion; 4. Ladle, square G14, room XL, fig. 209:1; 5. Necked jar, floor of room XL; 6. Plate, fig. 209, figurines found close to bench in room XL.
Other finds: One mould found in Mycenaean stratum, perhaps for casting of pins.
References: Frödin & Person 1938, 63-64, 66-67, 74-76, 90, figs. 43, 53, 54, 55, 206-207: 2-3; 209: 1, 3; 211; 212; 1-5; Hiesel 1989, 84-85; Shear Mylonas 1968, 280-286, 467-468.
Diary: 8

Discussion: This area was not completely excavated. In addition to the diary, photographs and plans confirm that the walls were neither well built nor high, and that not all of them were joined.[15] The measurements reported on the original excavation plan differ much as between the different walls and parts of House G. The excavation plan shows that the long Wall 59 diverges approximately 100-130 cm between the western and the eastern parts. The eastern part of the complex with Walls 67-69 shows a discrepancy in the orientation between these walls and the others. Wall 67 is documented on a level commensurate with the walls surrounding room XXXII in House G. Also, the column base found in Wall 67 is on a level comparable to the levels for room XXXII. Perhaps the wall and the base should be regarded as part of the megaron section? The measurements associated with Walls 68-69 are probably not to be connected with House G, as they are observed on a higher level and the walls in this area were reported as being in a worse state of preservation.[16]

Walls are not always easy to define on the photographs in the final publication. Wall 58 has been connected with House G as the north wall of the megaron. The question is whether the eastern part of Wall 58 was a later addition, (see House F, Wall 57), and room XXXI, was also assigned as part of House G. The upper level of this wall could be compared with Wall 58 where the bottom level is connected to the floor(s) in room XXXII. Also, photographs show that Wall 57 consisted of only one level of stones.[17] It may be questioned whether the wall should be regarded as part of the room complex; probably room XXXI had another layout.

The figures on the original plan reveal a layout for House G that does not correspond to the published plan for the house. The excavation plan and an unpublished photograph[18] indicate that the walls described may have been mixed up. In front of Wall 64 (north) and obviously on a much lower level is a wall that, to judge by the photographs, corresponds to Wall 67. It is quite possible that here we have a wall belonging to the first phase of the building that was neither published nor drawn. Walls 63-66 are reported as being flimsily built (or at least were found in that state) and not connected with others. It is also proposed that they were levelled off to make room for the floor, level 7.90 (corresponding to 1.25 on the excavation plan) of room XXXIX (House H).[19] The original plan shows, however, that these reported levels are not consonant with the layout assumed for House G; this is because the walls connected with the megaron area are found on a considerably lower level. Wall 65 is reported on the original plan at levels 0.90-1.15, whereas the final publication reports just one point of measurement, 7.91,

[15] Frödin & Persson 1938, 74, figs. 53-55.
[16] Frödin & Persson 1938, 64, 75.
[17] Frödin & Persson 1938, fig. 54.
[18] Photograph 1926, c7822; Frödin & Persson 1938, fig. 57, for another angle of the same area.
[19] Frödin & Persson 1938, 63-64.

rather than an interval. The level agrees with the floor level of 7.90, but not if the figures are applied to the original plan. The level of 1.25 for the floor is lower than the measurements given for Wall 65 on the original plan. It seems natural, therefore, to question whether this part of the complex belonged to House G. Instead, it appears reasonable to connect the floor with these walls.

The walls to the west of room XXXII have also been assigned to House G. Following the diary, where several floor levels and walls are mentioned, and also taking the pottery into consideration, Room XXX shows signs of continuity; probably the last floor excavated was of Late Helladic origin. On the western side of Wall 56, a row of stones was found on the same level as the other part of the wall. The row on the western side of Wall 56 has been interpreted as a bench like construction. The western row is, however, not connected to the wall and it cannot be ruled out that this row of stones was an independent sequence joining with the four large slabs (stairs?) in the northern Wall 53. Room XXX may be an extension of House G, but it may also have been an independent construction of the Late Helladic IIIC period. If the walls were part of a house the limestone pavement was a floor inside the house. But, if there was no building, the pavement might have been outside the house. As concerns the most western part of the complex, the information in the diary and the preserved height of Wall 52, on a considerably higher level than Wall 56, indicate that the wall and the room behind, XXVIII, may be Hellenistic constructions. A floor is reported 170 cm below the surface level, close to the Hellenistic lime kiln and this may be part of the Hellenistic house.

To conclude, and in contrast to the excavation report, we may exclude the possibility that this complex from the beginning consisted of room XXXII with an extension to the east; the latter is but fragmentarily documented on the excavation plan and on photographs. The layout of House G is probably not static and instead we may regard this as part of a building programme in progress during the LH IIIC period. As concerns the pottery connected with the lime floor in room XXXII, we may observe that the pottery is Middle and Late LH IIIC with Submycenaean and Protogeometric sherds present.[20] The latter material indicates continuity of habitation.

Shear Mylonas defined the complex as a category G house. On account of the size of the building and the two vestibules, she suggested that the building contained at least two separate establishments.[21] This conjecture is supported by the discussion above, as probably the western part of the complex, room XXX, was simply a later addition. It is also suggested that Wall 52 and the westernmost room, XXVIII, belonged to a later house, perhaps a Hellenistic structure.

Room XXXII is one of the largest Mycenaean rooms excavated, with two stone columns in the room, as well as a stone bench. According to Shear Mylonas, stone benches are found in room 32 in Panagia House III and in room 1 of the West House at Mycenae without any religious function.[22] The line of stones in room XXX has also been regarded as a bench similar to the one in room XXXII. However, as proposed in the earlier discussion, this may instead have been a free-standing wall and part of a connecting house. Room XXXII contained some interesting finds. Here was found a vase and idol deposit and the so-called Lord of Asine. According to the diary, the latter was found at level 180 cm, corresponding to the upper levels for the eastern-wall section of room XXXII. Close under the head were two smaller Mycenaean figurines: a black stone axe, a number of complete vessels and a couple of coarse-ware vessels. Further finds on a lower level were a stone axe and several vessels. The diary describes the find context as a level of clay mixed with charcoal on one side and small stones on the other. The objects were found in this filling on a bench-like construction close to Wall 58. The upper level reported on the excavation plan is 160-167 cm below the surface level. The excavation plan informs us that the top levels of Wall 61 varied between 161 and 207 cm below the surface level. Only the northern-most part of the wall, at 161 cm, corresponded to the bench. The rest of the wall was found on a deeper level than the bench. These levels are also significant for the other walls surrounding room XXXII.

The diary reports about the spectacular find twice.[23] It is noted that a bench constructed of several layers of flat stones appeared towards Wall 58 and the "upper Mycenaean wall", that is, Wall 61.[24] On one side was the vase and idol deposit and on the other, in the corner formed by Walls 61 and 58, there were a number of Mycenaean sherds and a large Mycenaean vessel deposited upside down without a bottom. Furumark assigned the deposited pottery to the transition to the Late LH IIIC period,[25] and Mountjoy considered them to be of LH IIIC Late origin.[26] Although there are vessels that probably belong to LH IIIC Middle, this period can be disputed as a date applicable to all finds.

[20] Boxes: As 1915, 1916, 3854, 4047, 4068, 4074, 4099, 4150, 4229A, 4229B, 3790, 3886, 3844, 4065, 4116. Of particular interest is a box containing remains from above the floor; this pottery is probably Early or Middle LH IIIC, As 2945. Several of the boxes contained a few LH IIIA/B sherds. Frödin & Persson 1938, 298-307, for the published pottery material from this area.

[21] Shear Mylonas 1968, 284.

[22] Shear Mylonas 1968, 283.

[23] *Diary* 8, 8 and 13 of April.

[24] Drawing *Diary* 8. H. 30 cm, W. 60 cm, L. 56 cm.

[25] Furumark 1944, 206.

[26] Mountjoy 1986, 181.

The mixed chronological character of the deposit is also to be observed in the presence of the so-called Lord of Asine.[27] The finds indicate the use of the building throughout both the LH IIIC Middle and the Late periods.

Another find to be mentioned is the mould for casting pins found in a Mycenaean stratum in this complex.[28] Pins made of different materials were also found in tombs. The single mould may be out of context and need not be associated with workshop activity in this specific building. The mould is, however, interesting as it indicates production somewhere in the area. Besides some LH III sherds, a small finger-ring of iron is reported in an entry of 26 April to have been found in a level mixed with charcoal, north-west of the megaron at c. 120 cm beneath the surface. The reported walls are, however, documented on lower levels and the ring is probably of a later date.

Shear Mylonas claimed that no hearths had been reported in the final publication.[29] But a hearth is mentioned as located in the north-eastern part of room XXXII and a charcoal and ash layer was reported to have been found on the lowest floor in the megaron, close to the upper Mycenaean wall.[30] In the filling were found bones, sherds and fired mudbrick. The layer ended in a pile of stones in the south-eastern corner of room XXXII. According to the excavators it may have been a fireplace and the wasters may have been removed down on the floor. Most of the lower floor level was cleaned at this point.
R. Hägg has suggested that room XXXII was used for a house cult,[31] a hypothesis supported by the finds of figurines, the Lord, miniature vessels, the upside-down vessel, the stone axe, the composite vase and so forth.[32] The main archaeological remains, the bench and the hearth, point to an installation for a house cult in the LH IIIC Late period. The hearth-like installation mentioned in the diary probably had both a religious and a domestic function, as we also find coarse ware and domestic ware in the material. Shear Mylonas suggests that rooms XXXIII and XXXIV, both of which are small and lack doorways, may have been used as storage areas.[33] Also the unnumbered room in the south-eastern corner of the building may have been a storage area. Their use should, however, most probably be connected with the later use of the construction and their size perhaps indicates household storage.

Summary: To summarise, we find a complex of rooms successively added to each other. The activity within the walls surrounding room XXXII can be assigned to Middle and Late LH IIIC. As has been mentioned, it is even possible that the most westerly part of the complex may have been a later, even a non-Bronze-Age, addition. The most easterly part of the complex needs more detailed investigation concerning the pottery that can be related to these levels. The information provided by *Diary* 8 indicates that we cannot rule out the possibility that the walls are of a much later date. It is reported that. in the "middle part" of the section excavated, that is, the area with Houses G and H, a purely Geometric level started at c. 80 cm down to c. 140-150 cm, followed by a Mycenaean level (17-20 March). Geometric levels found c. 130 cm below the surface, for example, east of the megaron (1 April and 14 May), were followed by Mycenaean levels on approximately levels 160-180, depending on area (20-22 March). The pottery that can for the moment be associated with the area is reported to have been found on deeper levels, c. 150-200. It is to be hoped that more research will shed new light on the reported higher levels.

The complex of rooms obviously had multiple functions and this was mirrored especially in the finds from room XXXII.[34] Religious aspects predominated in the finds around the bench, but the large number of kitchen and coarse-ware vessels found in the boxes confirms the domestic use and function. The hearth documented in the south-eastern part of the room may have been intended for domestic purposes and also for cultic rituals. The find of a mould for pins is also of interest, as it indicates that in this area production may have taken place. The rooms defined as storage areas are, as suggested, part of a later addition. Their presence further indicates the household and everyday aspect of the building. However, I would suggest that the size and layout of the house indicates that the inhabitants belonged to the local élite. The size may also indicate the household of an extended family group.

House H (*Fig. 3*)

Location: Lower Town. Sq. F-L10-13.
Period: Frödin & Persson 1938, period 7 = LH IIIC. New = LH IIIC:Late/Transitional/Geometric.
Layout: Seems to have been planned on the rectilinear principle. Uncertain whether the house was connected with the houses to the south-west as in Frödin & Persson 1938. Wall 72 is connected with House H.

---

[27] D'Agata 1996, 45-46; Frödin & Persson 1938, fig. 206. The figurine is dated to LH IIIC:M, but was found in the later context. In the material in the store at Uppsala was found one box, labelled "Vas o idol depå", As 3888. Unfortunately it contained mostly kitchenware. The few sherds of plain ware could be LH IIIC:L.

[28] Frödin & Persson 1938, 250.

[29] Shear Mylonas 1968, 682.

[30] *Diary* 8, 15 April.

[31] Frödin & Persson 1938, fig. 206 for the vase and idol deposit; *Diary* 8, 8-5 April; Hägg 1968, 44.

[32] Mountjoy 1986, 170. Obviously the composite vase usually appears in tombs. This may point to a religious function of the vessel and the context in which it was found.

[33] Shear Mylonas 1968, 284.

[34] The multiple functions were also suggested by Shear Mylonas 1968, 267-270, 283.

Walls: 70-74a. C. 1 m of Wall 71 is missing. According to Frödin & Persson, the walls are on nearly the same level.
Floors: Level 7.90 (1.25) in room XXXIX. Between the antae of the upper Mycenaean house c. 130-140 cm. In the house, on level c. 160 cm. another three lime floors and beneath them a layer with small pebbles.
Stairs: -
Doors: Walls 73b and 74a form a doorway between rooms XXXVII and XXXVIII.
Rooms: XXXVII-XXXIX. Room XXXIX equal in size to the main room of the House of Columns, Mycenae.
Architectural details: A column base found in room XXXVII, close to Wall 74a. The base is exactly equidistant from Walls 73 and 74. Two column bases found in the large rectangular room XXXIX. The columns lie exactly between Walls 70 and 73. Columns similar to those found in House G. A kiln found close to Wall 70 in room XXXIX.
Find: 1. Three-handled cup, square G12.
References: Frödin & Persson 1938, 64, 67, 76-77, figs .43, 53, 56, 57, 208: 4; Hiesel 1989, 70; Shear Mylonas 1968, 287, 468-469.
Diary: 8.

Discussion: The description of the house in the final publication suggests a picture of an impressive, large and homogeneous complex with some well-defined rooms in the southern part. According to the excavators, the building had three column bases similar to those in House G, adding to the significance of the building. A kiln was located in the largest room, XXXIX.

A more detailed examination of the walls and the floor levels shows that all walls defined as House H probably do not fit in. According to the final publication, floors were found on nearly the same level, but neither the diary nor the excavation plan support this contention. The diary mentions floor levels that in the final publication may have been associated with this house.[35] The floor levels in the upper Mycenaean house are on considerably lower level than the floor in room XXXIX.

The three column bases dedicated to the house are also of interest. The context has already been questioned by Shear Mylonas and, according to her, the base in room XXXVII was probably not part of the original building.[36] The measurements deserve mention, as in Frödin and Persson the two column bases in room XXXIX are reported with only slightly differing figures. Furthermore, in the description of the house, it is emphasised that the two bases were found on the same level, 8.00 m above sea-level, but when the columns are discussed, the level referred to is 6.98 m.[37] On the plan, 7.98 m and 8.01 m a.s.l., respectively, are given.[38] The final publication describes a situation with two column bases in the same room and at equal heights. The original plan does not agree with the reported figures. On the plan the two bases are not reported as belonging to the same levels as illustrated in Frödin & Persson 1938.[39] The column base in the southern part of the room was found on a level 93 cm below the surface level and that in the northern at 190 cm below the surface level, which gives a difference of nearly 1 m. The third base, room XXXVII, was found on a level 95 cm below the surface (7.96 in Frödin & Persson 1938), corresponding to the southern base in room XXXIX.[40]

The wall levels for the eastern part of the house reported on the published plan do not diverge from those for the western part of the house (Walls 71-74), as they appear at nearly the same height (c. 8.10-8.60). Wall 70 is here on a level c. 8.64 m a.s.l. It is to be observed that, although the excavation plan reported several measurements, only a few measurements are given for this particular wall. An examination of the original plan shows that Wall 70 had a level of c. 50 cm below the surface, that is, considerably higher than the other walls documented, as the top levels of these are c. 90-146 cm below the surface. The reported floor level for room XXXIX, 125 cm does not correspond to that of Wall 70, as the wall was quite thin and probably only one layer of stones was preserved.[41] In the diary, it is mentioned that walls of the Geometric period usually consisted of only one level of stones.[42]

Consequently, it is here suggested that the eastern part of the house H complex belongs to a later construction and the levels indicate that these walls may have been part of the Geometric settlement. I would suggest that Wall 65 may in fact be the eastern limit of House H; in the final publication it was instead regarded as part of House G. Following the original plan, the walls surrounding rooms XXXVII and XXXVI in House H are those labelled "upper Mycenaeaen house". The southern column base in room XXXIX may have been connected with this building. If so, it would then be thought of as being located outside the building, as would also the base in what was documented as room XXXVII. The northern base, room XXXIX, would then not be included at all; it was after all found on a level not at all consonant with the other measurements. On the final plan, the long Wall 71 was attached to House H. However, it is more plausible that only the westernmost part constitutes the southern wall of House H (the upper Mycenaean house), whereas the eastern

[35] *Diary* 8, 23 April, 27 May.
[36] Shear Mylonas 1968, 288.
[37] Frödin & Persson 1938, 66, 77.
[38] Frödin & Persson 1938, fig. 43.
[39] Frödin & Persson 1938, 78, fig. 43.
[40] Frödin & Persson 1938, 66, fig. 43.
[41] Frödin & Persson 1938, figs. 53, 57. Cf. photographs in archive.
[42] *Diary* 8, 9 June.

part may have been connected with the latter building and Wall 70.

To conclude the discussion thus far, it is here suggested that House H did not exist within the frameworks proposed by the report of Frödin and Persson. The floor levels found and the different walls described in the diary indicate as much. Instead, the complex may be divided into several building phases following very closely on each other and with walls re-used and re-modelled.

The last phase may have been Geometric as the levels of Wall 70, and the eastern part of Wall 71 correspond to the levels referred to in the diary, where references to Geometric material is made. In the profile, the Geometric layer started at c. 75 cm below the surface level, extending down to c. 130 cm. It is of more than passing interest to note the evidence for a Geometric layer east of the so-called, upper Mycenaean wall.[43] The layer is 20-25 cm deep and some walls were found in this particular context. Of interest is also the observation made that east of the megaron Geometric material appeared from level 130 cm down to level 170, where, without interruption, it changed to Mycenaean material.[44] More confusingly, however, we do not know with any degree of certainty whether these walls were drawn on the original plan or not. As regards the upper Mycenaean house, we find ourselves on firmer ground, as this can with some confidence be assigned to the Middle and Last phases of the LH IIIC. Equally interesting are the finds of Submycenaean and Protogeometric material.[45] East of the upper Mycenaean wall, later Helladic material is present at levels between 150 and 180 cm.[46]

The kiln mentioned earlier was on the published plan placed within the walls of House H.[47] The location of the kiln – inside a house complex – can be questioned. If the stratigraphical description with several building phases in the period LH IIIC to Protogeometric/Geometric is accepted, a location of the kiln outside walls in the final part of the Late Bronze Age (or even early Iron Age) is most likely.

It is difficult to date the walls, but we may here find a complex, including House G, to which rooms were added gradually. The simple need to expand to secure more space but also the usefulness of re-using constructions already in existence may be invoked in favour of such an interpretation. In the diary a thick layer of ash and charcoal is also mentioned and we can therefore not rule out the possibility that this part of the settlement was destroyed by fire before the Geometric period.[48] Complex H is best regarded as an extension of House G, which was in continuous use from the middle of Late Helladic IIIC onwards.

Summary: The layout of this part of the excavation, as described in *Diary* 8 and as pictured on the original excavation plans, does not exactly follow the descriptions of House G and House H as documented in Frödin and Persson. The excavation plan and the diary show, that the complex labelled House G most probably did not have the layout described in the final publication. House H suffered the same fate, as probably only a part of the structure was built simultaneously. Instead the information provided by the plans indicates that this part of the settlement developed continuously from the end of the Late Helladic period. The finds of Submycenaean and Protogeometric sherds provide evidence of still later activity in this part of the Lower Town and, as material from that period is present, some walls were probably constructed in the Geometric. Here, more investigation is needed and if material from the Geometric period that can be linked to the levels on the original plan east of the megaron is located, an interesting layout will be probable.

The larger part of the Lower Town area was not excavated more deeply than the walls on the original plan, although some deeper soundings may have been made as the presence of LH IIIA/B and even earlier material indicates.[49] The diary and photographs reveal that some of the walls found must have been removed before documentation. Of particular interest is the long sequence of habitation documented in this area. A multi-functional purpose may be found, as domestic activities are emphasised through the addition of storage areas whereas the kiln indicates home industry. The kiln may have been used for pottery production, as wasters have been found in the context surrounding this part of the excavation.[50]

House I (*Fig. 4*)

Location: Lower Town. Sq. D-H7-12.
Period: Frödin & Persson 1938, period 6 = LHIIIB. New = LH IIIC:Middle/Late/Transitional.
Layout: More or less square ground-plan.
Walls: 56, 56A?, 75-88.

[43] *Diary* 8, 16 April.
[44] *Diary* 8, 14 and 15 May.
[45] As 1360, 1363, 1364, 1365, 1375, 1377, 1423, 1575, 1712, 1717, 1910, 1914, 1917, 1934, 1947, 2044, 2090, 5337C, 5338A, 5580. Levels 100-250. Boxes As 1712, 4457, 5533, 5337A-C, 5580, 5624 with LH IIIA sherds and also LH IIA are of particular interest. The finds of Middle Helladic material in the area was observed also in the *Diary* 8 (11-12 May, 18 June, north-east of the upper Mycenaean house, levels 240-250).
[46] As 1729, 1742, 1760, 1766, 1767, 1769.
[47] Sjöberg 1997, 89-97.
[48] *Diary* 8, 12 June.
[49] As 5624 contained nice sherds of Vapheio-type cups. Level 180-200 cm, 'in front of the upper Mycenaean house'.
[50] As 1363, 3120.

Floors: House I, floor c. 140 cm, floor c. 160 cm below surface; House 3, c. 190-200 cm.
Stairs: -
Doors: No clear indication of doors or entrances to the house. However, the excavators discussed the possibility of entrances in Walls 75 and 79.
Rooms: XL-XLVIII. Room XLVI is perhaps the main room and XLVII a narrow corridor or passage. XLVIII a large room with the west wall missing, comparable to room XXXIX in House H. Room XLV is also a large area, with most of the east Wall 79 missing. Smaller rooms in the southern part of the house.
Architectural details: A column base preserved in main room XLVI. Along Wall 76 a ledge similar to those on Walls 56 and 61 in House G. Kiln built against Wall 80 in room XLII.
Finds: Room XLVI, open bowl LH IIIC:Late?, deposit of bobbins. Room XLV, a bronze dagger and a bronze pin.
Condition: Well preserved.
Refeences: Frödin & Persson 1938, 64, 66, 78-80, 90, figs. 43, 58, 66, 208:2; Shear Mylonas 1968, 289-292; 467-468; Hiesel 1989, 98
Diary: 7.

Discussion: The diary mentions three houses, I, II and III, which here will be labelled Houses 1, 2 and 3. These constitute House I. House 1, is amongst other things, room XLVI, House 2 is room XLVIII and House 3 is recognised with walls on a lower level in room XLVI. In House 1, Room XLVI, a deposit of so-called bobbins was found on a level approximately 140 cm below the surface. A possible column base was also found, on a level 116 cm below the surface. Something resembling a floor level was also documented on a level 0.60 cm below the surface. The height of the walls surrounding the room ranged from 0.26 cm to 200 cm below the surface and possibly the floor was connected with the walls surrounding the room. Another stone packing was approximately 160 cm below the surface level under the west wall of House I. To the east of House 1, a bronze dagger and pin were found.

A construction, most probably a pottery kiln, was found in Room XLII. It was made of clay and was partly destroyed when found.[51] Surrounding it was a stone pavement with a large vessel planted in it and close to the kiln a large quantity of ashes was found. A photograph of the excavation shows that the construction was built against the short wall connecting with Wall 80.[52] Following the details that can be recognised on the photograph, the short wall runs under Wall 83. Wall 83 seems to have consisted of only one level of stones, a very low wall. Probably the kiln should be connected with the unnumbered wall. Also, the level of Wall 82 does not seem to have corresponded to that of Wall 83, which has no measurements at all. Information on the original plan indicates that Room XLII probably did not consist of the walls outlined in Frödin and Persson.

According to the excavators, the walls in this area were well preserved, but the reported upper level of the walls seems to have been no higher than those documented elsewhere in the Lower Town area.[53] The levels noted for the pottery boxes cannot always be connected with the levels of walls on the plan. The walls of House 1 are all found on levels that correspond to those on the boxes. Pottery from House 2 was, however, found at a much deeper level than the walls of Room XLVIII.

The boxes of pottery relocated so far reveal that sherds on a level 50-60 cm below the surface in House 1 are mixed LH IIIC Late, Submycenaean and Protogeometric.[54] A floor may perhaps be connected with the level with the bobbins, c. 140 cm. Another floor was recognised at a level of approximately 160 cm. House 2 is represented in the material by a few boxes, level 200, with sherds containing plenty of coarse material. The datable pottery represents a sequence from LH IIIC Middle to Protogeometric.[55]

House 3 had pottery from a level of 200 cm below the surface.[56] The pottery is of a mixed character from LH IIIC:Middle/Late to Protogeometric. According to the diary, walls of this house were found inside House 1. A possible floor level was found approximately 80 cm under the west wall of House 1, which had an upper level of c. 80 cm. If we assume that the height of the preserved wall was approximately 30-40 cm, the level of the floor in House 3 should have been around 190-200 cm below the surface and possibly the floor should be connected with the pottery of level 200 cm.

The stratigraphy for this part of the Lower Town is still confusing. We find that the Late Helladic material does not always correspond to the levels for the walls, and the discrepancy in the case of material from House 2 is obvious. Here, as elsewhere, further analysis of the material is called for.

Summary: It is possible to establish that the walls on the published plan and the original plan are not part of the LH IIIA/B settlement. Also in this part of the excavation, sherds that can be assigned to the earlier periods have been recognised, but they are still quite few. Therefore, it is suggested that at most we may infer that the walls shown on the excavation plan probably belonged to the Middle/Late LH IIIC period. The

[51] Sjöberg 1997, 93-97.
[52] Frödin & Persson 1938, 67, fig. 66.
[53] Frödin & Persson 1938, 78, fig. 59.
[54] As 1785, 1794, 1807, 1878, 3595, 3597, 3606A, 3606B, 3607, 3700, 3698, 4006.
[55] As 1873, 4133.
[56] As 3618, 3687, 1780, 1847, 3589, 3590, 3953A, 3953B, 4016.

Submycenaean and Protogeometric periods are clearly represented and it cannot be ruled out that the walls were in use also during the transitional period.[57]

This complex of rooms is comparable to structure H, as walls may have been added over a long period of time. Furthermore, the multifunctional character, both domestic and industrial, is noticeable. Whereas the kiln indicates household production of pottery, room XLI was perhaps a storage area, emphasising the domestic character of the house. Also in this instance, the production of pottery was carried on in the later phase of the Bronze Age and perhaps also in the transitional period. The deposit of bobbins used for textile production supplements the picture of household production. As is the case in other parts of the Lower Town the pottery indicates continuity in building activity.

House K (*Fig. 4*)

Location: Lower Town. Squares G-I7-10.
Period: Frödin & Persson 1938, period 6 =LH IIIB. New = LH IIIC:Middle/Late
Layout: South-north. East of House I.
Walls: 89-96.
Floors: -
Stairs: -
Doors: A possible entrance between Walls 93 and 94.
Rooms: XLIX- LI.
Architectural details: -
Finds:
1. Stirrup-vase, square I7, LH IIIC:Middle/Late ?
2.Open bowl, square H7 close to Wall 94, LH IIIC:Middle.
8. Open bowl, square G7, LH IIIC:Late.
Condition: The eastern part badly damaged by the contruction of the Bath and therefore it is difficult to reconstruct a plan for the house.
References: Frödin & Persson 1938, 64, 80, 90, figs. 43, 58, 207:1, 6, 208:1; Shear Mylonas 1968, 292-293; Hiesel 1989,176-177
Diary: 5

Discussion: Our information concerning the building is meagre and we have to rely on the information provided in Frödin and Persson and in the diary. As outlined in the diary, this part of the excavation is of interest as concerns the chronological order. Apparently LH I/II material was found, as references are made to what were probably sherds of Vapheio cups.[58] The diary also refers to Mycenaean walls found on a much deeper level than in other parts of the excavation. The excavators explicitly comment, that in this area on a level c. 275 cm below the surface a lot of pottery was found and also that there was an observable difference between this level and the higher one excavated, as pottery of Granary and Salamis types were missing. However, the level of the pottery referred to does not agree with the observed level of the walls published and drawn on the excavation plan, as they range from approximately 50 cm below the surface level down to 190 cm. We have no evidence of wall levels corresponding to 200 cm below the surface in the area. Furthermore, it is necessary to try to locate the pottery associated with these levels. It is possible that this material will be LH IIIA/B, but the few vessels documented in the 1938 report are of LH IIIC Late type.

Summary: The stratigraphical picture is still very unclear and more pottery evidence that can be connected with excavation levels is needed. Our knowledge of the function of the house is of necessity limited, but a domestic function is most probable.

House L (*Fig. 4*)

Location: Lower Town. Sq. L-M10-12.
Period: Frödin & Persson 1938, period 6 = LH IIIB, New = ?
Layout: East of House G and H.
Walls: 103-105.
Floors: Under floor of room LII was found remains of walls.
Stairs: -
Doors: -
Rooms: LII.
Architectural details: The only room was most probably not joined to any other structure.
Finds -
References: Frödin & Persson 1938, 64, 81, 90, figs. 43, 60; Shear Mylonas 1968, 293-294.

Discussion: The construction is in a bad state of preservation. Whereas some parts were not excavated, as the road to the Panagia could not be excavated, probably the construction of the Roman Bath destroyed most of the architecture.

Frödin and Persson assigned these walls to the LHIIIB period and, as no pottery material possible to connect to this wall has so far been found, the date cannot be subjected to a more detailed examination. If we follow the information transferred from the original plan, we may observe that the walls were found on a considerably lower level, c. 320-350 cm below the surface level, than other walls interpreted as belonging to the Late Helladic settlement. The levels point to an earlier period. It is to be observed that the levels on the plan in Frödin & Persson are typically found between 9 and 10 m. It seems as if the figures have been mixed up. As with other measurements reported, I believe that the original plan should be followed. To speculate on the

[57] As 1784, 1794, 1807, 1878, 3595, 3597, 3607, 3700, 3698, 4006.
[58] Probably LH IIA, if we follow the description reported in the diary.

function of this single room is not possible, although Shear Mylonas suggests that in view of its size, room LII served as a large central room in a multiple complex.[59]

Summary: The date proposed in Frödin and Persson can not be checked as no pottery material has been located. The levels on the original plan indicate earlier periods. Also, as concerns function, no answer is to be found in the material.

House W

Location: Terrace III, small trench. Sq. S-T1-2.
Period: LH IIIC?
Layout: Constructed on top of House U (MH).
Walls: 21-23.
Floors: Consisted of earth.
Stairs: -
Doors: -
Rooms: Only one room.
Architectural details: The house has the same arrangement as House U.
Finds: 1. Open bowl, LH IIIC:M; 2. Open bowl, LH IIIC:L?
Condition: Only one room preserved. Damaged by Wall 24 which is probably of a later date.
References: Frödin & Persson 1938, 91, 93, 95-96, figs. 68, 69, 207: 4, 7.

Discussion/Summary: The two vessels documented in Frödin and Persson are the only indications that these walls are of an LH IIIC origin.[60] We may only speculate that this part of the settlement had a domestic function.

4.5 THE LOWER TOWN: A SUMMARY OF RECENT RESEARCH

A summary of the chronological study shows that also this part of the settlement is characterised by continuity of habitation. The diary informs us that Middle Helladic material was found, which can be confirmed in the sherd material. Also the following periods are represented, as sherds from both LH II and LH IIIA and B have been found.[61] As further material, not yet examined, exists, it is believed that more information concerning these periods will appear in due course.

The extensive habitation in the LH IIIC period should be noted. The hitherto examined material indicates that especially the Middle and Late LH IIIC periods were well represented. Indications of habitation in the Early LH IIIC period exist and it cannot, of course, be ruled out that further research and a wider knowledge of the pottery from this chronological sequence will shed light on this period. It is interesting to note the presence of Submycenaean and Protogeometric material, which may be interpreted as evidence for habitation also in the transition to the Iron Age.[62] If so, this tallies well with the results presented by B. Wells in a study of the Protogeometric period based on material from east of the Acropolis.[63] Continuity is also to be seen in the Levendis sector, where both LH IIIC and Protogeometric materials have been found.[64] The material from Asine shows that the Bronze and the Iron Ages are not clearly marked by an interruption. Rather than marking discontinuity, the transitional character of this period is much in evidence. Although no Submycenaean tombs have been found,[65] the pottery indicates that people lived in the area in this period. The finds of iron objects in contexts that may perhaps not be pure Early Iron Age also indicate transition and successive extension of know-how in society.

The stratigraphical analyses presented here show that it is not possible to confirm the layout of the houses in the Lower Town, as they were described in Frödin & Persson 1939. Instead, as shown, at least until the final part of the LH IIIC, the houses were probably extended from a basic concept with a room of megaron type at the core of the house. The classification proposed by Shear Mylonas[66] of Houses G and H as category G houses, multiple dwellings, elaborate and varied in layout, is therefore not disputed. They should, however, not be regarded as two chronologically speaking, strictly separate buildings. Similar dwellings have not been found elsewhere in the Argolid, even in the LH IIIB period, though our knowledge of houses of this period is good. The presence of large dwellings in an LH IIIC context, especially the Middle and Late phases, is therefore interesting. It is suggested that the size and the apparently conscious layout also mirror the status of the settlement in the region in this period. As has been observed in anthropological studies, the house may be seen as a social phenomenon.[67] But the role of the house also as an indicator of economic and political rank is to be reckoned with and the potentially status-marking significance of the house should therefore not be neglected.[68] Interesting is the presence of the bench in House G indicating cult. As has been observed by Blanton shrines in some cultures are rare and occur primarily in élite houses.[69] At Asine, only one construction like the bench has been recognised and

[59] Shear Mylonas 1968, 293-294.
[60] Frödin & Persson 1938, 300, fig. 207:4.
[61] French 1977, 136, observed typical Argive LH IIIB pottery of both phases in the material from the Lower Town.
[62] Styrenius 1967, 129, on some vessels from the Lower Town.
[63] Wells 1983.
[64] Hägg & Nordquist 1992, 59-60.
[65] Hägg 1974, 51.
[66] Shear Mylonas 1968, 467.
[67] Carsten & Hugh-Jones 1995.
[68] Nordquist 1990, 38 on the MH houses and tombs as exponents for different groups within the community; Shear Mylonas 1987, 153; Waterson 1995,47-68.
[69] Blanton 1994, 93.

this, combined with the size and content of House G, may strengthen the idea of the complex as the dwelling for a family of high rank. As concerns complexes G, H and I, we here have houses that seem to have been in use for a long period of time and to have had a multiple function. The large number of coarse and kitchen pottery found in connection with the lime floor and the hearth in room XXXII in complex G is indicative of the domestic character of the room and the house. The people inhabiting the houses may perhaps have belonged to extended families with high economic and social status. Interestingly, similar houses are not paralleled at other Argive settlements in use in the LH IIIC period. The existence of these houses at Asine may also be regarded as a symbol of the status of the settlement in a wider regional perspective.

Remains of economic activity in the Lower Town are quite scanty. Two possible, pottery kilns were located in complexes H and I and we may assume that they were probably in use at the very end of the Bronze Age, possibly in the transition to the Iron Age.[70] Santillo Frizell reports that there is evidence of a pottery workshop also in the Karmaniola area, since over-fired and vitrified fragments of a Submycenaean vessel were found.[71] The function of the kilns in the Lower Town has been discussed elsewhere.[72] It is sufficient to note that their location in a settlement context, including the area east of the Acropolis, fits in well with an agrarian economy based, at least in part, on self-sufficiency, yet one in which the need to use time and household members effectively was of importance for the economy of the family. The mould for the casting of pins indicates that jewellery was produced somewhere at the site.

In comparison with the flourishing LH IIIB period, society in the later part of the Late Bronze Age has been regarded having been in decline, with a simple economic and social structure to match. However, the archaeological evidence from Asine does not confirm this generalised picture. Instead, the tomb and settlement remains indicate that there was a society with both economic and social differences. The apparent differences in the sizes of houses and also tomb contents indicate that society, at least not at Asine, did not change to a poorer state, as concerned wealth and status after the destruction of the palaces.

Scholars have used different methods to assess wealth in archaeological contexts. Smith, for example, has proposed that food-preparation items and serving ware are useful categories for assessing wealth in agrarian societies. Traditionally in archaeology, painted pottery has been assumed to signify wealth and status and painted pottery is often serving ware. If so, it should then be possible to measure wealth by the amount of serving ware or painted pottery possessed by a household.[73] A random sample of sherds from room XXXII showed that more than a third of the total number of sherds was decorated and a third were kitchenware. But also large amount of fine and medium ware were found, both plain and decorated, indicating that those inhabiting the building complex possessed the means to supply the household with pottery that must have been more expensive.[74] If Smith's hypothesis is accepted, the amount indicated should reflect the wealth of the household. It is also to be observed that pottery boxes from other parts of the Lower Town included kitchenware, often of good quality. In the area of House I, it was found that approximately 40% of all pottery consisted of coarseware and kitchenware and included sherds of pithoi.

The larger houses may well have been intended for extended families. Such extended families have economic advantages, since, for example, they may spread the economic risks and their greater manpower may be used more efficiently. Also, they may handle a complex range of tasks, such as hunting, herding and agriculture, and domestic crafts, such as textile production, pottery-making and so forth, not to speak of cooking and baby-sitting. Another important factor in a traditional setting is the family as insurance for the older generation. The economic aspects of the extended family are obvious, but the political advantage is also of importance, as alliances are formed through marriage and may be useful in increasing the power of the family.[75]

4.6 CONCLUDING REMARKS ON THE SETTLEMENT OF ASINE

The survey of the Lower Town of Asine has revealed that this part of the settlement was in use for a long period of time. More recent excavations have shown

[70] Sherds are few but those found close to and inside the kiln indicate use in LH IIIC:Late/Submycenaean and also Protogeometric. As 5411, 1688, 1558, 1431, 3679, 3120. Some misfired and over-fired sherds were found in the area.

[71] Santillo Frizell 1986, 86, fig. 7.

[72] Sjöberg 1997.

[73] As. 3888, 2945, 1916, 1915, 991, 3854, 4047, 4068, 4074, 4099, 4150, 4229A, 4229B, 3790, 3886, 3844, 4021, 4065, 4116. It happen though that also less wealthy households were in possession of these items. In such cases, it should be possible to distinguish between households on the following grounds: 1. wealthier households will have a higher frequency of valuable goods; 2. the serving ware of the wealthier households will exhibit more use, as less wealthy households tend to use their goods less often.

[74] Approximately 50% of c. 2800 sherds were plain or decorated fine or medium ware (contents of 19 boxes of material from the lime floor, the hearth and the vase and idol deposit in room XXXII). As pointed out by Santillo Frizell 1986, 82, we must be aware of the mistakes when discussing quantities of decorated versus undecorated sherds. Hamilakis 1999, 59; Smith 1987, 307-322.

[75] Sahlins 1968, 63-65.

that also the Barbouna Hill and the area East of the Acropolis were inhabited for considerable periods.[76] Quite substantial, architectural features have been exposed for the LH II/LH IIIA1 periods, but the rich yield of pottery shows that the Levendis sector and the Barbouna Hill area were inhabited not only during the LH IIIA and B periods, but also in the LH IIIC. Also in this part of the settlement, traces of fire can be found, which may derive from a minor destruction of the LH IIIA1 settlement on the Barbouna Hill.[77] There is also evidence for habitation on the plateau in the LH IIIA2. Although almost no architectural remains have been found, according to Santillo Frizell, the LH IIIB period also is well documented in the area. Apparently some sort of destruction affected the plateau yet again, at the end of LH IIIA2.[78]

The Karmaniola and the area east of the Acropolis also proved rich in LH IIIA material, as regarded both quantity and quality. This particular part of Asine was apparently not affected by the destruction that struck the Barbouna area. Habitation at Karmaniola continued through LH IIIA2, although on a smaller scale. The LH IIIB period is represented by a decrease in pottery also in this area as in other parts of the settlement. It is also reported that in the excavated area, East of the Acropolis, continuity was observed to the Submycenaean period.[79] Further more, large, more complete, architectural remains from the Late Bronze Age are few in this area as in most others.[80]

The pottery material from the settlement indicates that the settled area of Asine may have been large and even extended outside the areas discussed here.[81] Unfortunately, for the time being the architectural remains do not allow more than speculation concerning the economy of the site in the LH IIIA and LH IIIB periods. To complete the picture, an evaluation of the tomb material is therefore necessary. This material is indicative of a society in which at least part of the population had the economic means to acquire imported goods made of precious materials. The material remains show that relations were established with other regions or settlements, and the location of the site by the sea may have had positive consequences for the local economy. The finds made of exotic materials in tombs are strong evidence of external contacts already at the beginning of the Late Helladic period. Asine, as a coastal settlement and therefore with a logistically and strategically advantageous location points to a function as an entrepôt for goods traded over long distances. Also its intra-regional role and standing are of interest, as we may perhaps assume that, thanks to its location and the activities that it is likely to have supported, Asine had the economic means to acquire more luxury items from other sites on the Argive Plain.

Irrespective of whether these commodities ended up in Asine in lieu of payment in transactions in which the Asineans acted as middlemen or were in demand by the locals because of their intrinsic value, the fact is that the quality and quantity of these commodities are on a par with those found at the major palatial sites inland. Relations with other settlements in the Argolid can also be deduced from the material. A probable LH IIIA1 sherd decorated with a stag found in the Karmaniola area is an interesting example of intra-regional exchange.[82] Parallels, although of an LH IIIB1 date, have been found at Mycenae and also at Tiryns and these sherds are assumed to have a workshop connection. Apparently pottery from the Mycenae area was distributed already in the LH IIIA1 period and it is possible that the Asine sherd had its origin in that area.[83] We may perhaps speculate that some individuals managed to sustain a higher rank, owing to their ability to participate in trade. From these groups the local élite emerged and these groups may have controlled both production and exchange.

The situation during the LH IIIB period is more difficult to evaluate, as fewer material remains have been preserved. Pottery from this period has, however, been found spread all over the settlement and as concerns the Lower Town area it is probable that future studies will expose more material. We should not forget that it is possible that the excavations conducted in this area did not reach the levels for LH IIIA and LH IIIB habitation. The tomb and the settlement material indicate a site in decline in the LH IIIB[84] and it is not unlikely that the contraction seen at several Argive sites and the regional production in imported materials may have affected the economy of Asine precisely because it served as an intermediary in trade or at least a gateway for trade. Larger quantities of material may have been imported more occasionally and possibly other ports may have been used.

The gap in material remains, following on the LH IIIB period, similarly indicates a short period of decline immediately after the destruction of at least some settlements in the Argolid.[85] Even so, as was observed

[76] Ålin 1968, 87-105; Dietz 1984, 23-52; Frizell 1978, 63-91; Hägg 1973, 81-82; Hägg & Nordquist 1992, 61-62; Santillo Frizell 1986; Styrenius 1975, 175-183.

[77] Hägg 1973, 81; Santillo Frizell 1980, 125-131; 1986, 84.

[78] Frizell, 1978, 90-91; Santillo Frizell 1986, 84.

[79] Åhlin 1968, 87-105; Dietz 1980, 71-72, 95-96, 98, 100, 104,-105; 1982, 57-69, 100-102; 1984, 43; Frizell 1978, 63-91; Santillo Frizell 1986, 84.

[80] Dietz 1982, 61, 101-102; Santillo Frizell 1986, 15, pl. 1.

[81] Sjöberg 1996.

[82] Santillo Frizell 1986, 40, fig. 27.

[83] Crouwel 1991, 27-28, 31.

[84] Dietz 1982, 101-102; 1984, 43.

[85] For a survey of the theories concerning the destruction, see Drews 1993. Discussions concerning the reason(s) for the destruction/changes are still in progress. Deger-Jalkotzy 1977; Eder 1998, 7-23; Walløe 1999, 121-126.

earlier, this may also partly be due to our lack of knowledge concerning the earliest part of the LH IIIC period. By contrast, the final period of the Bronze Age is now well documented at Asine. A recent study by A. Penttinen reveals that LH IIIC settlement accumulation could be documented also on the Acropolis and apparently the quality of the pottery was high.[86] An exception is the Levendis sector, as, so far, quite small amounts of LH IIIC pottery have been found. As observed by Santillo Frizell, this contrasts with the finds from the Lower Town, the Karmaniola, and the tombs.[87] In a study of the later material from the Karmaniola area, Santillo Frizell has established that the LH IIIC and the Submycenaean periods are represented in the material record,[88] something observed also by Dietz and Styrenius for the eastern part of the habitation.[89] I have also in this study pointed to the fact that Submycenaean material has been found in the Lower Town.

As noted earlier, our knowledge of the settlement in the LH IIIC Early period is very meagre, and this is in contrast to the state of affairs in the following Middle and Late LH IIIC. Although other plausible explanations may have been identified, this points to a short break or discontinuity following the destruction at the end of LH IIIB2. If an earthquake caused the destruction, the break is logical, as the previous settlement, or at least parts of it, may have been destroyed.

In LH IIIC Middle and LH IIIC Late, Asine was, again, a flourishing settlement with the economic means to start an active building programme. This follows from the general pattern that can be observed in the pottery production. The Middle phase of LH IIIC shows a large variety of shapes of a good quality. Also, as has been proposed earlier, the local society was not equal (i.e. equally destitute), but was rather characterised by a measure of social differentiation, although, we may assume, not as pronounced as that in the LH IIIA period. Although several sites were apparently in decline, we may also observe that others expanded or were re-settled. It is possible that Asine was again able to take advantage of her location and resume her position as an intermediary of goods traded over long distances.

Exchange as an economic factor may have functioned on several levels in all periods. In LH IIIA and LH IIIC, it is possible that goods made of exotic materials and, we may assume, also of a high value, were exchanged. Given the location and the differences in the goods, it seems appropriate to assume that exchange was conducted on several levels or over different circuits, depending on the purpose and value of the goods exchanged. For what end the exchange took place, however, is more difficult to establish. It may have been based on supply and demand, but may also have been engaged in as a means of creating and sustaining social networks or both. For all we know, different types and levels of reciprocity could also be accommodated within the trading system that we catch the occasional glimpse of in the material.

We are on firmer ground in discussing the local economy. It may be suggested that it was basically dependent on agriculture. Hunting and fishing, on the other hand, are by general consent presumed to have been of a more marginal importance. Unfortunately, the animal bones from the Late Helladic period have, as yet, not been seen through to publication. If animal bones from earlier Bronze Age contexts, as published by K. Moberg, are anything to go by, we may assume that domesticated animals were important. In the material, pigs and cattle were found to be the most common, followed by sheep. Game, such as deer, was not very common.[90] These figures are quite nicely reflected also in the survey of animal bones from Tiryns for the LH IIIB and LH IIIC periods, for which figures for each period are available and have been analysed in some detail.[91] The fact that deer are indeed present in the material from both sites is interesting in its own right, as these animals may have had a high status, as representations of deer on LH III pottery (amongst others, from Asine) suggest. Although the extent to which it was practised cannot be established, it is also likely that the average household was to a certain extent dependent on its own resources for food and other consumption goods, that is, self-supply was important in all periods.

Material from the Submycenaean period has been discovered in the Karmaniola area and Santillo Frizell observes that there is an indisputable continuity into the Protogeometric period.[92] Also in the excavated area, East of the Acropolis, the period has been documented.[93] This may be verified also in the Lower Town, where different locations show evidence of both the Submycenaean and the Protogeometric periods. As shown in the study of the houses in the Lower Town area, possibly some constructions were partly in use in the transitional period.

We may conclude that Asine, as a settlement, was active during the entire period LH IIIA-LH IIIC. Perhaps more interesting is the clear evidence that, whatever caused the break between LH IIIB and LH

[86] Penttinen 1996, 149-167.
[87] Frizell 1978, 91.
[88] Santillo Frizell, 1986.
[89] Dietz 1980, 108; 1982, 67-69, 1984; 26; Styrenius 1975.
[90] Moberg 1986; 1996.
[91] von den Driesch & Boessneck 1990, 92-93, 119-122.
[92] Santillo Frizell 1986, 85.
[93] Dietz 1982, 67-69.

IIIC, the disruption did not cause a disaster at Asine. The LH IIIC Early period is not well represented in the material, as is also the case of other settlements. This may be due to our poor knowledge of the pottery material, but it cannot be excluded that the phase following the disaster (if any) may have been very short and marginal, leaving no deep traces in the archaeological material. Instead, we may observe that the settlement was flourishing in the Middle and Late LH IIIC periods. The continuity of habitation into the Submycenaean and Protogeometric periods needs more analysis. The documented information indicates that the following Iron Age, at least at Asine, was bridged by continuation of habitation. It may even be hypothesised that the periods preceding the Geometric were of importance in transmitting information and knowledge between the Bronze Age and the Iron Age.

Chapter 5
THE SETTLEMENTS ON THE ARGIVE PLAIN

5.1 THE EMPIRICAL EVIDENCE

The Argolid has long enjoyed the close attention of archaeologists. As a result, the area has seen a large number of excavations over the past century or so. Naturally, attention was at first focused on the more prominent sites, the foremost amongst which was Mycenae. Over time, however, activity has come to include a variegated set of settlements, ranging from palatial sites to small hamlets. This is neither to imply that nothing remains to be done, nor that also those settlements that have attracted excavation have been exhausted. On the contrary, few sites have been explored in full. While this is entirely in keeping with the recognition that future archaeologists might command better methods and might pose new and perhaps more interesting questions that would require new rounds of excavation if they were to be answered, it leaves us with a problem: the degree of coverage of the Late Helladic Argolid cannot be said to be ideal.

The immediate consequence of this situation, as was noted in the introductory chapter, is that quantitative stocktaking is not a feasible way forward. This is so because we neither know the actual extent of the settlement at the height of Mycenae's influence over the Argolid, nor the sizes and characters of all settlements in full detail. The situation is compounded by the fact that we cannot pass judgement on the extent and representativity of the known and excavated sites, compared with the total number of settlements at the time. On the contrary, there are reasons to believe that what is known is strongly biased in favour of the top level of any actual or imagined hierarchy of settlements in the Argolid. Over time, sites of conceivably less importance have, of course, come into focus, but the fact remains that by far the greater part of all the energy spent by archaeologists on the Argolid to date has been allocated to the main sites, Mycenae and Tiryns. That there are still opportunities for archaeologists can be illustrated by the fortunes of what was originally typically seen as a minor site at the margins of the Argive Plain, Midea. Recent excavations have provided evidence that this was a rather more important site than was previously thought. This is all to the good, but it should caution us not to put our faith in the proposition that everything important has already been done.

The fact that recent decades have seen in surveys a new approach to regional archaeology does not change this basic contention. Surveys have added not only new material, as such, but more importantly, have added a new type of material for us to consider. They cover all manner of minor sites and installations, including those of marginal significance and those that are important by virtue of being of considerable areal extent, such as roads. Yet we are still not in a position to claim that we know the totality of what there is to be known.

It is against this background that the present thesis calls for a more pronounced focus on the qualitative aspects of the material and the insights that have resulted from the efforts of several generations of archaeologists in the Argolid. To do so, however, requires an examination of the results to date. This chapter is addressed to this particular issue. It is organised as follows. Each site is presented below, building by building, and the relevant information on each structure is given. This includes the dating and contextual material as given in excavation reports and other documentation primarily drawn from published sources.

5.2 THE QUALITY OF THE EXCAVATION REPORTS

Over and above the extent to which excavations have been carried out and their findings disseminated in published form, any assessment of the material remains of Late Helladic society in the Argolid needs to take the quality of the excavation reports into consideration. It immediately becomes apparent that they differ in quality quite considerably. This comes as no surprise, as we are concerned with material and publications ranging from the nineteenth century to reports of very recent date. Critically, new technology and also new excavation methods have been developed and, as a result, at sites where excavations have been resumed –examples include Midea and Tiryns – our knowledge of the habitation pattern has increased. This is true not only of the mature, Late Helladic period, but significantly also of the transition to the final part of the Bronze Age.

A survey of the publications concerning the excavations at Mycenae and Tiryns shows that reports published after the Second World War describe and analyse the material in a detailed way. Dating had become increasingly refined and along with new techniques the major reason for this was the increased use of the chronological framework for Late Helladic pottery worked out by Arne Furumark.[1] The publications that followed are often very detailed as concerns both plans and other types of information. In the case of Tiryns, studies by Kilian et al. have added new information on the stratigraphy and, thanks to this new and more detailed information, our knowledge, especially concerning the final phase of the Bronze Age has been usefully augmented. Similarly, the recent excavations at Midea have contributed to our knowledge of a settlement that was of great importance not only in the LH IIIB period, but during LH IIIC. Other settlements with reported building structures show a greater variety, as concerns the extent and quality of the published material. As the purpose of the following account is to discuss possible changes affecting Late Bronze Age society and to do so in considerable chronological detail, all information concerning these aspects is of importance. They will be drawn upon as far as possible, in order to extend the analysis beyond the point reached by the frameworks identified in Chapter 1 of the present thesis.

5.3 METHODOLOGICAL AND CHRONOLOGICAL COMMENTS

It should be noted that the discussion and analysis in the following pages is based exclusively on earlier published material. Also, it is to be observed that a more detailed dating for architectural installations is not always available. In those cases in which a specific period is given, it will be recorded, otherwise a more general period reference will be given, i.e. LH IIIA, instead of LH IIIA1 or LH IIIA2. It goes without saying that the dating of different categories of constructions is at times difficult or impossible. For example, the palace at Mycenae cannot be put down to any one period, as the different phases of construction can be attributed to a range of periods rather than just one. It may well be that the architectural history of the citadel is so complex that it will never be possible to describe it in detail. Yet it is useful, and often indeed possible, to analyse individual houses and their relationships to the settlement as such.

The exercise is made more difficult by the fact that Linear B material from Argive settlements is not usually characterised by abundance. Especially in the cases of Mycenae and Tiryns, this may seem strange, as it has been widely (if perhaps implicitly) assumed that these settlements are likely to have yielded undetected archives comparable to those found at Pylos and Knossos. The reason for this state of affairs has been laid at the door of oversight or poor methodology during the early excavations. Out of ignorance or because of technical shortcomings, tablets may have been thrown away as debris. It has also been assumed that most tablets were probably not baked in the destruction, leaving few for nineteenth or twentieth century archaeologists to excavate in the first place. This irritating situation has been further compounded by the fact that the ruins have been disturbed by later rebuilding and also by destructions.

Even so, it cannot be ruled out that the original number of tablets may have been a whole magnitude smaller than at Pylos and Knossos. Excavations undertaken during the last century have for the most part been both careful and detailed. Still, the number of tablets found is small, compared with those at other sites, such as Pylos. It may therefore be relevant to raise the question whether there was in fact a large archive at any of the Argive sites or whether the few finds of tablets actually mirror the situation prevaling at the time of the destruction? Perhaps, and for reasons that escape us, there was no need to document transactions in the fashion or the quantity that was done at Pylos. Alternatively, can it safely be ruled out that the finds left behind at Mycenae and Tiryns do not simply reflect a part of the year at some remove from the season when the annual recording took place? Whatever the case, the fact remains that textual evidence from Mycenae is scanty. Just as importantly, most of the tablets found, for the most part not *in situ*, derive from LH IIIB1 contexts outside the citadel. The situation at Tiryns is, from the quantitative point of view, even worse and only a few tablets and fragments have so far been identified. The latest excavations, although more advanced methodologically than anything in the past, have not exposed any amount of new material of this particular nature. Recent excavations at Midea, on the other hand, have yielded new Linear B material.

Areas and rooms identified as workshops have been found at several sites. In the following pages, the analyses published by other scholars and excavators of sites will be used as the point of departure. This implies that, in the following summary of published material, proper areas used for storage will also be taken note of, alongside workshops. In cases in which finds of idols are emphasised in the publication, a cultic function has been assumed. A domestic function is attributed to buildings and rooms where pottery, hearths and other indications of everyday activity have been identified. The label "official" is used when a building has been identified in published archaeological accounts as connected with the administration and a central authority. These definitions are, of course, subject to discussion and should for the present purposes be regarded only as an indication of possible activity. Most probably, many buildings had a multifunctional purpose.

Each settlement will be represented by a catalogue in which the buildings are presented. This will be followed by an analysis in which the settlement remains will be discussed in more detail.

---

[1] Furumark 1972a; 1972b; 1992.

5.4 MYCENAE

Methodological and chronological comments

The citadel walls most likely belong basically to three periods. The first can be dated to the LH IIIA2 period, followed by a second extension in the middle of the LH IIIB period, c. 1250 BC, that nearly doubled the size of the citadel. Towards the end of LH IIIB2, c. 1200 BC, the last phase was added and the citadel assumed its final form. It is conceivable that the first, larger, Late Helladic structure was built at the beginning of the Late Helladic period. However, it is to be noted that the architectural evidence for a palace is very scanty. The construction of a palace-like building may have started at the beginning of LH IIIA1. When the first citadel wall was built in LH IIIA2, a remodelling and extension of the palace also took place. The second phase is signified by an intense building activity and we have the first clear evidence of a larger palace construction. Mycenae, like other sites, was damaged by an probable earthquake at the end of LH IIIB1. The third reconstruction and partial remodelling of the citadel are dated by the different excavators to the end of LH IIIB2 or the beginning of LH IIIC. The third and final remodelling was an extension of the north-eastern citadel area. The published plans of the development of the citadel of Mycenae are interesting, as they imply that the settlement did not fall into decline after the destruction at the end of LH IIIB2. Instead, the picture mirrored in the excavation reports suggests that as concerns building activity after the destruction at the end of LH IIIB2 Mycenae was probably prospering. The palace was restored, new houses were built and some buildings destroyed earlier were rebuilt and decorated.[2]

Discussion and summary

The settlement shows continuity of habitation during the entire Late Bronze Age. Although our knowledge of architectural installations in the first few periods of Late Helladic Mycenae, as shown in the table above, is limited, this does not imply that it was not inhabited during this particular phase of the Bronze Age. On the contrary, the following periods are rather well represented by architectural remains. Several houses have been assigned to the LH IIIB1 period and some of them seem to have been in use already in the LH IIIA2 period. Some buildings were damaged by a fire, perhaps caused by an earthquake, towards the end of the LH IIIB1 period. The palace complex was extended and the Lion Gate may have been constructed towards the end of LH IIIB1, beginning of LH IIIB2. It is interesting to note that the houses with the largest number of Linear B tablets found at Mycenae were not rebuilt. However, several houses continued to be in use in LH IIIB2 as well.

Also the following period, LH IIIB2, was characterised by intense building activity, including rebuilding and new constructions of both monumental and non-monumental character. At the time, the citadel area was used to an extent, both in terms of territorial coverage and in intensity of land use, not recorded for earlier periods. Habitation outside the citadel walls has been demonstrated and the building of the last tholos tombs can probably be assigned to this period.

The LH IIIB2 period ends with a catastrophe, quite possibly caused by an earthquake, affecting most buildings to some extent. It is of considerable interest to note that this second disaster was not followed by an abandonment of the settlement either. Rather the material indicates that several of the areas previously occupied were re-used and rebuilt also in the LH IIIC period, in addition to which new houses were constructed. The Submycenaean period has left fewer traces, but there is some evidence concerning walls and tombs.[3]

The destruction at the end of LH IIIB1 did not cause Mycenae to be deserted. The same pattern is repeated after the destruction in end of LH IIIB2 as some houses were destroyed and abandoned, but the majority, eleven houses in fact, were continuously in use from LH IIIB2 until, in some cases, the end of the LH IIIC period. It is therefore suggested that this break did not cause an abrupt change in the life of the settlement or in that of the inhabitants either. The infrastructure was affected, but life seems to have continued. In view of the material referred to above, it seems appropriate to suggest that the re-use of houses may be interpreted as an indication of continuity not only in habitation pattern but also in life style. The chronological division is based on changes in pottery style and we may perhaps assume that these changes need not be associated with any radical change in lifestyle of the inhabitants of these houses. We know from modern parallels that earthquakes often cause severe destruction of infrastructure, but it seems that people re-settle quite soon. Old houses are re-used, as the construction of a new dwelling is often not possible, owing to limited economic means.

The Linear B material has long been regarded as a major source of information concerning the state control of economic transactions and the production of certain goods. Thanks to the Linear B tablets found, the House of the Oil Merchant and the House of the Sphinxes were early on described as appendages to the palatial administration and not as houses for private citizens.[4] This contention, however, found an early critic in Wace and Verdelis, who pointed out that the fact that tablets were found in palaces at Knossos and Pylos did not imply that all buildings in which tablets were found must be royal. Instead, they argued, most people might have been

[2] French 1998, 4; Hope Simpson & Dickinson 1979, 29; Iakovidis 1983, 27-37, 50, 56-57, 70-72; Mylonas 1966a, 22-33; Schaar 1979, 80-95; Scoufopoulos 1971, 45-46; Wace 1921-1923, 12-13.

[3] Hägg 1974, 65-67.

[4] Ventris & Chadwick 1973, 110.

Table 5.1: Mycenae: the material

PERIODS	HOUSES	LINEAR B	STORAGE	WORKSHOPS	PURPOSES
LH I/II	House under Ramp House				Domestic
LH IIIA	Palaia Oikia				Domestic
LH II/IIIB1	Cyclopean Terrace Building		X		Domestic
LH IIIA2/IIIBl	House of Lead		X		Domestic
LH IIIA2/IIIBl	House of Wine Merchant		X		Commercial
LHIIIA2/IIIBl	Ramp House		X		Domestic
LH IIIA:2	Petsas' House		X/Unused pots		Commercial
LH IIIB1	House of the Oil Merchant	X	X/Oil	Oil/Perfume	Official/Domestic
LH IIIB1	West House.	X		X/Oil	Industrial/Official/ Domestic
LH IIIB1	House of Sphinxes	X	X	X/Ivory	Industrial/Official/ Domestic
LHIIIB1	House of Shields	X	X	X /Ivory/Stone/ Faience	Industrial/Official
LH IIIB1	Panagia House I		X		Domestic
LH IIIB1/2	Panagia House II		X		Domestic
LH IIIB1/2	Panagia House III		X	X	Industrial/ Domestic
LH IIIB1/IIIC:E/M	Citadel House Area		X	X/Jewellery/ Ivory/Lead	Industrial/Storage/ Cult
LHIIIB1/IIIC:M	South House	X	X		Official in LH IIIB
LH IIIB1/2	House with the Idols		X	X /Ivory	Cult/Industrial
LH IIIB1/C	House of Tsountas		X	X?/ Ivory	Industrial?
LH IIIB2	Megaron Room 2		X	X/ Ivory	Industrial/Cult
LH IIIB2	North store-rooms		X		Storage
LH IIIB2	Artists' Workshop			X/Ivory/Bronze/ Seals/Jewellery	Industrial
LHIIIB2/IIIC	The North-West Slope		X		Storage
LH IIIB2/IIIC:L	House of Columns	X (*not in situ*)	X		Official
LHIIIB1/2/IIIC:M	House of the Warrior Vase		X		Storage
LH IIIB2/IIIC:M	Granary		X		Storage
LH IIIB2/IIIC	House A		X		Domestic
LH IIIB2/IIIC	House B		X		Domestic
LH IIIB2/IIIC	House C		X?		Storage
LH IIIB2/IIIC	House D		X?		Storage
LH IIIA/IIIC	House M		X		Storage/Official
LH IIIC:E	House N				Storage/Official
LH IIIC	House H				
LH IIIC	Building Omega				
LH IIIC	Building Psi				

House under Ramp House: One of the earliest LH buildings, located inside the citadel. Only one room preserved.
Source: Hiesel 1989, 187.

Palaia Oikia: Located under West House. Only two rooms preserved.
Source: Hiesel 1989, 30-31.

Cyclopean Terrace Building: The area was already occupied in LHII/LH IIIA. Located outside the citadel. Residential, destroyed at the end of LH IIIB1.
Sources: French 1961, 82-83; Hiesel 1989, 186; Shear Mylonas 1968, 191-194; Wace 1921-1923, 403-407; 1953, 15-18; 1954b.

House of Lead: Located near south end of Panagia Ridge, outside the citadel. Building poorly preserved. Larger vessel of lead found as well as fragments of a metal inlay, probably silver with gold inlay. Storage room with approximately ten vases of domestic type, no large pithoi. Pottery indicates that the building was in use until the end of LH IIIB1 when it was destroyed, like Panagia House I. Earlier LH IIIA activity has been demonstrated by finds of LH IIIA pottery. According to Hiesel, the building may be compared with the House of the Oil Merchant. Probably purely domestic purpose.
Sources: Hiesel 1989, 187; Mylonas 1966a, 83; Wace 1956, 119-122.

House of the Wine Merchant: Located outside the citadel. C. 50 sealed stirrup jars, 8 tall pithoi found. Perhaps for storage for commercial purposes. Destroyed by fire, perhaps at end of LH IIIB1, like Petsas's House.
Sources; Hiesel 1989, 187-88; Mylonas 1966a, 80; Shear Mylonas 1968, 185; Wace 1953, 15-18.

Ramp House: Located inside the citadel. LH IIIA2 house, rebuilt in LH IIIB, perhaps destroyed at same time as Panagia House I. 43, 44 and 45 storage areas. Domestic purpose?
Sources: Hiesel 1989, 79-80; Iakovidis 1983, 43; Mylonas 1966a, 79; Shear Mylonas 1968, 199-205; Wace 1921-1923, 74-76, 79-84.

Petsas' House: An unusual and very large building, more than 15 rooms in the basement, Perhaps not a private building? Located outside the citadel. The basement rooms served as storage areas and contained numerous unused, LH IIIA2 pots (over 700 but only 20 shapes) and a large number of figurines. Perhaps stored for commercial purposes, a potter's store?
Sources: Crouwel 1991, 27; French 1963, 46-47; 1965, 171-184; Hiesel 1989, 153-154; Shear Mylonas 1968, 187-191.

House of the Oil Merchant: Room 1, 11 pithoi, heating installation, oval sump, one tablet with oil ideogram. Corridor, 30 stirrup jars. Room 2, large number of tablets, dealing with oil, wool, spices, and list of bakers. Room 4, many storage jars. All basement rooms for storage, including the corridor with the deposit of stirrup jars that suggests direct contacts with Western Crete, Chania. Linear B tablet with personnel list, same names that are recorded also in tablets of the West House. The content of Room 1 indicates oil storage. Perhaps also Room 4 was used for same purpose. The spices mentioned may have been used for perfume production. C. 30 tablets dealing with the wool and textile industry, recorded in Room 2, may indicate storage of wool. Multifunctional building, like the others in this group, both an official and a domestic character. Tournavitou suggests that the quantities of commodities mentioned, the extensive range of activities, and the storage facilities indicate that the building was closely connected with the central authority. On the contrary, Shear Mylonas suggested that the activities in the area were of a private nature. Destroyed in same fire as the other houses in this complex, i.e. at end of LH IIIB1.
Sources: Bennett 1958, 45; Chadwick 1963, 54-67; French 1967, 151-153; Hiesel 1989, 119-121; Mylonas 1966a, 80-81; Shear Mylonas 1968, 144-163; Tournavitou 1995, 28-41; Wace 1955, 184-185; Wace & Wace 1958, 6-9.

West House: Room 1, Linear B tablets found *in situ*, perhaps the record-keeping part of the house, a large deposit of fine-ware stirrup jars. Room 2, two craters with clay. Room 3, a huge pithos, in the corridor an unusual hearth. It is suggested by Shear Mylonas that there may have been a connection with the oil production in the House of the Oil Merchant. Room 4, perhaps the kitchen, as remains of food and various pots were discovered, but the area may also have been the part of the house where the oil was mixed and heated. Room 5, many kylikes, also Linear B finds. Tournavitou points out the unusually large deposit of fine-ware vessels that sets this house apart from other contemporary domestic buildings in the area (i.e. the Panagia Houses, the House of Lead). The Linear B tablets are personnel/ration lists and Tournavitou speculates on the connection between the tablets and the vessels in their

capacity as containers of liquid rations. Some names recur in the House of the Oil Merchant records and imply that the two archives were contemporary and also a possible connection between these two, as suggested by Shear-Mylonas. Four personnel, seven ration tablets. Seven clay seals; the words inscribed were mostly names of pots. Interesting, as the finds in the house are of domestic character. Both an official/administrative and a domestic character. Destroyed by fire at end of LH IIIB1.
Sources: Chadwick 1963, 54-67; French 1967, 157-168; Hiesel 1989, 128-129; Mylonas 1966a, 81; Shear Mylonas 1968, 131-144; Tournavitou 1995,1-28; Verdelis 1963, 13-29.

House of Sphinxes: Room 1, large number of both painted and unpainted vessels, only four closed, storage vessels, three flat disks perhaps served as stands for large vases, two large jars, carved ivories, seven clay sealings with impressions and Linear B signs. South of Room 1 a large rectangular room, according to Mylonas, similar to Rooms 90-110 at Pylos and perhaps also here served as a workshop area. Room 6, nine Linear B tablets, not *in situ* (fallen down from above), records of regular taxation in herbs and spices, possibly pottery and personnel management. Room 8 contained large quantity of pottery. A general store-room function for the basement area. Rooms 1 and 8 pottery store- rooms. Rooms 2, 4, and 6 were used for storage of other items than pottery, perhaps perishable. Ivory-working on the ground floor over Room 1. The Linear B tablets were found with a small number of storage pots and may not be associated with the contents of those. One tablet was probably a list of personnel or labourers. Two deal with rations. Six tablets in Room 6, deal with spices and one with a liquid commodity. A general store-room function for the basement, Rooms 1 and 8. Ground floor, over Room 1, was associated with the storage or perhaps working of ivory. Tournavitou suggests that the finished state of the objects indicates that the area was probably meant for preliminary storage, not workshop activity, whereas the other rooms with finds of ivory and worked, carbonised wood and used pumice, are indicative of secondary workshop activities. Further more, the large number of pots found in Room 1 were probably used for trade. The house has both an administrative, industrial and private/domestic character, like the West House and the House of the Oil Merchant. The destruction is dated by Tournavitou to the middle of the LH IIIB period.
Sources; Bennett 1958, 46; French 1967, 153-157; Hiesel 1989, 123-124; Mylonas 1966a, 81; Shear Mylonas 1968, 163-176; Tournavitou 1995, 41-67; Wace 1954a, 238-241; 1955, 185-189; 1956, 113-116; Wace & Wace 1958, 9-13.

House of Shields: Architecturally contemporary with the West House. Lacked a cooking area and a floor deposit of domestic pottery, but contained an extraordinary number of finished objects in luxury materials such as ivory, faience and stone. Enormous quantity of worked ivory and faience, but with no indication of manufacture. Finds of tools, such as bronze knives and saw, obsidian blades. One Linear B tablet indicates inter-regional trade in cloth between the building and Thebes. A non-domestic and non-religious character, but instead a secondary workshop and storage area. Destroyed at end of LH IIIB1.
Sources: Hiesel 1989, 163; Mylonas 1966a, 81; Shear Mylonas 1968, 176-179; Tournavitou 1995, 16-28, 287-289; Wace 1954a, 234-237; 1955, 180-184; 1956, 107-113; Wace & Wace 1958, 5-6.

Panagia House I: Earliest of the houses in the Panagia area. Built in LHIIIB1 and destroyed at the end of that period. No re-building. Small subsidiary areas, store-rooms, for domestic purposes.
Sources: Hiesel 1989, 121-123; Shear Mylonas 1968, 5-20; 1987.

Panagia House II: Large house with two clearly defined periods. Several rooms interpreted as storage areas owing to the door construction, but only a few, large, storage vessels found. First phase of house built in LH IIIB but after the construction of House I, rebuilt after earthquake and made smaller. Also the storage rooms underwent a change and were reduced in size.
Sources: Hiesel 1989, 149-153; Shear Mylonas 1968, 20-66; 1987.

Panagia House III: No exact construction and destruction dates, probably LH IIIB2. No well-defined, floor deposits. Smallest of the three Panagia Houses. Some rooms interpreted as storage-and workrooms.
Sources: Hiesel 1989, 77-79; Shear Mylonas 1968, 66-92; 1987.

Citadel House Area: Includes the South House, South House Annex, the House with the Idols and the Tsountas' House. The Citadel House was from the beginning also called Wace's House. This section of the site may have been outside the citadel until the middle of the LH IIIB period. The first stage of building activity is to be associated with LH IIIB1 pottery. A lead bun ingot was found. After the first destruction, the building was slightly altered. Finally destroyed at end of LH IIIB2. Building period can be associated with LH IIIC pottery. Probably several large store-rooms, and at least one seems to have been used in LH IIIC. Open area 36, Floor 2, LH IIIB2 period, on it were found complete and shattered vases, bronze implements, numerous, tiny, disc beads, steatite spindle-whorls, little strips of

ivory, horn implements, steatite mould. The area seems to have been an open space used as a workshop. Area Gamma 10 and 11, LH IIIC structures Room 7 and corridor 6. Number of LH IIIB2 rooms. Area Gamma 12, pottery from the LH IIIB1 period, also LH IIIC in this area. Area Gamma 3, Room II, masses of pottery, valuable objects such as boar's tusk, ivory strips and inlays. In Room I was found the lower canine of a hippopotamus. Two floors possibly belong to the LH IIIC period. Area Gamma 21, LH IIIC walls as well as a round hearth probably also of LH IIIC date. Rooms 22 and 21 part of South House, pottery dates to LH IIIB1. Area Gamma 22, LH IIIB constructions, LH IIIC:E walls. Room with the Fresco, a lead vessel with a faience plaque of Amenhotep III (middle of LH IIIB). Room 32, two vessels, a weight and a conulus (middle of LH IIIB). Lead vessels in destruction layer, LH IIIB1. In LH IIIB2 large quantity of lead objects. Area Gamma 23, LH IIIC walls, some pottery assigned to LH IIIC:E. Area Gamma 32, LH IIIC pottery, washed down from higher up the slope. For Linear B tablets, see below, South House. A large number of lead objects were found and also a large quantity of the metal. The date of the area extends from LH IIIB2 to LH IIIC:E/M. Pictorial pottery from LH IIIC:M has been found. The objects found in the Citadel House may have been manufactured, but more probably stored and allocated as wasters etc. have not been found. These activities after LH IIIB1.
Sources: Chadwick 1963, 54-67; Crouwel 1991, 28; French 1963, 51-52; 1981, 41-48; 1998, 3; 1999, 222-223; Hiesel 1989, 160-161, 19-20; Iakovidis 1983, 44, 48; Mossman 2000; Shear Mylonas 1968, 195, 219-225; Taylour 1963, 35-46; 1969, 91-97; 1971, 266-268; 1981,8-11; Wace 1955, 177-179.

South House: Included in the Citadel House complex. Built in the early part of LH IIIB1. Room 1, ivory fragments, one Linear B sealing, one Linear B tablet, not *in situ* (Oi 701). Seven other tablets (Oi 702-708) found in Room 4 outside house. Linear B tablets; ration list, list of blue-glass paste workers etc. The only tablets found within the citadel. Fragments of Close Style vase indicate use in LH IIIC:M. Storage vessels, melted lead. Basement rooms functioned as storerooms. No finds discovered *in situ*. Destroyed at end of LH IIIB2, re-used in LH IIIC.
Sources: Chadwick 1963, 54; Hiesel 1989, 85-87; Iakovidis 1983, 43-44; Mountjoy 1976, 77; Mylonas 1966a, 79; Shear Mylonas 1968, 212-219; Taylour 1963, 35-46; 1981, 16; Wace 1921-1923, 86-96.

House with the Idols: Built in or after LH IIIB1. The complex contained several rooms of a religious character with finds of idols, although not as many as should perhaps have been expected. Snakes, jewellery, large fresco showing a religious scene, pottery of a poor quality (in Room with the Fresco, Room with Idols, Megaron). Finds of tools and raw material, mostly ivory and moulds often partly worked. According to E. French, the light is not adequate for an indoor workshop and possibly this activity took place somewhere else and the finished objects were later returned for storage. After destruction, at end of LH IIIB2, the area was filled in and only slight re-occupation took place at a much higher level. Cultic purpose, but also workshop activity as we have finds of tools and unfinished objects, evidence of storage.
Sources: French 1981, 41-48; Iakovidis 1983, 47-48.

House of Tsountas: Built in LH IIIB1. Shear Mylonas suggests that the house originally stood outside the citadel. Basement: four rooms contained one pithoi each, store-rooms. Complete LH IIIB2 vases were found. Ivory fragments in Room II. Large number of sherds of large pots found in vestibule of the "Temple". Destroyed at end of LH IIIB1 and rebuilt in LH IIIB2. Destroyed again, at end of this period and a LH IIIC construction was added.
Sources: French 1981, 41-48; Hiesel 1989, 125-126; Iakovidis 1983, 44, 47; Mylonas 1966a, 79; Shear Mylonas 1968, 226-235; Taylour 1981, 19-20.

Megaron Room 2: Building with a large room with hearth and divided into two parts. The southern part consists of the basement, where larger quantities of ivory inlays, beads, boars' tusks and broken pottery were found. This part was obviously a workshop or store-room. May indicate a combination of cultic and profane purpose.
Sources: French 1981, 41-48; Hiesel 1989, 62; Taylour 1981, 18-19.

North store-rooms: Jars *in situ* used to contain dried fruit and cereals, two fragments of an inscribed tablet, ivory, bronze, lead, other small finds and large quantity of pottery. Destroyed by fire at end of LH IIIB2. Not restored later.
Sources: Hiesel 1989, 162-163; Iakovidis 1983, 67.

Artists' Workshop: Whole vessels date destruction of building to end of LH IIIB2. Other finds are worked ivory and ivory chips, cuttings of gold leaf, slag from bronze-smelting, a matrix, fragments of semi-precious stones, blue pigment, lumps of substance compounded of sulphur and colophon used as a solder, probably in inlay work, a few bronze tools. Probably workshops.
Sources: Iakovidis 1983, 63-64; Mylonas 1966b, 419-426.

The North-West Slope: Construction level, end of LH IIIB and beginning of LH IIIC. Row of rooms interpreted as store-rooms. One room compared with the galleries at Tiryns, but according to Wace and Rowe the chamber was not a gallery and the purpose is diffuse. Maybe for shelter, or for storage.
Sources: Iakovidis 1983, 50-53; Wace & Rowe 1954, 254-257.

House of Columns: Largest excavated house at Mycenae and a luxurious complex. A large storeroom with stirrup jars, one with an inscription, another store-room with a row of jars. Part of a Linear B tablet with reference to cloth. Iakovidis and others suggest that the house was part of the palace and therefore not the residence of an individual. The building communicates with the Artists' Workshop. Destroyed by fire at end of LH IIIB2. Partly repaired and remodelled in LH IIIC and in use throughout this period.
Sources: Bennett 1958, 45-46; Hiesel 1989, 115-119; Iakovidis 1983, 64-66; Mylonas 1966a, 78-79; 1966b, 426; Schaar 1979, 72-75; Shear Mylonas 1968, 249-262.

House of the Warrior Vase: Basement, store-rooms, whorls, bronze vessels, a jar contained carbonised olives. Pottery from LH IIIC:M the Warrior crater. The building was probably destroyed at this point. Storage.
Sources: Hiesel 1989, 126-127; Iakovidis 1983, 43; Mylonas 1966a, 79; Shear Mylonas 1968, 205-211; Wace 1921-1923, 84-85.

Granary: Probably constructed in LH IIIB2, destroyed but later used until LH IIIC:M. Carbonised barley and wheat. A large number of whole vases were found, of the Granary Style, LH IIIC:M. Storage.
Sources: Hiesel 1989, 145-147; Iakovidis 1983,42, 71; Wace 1921-1923, 40-59.

House A: Constructed like House B at end of LH IIIB2 and in use for a long period. The only preserved room, A, contained six large jars and was apparently a storage room. Domestic character.
Sources: Iakovidis 1983, 53-54, 71; Mylonas 1966a, 32-33.

House B+ North-East extension: Constructed at the end of LH IIIB2, and continued to be in use for a considerable length of time. Destroyed at the end of the period, afterwards rebuilt or repaired and continued to be in use until the end of the LH period. Two rooms contained a large quantity of pottery. Three store-rooms. Domestic character.
Sources: Hiesel 1989, 113-115; Iakovidis 1983, 49, 54-55, 71; Mylonas 1966a, 32-33.

House C: Used in LH IIIB2 and reused in LH IIIC. Narrow rooms, storage facilities?
Sources: Hiesel 1989, 159-160; Iakovidis 1983, 63, 66-67, 71; Schaar 1979, 71.

House D: The basement level preserved, one bronze tool found, probably built in LH IIIB, partly in use in LH IIIC. Storage?
Sources: Hiesel 1989, 161-162; Iakovidis 1983, 63, 66, 71; Schaar 1979, 71.

House M: The dates of the various parts of this house are uncertain. The first phase may have been constructed in LH IIIA. The construction of the main complex probably was in LH IIIB2. The galleries at Tiryns, constructed in LH IIIB2, perhaps inspired Rooms 11-13, built within the fortification wall. The corridors, the road, the terraces and store-rooms were in use also in LH IIIC. Room 3, several fragments of idols and animal figurines, necklaces, one lead vessel and fragments of several others, two fragments of faience plaque bearing the cartouche of Amenophis III (1405-1367). Room 7, one seal, an ivory figurine of woman; these finds are dated by sherds to LH IIIB2. Room 4, a raised clay area and its position in the main room is obviously similar to that in the megaron. **House M, extension:** This part of the building complex was added later. Store-rooms 15-18 lie west of House M, separated by a corridor. Access also this way indicates that the rooms belonged to the house and were not public. It is suggested by Shear Mylonas that the house may have belonged to an official.
Sources: Hiesel 1989, 52-54, 147-149; Iakovidis 1983, 51-52; Shear Mylonas 1968, 235-248; Wace 1953, 254-257.

House N: Probably LH IIIC:E. Iakovidis suggested that it was used to house the garrison.
Sources: Hiesel 1989, 162; Iakovidis 1983, 50, 71.

House II: Located close to the northern citadel wall. Poorly preserved LH IIIC construction.
Source: Hiesel 1989, 188.

House Omega: Built in an area where destroyed House of Columns was constructed.
Source: Hiesel 1989, 188.

House Psi: Built in an area where, in LH IIIB2, the destroyed House of Columns was constructed. *Source*: Hiesel 1989, 188.

able to read and also to write the tablets and the character of the houses was domestic and private. We must not jump to the conclusion that only those responsible for the official and administrative part of society had a need to keep records and means of keeping them. This could also be true of others, such as merchants, traders and the like.[5]

The proposal has recently been criticised by Palmer who argues that some of the names, commodities and etc. listed on the tablets from each house also occur on tablets from the other houses in this complex. Apparently no scribal hand appear on tablets from more than one house and according to her the houses were linked administratively and could not be individual and independent merchants' establishments. But this lack of interconnection of scribal hands point towards a looser administrative organisation. Also, the fact that some tablets reveal the same assessment and collection system as seen at Knossos and Pylos point towards palace business.[6] To adjudicate between both these two plausible, yet mutually exclusive interpretations, more material is clearly needed.

In an important and impressive work, Tournavitou has recently analysed the West House, the House of Shields, the House of the Oil Merchant and the House of Sphinxes.[7] Although she does not exclude the possibility that the owners may have been private individuals, she also arrives at the conclusion that they were probably royal dependants, employed directly or indirectly by the palace, and, as such acted on behalf of the palace. As a matter of fact, she suggests that the status of the individuals was closely related to state control.[8] In keeping with this proposition, the Linear B tablets are interpreted as the records of a centralised economic system where labour and goods were strictly controlled by the central redistributive agency. Tournavitou also interprets the larger size of this group of houses, as compared with the Panagia group, and the attendant architectural elaboration as evidence of the higher status of the building complex.[9]

The chronological and spatial setting of the tablets is also of considerable interest. The largest number was found in the four LH IIIB1 buildings destroyed at the end of the period and located outside the citadel area. As remarked earlier, also the tablets found in the Citadel House area may be of the earlier date.[10] The presence of tablets in a LH IIIB1 context indicates that the habit of recording disbursements of material and so forth was in operation already before or very close to the first destruction, which occurred at the end of the period. Tournavitou has suggested that their presence in a non-palatial area reflects economic prosperity and self-confidence and that the area inside the citadel walls may have become too small to contain all the activities of the central authority. The tablets provide some information on issues such as ration lists, lists of personnel, different products and so on.[11] The detailed study by Tournavitou of the houses and their contents shows that the tablets record locally produced products and not objects or products of exotic origin. By way of an example, the allocation and distribution of wool and oil to individuals are documented but there is no mention of the valuable ivory, stone and faience material. This is somewhat surprising, precisely because the products are valuable and if under the control of a central authority, we should perhaps expect records to have been kept. The *lacunae* may, of course, be explained with reference to the small number of tablets found at Mycenae. A similar chronological situation seem to have prevailed at Thebes, where tablets were, also, in use only in LH IIIB1, as the settlement was obviously destroyed at the end of the period and later not rebuilt.[12]

One of the tablets found in the House of the Oil Merchant, Fo 101, records allocations of oil to a woman working with textiles, other tablets from the same house list men and women who received wool. Tournavitou interprets the disbursement of wool as meaning that the House of the Oil Merchant regulated the major part of wool traffic at Mycenae.[13] C. Varas, on the other hand, has suggested that wool was probably allocated in exchange for work performed for or a service rendered to the palace.[14]

At this juncture, it may be added that it is unwarranted to simply assume total palatial control. The idea of individuals working for some kind of payment, and doing so for or on behalf of an individual entrepreneur, is no more far-fetched than to assume full centralisation or, for that matter, any combination of the two. The fact that tablets list same names, commodities etc. and also reveal an assessment/collection system similar to those at other centres need not indicate total palatial control and centralisation. It is plausible that the entrepreneur, as an individual acting on his own account, might have had a need and perhaps also the ability to keep records is not a

[5] Verdelis 1963, 28-29; Wace & Wace1958, 3-4.
[6] Palmer 1994, 177-178.
[7] Tournavitou 1995.
[8] Shelmerdine 1997, 542; Tournavitou 1995, 296-298.
[9] Tournavitou 1995, 294-296.
[10] Tournavitou 1995, 298; Varas 1994-1995, 137.
[11] Bennett 1958; Chadwick 1963; Tournavitou 1995, 257-269.
[12] Demakopoulou 1990a, 307-317.
[13] Tournavitou 1995, 290.
[14] Varas 1994-1995, 143.

new idea. As pointed out earlier, Wace proposed that the knowledge of Linear B writing was not necessarily limited to a few individuals of society. Others, including Varas who primarily deals with the question concerning dialects in the tablets, also take this position. Varas suggests that the inhabitants of the houses outside the citadel used both the standard and the substandard language. Whether the use of the dialect of the people was due to the distance from the palace or was meant to imply that these houses were in some sense more private, is not stated.[15] Yet the suggestion is interesting not least because the tablets indicate that we have certain individuals receiving textiles or oil from someone. Perhaps that someone was simply the palace, which in such a case may have contributed commodities as payment for work performed by these individuals. On the other hand, might it not also have been the case that the owners of these houses were the distributors of these goods? They may have received goods in transactions, perhaps with the palace, and used them as payment for different services. The oil and the wool so often recorded at the various palatial sites may thus have been the necessary merchandise used between economic actors on different societal levels. Also the wine, as suggested by Palmer, produced locally at Mycenae, could have been used for trade.[16] Speculation apart, this range of possibilities should warn us not to restrict ourselves to only one interpretation, no matter how plausible, unless further evidence to that end can be produced.

In the case of Mycenae, Tournavitou has suggested that tablet x508, found in the House of Shields and possibly recording cloth sent to Thebes, may be adduced as an important piece of evidence of inter-regional trade. Also, considering the size and the contents of finished objects in luxury materials in the building in which the tablet was found, it is suggested by Tournavitou that the House of Shields was connected with import and export trade. The unique character of the building and the Linear B texts could then suggest a considerable degree of control exercised by a central authority.[17] In an article, M.-L. Bech Nosch puts forward the proposition that the production and distribution of products operated at different levels and were both centralised and decentralised.[18] For example, ivory found at Mycenae and other large settlements may thus be explained as a actual, physical centralisation of production. From this proposition it does not follow, however, that such production was necessarily carried out by a central authority. It is equally plausible (or equally implausible) that a private workshop controlled production.

Consider the conditions under which the latter contention might be proved true. Raw material may have been traded and purchased by the palace and later bought by an independent workshop. The finished products may then have been sold back to the palace or acquired by others interested in these products. In such a scenario it is not to be excluded that the owners of the houses recorded, indeed wrote down, the information contained in the tablets. Indeed, the lack of mention of ivory in the tablets points towards a non-palatial control. This is, especially so, as ivory production in LH IIIB1 is documented only at Mycenae. Whether this is to be interpreted as indicative of specialisation or concentration, perhaps also monopolisation, cannot be firmly established, but the chances are that the expenses involved in procuring the raw material would favour few production locations. Similarly, if demand was limited (due to its character of a luxury) or the palace had assumed control over the use and consumption of ivory (use being the right of the ruling elite or royalty), the outcome is likely to have favoured production at just one location.

Finds of Linear B tablets assigned to the LH IIIB2 period are very few and as apparently several of these few were no found *in situ*, the date may be questioned. These tablets detail lists of rations and blue-glass workers, and include references to cloth and so forth. Blue-glass was apparently used for decorating furniture and perhaps the finds in open area 36, floor 2, may indicate that some type of furniture may have been repaired or produced in the South House. The mention of blue-glass is interesting in its own right. It was one of the products traded ower long distances. The association with a major site indicates that the palace may have used the product as an exchange item when trading with other settlements or for its own consumption. The evidence from the House of Columns is restricted to part of a single tablet mentioning cloth. The Citadel House was destroyed at the end of the LH IIIB2 and fragmentary Linear B tablets were found.

Storage areas are of particular interest by virtue of their often being associated with centralised and redistributive systems. The relevance of using storage facilities as a group of data reflecting the exchange system has been discussed by Earle and D'Altroy. They assume that useful knowledge will appear by studying the structures used and they postulate that the household economy would have required small-scale and dispersed, storage areas adjacent to the individual household. Centralised and relatively large-scale, storage facilities would be expected in connection with redistribution and this also reflects the degree of political centrality.[19] If we accept the chronological frameworks for the houses at Mycenae, we may conclude that the houses dated to the LH IIIB1 are represented with storage facilities. However, they are neither large nor located inside the citadel. Their size makes it doubtful whether we should accept them as storage areas for an economy based on centralisation and the redistribution of goods.

[15] Varas 1994-1995, 157.
[16] Palmer 1994, 184-185.
[17] Tournaviotu 1995, 261-262, 288.
[18] Bech Nosch 2000, 54-55.
[19] Earle & D'Altroy 1982, 265-290.

One exception may be Petsas' House, which had large facilities for storage. It should be noted, though, that the substantial number of pots deposited there belongs to the LH IIIA2 period; as such, it calls the further use of these facilities during the subsequent period into question. Rather more interesting is the House of the Oil Merchant, where large quantities of storage vessels and also Linear B tablets dealing with oil have been found. In this complex were also found tablets mentioning wool and the textile industry. A multifunctional use should therefore not be excluded. Also the House of Sphinxes seems to have had a mixture of functions, including activities of an administrative, industrial and household characer. With respect to these storage facilities, Shear Mylonas has proposed that specialisation in the Late Helladic period led to greater productivity and more goods. These changes should then have been reflected in larger storage facilities and specialised work areas.[20]

Finally, the suggestion by Tournavitou that the reason for building these houses outside the wall was that the area within the citadel had become too small in the LH IIIB1 period can be questioned. The citadel area seems to have been quite empty as far as constructions in the LH IIIB1 go. This is so in that the major extension took place in connection with the last building phase, at the end of LH IIIB2. At the time when the houses outside the citadel area were in use, that is, until the end of LH IIIB1, there should have been space enough for different activities, if space really was needed or required. We may further propose that the location of the houses and the small storage areas did not exclude private entrepreneurs or self-employed artisans working for the palace. For the sake of argument, it can be suggested that the palace may have traded the raw material, as they had the contacts and the means to trade in luxury materials, but did not have the technical or the artistic skill to work them. In such a case, they were dependent on the specialists. The individual nature of such activities has also been pointed out by Shear Mylonas.[21]

Other buildings located outside the citadel and probably built in LH IIIB1 and in use until the end of LH IIIB2 include the Panagia Houses. In addition to pottery, a variety of finds has been made. They include, for example, clay sealings. It has also been observed that no large storage jars were found, which may seem peculiar, as also storage facilities are mentioned. According to Shear Mylonas, the storage areas suggest that large quantities of foodstuffs were stored. Furthermore, a large number of decorated pots were found, although not of the size found, for example, in the West House. Shear Mylonas goes on to suggest that the houses are important, as their existence implies a certain degree of individual economic enterprise. Scraps of jewellery, glass-paste inlay, gold leaf and seal-stones, fragments of a bronze bowl, half of an ivory figurine, and so forth indicate a measure of affluence, although limited. Shear Mylonas concludes that the Panagia Houses, although modest, mirror the lives of these inhabitants.[22]

Houses attributed to the LH IIIB2 period are those located inside the citadel. According to the theory of a redistributive economy these should have been furnished with large storage facilities. However, no dramatic change in capacity or number of buildings with storage areas can be found as we move from LH IIIB1 to LH IIIB2. The size of the House of Columns, is significant. Probably the building communicated with the Artists' Workshop, also destroyed at the end of LH IIIB2. The storage capacity in the House of Columns is associated with stirrup jars and probably the storage areas were in use in the LH IIIB2 period. Clear evidence of storage has been found in the North store-rooms, as here the remains of fruit and the like in jars clearly indicate the storage of dried items.[23] Also the large number of pots may strengthen this picture. The Gamma and Delta houses to which Kilian assigned storage areas, may very well have been used as such, although other remains than the constructed plan apparently do not indicate storage.[24] It is possible that these buildings were part of the palace. If used for the storage of food items, these items were probably for the consumption of the inhabitants of the citadel as their capacity is not such to enable them to store products for a larger population. An interesting point about these houses is that they were most probably in use also in the following LH IIIC period. We therefore cannot exclude the possiblity that their function may, also, have been the same. Another area to be mentioned is the North-west slope. Here, excavations exposed a row of rooms that may have been used as storage areas, although no direct evidence of stored products has been found. The sequence of rooms is dated by the pottery to the end of LH IIIB2 and the beginning of LH IIIC. The constructions have been compared with the galleries at Tiryns, but, as observed, the vaulted room is not a gallery, as it does not run within the wall.[25]

Several buildings were affected by the destruction at the end of LH IIIB2 but were later re-used and rebuilt. The House of Columns was apparently in use throughout the LH IIIC period, and habitation was demonstrated also in the Citadel House Area, where LH IIIC Early pottery was found. In the same area evidence of LH IIIC Middle habitation in the South House has been secured. Other buildings with LH IIIC Middle pottery are the House of the Warrior Vase and the Granary. Also Houses A, B, Gamma, Delta, M and N were apparently built in the LH IIIB2 period, destroyed and then re-used although mostly with different layouts. Finally, there are also the remains

[20] Shear Mylonas 1987, 154.
[21] Shear Mylonas 1968, 181-182.
[22] Shear Mylonas 1987, 144-154.
[23] Iakovidis 1983, 67.
[24] Iakovidis 1983, 66-67; Kilian 1987a, 113; 1987b, 26, fig. 3b.
[25] Iakovidis 1983, 51-52; Wace & Rowe 1954, 254-257.

of three buildings designated LH IIIC, House H, Omega and Psi. During LHIIIB2, the area, known as the North-east Extension was used for storage and it is reported that it was in use also after the destruction. Not only was the citadel occupied in this period, but habitation activity has also been demonstrated outside the walls. The houses in the LIIIC Early period are therefore characterised by continued use, as many of the houses, some even built in LH IIIB1, were still in use. All these houses were equipped with storage areas and it is assumed that they were used in the LH IIIC period. It should be observed that also at this stage of the Late Bronze Age, storage facilities at Mycenae were used and, it seems, to nearly the same extent as in the previous period.

Several of the houses have areas that have been interpreted as workshops and in some cases as secondary workshops, as is the case of the House of Shields, the House of Sphinxes and perhaps also the House with the Idols. We may note that LH IIIB1 houses are represented with workshop areas located outside the citadel area. The products dominating the archaeological remains are ivory in different stages of preparation and oil and perfyme.

For the LH IIIB2 period, there are indications of workshop activities in three buildings. In the Citadel House Area, an open area may have been used as a workshop for various products. Amongst other things 181 lead objects (more than 100 kg) were discovered, sometimes in association with material from other industrial activities, such as ivory, glass-bead and possibly gold (jewellery) manufacture. However, according to Mossman, it seems that all these materials were stored and not manufactured, as there is no evidence of manufacturing activities. Not only vessels were found but also lead weights and Mossman argues that these served as standards rather than as parts of a working set.[26] According to Tournavitou, the jewellery mould found in area 36 was probably out of context.[27] Betts and Younger identified some evidence for seal production in the House of the Columns at Mycenae, dating it possibly to the early LH III. Furthermore, they proposed that seals made of semi-precious stones ceased to be made c. 1300 BC.[28] Some doubts concerning the date and also the production arise with respect to the House of the Columns, as it has been dated to the second part of the LH IIIB period and was later remodelled in LH IIIC.[29] It is questionable whether production was carried on in the building, as no evidence has been attested. It is more plausible that the production of seals was in progress, but in the area immediately to the west named the Artists' Workshop. Here, fragments of, amongst other things, semi-precious stones, such as opal, steatite, rock crystal and quartz, have been found and a floor deposit dates the destruction of the building to the end of the LH IIIB2 period. Although otherwise suggested by Betts and Younger, the fragments of production in this area make it tempting to accept seal-making after 1300 BC. It has also been suggested by Tamvaki that a workshop may have been active down to the end of LH IIIB and perhaps into LH IIIC.[30] The two houses, Megaron Room 2 and the Artists' Workshop, indicate involvement also in ivory and gold production. In the latter building, slag from bronze-smelting, a matrix, material used as solder probably in inlay work and a few bronze tools has been found. These finds may indicate metal-working in the area.

Bronze objects and a large number of ivory objects were found in chamber tombs antedating LH IIIB. Evidence of bronze production should perhaps therefore be expected. However, the archaeological data from the settlement have not produced any evidence of such production in the earlier period. Neither is evidence for bronze production during LH IIIB2 anything more than fragmentary, in that remains of a matrix and some slag have been found in the Artist' Workshop. Also lead in large quantities has been found, but it was apparently not possible to associate it with production. This observation is of considerable interest, as it would perhaps be logical to expect evidence of a large-scale production at Mycenae. This is especially so if we connect specialised work with the operation of a centralised economy. Of course, the possibility that during all periods metal working was in progress outside the citadel walls should not be excluded. It was not out of the question that the finished products stored within the walls of the citadel were produced by wandering workmen, artisans and other specialists. The élite and those inhabiting the palace area could also have had precious materials at their disposal. As pointed out by Shelmerdine, Linear B tablets have been found only within the citadel area and the production of valuable objects had moved within the premises of the citadel at Mycenae. Together with the extension of walls and other related structures, this has been interpreted as a sign of uncertainty, similar to that found at Pylos. The location of production within the palace site at Pylos has been explained as a process due to stress on the palatial economy, as the conditions changed in the later part of the 13th century.[31]

This idea of Shelmerdine's is intriguing and suggestive of what may have transpired. I would, however, like to suggest a scenario in which the economy of the Argolid may already have been under stress in the period immediately following the disaster at the end of the LH IIIB1 period. Contrary to the suggested model, it is here proposed that the empirical evidence from the LH IIIB2 should be interpreted as signs of rapidly growing prosperity. The settlement shows intensive building activity, which should be indicative of improved

[26] Mossman 2000, 96, 101-102.

[27] Tournavitou 1997, 233.

[28] Betts & Younger 1982, 115

[29] Iakovidis 1983, 65.

[30] Tamvaki 1974, 292-293.

[31] Shelmerdine 1987, 559, 565-568; Wright 1984, 29.

economic conditions and possibly of improved welfare for the inhabitants. The monumental building programme probably took place after the destruction in the middle of the LH IIIB period and needed a larger number of workers, hired by the palace. Even though, strictly speaking, this belongs to the realms of speculation, we may perhaps venture the guess that the construction of the Lion Gate, tholos tombs and so forth took place during the low seasons in the agricultural cycle when labour was available, or that any other groups of people needed for large-scale building, such as specialists, were available.

The workshops and storage facilities for produced goods located inside the citadel may indicate palatial interest. The palace could well have obtained a dominant position as concern production of certain products such as ivory and jewellery objects. It should be underlined, however, that the material at hand does not provide irrevocable proof of palatial involvement, let alone that the palatial involvement should have dominated all sectors of production and economy. The raw material imported by the palace may also have been worked by hired, skilled craftsmen perhaps wandering between different periodical markets, where demand for their skill existed. Both ivory and blue-glass, mentioned in a tablet, were of an exotic origin and therefore traded over long distances. We may assume that those who could engage in such transactions were those with the economic means to invest in hazardous trade expeditions. Or, merchants were dependent on those with the economic means to invest in the material. It could even have been a group of persons with the equal economic possibilities and interest in investing in such expeditions. Whether this implies the involvement of a central authority or individuals with the required economic means cannot be established however.

Finally, some words concerning the continuity of the site. As is shown above the houses so far excavated indicate continuity at Mycenae. I would like to suggest that the evidence points towards a situation with no sharp breaks, even though the site was struck by calamities. Although several houses located outside the citadel ceased to be in use after LH IIIB1, we find that some were in use also after the destruction, as was the case with the Panagia Houses II and III. Following the analyses presented by Shear Mylonas, they show evidence of a certain level of prosperity. Furthermore, houses in the so called Citadel House area built in the LH IIIB1 period were not abandoned but rebuilt. Evidence of production in the LH IIIB1 is limited to perfume, oil and ivory. If the archaeological record is anything to go by, most of the craft production was concentrated to the second part of the LH IIIB period. The period has left traces of metal-working, jewellery and ivory production. Large-scale storage facilities indicating a centralised, redistributive economy cannot be associated with the LH IIIB1 period and the same pattern emerges for the second part of the LH IIIB period.

The transition from the LH IIIB to the last phase of the Late Bronze Age has been much discussed. Desborough suggested in an early study that it was not possible to discuss architecture in LH IIIC, as only one site on the Mainland, Asine, had buildings constructed in this period. According to Desborough, the destruction at the end of the LH IIIB period was substantial and settlements were deserted.[32]

However, as has recently been pointed out by Birgitta Eder, the material from Mycenae shows that the site was not abandoned. If anything, the evidence indicates continuity in a majority of buildings and small houses scattered over the citadel area.[33] This picture is also confirmed by French.[34] It is also possible that a pottery workshop was located at Mycenae that specialised in the manufacture of so-called Close Style vessels.[35] For this reason, it is not to be excluded that some of the activities conducted in LH IIIB2 may have survived. The Citadel House Area was in use after LH IIIB2 and it is possible that some activities, such as inlay work and the like, continued in the LH IIIC period. In Tsountas House finds of ivory fragments indicate some kind of production during LH IIIB2, but it is not possible to say whether the activity survived the destruction. The House of Columns had an official character in the LH IIIB2 period and was probably connected with the Artists' Workshop. The latter was destroyed in the disaster, whereas the former survived and therefore, the possible connection with workshop activities may have also survived. Continuity in storage is found in several buildings – the South House, the House of Warrior Vase, the Granary, Building Gamma, Building Delta and House M – and the capacity should not have diminished very dramatically between LH IIIB2 and LH IIIC.

As concerns the transition to the Submycenaean period, the evidence of building activity is scanty.[36] The citadel area was now used for burials and according to Desborough, this in itself is evidence of occupation. The argument is that it was not very likely that people would have used the citadel for burials if their houses were at a great distance.[37]

5.5 TIRYNS

Methodological and chronological comments

As in the case of Mycenae, it is very difficult to find any precise dating for the construction of the different phases of the citadel and the phases suggested by scholars are not homogenous. Still, it seems as if the chronology of

[32] Desborough 1964, 31.
[33] Eder 1998, 36.
[34] French, 1999, 222-223.
[35] Crouwel 1991, 29.
[36] Hägg 1974, 65-66.
[37] Desborough 1973, 91-101.

Table 5.2: Tiryns: the material

PERIODS	HOUSE	LINEAR B	STORAGE	WORKSHOP	PURPOSES
LH I/II	Haus in Graben F(3)				
LH II/IIIA	Graben F(2)				
LH II	Haus D1		X		
LH IIIA1	Haus 49				Domestic
LH IIIA2	Graben F(1)				Domestic
LH IIIA2/IIIB1	Rooms 190, 209-210, 213-218			X/Old metals/ Bronze	Industrial/Domestic
LH IIIB1	Room 226	X	X		Storage
LH IIIB1/2	Haus M	X	X		Storage/Domestic
LH IIIB2	Bau I			X/Metal/Pottery	Industrial/Domestic
LH IIIB1/2	Bau II				Domestic
LH IIIB2	Bau III	X		X/Lead	Industrial
LH IIIB2	Bau IV				
LH IIIB2	Bau V				Domestic
LH IIIB2 **LH IIIC:E/M**	BauVI	X		X/Ivory/Bone/Lead/ Bronze/Iron	Industrial/Cult/ Domestic
LH IIIB2/IIIC	Bau VII				Domestic
LH IIIB2	Bau X		X		Storage/Domestic
LH IIIB2	Bau XI			X/Gold/Bronze	Industrial
LH IIIB2	Area LXI 43-LXII44:			X/Bronze/Lead	Industrial
LH IIIB2	Area LXI 35-LXII36			X/Lead	Industrial
LH IIIB2	Rooms 150-154		X		Domestic/Storage
LH IIIB2/IIIC:E	Bau XII				Domestic
LH IIIB2/IIIC:E	Room 10a			X/Cupola oven	Industrial?
LH IIIB2/IIIC:E	Room 119				Cult
LH IIIB2/IIIC:E/M	Kammer 4		X	X/Work-area?	Industrial?/Storage
LH IIIC	Rooms 78a-c				Domestic
LH IIIC	Haus O	X			Domestic
LH IIIC:E	LXI 40/11-41			X/Pottery kiln	Industrial
LH IIIC:E	Room 11				
LHIIIC:E	Rooms 74-77				Domestic
LH IIIC:E?	Room 93-96				Domestic
LH IIIC:E	Room 97				Domestic?
LH IIIC:E	Room 117				Cult
LH IIIC:E/L	Kammer 14/R 224.				Domestic
LH IIIC:E/M	Room 110				Cult
LH IIIC:M	Megaron W				Cult
LH IIIC:M	Bau VIa				Domestic/Industrial
LH IIIC:M	Rooms 88/89				Domestic
LH IIIC:M	Rooms 106/106a/124		X	X/Lead	Storage/Industrial/ Domestic
LH IIIC:M/L	Room 110a				Cult
LH IIIC:M	Room 115				Cult?
LH IIIC:M	Room 126				Domestic
LH IIIC:M	Room 127				Domestic
LH IIIC:M	Rooms 127a,b				Domestic
LH IIIC:M	Rooms 11/135				
LH IIIC:M	Room 137			X/Cupola oven	Industrial?/Domestic
LH IIIC:L	Room 104				Domestic
LH IIIC:L	LXI 36/55.56				
LH IIIC:L	Room 124				Domestic
SubMyc	LXI 35, 36				
SubMyc	LXII 36/63, 74				
SubMyc	LV III 41/37-48				

Graben F(2): Difficult to decide type of building.
Sources: Gercke & Hiesel 1971, 4-6; Hiesel 1989, 35-36.

Haus D1: A simple construction with a storage room. Beneath this construction is Haus D2, built in the later part of MH and possibly re-used in the transitional period.
Sources: Gercke, Gercke & Hiesel 1975, 18-19, 26; Hiesel 1989, 34-35.

Haus 49: A large construction consisting of nine rooms, although only six were excavated. LH IIIA1.
Sources: Hiesel 1989, 87-88; Podzuweit 1977, 125-134.

Graben F(1): A small house. LH IIIA2.
Source: Hiesel 1989, 35.

Rooms 190, 209-210, 213-218: Room 190, a fireplace, two steatite pearls, a spindle, two graters, two pieces forming the handle of a bronze knife, two animal figurines, a Psi idol. Room 209, three steatite pearls, several pieces of lead, fragment of a large bronze vessel, animal figurine, a grater, a couple of clay vessels, all evidence of daily life. Room 210, a cauldron found on the floor, a pile of ashes with a steatite button, an animal figurine, and a Tau idol. Against the east wall a 0.40 m high oven in which was found a well-preserved melt crucible and a fragment of the handle to a bronze knife. The oven was obviously used for the melting of old metals. The clay-lined hole in the floor, as in Room 221, may have been used as a mixing trough for baking. Room 214, with a hearth and sherds from storage vessels, a Psi idol, six animal figurines, a glass pearl, a lead vessel, fragments of a clay mould for a lance. In the later phase a pithos was embedded in the floor. Room 215, two bronze bars (19,450 kg) on the ashy floor without hearth, a fragment of a lead cauldron, an animal figurine, a steatite pearl, bronze slag, a bronze fragment, the slag remains of an oval melt crucible. Room 217, a steatite pearl, lead scrap, one Phi idol. Room 218, an animal figurine, a bronze staff, a steatite pearl, a seal. In Area LXII 43/82 an oven was found with lead remains, a few tools, idols, etc. The chronology of the room complex differ slightly as Rooms 213, 217-218 were in use in LH IIIA2 and the other rooms seems to have been added during the LH IIIB1 period. The last Rooms to have been in use: 190, 210, and 214-216, end of LHIIIB1. Workshop and domestic.
Sources: Kilian 1983, 305, fig, 29; 1988c, 126-139.

Room 226: Located outside Kammer 14. Finds of one Phi idol, a lamp. In the Kammer were found two lead vessels, other large vessels, two holes for, probably, pithoi. The area was probably used for storage. In the debris of Room 226 were found fragments of a Linear B tablet.
Source: Kilian 1988c, 114.

Haus M: A construction found to the east of the citadel wall. Some rooms identified as storage areas. The size of the house is not known, but it might have been quite large. Linear B tablet found under the south wall, another fragment found close by with LH IIIB pottery. No more precise dating than LH IIIB.
Sources: Gercke & Hiesel 1971, 15-17; Gercke, Gercke & Hiesel 1975, 17, 21; Hiesel 1989, 24.

Bau I: Room 8, a hearth, a grindstone and a grater. Room 9, one large mortar, one grinding stone, and two pithoi. Room 10, large quantities of ashes, several Psi figurines, finds of bronze and lead, a fibula, a small mortar and several pestles, and hard fired smelted pottery. A house used for domestic purposes but also for workshop activities as indicated by finds of tools, ashes, metal remains and fired clay. It is possible that there was a second floor used as a living area. Work area/domestic. Destroyed at end of LH IIIB2. Above was a new building, Rooms 93-96, built.
Sources: Gercke & Hiesel 1971, 48-50; Grossmann 1980, 156-160; Grossman & Schäfer 1971, 48-50; Hiesel 1989, 154-155; Kilian 1979, 400, fig. 20; 1981, 175-178; 1988c, 120.

Bau II: Rooms 221a, 222a. The small house had an oven/kiln associated with the last phase. In Room 221a were also found a grindstone, an animal idol and a pricker made of bone. According to Kilian the finds are to be associated with daily activities. Two floor levels contained LH IIIB1 pottery. Destroyed at end of LH IIIB2.
Sources: Avila, Grossman & Schäfer 1980, 1-87; Gercke & Hiesel 1971, 50-52; Hiesel 1989, 21; Kilian 1979, fig. 16, 20; 1988c, 117.

Bau III: Room 3, five lead vessels, remains of lead, two animal figurines and a nail of bronze were found. Large number of small and handmade vessels. Lead waste, waste from casting, metal strips with patterns of chisel, lead wires, a bronze drill and pricker and other finds associated with craft activity were located outside Room 3. A couple of bone pins, similar to those found at Mycenae and Midea were found and may, perhaps, have been used to inscribe

Linear B tablets. One sherd with Linear B sign found outside. Close to Bau III (north) is a possible lead-working area/workshop (LXII35/LXI36). Destroyed at end of LH IIIB2.
Sources: Gercke & Hiesel 1971, 52-54; Grossman & Schäfer 1975, 55-596: Hiesel 1989, 31-32; Kilian 1979, 397, 400, fig. 16, 20: 1983, 295-301.

Bau IV: Only a fragment of this building found. Destroyed at end of LH IIIB2.
Sources: Gercke & Hiesel 1971, 54-56, 68: Grossman & Schäfer 1975, 58. 94.

Bau V: A long narrow building consisting of three rooms. Bordered Bau VI in south. In Room 92, a hearth. Destroyed end of LH IIIB2.
Sources: Hiesel 1989, 136; Kilian 1979, 394, fig. 20; 1981, 178-180.

Bau VI: Located in the Unterburg. A building with private function but also cultic and workshop purposes. Room 122, two small storage vessels, a mortar, and two prickers, a domestic room. Room 123, a small altar with cultic horn, no other finds that could be associated with religious activity; this may have been a house altar. Room 121, domestic pottery; one seal was found. Finds of ivory and bone objects. Some ivory plates were found in the LH IIIC Early context. Room 130, finds of pottery, amongst others, an animal rhyton, a sickle, a pricker, a saw-blade, a grindstone, but no hearth; interpreted as a storage/work area. Rooms 191 and 192, remains in the form of tools, metals such as lead and bronze wasters and also iron slag and a lead weight, indicate workshop activity. Also, Linear B tablets and fragments of a different textual characters were found, personnel, wheels, probably chariot frames, mixed commodities such as figs and perhaps skin. It has been suggested that the building functioned also as a writing/archive room. Destroyed at end of LH IIIB2. Building partly in use also in the LH IIIC:E/M, as Bau VIa. Multifunctional building.
Sources: Godart, Killen & Olivier 1983, 416-426; Hiesel 1989, 136-138; Kilian 1978, 458; 1979, 385, 389, 400-404, fig.1, 20, 27; 1981, 174, 180; 1982, 396, 400-403; 1983, 279-280, 303-306, 308.

Bau VII: Only one room preserved, 120, with hearth and skeletal remains of two sheep. Classified as a living area. Destroyed at end of LH IIIB2. Apparently the construction was repaired after the destruction.
Sources: Hiesel 1989, 21; Kilian 1979, 400, fig. 20; 1981, 174-175; 1982, 399.

Bau X: A large house with several rooms. Rooms 150-154, possibly for storage. Room 150, a hearth and two complete kylikes. Room 151, perhaps shelves with pottery. Room 152, a tripod hearth in the middle of the room, another at the south-east wall, an amphora, several large jugs, etc. Room 153, a partly built-in stone chest. Room 154, a pile of ashes, plenty of pottery. Part of the building may have been used to store small quantities of goods, and the rest of the house was used for everyday purposes. Storage.
Sources: Hiesel 1989, 32; Kilian 1982, 403-411.

Bau XI: Location LXII 437LXII35. A hearth in R 78a contained worked remains of gold foil and bronze. Perhaps used for metal-working?
Source: Kilian 1988c, 111, n.14.

Area LXI 43-LXII 44: Hearth, idols. Tools and remains of metal, bronze slag, bronze and lead vessels indicate that the area was used for bronze-working, but also lead.
Source: Kilian 1983, 307-308.

Area LXI 35/LXII 36: The open area north of Bau III with a large hearth, and remains of lead working. Lead vessel, metal bars, an un-used crucible, etc. Work area.
Source: Kilian 1988c, 114-117.

Rooms 150-154:: A room complex. One storage room with pithoi.
Sources: Kilian 1981, 181.

Bau XII: In the LH IIIB2 filling, two clay models of boats were found. A room was probably added in LH IIIC:E. South of the building was an area with LH IIIC:E pottery.
Source: Kilian 1988c, 121-123.

Room 10a: A cupola oven and a fireplace located close to the room. Perhaps a work area.
Source: Kilian 1981, 164-165.

Room 119: A provisional arrangement after the LH IIIB2 destruction. Several idols. Cultic purpose. Transitional LH IIIB-LH IIIC Early.
Source: Kilian 1981, 162, 165.

Kammer 4: Probably in LH IIIB2. LH IIIC:E level; by a fireplace was found a spindle, a polishing stone, half a stone weight, an antler with saw and incision marks. LH IIIC:M level: two large containers and grater found. Area probably used for storage, perhaps also production.
Sources: Kilian 1982, 397-399; 1983, 291-293, 1988c, 111.

Room 78 a-c: A construction consisting of three rooms.
Source: Kilian 1988c, 111.

Haus O: A simple LH IIIC construction with a hearth or a possible oven. A Linear B fragment found with LH IIIC material, probably out of context. Located outside the citadel. Area H.
Sources: Gercke, Gercke & Hiesel 1975, 10-12; Hiesel 1989, 24-26.

LXI 40/11-41. A pottery kiln located close to the citadel wall, between Rooms 10a and 119. Remains of over-fired and misfired sherds, clay pits filled with ashes.
Source: Kilian 1981, 165-166, figs. 14, 18; Podzuweit 1981, 219, figs. 56-57.

Room 11: Room located partly above Bau III.
Source: Kilian 1979, 394-395, fig. 16.

Rooms 74-77: First building activity after the catastrophe. In Room 76 an oven. In the rooms were also found a grindstone and a weight made of lead for a net.
Source: Kilian 1988c, 121.

Rooms 93-93: Built above Bau I after the destruction at end of LH IIIB2.
Sources: Grossmann 1980, 162-163; Kilian 1981, 162.

Room 97. Finds indicate that the room is earlier than 88/89 and later than Bau I and V, LH IIIB2. Probably domestic function.
Sources: Hiesel 1989, 22; Kilian 1979, 383, fig. 1.

Room 117: A room with a cult bench. Finds of miniature vessels, a rhyton, and idols. Cultic purpose.
Sources: Hiesel 1989, 55-56; Kilian 1979, 389-390, figs. 10-11.

Kammer 14/Room 224: A fireplace, a clay bench for vessels. A lot of fine ware. Located in same area as Rooms 11, 135 and 78a-c. The area was in use during the entire LH IIIC period.
Sources: Kilian 1982, 397-399; 1988c, 111-114.

Room 110: Room built close to the citadel wall. Large idols found with cultic purpose. Outside the south wall and under the floor of the room were found a rhyton and miniature vessels indicating cult continuity in this area at least from LH IIIC Early. Destroyed by fire LH IIICMiddle.
Sources: Hiesel 1989, 22; Kilian 1978, 463-464.

Megaron W: Located outside the citadel wall on the east side, Area H. A very large room, with a hearth, comparable to the Megaron of the LH IIIB period. Close Style and Granary Style indicate Middle LH IIIC. Similar to megaron-type building in Midea.
Sources: Gercke & Hiesel 1971, 11-15; Gercke, Gercke & Hiesel 1975, 8-10; Hiesel 1989, 63-65.

Bau VIa: Complex of Rooms 107, 103 and 116. Room 107 built above Bau VI with fireplace and beside it a grindstone. Room 103, also with a fireplace. Room 116 no hearth, perhaps a storageroom.
Sources: Kilian 1978, 458; 1979, 385, fig. 1.

Rooms 88/89: Two narrow rooms part of same complex. Located close to the citadel wall. Two hearths. Two millstones. The pottery LH IIIC Middle.

Sources: Hiesel 1989, 197; Kilian 1979, 381, 383, fig. 1.

Rooms 106, 106a, 124: Complex of rooms built close to the citadel wall. The pottery collection was rich in forms, amongst others, three craters, a clay cork for a stirrup jar with a seal impression. A saw-blade of obsidian. Room 106, three pithoi sunk into the floor, a square oven with melted lead indicating metal-melting. A house with combined use, for living, storage and work activities. To the rooms were later added Room 124, also with a hearth and a grindstone. Workshop.
Sources: Hiesel 1989, 33; Kilian 1978, 459-460; 1979, 383-385, figs. 1, 7; 1981, 153.

Room 110a: A small house built close to the west wall of the citadel and above the earlier cult Room 110. So-called megaron room. Figurines, perhaps indicating cult continuity. Destroyed at end of LH IIIC Middle.
Sources: Hiesel 1989, 55; Kilian 1978, 460-461; Kilian 1981, 153.

Room 115: Located north of Room 110. Small finds of faience pearl, glass bead, a Psi idol and some other small clay objects. Cult? Destroyed LH IIIC Middle.
Sources: Hiesel 1989, 23; Kilian 1978, 463, 465-466, fig. 18; 1981, fig. 5.

Room 126: Room opening into the open area 2. A large crater found, as well as vessels for liquid, several hydrias, a considerable number of cups, a large number of steatite knobs, a animal figurine. Perhaps storage for vessels.
Source: Kilian 1981, 154, 157, 159.

Room 127: The largest room construction. A grater was found. Several hearths. Room destroyed by fire at end of LH IIIC Middle.
Sources: Hiesel 1989, 23-24; Kilian 1981, 154, 159; 1982, 395; 1983, 280-281.

Rooms 127a,b: In Room 127a a fireplace and a millstone. In Room 127b, a huge ashpile and fireplace. No kitchenware in these room but plenty of cups. Domestic.
Sources: Hiesel 1989, 33-34; Kilian 1981, 156; 1983, 280.

Rooms 11/135: Located south of the LH IIIC complex 78a-c.
Source: Kilian 1988c, 111.

Room 137: A cupola oven. Large number of vessels; five hydria, three craters, several skyphoi, kylikes and cups. Perhaps a work area?
Source: Kilian 1981, 156, 159.

Room 104: A room with a fireplace, Beside it a Psi-idol and a whetstone were found. This late construction indicates a break in continuity of house-building in this area. LH IIIC Late.
Source: Kilian 1978, 459.

LXI 36/55.56: A fireplace found, no architectural remains.
Source: Kilian 1983, 279.

Room 124: Built above Rooms 106/106a. A hearth, a large storage vessel and a millstone.
Sources: Kilian 1979, 385; 1981, 153.

LXI 35, 36: House remains. SubMyc.
Source: Kilian 1988c, 107:

LXII 36/63, 74: House remains. SubMyc.
Source: Kilian 1988c, 107.

LVIII 41/37-48: Remains of an abside building. SubMyc.
Source: Kilian 1988c, 107-108.

the citadel can be divided into three major phases.[38] The first defence walls were probably built towards the end of the first quarter of the 14th century, LH IIIA1, followed by a second citadel in LH IIIB1. Probably during the second period, the area was almost doubled, with an increased number of rooms, strengthening of the fortifications and so on. Traces of fire and destruction perhaps caused by an earthquake at the end of the LH IIIB1 period have also been reported here. Probably from the middle and during the second half of the 13th century the settlement experienced a third and final building phase when the *Unterburg* and also the southern part with the galleries were built. It seems that the settlement was struck by a major catastrophe, probably an earthquake, towards the end of LH IIIB2, c. 1220-1200.[39]

These events seem to have accelerated in the end of LH IIIB2. Kilian identified destruction at the end of LH IIIB2 caused by an earthquake and later Zangger also has suggested that the earthquake may have coincided with a flash-flood, dated by him to the end of LH IIIB2 or Early LH IIIC. The flood may have been a single event causing destruction, as the areas north and east of Tiryns were buried under several meters of mud. The consequences must have been serious and, as a result a dam and a canal were constructed and the course of the stream was redirected. However, it has recently been raised doubts concerning one singe catastrophy. Instead it has been suggested that the area was affected by periodic flooding events between LH IIIB1 and the beginning of LH IIIC.[40] by periodic The destruction was followed by re-occupation and the settlement was even extended, as the area between the citadel and the coastline was inhabited.[41] It is possible that both LH IIIC Early and LH IIIC Middle ended with fresh earthquakes.[42] The area was gradually deserted during the LH IIIC Late period. After the LH IIIB2 destruction, the Unterburg seems to have continued to be in use. The Oberburg nearly ceased to be in use and only a very small megaron replaced the LH IIIB2 structure. Apparently an earthquake caused destruction also at the end of the LH IIIC period.[43] Remains of Submycenaean habitation are few but tombs identified as belonging to this period show that the area was still used.[44]

Discussion and summary

The architectural remains representing the initial phases of the Late Helladic period are few. As shown above, only a couple of building remains are dated to LH I/II and also the LH IIIA period is presented by few constructions.[45] Under the LH IIIB floor of Bau III, LH IIIA pottery was found. Here was also found a figurine of faience with a cartouche of Ahmenophis II. According to Kilian the material is not Egyptian faience, but Syrian.[46] The LH IIIB1 period is equally represented by few constructions, although the LH IIIB pottery found in the deposits surrounding the citadel indicates that these areas may have been inhabited then.[47] Among these houses, two have areas identified as being for storage, whereas remains of production have not been observed. Linear B fragments were found under a wall of House M and they were not *in situ*. The date of the construction has not been established, but it is somewhere in LH IIIB. A recognisable change has been observed in the LH IIIB2 period, as at least nine buildings have been identified. Storage facilities have been recognised only in Bau X, whereas workshop activity has been recorded in several locations, with remains of metal production in the majority. The period is represented with Linear B material only in one building, Bau VI.

The LH IIIC settlement was extensive, as excavations have shown that not only the Unterburg was inhabited, but also areas outside the citadel. Kilian identified the Early and Middle LH IIIC periods also north of the citadel.[48] The southern part, the so-called Lower Town, has also been identified as part of the LH IIIC settlement and the citadel was surrounded by LH IIIC occupation.[49]

As has been shown in the table the Submycenaean period has been identified also at Tiryns, as remains of building activity have been documented and also the pottery representation seems to be promising.

The Linear B material found in Tiryns is fragmentary and more detailed information concerning its purpose is not available. Obviously one fragment of a sherd with Linear B inscriptions was found outside the citadel area.[50] Another sherd with Linear B signs was discovered close to Bau III in an LH IIIB2 context.[51] In this case, the situation is similar to Mycenae and the reason for the lack of tablets may be the same. The chronological situation is confusing as the available material has been found in mixed contexts and probably most of the fragments were not found *in situ*. The few finds and their locations make it difficult to even try to speculate on their function in the economic system. Some interesting observations may, however, be made. For example, we have the fragment TI X 6, in which the term *tu-ru-pte-ri-ja* is mentioned. This is interpreted as alum, a mordant used as a dye-fixer in

[38] Hope Simpson & Dickinson 1979, 41-42; Iakovidis 1983, 3-13; Jantzen 1975, 53-57; Slenczka 1974, 157; Voigtländer 1973, 242-244, 264-266.
[39] Kilian 1979, 404; 1981, 192; Slenczka 1974, 159.
[40] Maran 2002-2003, 223.
[41] Balcer 1974; Zangger 1994, 207-211.
[42] Kilian 1978, 466; 1981, 159.
[43] Zangger 1994, 207-210.
[44] Hägg 1974, 79-82, fig. 12.

[45] Kilian 1988c, 142, evidence of LH IIIA2.
[46] Kilian 1979, 405.
[47] Zangger 1994, 198-199.
[48] Kilian 1978, 449-453, 468, fig. 26.
[49] Gercke & Hiesel 1971, 1-19; Gercke, Gercke & Hiesel 1975, 7-36.
[50] Godart & Olivier 1975, 38.
[51] Grossman & Schäfer 1975, 64, no. 13, fig.3.

cloth production. The term is also found on two tablets from Pylos and one from Knossos, and alum was most likely an imported product.[52] Otherwise, the few tablets seem to cover a wide range of subjects, such as land-tenure, oxen, personnel, wheels etc.[53] However, it is not possible to use the material as a means of identifying specialisation, carried on under the auspices of the palace.

We may also note that not all tablets or fragments were found within the citadel area. For example, Haus M is located outside the citadel wall, as well as Haus O. The tablets and the fragments all probably represent the latter part of the LH IIIB2 period, although the fragments located in House O were found in an LH IIIC:E context.

Specialised workshop activity in the LH IIIB1 period has been recorded in the area of Rooms 190, 209-210 and 213-218. The room complex, 190 and 209-217, is interesting as here an oven with a well-preserved melt crucible was found. Furthermore, finds of two bronze bars, bronze slag and slag remains from an oval metal crucible were made. Excavations have located several areas of workshop activity in the LH IIIB2 period. The Area LXI35/LXII36 north of Bau III was apparently used for lead-working and the same activity seems to have taken place in Bau III. Room 10 in Bau I also had indications of metal-working. Mixed metal-working was probably the craft activity that took place in Bau V, but here there were also indications of ivory-working. Further evidence of metal-working has been detected in location LXI43/LXII44, where remains of metal, bronze slag, bronze and lead vessels indicated metal-working. Finally, Bau XI had indications of working in gold and bronze. The LH IIIC period is rather well represented, as regards workshop activity. There are traces of a work area in Room 10a which may be dated to LH IIIB2/LH IIIC Early and also in Kammer 4, LH IIIB2/LH IIIC Middle. Probable lead-working in LH IIIC Middle is evidenced by the finds in Rooms 106/106a/124, and Room 137 was perhaps a work area during the same period. A question mark is Bau VI were metal-working ws recorded in LH IIIB2. The bulding was partly in use in LH IIIC Middle as Bau VIa and it is posible that the tradition of metal-production continued. To conclude it may observed that the level of metal-working at Tiryns is notable, as installations for production have been found, although the quantities of a metal such as lead are not as large as at Mycenae.[54]

A pottery kiln was reported by H. Dragendorff and another possible kiln has been found close to the citadel wall.[55] Dragendorff reported that the kiln contained mostly unpainted kylikes, bowls and cups, but also a few larger vessels, all Late Helladic. The kiln found has not been dated but according to the excavator, it was located close to the wall that was built between the upper and the lower part of the citadel. If we follow the building phases for Tiryns, an LH IIIB2 date may perhaps be suggested, as the thick wall was constructed c. 1250. The later kiln contained only a small amount of kitchenware, whereas fine ware, such as craters, skyphoi, kylikes, cups etc., predominated. This kiln is probably of a later date, LH IIIC Early.[56]

Storage areas have been identified. But they are not large and it is difficult to imagine that they were intended for storage on a grand scale. Kilian in an article designated several rooms as to have been used for storage and, according to him most of them were located in the southern and eastern parts of the citadel.[57] The evidence for actual use, i.e. food remains, vessels etc, is, however, scanty in the so-called galleries. This part of the citadel was constructed as the third and final part at the end of LH IIIB2 and we may perhaps assume that, if the areas designated as storage facilities really were used for this purpose their period of use must have been very short as regarded the so-called palace period. Furthermore, it is difficult to imagine a situation with the redistribution of products on a large scale to a large number of people living outside the citadel walls, as the storage capacity was probably not sufficient. If, indeed, these were used as storage areas, it may perhaps be suggested that the products were intended for use among the members of the palace.

Settlement remains indicate continuity from LH II onwards. The LH IIIA period is not well represented, as regards architectural remains. An interesting feature is the few buildings representing the LH IIIB1 period, as it could perhaps be expected that, if Tiryns was part of the centralised palace economy, this should have been reflected in an extended settlement already in the first phase of the LH IIIB period. Tiryns as a settlement seems to have flourished in the LH IIIB2 period and the citadel area was extended to the north. The third building period apparently started in the middle of the 13th century and reached its final form during the LH IIIB2 phase. The building activity reached its peak in this period and was on the same level as at Mycenae. The number of buildings in use was larger than in the previous period, and an interesting fact is, the many areas identified as workshops. It seems as if there was a specialisation in metal-working in this period. We have evidence of, especially, lead-working, but also gold and bronze

[52] Godart, Killen & Olivier 1979, 451-452, 454, 456; Landenius Enegren 2000, 32; Palaima 1991, 279; Palmer 1994, 92-93.

[53] Gercke, Gercke & Hiesel 1975, 21; Godart & Olivier 1975, 37-53; Godart, Killen & Olivier 1983, 413; Naumann, Godart & Olivier 1977, 101, 229-234.

[54] Mossman 1998, 275. Tiryns c. 37 kg and Mycenae c. 98 kg; 2000, 100-101.

[55] Dragendorff 1913, 338-341, figs. 3-4; 1914, 133-135, fig. 1.

[56] Kilian 1981, 165-166; 1982, 412.

[57] Iakovidis1983, 7; Janzen 1975, 22, notes that the function of the galleries was not clear and they may, perhaps, been used for protection; Kilian 1987b, 25, 27-28, fig. 5.

manufactures. Remains of iron slag were found in Bau VI, which was in use in LH IIIB2 and also LH IIIC Early and Middle, as Bau VIa. Possibly the iron could be assigned to the LH IIIC Early/Middle period. The clear indication of metal production contrasts with Mycenae where manufacture, according to the evidence, most probably did not take place within the citadel.

Tiryns was also destroyed at the end of the LH IIIB2 period, but here, as at Mycenae, we may conclude that not all the buildings were abandoned. On the contrary, in the initial part of LH IIIC, there was a a redesign of the settlement with extension of the number of buildings in use.[58] We find a quite large and, as it seems, well-organised settlement indicating continuity. The first sign of change is seen in the individual building, Room 104, built towards the end of the LH IIIC period.[59] As concerns workshop activity, pottery and metal-working has been recorded. Most buildings and rooms seem to have been of an everyday character. Several rooms with finds of idols etc, indicate a cultic function. [60] There is a parallel found at Asine, where cult activity has been traced in House G. Finally, we also have remains of buildings assigned to the Submycenaean period and the pottery evidence also indicates habitation in this period.[61]

5.6 MIDEA

Methodological and chronological comments[62]

The first sounding at Midea was made at the beginning of the twentieth century followed some decades later by excavations conducted by A.W. Persson and subsequently by N.M Verdelis and P. Åström.[63] The excavations were resumed in 1983. The settlement and its surroundings were inhabited for a considerable time. The latest excavation campaigns have indeed been rewarding and the stratigraphical picture that has emerged is of considerable interest. A significant number of Final Neolithic sherds have been found, as have a few EH sherds. The finds indicate that the acropolis was occupied long before the Late Bronze Age. Also the MH period is represented by finds of sherds and also tombs.[64] The most recent rounds of excavation, begun in the 1990s, have extended our knowledge and revealed a large number of sherds dated to the LH II A/B and LH IIIA1 periods. Pottery from the LH IIIA2 and LH IIIB1 periods have been found as well. Although architectural remains are few, the pottery found is a clear indication of settlement activity earlier than LH IIIB. The excavations have shown that beneath the LH IIIB megaron was an earlier, LH II building. The latest reports concerning the date of the architectural features in both the West Gate area and on the Lower Terrace indicate that, in the LH IIIB period and especially the LH IIIB2 phase, Midea was an important site.[65] The recent excavations in the area of the West Gate indicate that the fortifications were built in the middle of LH IIIB, contemporary with other extensive building programmes on the Argive plain. The West Gate Area seems to have been in use only in the LH IIIB2 period as no traces of rebuilding was found. It should be noted, however, that LH IIIC pottery material has been found sporadically in the area.[66]

Mycenae and Tiryns appear to have been affected by some kind of destruction c. 1250, possibly an earthquake, and probably this event also had an impact on Midea. Somewhat later, towards the end of the LH IIIB2 period, Midea was, like Mycenae and Tiryns, severely damaged by an earthquake.[67] Until recently, it has been assumed that there was no habitation after the LH IIIB2 destruction. But, as is shown by the recent excavations, the material evidence shows very clearly that the settlement was in use again in the LH IIIC period; in turn this suggests cultural continuity.[68] Ceramic finds from the Lower Terrace indicate that the area was not inhabited in the earliest part of the LH IIIC:E. Instead, the area seem to have been occupied in the later part of LH IIIC Early, during LH IIIC Middle and LH IIIC Late. Apparently another disaster struck in LH IIIC Middle, destroying much of the settlement. The site was not abandoned however as evidence of pottery material of the LH IIIC Late periods has been found.[69] The Submycenaean period is not represent in the material found so far.[70]

Discussion and summary

The excavations at Midea have revealed continuity in habitation and the material remains clearly provide evidence not only of the importance of the site in the LH IIIB period but also of its obviously extensive use in the LH IIIC period. Of particular interest is the fine representation of the LH IIIB2 period in the abundance of pottery material found. This is of some consequence as, so far, only a few groups of LH IIIB2 pottery have been identified in funerary or domestic contexts in the Argolid

[58] Kilian 1988c, 150.
[59] Eder 1998, 39; Kilian 1978, 466.
[60] Kilian 1979, 388.
[61] Papadimitrou 1988, 227-243.
[62] I am most grateful to Professor Gisela Walberg for extensive comments and advice concerning her part in the Midea excavations.
[63] Åström 1968, 54; Persson 1942, 3-16.
[64] Åström, Demakopoulou, Divari-Valakou, Fischer & Walberg 1990, 16; Demakopoulou 2001, 180; Demakopoulou, Divari-Valakou, Åström & Walberg 1997-1998, 82-83; Hägg 1962, 88-89; Hope Simpson & Dickinson 1979, 40.
[65] Demakopoulou 1995; 2001; Demakopolou & Divari-Valakou 1999, 209-212; Demakopoulou, Divari-Valakou, Åström & Walberg 1997-1998, 8; Walberg 1998a; 1998c, 175-176; Walberg & Giering 1998, 85-86.
[66] Demakopoulou 1995, 152, 157.
[67] Åström, Demakopoulou, Divari-Valakou & Fischer 1992, 14; Demakopoulou 1995, 154,157, 161; Walberg 1999, 157-158.
[68] Åström & Demakopoulou 1986, 25; Demakopoulou 1995, 157; Demakopoulou & Divari-Valakou 1999, 211; Walberg 1998c, 177-178; 1999, 159.
[69] Walberg 1999, 159-160.
[70] Personal communication from Professor Gisela Walberg.

Table 5.3: Midea: the material

PERIODS	HOUSES	LINEAR B	STORAGE	WORKSHOP	PURPOSES
LH I/II/IIIB	Room XIII, tr. Mx and Mw				
LH II/IIIC	Room XIV, Mt, Mv				
LH IIIA2	Terrace 10, Trench Nb, Str 3				
LH IIIB2/ LH IIIC:E	West Gate Area, general	X	X	X	Administrative/Industrial/ Defensive/Storage
LH IIIB2	West Gate: Room I		X	X	Storage/Industrial
LH IIIB2	West Gate: Room II			X	Storage/Industrial/Cult
LH IIIB2	West Gate: Room III			X	Domestic/Industrial
LH IIIB2	West Gate: Room IV			X	Domestic/Industrial
LH IIIB2 LH IIIC:E	West Gate: Rooms VIa/b	X	X	X/Jewellery/Seal/ Glass/Textile	Storage/Industrial
LH IIIB2 LH IIIC:E	West Gate: Room VII				
LH IIIB2	North-Eastern Citadel, Room 1		X		Storage
LH IIIB2	North-Eastern Citadel Room 6				
LH IIIB2	North-Eastern Citadel, Room 7		X		Storage
LH IIIB2	North-Eastern Citadel, Room 8				
LH IIIB2/C	Terrace 9, Room II		X	X	Domestic/Industrial /Cult/ Administrative/Storage
LH IIIB2/C	Terrace 9, Room VIII		X		Domestic/Cult/Storage
LH IIIB2/C	Terrace 9, Room IX		X		Domestic/Storage
LH IIIB2/C	Terrace 10, Trench Na/Nb	X	X	X/Lead/Bronze	Storage/Administrative/ Domestic/Industrial
LH IIIB2 LH IIIC:M	Terrace 10, Room IV, corridor				
LH IIIB1:2 LH IIIC	Terrace 10, Room V Megaron				Administrative/ Cult
LH IIIB2	Terrace 10, Room VI.		X	X	Domestic/Industrial Administrative
LH IIIB2/C	Terrace 10, Room VII	X	X		Administrative/ Domestic
LH IIIB2/C	Room XI				Domestic
LH IIIB2	Room XVIII			X	Industrial?
LH IIIB2	Room XX				Cult

Room XIII: Pottery indicates that the area seems to have been in use in LH I-II and the building may have preceded the LH IIIB megaron. The area seems to have been, at least partly in use in LH IIIB.
Source: Demakopoulou, Divari-Valakou, Åström & Walberg 1996; 1997-1998.

Room XIV: Str. 3, LH IIIC, finds included a bronze awl, a whorl, part of an animal figurine, fragments of bone, pottery and plaster, representing destruction debris. Str. 5 finds included a lead clamp. Str. 6, MH III-LHI/II, remains of a construction. Str. 4-5, probably LH IIIB.
Source: Demakopoulou, Divari-Valakou, Åström & Walberg 1997-1998, 78-79, 89-90 .

West Gate Area: In the area, a large amount of LH IIIB2 pottery dated the destruction to this period. The area was not rebuilt, but LH IIIC:E sherds have been found. Finds included a large number of storage vessels, such as pithoi and large jars, and household vessels, such as tripod cooking pots and cooking grills. A large fragment of a pictorial krater has perhaps parallels at Mycenae and Tiryns, attributed to the same workshop. Remains of products stored have been found: carbonised figs, olives, grape pips and grain. In the excavated gate area were found many lead objects, such as large vessels (crushed and shapeless), minor objects, such as clay figurines, bronze arrowheads and tools made of bronze and stone. The presence of various finds and also the large number of storage vessels and the quantity of household pottery have been interpreted as indications that it not only served a defensive purpose but was also as place of permanent residence. Also rooms were excavated close to the citadel wall. These rooms are interpreted as possible storage rooms and workshops, owing to the finds of many pithoi, other storage vessels, stones, many bones, bronze and stone tools. Also a large number of spindle-whorls and loom-weights, together with a spider motif on a nodule, interpreted as an indication of textile production. A steatite jewellery mould, beads of amethyst, carnelian steatite, bone objects, etc. may indicate jewellery production. Also, several inscriptions in Linear B as well as seven seal-stones were found, indicating an administrative function for the area. Most of the pottery found is of LH IIIB2 date. In this a large number of pottery representing earlier periods has been found, The finds indicate that especially the MH and the Early Mycenaean settlements were quite substantial. Apparently the West Gate Area was not rebuilt after the destruction as no architectural features have been recognised.
Sources: Åström & Demakopoulou 1986, 20-25; Åström, Demakopoulou, Divari-Valakou, Fischer & Walberg 1990, 13-14; Åström, Demakopoulou, Divari-Valakou & Fischer 1992, 13; Demakopoulou 1995, 155-157; Demakopoulou, Divari-Valakou & Walberg 1994, 31; Demakopoulou & Divari-Valakou 1994-1995, 324-325.

West Gate: Room I, only the floor level preserved, no walls, a few clay vessels, stone tools including a large millstone, and two pestles. Many fragments of pithoi and cooking pots, large fragment of a storage stirrup jar. Storage, workroom.
Source: Åström, Demakopoulou, Divari-Valakou & Fischer 1992, 14.

West Gate: Room II only a floor found. In the middle of the room was a large unworked stone. It had perhaps a ritual function. Most finds found around the stone. Few vessels, stone tools, a large millstone, two pestles. Many fragments of pithoi and cooking pots. Large fragment of storage stirrup jar.
Source: Demakopoulou, Divari-Valakou & Walberg 1994, 20.

West Gate: Room III, the floor deposit contained mostly LH IIIB2 pottery and other finds such as figurines, millstones, stone tools and metal objects. Large quantities of sherds, especially pithoi other storage vessels, cooking vessels and unpainted domestic pottery. May indicate domestic/workshop activity.
Sources: Demakopoulou, Divari-Valakou & Walberg 1994, 20; Demakopoulou, Divari-Valakou, Åström & Walberg 1997-1998, 57-58.

West Gate: Room IV, the floor deposit contained mostly LH IIIB2 pottery, also here finds of stone tools and metal objects, as well as two large millstones. Large quantities of sherds, especially pithoi other storage vessels, cooking vessels and unpainted domestic pottery. May indicate domestic/workshop activity.
Sources: Demakopoulou, Divari-Valakou & Walberg 1994, 20; Demakopoulou, Divari-Valakou, Åström & Walberg 1997-1998, 57-58.

West Gate: Rooms VIa/b, in both rooms a large quantity of LH IIIB2 painted pottery was found, as well as a large number of unpainted domestic pots. The pottery also included types usually dated to LH IIIC:E. The large amount of coarse ware included household vessels. Stone mortars, pestles, pounders and whetstones. The large lead vessels served for storage. Large storage vessels *in situ*. Numerous small objects of stone and bronze, amongst other things two complete chisel and bone tools, many steatite spindle-whorls, a bronze mirror, beads of glass and semi-precious stones, obsidian and flint were found in great numbers. A steatite mould for glass production. Pieces of glass have been found on the settlement indicating that they were mould-made. Two seals, one of agate, depicting a wild goat and the other of steatite with linear motifs. Many, fragmentary, human and animal figurines. Also finds of the remains of food, such as olive pips, many figs, bones of small animals and seashells. In Room VIb were found storage stirrup jars similar to those found at Mycenae. One vessel bears the Linear B inscription *wi-na-jo* and a similar inscription

was found on a jar found in Knossos, another in Armenoi. It seems that the jars came from the same workshop on Crete. A clay nodule with a Linear B inscription with the impression of a spider, and the GRA ideogram (wheat). According to the excavators, the two rooms may have served as storage and workshop rooms for textile and jewellery or glass production.
Sources: Demakopoulou, Divari-Valakou 1994-1995, 324; Demakopoulou, Divari-Valakou, Åström & Walberg 1997-1998, 57-68.

West Gate: Room VII, large amount of LH IIIB2 painted pottery, as well as plain domestic. Also here were found types associated with LH IIIC:E. Here was found a pithos base with incised potter's marks. A large number of household vessels, coarse ware, pithoi *in situ*, other storage vessels, such as large stirrup jars. Stone tools such as a millstone, pounders and pestles, a stone mortar, clay loom-weights, steatite spindle whorls, figurines, two lead weights. Probably used as a storeroom.
Source: Demakopoulou, Divari-Valakou, Åström & Walberg 1997-1998, 68-72.

North-Eastern Citadel: Room 1, an ash layer, carbonised remains of figs, horsebeans, olive stones, grain. Storage.
Sources: Åström & Demakopoulou 1986, 19; Demakopoulou, Divari-Valakou, Åström & Walberg 1997-1998, 73-74.

North-Eastern Citadel: Room 6, several pieces of lead, terracotta figurines, bronze objects, steatite buttons or whorls, bone pins, a stirrup jar and a stone quern. Latest pottery from LH IIIB2.
Sources: Åström, Demakopoulou, Divari-Valakou, Fischer & Walberg 1990, 9; Åström, Demakopoulou, Divari-Valakou & Fischer 1992, 11.

North-Eastern Citadel: Room 7, several lead vessels; a large area of yellow ochre was found on the floor, probably from a large broken pithos. Storage.
Sources: Åström & Demakopoulou 1986, 19; Demakopoulou, Divari-Valakou, Åström & Walberg 1997-1998, 73.

North-Eastern Citadel: Room 8, traces of yellow ochre were found. Several lead vases and also fragments of lead. Objects of stone: polishers, grinders, a whetstone, steatite buttons, obsidian blades, and a hematite seal. Bronze objects, two terracotta figurines, and faience beads. No clear indication of purpose and use of room.
Source: Demakopoulou, Divari-Valakou, Åström & Walberg 1997-1998, 73-74.

Terrace 9: Room II, under LH IIIB destruction debris, the LH IIIC floor and fill were found. No pottery later than this period. Two groups of finds: 1) Luxury items, amongst other things, decorated pottery, glass-paste jewellery, beads, figurines and ivory. 2) Domestic items, such as coarse ware, pithoi, chipped and ground stone tools, carbonised food and lead vessels suggest cooking, storage and processing activities. The four bone objects may be styluses and indicate recording activity. It is suggested that the lead vessels and the luxury items indicate cult activity in the room. However, it is not out of the question that the assemblage fell from a second floor and the domestic items may have been in the lower room, indicating a domestic and/or workshop function. LH IIIC material was found above the destruction level, but no architectural features were recognised.
Sources: Mossman 1998, 270; Tzonou 1998, 87-88; Walberg 1998c, 177; Walberg & Giering 1998, 80-82.

Terrace 9: Room VIII, an unsealed LH IIIB2 floor. Finds of a pictorial stirrup jar and a large bovine figurine in the LH IIIB level may together with the lead vessels and other finds in Room II indicate a cultic function for Terrace 9, although not exclusively, as the ground floor may also have functioned as a storage area, (a stopper was found). Room VIII was used also in LH IIIC, although the level was disturbed by Roman finds. Finds of plain and coarse ware, indicating food-preparation activity.
Sources: Tzonou 1998, 88; Walberg & Giering 1998, 82-83.

Terrace 9: Room IX, north of room VIII. Two LH IIIB floors. Also LH IIIC pottery. Coarse and plain ware predominated in the ceramic assemblage, indicating food-processing and storage. Also the LH IIIC assemblage consisted of coarse and plain ware.
Sources: Tzonou 1998, 89; Walberg & Giering 1998, 83.

Terrace 10: Trench Na/Nb. Tr. Na, str. 5, obsidian arrowhead, faience spindle whorl, and some LH IIIB2 pottery. Str. 6, a large amount of LH IIIB2 pottery. Some figurines, two shapeless pieces of lead, one lead spoon, two stone weights, two spindle-whorls, quern; Nb, Str. 3. Large amount of coarse ware; baking pan and charcoal may indicate an outdoor cooking or food-preparation area. Finds of LH IIIA2, LH IIIB and LH IIIC pottery. Probably an LH IIIC

stratum. Str. 4. LH IIIB coarse ware predominated also finds of lead slag in the southern part. LH IIIB pottery predominated in the northern part, many small finds, such as bronze pin fragments, a limestone disk, obsidian arrowhead and a loomweight. The area was levelled in LH IIIC, as indicated by the pottery. Str. 5. Mostly LH IIIB pottery but also LH IIIC ware. Two, coarse-ware, tripod, cooking-pots, fragment of baking-pan. Fragment of bronze sheet, maybe part of a bronze armour. A domestic stirrup jar (FS 164) with the Linear B syllabogram *ka* was found. It may indicate storage and/or administrative activity in the area (see also rooms VI and VII). Str. 6. LH IIIB fill and floor. Could the lead slag, and the bronze sheet and the part of an armour indicate production nearby?
Sources: Walberg 1992b, 38; 1998b, 35-38, 43-46.

Terrace 10: Room IV, a corridor, a connection between the Megaron and other areas. Used in both LH IIIB and LH IIIC Middle.
Sources: Tzonou 1998, 90-91; Walberg 1998b, 47-49; Walberg & Giering 1998, 84.

Terrace 10: Room V Megaron, main room. South and parallel to room IV. The construction of the area was of a palatial character, (public, administrative and/or bureaucratic functions). Supported by the finds of Linear B nodules and the inscribed stirrup jar in the area.
A building dating from the LH II period preceded the Megaron and the latest excavations have also shown that the acropolis was already inhabited in the MH period. The building was first constructed in LH IIIB1, followed by rebuilding indicated by new floors, enlargement of the main room, a large platform and a hearth. Also this building was damaged towards the end of LH IIIB, later followed by substantial repairs and levelling. The LH IIIC plan and the interior of the building have a parallel in Megaron W at Tiryns. The final destruction of the building took place in LH IIIC. At least three floors were defined: 1) LH IIIC. 2) Destruction debris LH IIIB2. 3) Another LH IIIB2 floor. Finds of pommels. The platform is interpreted as probably an indication of a ritual function. Apparently no indication of storage was found. Food preparation in LH IIIB/C is suggested by the finds of a number of querns and pounders.
Sources: Tzonou 1998, 89-90; Walberg 1998b, 50; Walberg & Giering 1998, 85-86.

Terrace 10: Room VI, on the LH IIIB floor, a millstone was found, suggesting domestic or specialised work activity. The Linear B syllabogram found east of room VI may indicate that the area also had an administrative function. No clear floors.
Sources: Tzonou 1998, 92-93; Walberg 1998b, 46; Walberg & Giering 1998, 84-85.

Terrace 10: Room VII, Str. 3, LH IIIC, disturbed by Roman remains. Str. 4, LH IIIC, levelling of LH IIIB debris, Roman disturbance. Large quantity of coarse-ware fragments and a few obsidian flakes. Str. 5 is contemporary with floor no. 1 of the Megaron (LH IIIC), with a base for a roof support. Str. 7, a LH IIIB floor and destruction debris, corresponding to floor no. 2 of the Megaron (LH IIIB2). Finds of a nodule with Linear syllabograms *ro* and *zo* and perhaps ideogram 125 CYPERUS, a commodity mentioned in connection with perfume. Another nodule with syllabogram *pa-zo-jo* and with a seal impression of a quadruped with suckling young, the logogram *130 OLEum. Also a coarse-ware stirrup jar with the Linear B syllabogram 77 *ka* was found east of Rooms VI and VII, (see Tr. Nb. Str. 5). Str. 8, the finds included another nodule with the impression of a goat, a small arrowhead, a quern, pounders, a whetstone. Str. 9, a LH IIIB floor, probably contemporary with no. 3 of the Megaron (LH IIIB2) finds of amber, rock crystal and stone beads. Str. 11 revealed part of a LH IIIA2 flask, obsidian denticulate and also blades and flakes, a bronze rivet. The finds of seals and the nodule may indicate accounting and administration. Pounders, a quern, a whetstone etc. suggest household activities in the LH IIIB.
Sources: Demakopoulou, Divari-Valakou & Walberg 1994, 39; Demakopoulou, Divari-Valakou, Åström & Walberg 1997-1998, 83-84; Walberg 1992a, 93; 1996-1997, 133-134; 1998a, catalogue no. 650; 1998b, 31; 1998c, 177; Walberg & Giering 1998, 85.

Room XI: Str. 3, LH IIIC floor, among the finds were three stone pounders suggesting that the room may have been used for food preparation. Str. 4 corresponds to the latest of the two LH IIIB floors in the Megaron (LH IIIB2). The find of a quern, several stone pounders and a spindle whorl indicate that the room was probably used for food preparation also in this period. Str. 8 corresponds to the first LH IIIB floor in the Megaron (LH IIIB2). Also then the room may have been used for food preparation in connection with different activities in the Megaron.
Sources: Demakopoulou, Divari-Valakou, Åström & Walberg 1997-1998, 75-76; Walberg 1998b, 31.

Room XVIII: Several strata and floor levels. Str. 5-7 are LH IIIB2. Finds in Str.2, two heads of female figurines, torso of another female figurine, a bronze weight. Str. 5, probably a floor, a column base, finds included a pestle. Str. 6, finds included a piece of worked bone and a stone crucible. Str. 8, MH II pottery. Perhaps industrial purpose?
Source: Demakopoulou, Divari-Valakou, Åström & Walberg 1997-1998, 86-89.

Room XX: Str. 5, an LH IIIB floor and filling. Str. 6 covered the whole area of R. XX. Finds of a large amphora and also a possibly unfinished seal. At the top of Str. 7 was another LH IIIB floor and filling. Trench Nj defined the northern part of R. XX. From Str. 4, a semicircular formation of flat stones, the construction continued down to Str. 7. Str. 5 a LH IIIB floor. Str. 7 another LH IIIB floor, corresponding to the LH IIIB floor in Str.7 of Tr. Ni. The finds of the platform, spouted bowls, lead vessels and figurines may suggest that the room was part of a sanctuary. *Source*: Demakopoulou, Divari-Valakou, Åström & Walberg 1997-1998, 86, 90.

and beyond.[71] The rich yield of pottery and other finds associated with the LH IIIB2 stratum at various locations also indicates that Midea was a prospering settlement during the mature Late Helladic period. Traces of destruction at the end of LH IIIB2, probably caused by an earthquake that also brought down parts of Tiryns and Mycenae, can be detected.[72] The area was cleared of debris and the most recent excavations have shown that also the LH IIIC habitation may have been impressive; Early, Middle and Late LH IIIC material can been recognised.[73]

Although no tablets have been found the finds of nodules indicate that the administrative system at Midea may have been on a par with those at Mycenae and Tiryns. This conclusion is further strengthened by the number of seals found. Excavations at Midea have yielded at least seven, quite possibly as many as eleven, to be compared with the eight found at Mycenae and the total absence of seals at Tiryns. The seal with the impression of a spider and the ideogram GRA (= wheat) may perhaps be associated with textile manufacture, assumed to have been conducted in the West Gate Area (on which, see below). According to the excavators, the seal indicates exchange of textiles and grain or rations of grain for the textile workers. The storage stirrup jar (MI Z 4) is associated with Crete and was probably imported from Chania. The finds of Linear B material, although fragmentary, are interpreted as additional evidence for the position of Midea as a palatial site in the Argolid. The excavators conclude that the finds of Linear B records may indicate that more material may be discovered in the future.[74]

The two Terraces 9 and 10 have provided us with material indicating domestic/official/ administrative and storage use, as well as some kind of religious activity. Storage areas have been identified at several places and they are all located in constructions dated to LH IIIB2. Storage is indicated not only by the finds of large lead vessels and stoppers but also by finds of pithoi, coarse ware and stirrup jars. Further material pointing to a storage function has been located close to the West Gate. K. Demakopoulou has explained their presence as due to the need to store products collected from the fertile plain. The West Gate Area is interpreted as the permanent quarters for the officers not only in charge of the defence and security of the citadel, but also in charge of the receiving, recording and storing of agricultural products from the plain.[75] In the East Gate Area, two rooms have been located that may have been storerooms.

Most of the rooms found in the West Gate Area were probably used as storage facilities and workshops. As well as tools, large numbers of loom-weights and spindle-whorls, many pithoi and other storage vessels were found here. Together with the clay nodule found, these finds have been interpreted as indications of textile production. Additional evidence for textile production is also to be found in the report of the excavations carried out by Åström and Verdelis in the East Gate Area where a number of spindle whorls, or buttons, were found. In the East Gate Area, trenches E and F revealed two rooms where several lead vases were found. The total number of, mostly crushed, lead objects found at Midea is impressive. Wasters of lead found in trenches H and Va support the idea of metal-working similar to that occurring at Tiryns during the LH IIIB and LH IIIC periods. The excavations on the Lower Terrace have been similarly rewarding and a large number of objects made of lead were registered. A lead bun ingot found indicates trade or workshop activity in the East Gate Area.[76]

The presence of a seal-cutting workshop is indicated by several unfinished seal-stones. It is similarly suggested that the imported bun ingot reveals the presence of a glass workshop. Jewellery is also thought to have been produced, as there are finds of partly finished pieces of fluorite, a mould and raw material, such as gold, faience and so on.[77]

The objects found and the raw materials used for different categories of objects indicate not only a high level of craft specialisation but also the extent to which external contacts took place. On the latter score, these seem to have been significant. Of particular interest is the recent finds of stirrup jar sherds inscribed with Linear B signs. Although such jars are typically thought of as having been imported from western Crete, excavators are of the

[71] Demakopoulou, Divari-Valakou & Walberg 1994, 27.
[72] Demakopoulou, Divari-Valkou, Åström & Walberg 1997-1998, 59; Walberg 1998c, 177.
[73] Walberg 1998c, 178.
[74] Demakopoulou 1995, 161; Demakopoulou & Divar-Valakou 1994-1995, 327.
[75] Demakopoulou 1995, 157.
[76] Mossman 1998, 271-276; Mossman 2000, 102.
[77] Demakopoulou 1995, 160-161.

opinion that this at least indicates contacts with other local centres.[78] In this connection, it should be noted that more similarities have been found between Tiryns and Midea than between Midea and Mycenae.[79]

The picture of Midea to emerge from the recent excavations and the publications made available to date is one of a settlement inhabited already in the late MH and early LH periods but with full expansion in the second phase of the LH IIIB period. If this is correct, Midea shares this characteristic with other sites on the Argive Plain. We have clear evidence of different types of settlement activity, such as building constructions, production of goods, economic exchange and daily household activity. Evidence for exchange and trade is given in the lead and clay weights, the balance weight and the imported goods. The finds of pottery, with Crete as the probable place of origin, further indicate external relations. Some finds of pictorial pottery from LH IIIB are likely to have been sourced at the Myc/Ber workshop; later dated samples, LH IIIB2 and LH IIIC, originated from the Tir/As workshop.[80] As such, these samples record intra-regional exchange. Also, the large female figurine found in Room VIa has parallels at Mycenae and Tiryns. The fragment of an amethyst vessel, possibly a Minoan work from the 16th or 15th century BC, is worthy of note, as an amethyst fragment has also been found at Mycenae. The fragment at Midea was probably considered as valuable.[81] Could it have been regarded as a heirloom?

To the objects mentioned should also be added the large number of lead vessels, the beads made of semi-precious stones, the ivory sword pommels and other artefacts. All are objects that were either made locally out of imported material or produced elsewhere. The elevated status of the settlement is underlined by the large number and high quality of the objects found. Although local variations can be identified, the fact that the same activities were practised at Midea as at the palatial sites of Mycenae and Tiryns puts the former on a par with the two latter. The architectural remains point in the same direction. A megaron-type building have been excavated and in the LH IIIB2 layers also storage and workshop areas have been identified.

It is also interesting to observe that there is ample material evidence to suggest that the site was not forced into decline after the LH IIIB2 destruction. Instead, the architectural layout of the new settlement is indicative of cultural continuity. Furthermore, the good quality of the pottery representing the final LH IIIC period provides a hint as to the status that Midea enjoyed. The strategic location of the site must have been of importance in all periods.[82] Demakopoulou regards the acropolis as a symbol of the monarch who controlled not only the palace but also the surrounding region and the settlements grouped around the acropolis. It was the node of the centralised economy and administration, and here agricultural products were collected for distribution to the subject population. Midea was such a centre in the LH IIIB2 period and, according to Demakopoulou, the settlement is best seen as equal to its peers Mycenae and Tiryns.[83] Walberg similarly notes that the fortification and its location close to major areas of cultivation and the Royal Tombs at Dendra are further evidence to the effect that Midea can be considered "one of the great Mycenaean citadels of the Argolid along with Tiryns and Mycenae in the LH IIIB period".[84]

5.7 ARGOS

Methodological and chronological comments

Excavations at Argos have been severely handicapped by the fact that it is a modern urban centre. A large part of the Late Helladic settlement is in all likelihood covered by modern structures or is likely to have been upset as a result of continued habitation of the area for extended periods of time since the Late Bronze Age.

Discussion and summary

The architectural evidence is meagre and it is not possible to trace the plan of the Late Helladic settlement. We can only establish that the few remains of constructions found indicate continuity from the LH IIIA1 to the LH IIIC period.

5.8 PROSYMNA

Methodological and chronological comments

The site has remains of prehistoric settlement activity reaching from the upper terrace, where later the Temple of Hera stood, southwards to the area below the later South Stoa. The remains of the settlement were in a bad condition and our knowledge of the site In the Late Helladic period, as opposed to the evidence from the cemetery, is limited.[85]

---

78 Demakopoulou & Divari-Valakou 1992-1993, 304.
79 Demakopoulou & Divari-Valakou 1992-1993, 304; Walberg 1998c, 177.
80 Mommsen & Maran 2000-2001.
81 Demakopoulou 1995, 160.
82 Walberg 1998c, 176.
83 Demakopoulou 1995, 151-152, 161.
84 Walberg 1998c, 177.
85 Renard 1995, 55-56; Shear Mylonas 1968, 270-271.

Table 5.4: Argos: the material

PERIODS	HOUSES	STORAGE	WORKSHOPS	PURPOSES
LH IIIA1	Odos Niobis 60	X		Domestic
LH IIIA2	Odos Diomidous 136			Domestic
LH IIIB/LH IIIC	Aphrodision Maison 1			Domestic
LH IIIB/LH IIIC	Aphrodion Maison 2			Domestic
LH IIIC:E	House-Odos Irakleous			Domestic

Odos Niobis 60: Built in early LH IIIA and destroyed at the end of the period. The very thick walls, 1 m, do not correspond to the size of the rooms. May be some kind of storage rooms.
Source: Hiesel 1989, 175.

Odos Diomidous 136: Only one wall.
Source: Hiesel 1989, 175-176.

Aphrodion Maison 1: Two floor levels, LH IIIB covered by a thick layer of ashes and LH IIIC with an oval hearth. Three rooms in a row.
Source: Hiesel 1989, 103-104.

Aphrodision Maison 2: Only two parallel walls.
Source: Hiesel 1989, 176.

Odos Irakleous: Pithos sherds found and charred beans. Two LH IIIC floors. Somewhat megaron-like character with two or three rooms. Also in the area of Odos Irakleous: walls consisting of at least six building phases, LH IIIA-C, but also earlier periods.
Source: Hiesel 1989, 175-176.

Table 5.5: Prosymna: the material

PERIODS	HOUSES	STORAGE	WORKSHOPS	PURPOSES
LH IIIB	One house on Acropolis			Domestic
LH IIIB	One house- Kephalari			Domestic
LH IIIB	House A			Domestic
LH IIIB	House B			Domestic
LH IIIB	House C			Domestic
LH IIIB	House D			Domestic
LH IIIB	House E			Domestic

Acropolis: Only partly preserved.
Source: Hiesel 1989, 193-194.

Kephalari: Only partly preserved.
Source: Hiesel 1989, 194.

House A: Located between Stoas II and III. Badly preserved walls. Possibly two-room house with portico.
Sources: Blegen 1937, 11; Hiesel 1989,102-103; Shear Mylonas 1968, 271.

House B: Similar in plan to House A.
Sources: Hiesel 1989, 102-103; Shear Mylonas 1968, 272.

House C: The walls indicate that this building was probably in use at the same time as House B.
Sources: Hiesel 1989, 102-103; Shear Mylonas 1968, 273.

House D: Also an incomplete plan preserved. Two central rooms. Similarities in plan to Panagia House I and the Ramp House at Mycenae.
Sources: Blegen 1937, 12; Shear Mylonas 1968, 274,

House E: Only one room and part of another preserved. Many potsherds on the floor.
Sources: Blegen 1937, fig. 15; Shear Mylonas 1968, 276.

Discussion and summary

More walls than those mentioned above were found. Caskey and Amandry report that remains of small Mycenaean houses were found, indicating habitation along the terraced eastern slope. They also mentioned a narrow roadway.[86] According to Shear Mylonas, the houses at Prosymna belong to the same type as those at Mycenae. However, the buildings at Prosymna are smaller and much simpler. Nor do we find houses with enclosed courtyards, or basement rooms, or several storeys.[87] Blegen suggested that the palace of the local ruler should have been constructed on the upper terrace, where the archaic temple was later to be constructed.[88] In addition to the profane building activity, Prosymna had a larger number of chamber tombs as well as a tholos. Caskey and Amandry further report that pottery datable to the LH IIIA and LH IIIB periods were found and so were sherds representing the LH II period. The settlement seems to have been abandoned by the end of LH IIIB, without reoccupation in the LH IIIC period. No material of immediate post-Mycenaean vintage has been found.[89]

5.9 BERBATI

Methodological and chronological comments

Whereas architectural remains are few, the kiln has received some attention and remains the best published part of the settlement.

Discussion and summary

The settlement and domestic activity at Berbati are documented in only a few architectural remains.[90] A kiln has been found dated to the LH II period; probably abandoned in the LH IIIA1 period.[91] On the same site, another large complex composed by several rooms followed later. No kiln can safely be associated with this building, although production is assumed to have continued at the settlement in LH IIIA1 as wasters have been found.[92] The building dated to the LH IIIA/B period consists of a large courtyard, enclosed by small rooms. Two roads delimit the building. The function of the second building may also have been domestic, as cooking facilities were found. In the complex was a storage room, with one large pithos, and also a huge crater, partly sunk into the floor and with a pierced bottom. The vase deposit is interpreted as probably an arrangement for cult purposes and also two installations have been identified as altars. The settlement was most likely abandoned in the later part of the LH IIIB period.[93]

Increased settlement activity, in which slopes and valley floors and even more remote areas were used, characterised the settlement pattern in the Berbati valley in late LH IIIA2 and LH IIIB1. The change has been explained in terms of expanded economic activity with an increase in the number of farmers, as well as an expansion of the area cultivated. The economy is described as most probably redistributive in character with pottery and agricultural products being sent to Mycenae. Intensification driven by the needs of the palace necessitated the utilisation even of the most remote areas of the valley; similarly, the increased settlement activity is explained as a result of the economic and political interest of Mycenae.[94] The dependency on Mycenae was similarly emphasised also in an earlier report, where the inhabitants of the valleys of Berbati and Limnes are said to have supplied Mycenae not only with raw materials, agricultural products and

[86] Caskey & Amandry 1952, 170-171.
[87] Shear Mylonas 1968, 277.
[88] Blegen 1937, 20.
[89] Caskey & Amandry 1952, 169-173, pl. 44.
[90] Hiesel 1989, 99-100, 179;Renard 1995, 56-58; Säflund 1965, 120; Shear-Mylonas 1968, 267-268.

[91] Åkerström 1940; Schallin 1997.
[92] Mountjoy 1999, 65.
[93] Åkerström, 1968, 49; Persson & Åkerström 1937-38, 59-63; Schallin 1997, 65.
[94] Schallin 1996, 170-172.

Table 5.6: Berbati: the material

PERIODS	HOUSES	STORAGE	WORKSHOPS	PURPOSES
LH II/IIIA1	Wall/kiln		X Pottery	Industrial
LH IIIA2/B				Domestic/Cult

Table 5.7: Lerna: the material

PERIODS	HOUSES	STORAGE	WORKSHOPS	PURPOSES
LH IIIA2/IIIB1	Area D; R 1			Domestic
LH IIIA2/IIIB1	Area 5			Domestic

Area D: Constructed in LH IIIA2 and ended in early LH IIIB1. However, a second partial floor indicates a scant re-occupation.
Sources: Caskey 1955, 27; Wiencke 1998, 126-132.

Area 5: An open space or courtyard, perhaps small rooms belonging to one or several houses. The floor is LH IIIA2 or somewhat later. Also here a second floor is datable to early LH IIIB1.
Source: Wiencke 1998, 146-147.

manufactured goods but also with labour. In exchange, they received imported goods, military protection and everyday products such as pottery. Evidence for this control had also been found in the road that connected Mycenae with Corinth but, above all linked Berbati with Mycenae and made feasible the transport of all goods of interest to the citadel.[95] The decrease in archaeological finds, observable in the LH IIIB2 period, is interpreted as a change in the demand for the previously needed, marginal land.[96]

5.10 LERNA

Methodological and chronological comments

As sherds reflecting the LH I-LH II periods have been found, the site of Lerna is thought to have been occupied continuously from the Middle Helladic period into the Late Helladic period. Even so, given the rather few sherds dating from the LH IIIA1 period recovered, there appears to have been at least one period characterised by low population. Although only a few sherds indicate activity during LH IIIB2, the main focal point of activity during the Late Helladic period seems to have been Area D. The lack of material remains representing the LH IIIC period suggests that the settlement was abandoned. The recently compiled material evidence, reported by Wiencke, indicates that a more complete presence of architectural features (comparable, for example, to the houses at Mycenae, Asine and other sites), has not been located.

Discussion and summary

The extensive and prosperous Middle Helladic settlement was followed by habitation also in the Late Helladic period. The first phases of the Late Helladic period are followed by scanty architectural remains and some tombs dating from the Mycenaean period (Lerna VII).[97] According to Wiencke, the presence of a shaft grave at Lerna may indicate a certain independence for the site in the early Mycenaean period. The scarce evidence of occupation in LH IIIA1 is interpreted as a possible sign of local élites failing to sustain their power. It is suggested that the settlement may in the LH IIIA2 period have become a political dependency of Argos. Lerna was occupied also in the LH IIIB1 period and the finds in area D and a horse burial with fragments of at least 37 kylixes and other vessels are interpreted by Wiencke as a confirmation of the importance of Lerna in this period. In contrast, by virtue of the few remains from the following LH IIIB2 period, signs of local stagnation have been found. This was brought to a head in LH IIIC when the site seems to have been totally abandoned.[98]

5.11 IRIA

Methodological and chronological comments

A site with few architectural remains.[99]

[95] Wells, Runnels & Zangger 1990, 237; 1993, 54, 58.
[96] Schallin 1996, 170-172.

[97] Caskey 1954; 1955; Renard 1995, 67-69; Wiencke 1998.
[98] Caskey 1954, 11; Hope Simpson & Dickinson 1979, 47; Wiencke 1998, 208.
[99] Döhl 1973; Hope Simpson & Dickinson 1979, 50.

Table 5.8: Iria: the material

PERIODS	HOUSES	STORAGE	WORKSHOPS	PURPOSES
LH IIIB2 **LH IIIC:E/M**	House M with side room A			Domestic

Table 5.9: Material from settlements without preserved architectual remains

LH II	Vreserka, Gymno, Aria, Kandia, Synoro, Kazarma, Kokla
LH IIIA1	Monasteraki,Magoula, Vreserka, Schoinochori, Gymno, Ayios Andreas, Nauplion, Aria, Kandia, Kazarma, Kokla, Ligourio
LH IIIA2	Phychtia, Monasteraki/Magoula, Vreserka, Schoinochori, Gymno, Ayios Andreas, Nauplion, Aria, Kandia, Kazarma, Ligourio
LH IIIB	Phychtia, Monasteraki/Magoula, Vreserka, Gymno, Kephalari, Achladokombos, Ayios Andreas, Nauplion, Kandia, Kazarma, Ligourio
LH IIIC	Phychtia, Nauplion, Kandia
Sybmycenaean	Nauplion

Discussion and summary

The site was already inhabited in LH I. Excavations have revealed a LH IIIB building and an associated cistern, which was partly filled with debris from a destruction and the pottery indicates a date at the beginning of LH IIIC. Mountjoy has recently found a transitional LH IIIB2 to Early LH IIIC period represented here as well as also LH IIIC Middle pottery.[100]

Located close to the coast, this may have been a small harbour or fishing village. The settlement was destroyed by fire in Early or middle LH IIIC. The pottery is dominated by open shapes; decorated pottery is more common than undecorated ware. The material illustrates the standard of living in a non-palatial, household context.[101]

5.12 SETTLEMENTS WITHOUT PRESERVED ARCHITECTURAL REMAINS

Methodological and chronological comments

No large excavations have been reported and the published material is meagre. The following sites have in some cases tombs preserved from the LH period, in other cases only some few surface finds have been found.[102]

Discussion and summary

Several of the above-mentioned sites are promising, and further excavations and the publication of hitherto excavated material is likely to prove rewarding. Kokla is a case in point. Here, archaeologists have found chamber tombs and also a tholos, of which parts have been published.[103] Unfortunately, no remains of a settlement have been recorded, but it is conceivable that the site was prominent at least during the period when the tholos and other tombs were in use. At this juncture, also Nauplion must be mentioned, as it has been reported to be the site of a large chamber-tomb cemetery.[104] The location of the site makes it ideal as a harbour and fishing settlement. However, to date no finds to that effect have been found.

5.13 THE SETTLEMENTS OF THE ARGIVE PLAIN: A SUMMARY

The above survey of houses shows that evidence of habitation in the periods preceding LH IIIB is very meagre. The settlement material does not allow of any detailed analysis of function or economic activity in the LH IIIA period. Mycenae is one of the few sites with recorded remains of houses. Although the evidence is very fragmentary and piecemeal, a commercial role may be suggested for the House of Lead and House of Petsas's. At Berbati, a pottery kiln was probably in use in the LH IIIA period and the economic significance of this kiln has earlier been pointed out. The proposed dependency of Mycenae may be questioned as the pottery material from Mastos may also have been exchanged via other channels than Mycenae. The pre- LH IIIB m5 road (*fig. 5*) connected Berbati with the southern part of the Argive Plain,[105] and supports the contention that the distribution of pottery and other locally made products need not have been dependent on Mycenae. Instead, it is possible to argue in favour of a scenario in which the

[100] Döhl 1973; Hiesel 1989, 15-16; Mountjoy 1999, 36, 47.
[101] Döhl 1973, 191-194.
[102] Hope Simpson & Dickinson 1979 for site information, Renard 1995, 61, 65-67.
[103] Demakopoulou 1990b; 1993.
[104] Alden 1981, 292-306.
[105] Lavery 1995.

locally produced goods in the Berbati-Limnes area were exchanged with also other sites than Mycenae.

The survey of houses shows that the character and function of the buildings are not homogeneous, not only across time and space but also within individual settlements. If the analysis presented by Tournavitou is accepted, the houses in use in the LH IIIB1 period at Mycenae seem to have been private buildings occupied by individuals or functionaries (or craftsmen, merchants, etc.), who by virtue of their official standing were closely connected with the palace. As we have precious little evidence on their official status, however, it is less far-fetched (or at least safer) to assume that the official function (if any) was marginal or secondary. Instead, the houses primarily served as living spaces of independent households. This does not preclude the possibility that a range of activities took place there, including those that were for the benefit of or on behalf of the palace, and multifunctional use can indeed be deduced from the material found. We find small-scale industry composed of a mixture of activities such as oil or perfume manufacture and ivory production, in parallel with a domestic purpose. The occupants may, of course, have been entrepreneurs with the palace as one of their a customers. Shear Mylonas has in her study of Late Helladic houses categorised some of the houses at Mycenae built in the LH IIIB1 period as of the more elaborate types, E and F, for example , the House of the Oil Merchant, the House of Sphinxes, the Tsountas House and the West House.[106] All these buildings were located outside the citadel and contained valuable goods and Linear B tablets. They have been characterised as industrial, official and domestic. At Tiryns the LH IIIB1 settlements seem to have been limited, as only a few houses or rooms have been documented and they have a domestic and industrial character. At Midea, by contrast, the evidence of habitation in the periods preceding LH IIIB is very poor.

The finds of Linear B tablets in LH IIIB1 contexts at Mycenae are of particular interest. So far, they are the only tablets from this period that have been found on the Argive Plain. The tablets found in LH IIIB1 contexts indicate the need for recording already in this period. The locations of the houses where the tablets were found, outside the citadel, point in the direction of a function that need not have been of an official and palatial character. However, as argued earlier, there may have been an interest on the part of those inhabiting the citadel in being involved in trade. This does not necessarily imply, however, that they controlled the trade.

As indicated by the archaeological material available, production in LH IIIB1 was concentrated at Mycenae on olive oil, perfume and ivory. According to E. French, the small stirrup jars found in the West House were produced at Mycenae.[107] Probably a pottery workshop was located somewhere in the vicinity of Mycenae/Berbati in LH IIIB as evidenced by pictorial pottery samples found at Midea and also the eastern part of the Mediterranean. Also unpainted sherds from the same workshop group have been found at Tiryns. The lead bun ingot found at the Citadel House in LH IIIB1 context, mentioned by S. Mossman, may indicate production in this metal, although remains of manufacture are not obvious. At least it is evidence of external contact, either via another Argive site, or direct exchange with Laurion from where a majority of lead in the Late Bronze Age Argolid seems to have been mined.[108] At Tiryns, the production in old metals has been documented, but new production indicated by bronze bars is also evidenced. At Midea, no evidence of production has been registered in this period.

Production in olive oil, perfume, wine and ivory at this point gave Mycenae an opportunity to use goods as valuable exchange items in transactions with other settlements within the region or in long-distance trade. We may, however, assume that olive oil and wine was produced in a local context. It has been suggested that the Berbati-Limnes area was dependent on Mycenae through a redistributive system. The evidence from the LH IIIB1 period cannot be used to verify such an assumption, as evidence of large-scale storage, that can be associated with a centralised and redistributive economy, is not to hand, nor can the Linear B tablets be interpreted as records of a centralised economy. Mycenae obviously had the economic means to acquire also exotic and expensive goods. Indeed, the raw material may have been worked into finished goods at Mycenae. It is also possible that raw material was exchanged between Argive sites. On a more speculative note, it is conceivable that itinerant workmen could have produced the finished objects and these temporally limited and periodical workshops (if any) are unlikely to have left any major traces. Exchange of a long-distance character is indicated in the material; to mention only a few, for example tablet X508 on which exchange with Thebes is indicated, and in the stirrup jars from western Crete found in the House of the Oil Merchant.[109] Tiryns, where metals were worked in LH IIIB1, may have used the finished products in regional exchange transactions. In the LH IIIB period the road pattern developed (*fig.* 5) and new roads were used that facilitated contacts between settlements.

The LH IIIB1 period ended in destruction, yet apparently it did not cause any major break in the activities on the Argive Plain. The archaeological evidence indicates continuity at Mycenae, where some houses were re-used, others were abandoned and a significant number were new constructions. The LH IIIB2 period saw extensive use not only of the area outside the citadel but also in the

[106] Shear Mylonas 1968, 464-465.

[107] French 1991, 124.

[108] Mossman 2000, 87-88.

[109] Haskell 1997, 101-111.

citadel area itself, which was extended as new buildings were constructed, some of an obviously monumental character. Also at Tiryns, as well as at Midea, intensive building activity characterised this period. Not only were regular buildings constructed, but also more monumental ones and the megaron like room has also been identified at Midea.

Workshop activity at Mycenae was concentrated to the citadel area, where continued ivory manufacture has been recorded, but bronze, seal and jewellery and perhaps furniture production also took place there. At Tiryns, metal production seems to have been the main occupation. Remains of lead production indicate specialisation, but the presence (and hence possibly use) of gold, bronze and iron is documented. It is possible that the iron was produced in the LH IIIC Early and Middle periods as Bau VIa was in use then. Still, even then the evidence for iron production is early and indicates the phenomenon of a continuous transfer of technological know-how. Moreover, remains of ivory and bone indicate the production of jewellery, inlay for furniture or the like and a kiln bears witness to pottery production. Midea is the third settlement of interest as recent excavations have displayed evidence of a prospering and important settlement on this site in the LH IIIB2 period. Production has been recorded in several areas. Finds from the West Gate Area are suggestive of jewellery and textile production. Evidence of production, tools and so forth has been found also in other areas, but there seem to be few traces of raw material that could help to identify the type of goods produced. Mossman mentiones that the largest quantity of lead finds have been found at Mycenae, and then Tiryns and Midea. In the case of Tiryns the context is LH IIIB2 to LH IIIC and associated with bronze-working industry. At Mycenae the metal was found also in LH IIIB2 context together with industrial activities such as ivory and glass-bead and possibly jewellery manufacture. But, according to Mossman all these material were stored not produced at the Citadel House. Also at Midea large number of lead objects have been found and a lead bun ingot, found at the East Gate Area, indicate metal-working or trade.[110] At Mycenae and at Tiryns only some few tablets and fragments of Linear B have been recorded and then mostly not *in situ*. At Midea no tablets have been found so far, but nodules and seals indicate that the need for recording was felt also at this settlement.

Larger storage areas dedicated to the LH IIIB2 period and such that could verify the assumed economic centralisation in this period are yet to be discovered at Mycenae. Generally speaking, the size of the storage-rooms is small, and it may be suggested that they were primarily used for storage of prestige (rather than staple) goods, either produced at the site or traded from other regions. Of course, some might have been used for the storage of agricultural products for those living in the building, or for distribution to members of the community in need, social storage as suggested by Halstead.[111] This is in contrast to Tiryns, where Kilian suggested that large-scale storage capacity was located in the galleries built at the end of LH IIIB2.[112] As storage facilities, these have been associated with a redistributive economy, but their capacity is quite limited. If used for storage of agricultural products in times of need, the number of receivers was probably small and may primarily have been intended for the inhabitants of the citadel. Also at Tiryns, the areas may have been used for the storage of other products, but as is the case with agricultural products, this is hypothetical, as no material indications of storage have been recorded. At Midea, storage areas have been identified only in the LH IIIB2 buildings. Although otherwise suggested by Demakopoulou, the capacity of these rooms does not come across as large and their storage function was probably also of a multifunctional character excluding use as storage rooms for a large part of the inhabitants of the settlement.

In a parallel development to that at the end of LH IIIB1, the destruction at the end of the LH IIIB2 period did not cause the inhabitants to abandon the larger settlements. But, settlement activity has also been located at sites as Argos, Asine and Iria.[113] The rebuilding level was, however, not comparable with the that observed following the first round of destruction (that marking the transition from LH IIIB1 to LH IIIB2), when probably also a monumental building programme was initiated. Mountjoy has recently at three sites, Iria, Tiryns and Midea, identified a transitional phase between LH IIIB2 and Early LH IIIC.[114] A problem in identifying such a transitional phase is that our knowledge concerning the LH IIIC Early period is meagre owing to lack of published stratified material. Still, it cannot be excluded that also the LH IIIC Early period was short and in some sense a transitional phase.

Although the disaster had more severe effects than the one at the end of LH IIIB1, continuity may be observed as houses were re-used.[115] That is observable at Mycenae, where several houses seem to have been in use from LH IIIB to LH IIIC. Also at Tiryns, re-use is recorded at several spots. At both settlements, also new buildings were constructed. The houses and rooms at all sites are for the most part of a domestic character. An exception is Tiryns, where evidence of metal production is recorded in the LH IIIC Early and Middle periods. Also, finds of ivory in an LH IIIC context in Bau VI, later re-placed by Bau VIa, may indicate continued production at the site. A

[110] Mossman 2000, 98-102.

[111] Halstead 1988, 524; 1992a, 68-70, 73-74; 1992b, 113-115.

[112] Kilian 1987b, 25, 27-28.

[113] Kilian 1980, 171.

[114] Mountjoy 1999, 36.

[115] Drews 1993, 21-24.

kiln from the LH IIIC period was used in pottery production. In a parallel to the situation at Asine, by LH IIIC we also find rooms assigned a cultic function. As for Mycenae, no evidence of possible production or of a cultic function has been found. It has been suggested that Houses M and N had an official function and that they were provided with storage facilities. We do not, so far, know the level and periods of re-building at Midea, but it seems as also this settlement continued to be used in LH IIIC as habitation at Midea in the LH IIIC period has been identified on Terraces 9 and 10. The function of the areas needs further research, but a mixed character is conceivable. Production may have continued alongside any of the domestic functions. Question marks remain, however, with respect to the issue whether the cultic function identified in LH IIIB2 survived the destruction. Another site of importance, but handled in the previous chapter, is Asine as the site was used in LH IIIC Middle and Late periods.

Large storage facilities have been recorded at Mycenae as Houses M and N and also the House of Columns may have had this function. This does not quite square with the view that large storage rooms should be expected during LH IIIB but not beyond that point. It was during the earlier of the two periods, after all, that the economy was characterised by large-scale storage as the prime expression of redistribution under a centralised power. Although it is not self-evident what can be made of this observation, mere logic suggests that either redistribution was continued into the latter period (with all the consequences that that may have for our understanding of that particular period, as compared to the previous ones) or we have been mistaken in associating large-scale storage facilities with redistribution. It may, of course, be objected that physical continuity of facilities does not necessarily imply continuity of use, but then we may rightfully ask why we should associate a particular archaeological form with a particular use at one point but not at another. The LH IIIC period was, as well, hit by destruction in the end of the Middle LH IIIC, probably caused by an earthquake.[116] The material remains indicate that rebuilding took place at Tiryns whereas Mycenae show rather few remains from the last sub-period. Midea is still a question mark, whereas at Asine settlement activity has been identified.

The end of the LH IIIC period may well have been turbulent and the archaeological evidence supports the picture of decline at Asine, Mycenae, Midea and Tiryns.[117] As for the Submycenaean period, few indications of activity have been recorded in the settlements for this period. There are some evidence, however, for habitation at Mycenae while at Tiryns we find structures of Submycenaean origin.

In addition to the settlements mentioned above, several smaller settlements have been identified on the Argive Plain. However, the published material is meagre and it is only possible to identify them as minor sites. One exception is Nauplion, as the site was most probably of importance in the Late Helladic period. Unfortunately, the archaeological material is very poor, except that a larger number of chamber tombs have been identified, if not yet published. The existence of the cemetery and the location of the site point towards some degree of importance. By the end of the LH IIIB period, a majority of these minor sites were abandoned and only a few show traces of activity in the end of the Bronze Age.

---

116 Kilian 1980, 186.

117 Eder 1998, 86-87; Mountjoy 1999, 48.

PART III

TOMBS

CHAPTER 6
TOMBS: THE SOCIO-ECONOMIC IMPLICATIONS OF CHAMBER TOMBS

6.1 INTRODUCTION

'Death in Mycenaean Greece', Mee and Cavanagh point out, 'could not be described as a neglected subject'.[1] Indeed, issues concerning the social aspects and the significance of different types of tombs have attracted the attention of scholars ever since the first chamber tombs and tholoi were excavated.[2] This is not to imply, however, that all the problems have been resolved. Issues that continue to attract attention include, for example, the possibility of establishing the social status of those buried and whether tombs served as markers for different hierarchical structures in Late Helladic society. As has been shown earlier, the tomb material has been explicitly used by analysts as an indicator of the status of individual settlements and hence as a means of deducing hierarchical settlement patterns on the Argive Plain. Methodologically, approaches concentrating on the quantitative measuring of grave goods and tomb types have been favoured, but a qualitative and subjective value has also been applied to grave goods. There are a fair number of studies that bring up problems concerning tomb data as measures of status and wealth as the determinant of the social position of the deceased. Generally, the tombs have been seen as symbols of the economic-political position of the deceased, or of a whole group.

The authors of previous studies on the settlement system in the Argolid have regarded Late Helladic tombs as a critical type of material that could be used to identify the relationship between major and minor settlements. For this reason alone tombs should not be neglected in a discussion concerning issues of spatial differentiation and the establishing of social status. In fact, tombs and the material objects left behind in them make it possible to extend the scope of previous research.

The point of departure of the following analysis will be the previously used definitions of tombs as status markers in the Argive socio-political landscape. This is done with a view to establishing the usefulness and validity of previous work. After this, the grave goods will be discussed not only as a possible measure of wealth and status but also as an indicator of the predominant mode, or modes, of economic transaction. Setting out from an in-depth analysis of the situation at Late Helladic Asine, as it is evident in published material, the empirical part of the work will provide for the necessary inputs to a discussion of the local developments, as set in regional context.

6.2 MORTUARY DATA AS INDICATORS OF SOCIO-ECONOMIC STATUS

Ever since chamber and tholos tombs were first excavated, scholars have raised the issue of their status. Interest has mainly focused on their social significance and their symbolic value in the political landscape of Late Helladic society.[3] Tholos tombs have since their discovery been regarded as representatives of an élite or aristocracy in Late Helladic society. The argument that the tholos is a "royal" or "princely" type of tomb has also been put forward.[4] Some scholars have argued that chamber tombs are best understood as tombs for an élite, while others take the view that they are common type also made use of by the rest of the population.[5] Specifically, some have regarded them as a type of tomb for a middle class who seems to have been quite affluent, or that alternatively was used by a very large part of the total population.[6] It is against this background that the use of the tombs as symbols of different tiers in settlement hierarchies should be seen; the conflicting interpretations are likely to have their impacts on models such as those devised by Bintliff and Kilian.

Alden, who studied the fluctuations in the use of chamber tombs and who pointed out that the peak in their use was reached in LH IIIA, presents a more systematic study of the tomb material from the Argolid.[7] From the point of view of the region, the material from the Argolid shows a peak in LH IIIA2 (rather than LH IIIA1) followed by an incipient decline in LH IIIB, which continued in LH IIIC. According to Alden, one

[1] Mee & Cavanagh, 1984, 45.

[2] See for example, Alden 1981; Bintliff 1977; Cavanagh & Mee 1990; Kilian 1988; Mee & Cavanagh 1984; 1990, Voutsaki 1992; Wace 1921-1923.

[3] Alden 1981; Bintliff 1977; Cavanagh & Mee 1990; Kilian 1988a; Mee & Cavanagh 1984; 1990.

[4] Alden 1981, 7; Bintliff 1977, 135, 156, 288; Darcque 1987, 185-189; Mee & Cavanagh 1984, 50, 56; 1990, 240; Pelon 1990, 107-112; Voutsaki 1992, 7.6, 10.2.2.

[5] Voutsaki 1995a, 62.

[6] Alden 1981, 19; Bintliff 1977, 138, 288-289; Dickinsson 1983, 63.

[7] Alden 1981.

reason for these fluctuations may have been the changing conditions in Late Helladic society itself. For example, the increase in the number of chamber tombs in use in the LH IIIA2 period could be explained in terms of an better-organised agriculture imposed upon society by the palace. As a result, the possibilities of giving better support to a larger population emerged.[8] The extravagance of the form of burial and also the grave goods in certain instances indicate – or so Alden contends – that the group that used chamber tombs was fairly affluent. The tholos tomb is not included in her study, but she maintains that they would have been built for the most privileged members of Late Helladic society.[9]

Dickinson, on the other hand, argues that any attempt to make a distinction in wealth between the users of different types of tombs is fraught with difficulties, as there are actually sites where cist tombs are quite as generously endowed as other types of tombs. Furthermore, large tholoi seem to have been richly furnished, but we also find chamber tombs, even in the LH III period, which seem to have been very rich. Therefore, according to Dickinson, it is not possible to discern a pattern were we find that particular forms of tombs are always rich or poor. He also points out that both the regional and the local diversities in tomb types in the Argolid are not quite as pronounced as in Messenia. There is simply a greater degree of homogeneity in burial customs in the former as compared with the latter. Inherent differences, such as the size and character of the territory, may explain the distinction between the two in development and diversity, but the Argolid also shows a development of architectural and engineering skills, wealth and power not evident in the other regions. The choice of a particular tomb type is therefore, or so Dickinson concludes, best explained not in terms of status, class or wealth, but rather by regional or family traditions, or even convenience; after all, there are chamber tombs with goods that do not suggest a very high status on the part of the deceased.[10]

The argument that most individuals were buried in chamber tombs is also advanced by Mee and Cavanagh, but unlike Dickinson they argue that it would be unwise to exclude the possibility that status, both economic and social, could have been expressed by the size and richness of the individual chamber tomb.[11] In their analysis of chamber tomb material, they also made the observation that the number of chamber tombs in use and their indicated wealth tended to fluctuate considerably between the Late Helladic periods. The number of chamber tombs in use shows an increase during the LH IIIA period, only to be followed by a decrease in LH IIIB.[12] In the material analysed they also observed that there was a distinct trend from larger and richer tombs in use in the earlier periods to poorer tombs in LH IIIA and LH IIIB.[13] According to Mee and Cavanagh, several explanatory factors can be identified. They do not favour the idea of population growth (an explanation put forward by Alden), but instead suggest that the section of the society using the tombs might have changed. The disparities in the size and wealth of the tombs may have mirrored loose political alliances consisting of an association between both the poorer and the richer groups in the society. The sharp rise in the number of tombs in use in the LH IIIA may then be explained by a spread of the tomb type to other sections of society owing to new burial traditions or a less restricted use of the tomb type, but cultural hegemony – quite possibly issuing from or developed under the influence of the palaces – may also explain the presence of a standardised tomb type.[14] As such, both explanations have an air of plausibility, but have very different implications as far as the type of society that they assume. It would therefore be of considerable interest to investigate whether there is any additional evidence that may help us to distinguish between the two.

In a recent book Cavanagh and Mee also propose that it is possible that the palaces, directly or indirectly, were responsible for an increase in the number of settlements in mainland Greece. The number of settlements was mirrored in the number of cemeteries, which increased during this period. The sizes of the cemeteries are of interest, not least because they imply that most people were buried in chamber tombs in this period. The number of offerings obviously decreased during the LH III period and, according to Cavanagh and Mee, this may be have been a result of legislation against ostentatious aristocratic burial, as the rulers may have thought that their authority was threatened.[15] According to them most Mycenaeans were buried in chamber tombs in this period and at this level of society, grave offerings were still an indication of status, more so than the tomb type.[16] Another explanation, proposed by French, may be that fewer grave goods were placed in tombs during this period[17] and accordingly tombs from this period may be more difficult to recognise. Mee and Cavanagh, for their part, argue that this explanation cannot be proved. What is more, they suggest, the Argolid is something of an exception: mainland Greece as a whole does not show such a decline as that that can be observed in the north-

[8] Alden 1981, 218, 322-324.
[9] Alden 1981, 7.
[10] Dickinson 1983, 62-66.
[11] Cavanagh & Mee 1990, 56; Mee & Cavanagh 1984, 56, 61-62.

[12] Mee & Cavanagh 1984, 54, 57.
[13] Cavanagh & Mee 1990, 62; 1998; Mee & Cavanagh 1990, 234.
[14] Mee & Cavanagh 1990, 234.
[15] Cavanagh & Mee 1998, 126; Mee & Cavanagh 1990, 234.
[16] Cavanagh & Mee 1998, 127.
[17] French 1969, no. 64, 71.

eastern Peloponnese.[18] Yet the explanation suggested by French has much to be said for it. Like others, I would not exclude the importance of earlier deposits as heirlooms. Also, it may be observed that new categories of objects could have replaced other deposited earlier and deposits may also have been made of materials not preserved. An interesting and important point made by Ucko is that ethnographically it is possible to observe that burial rites may change quickly and are relatively unstable.[19] This characteristic may well have been valid also for the burial traditions of the Late Bronze Age.

Cavanagh and Mee also discuss the distribution and significance of the tholos tombs and do not exclude the possibility that the tholos tomb, as early as the first phases of the Late Helladic period, became an exclusive burial type for the Mycenaean elite and aristocracy. The general distribution shows an increase in the number of tholoi in the LH IIIA period, followed by a decrease in the LH IIIB. They suggest that it may have been during the course of LH IIIA2 and LH IIIB that the tholos actually became the exclusive type of tomb for kings. A closer look at the distribution of this tomb type in the Argolid displays a decrease already between LH IIIA1 and the following phase. The restricted geographical distribution can conceivably be interpreted as a result of the emergence of larger states with a commensurate, diminishing need for many and dispersed tombs of this type; it goes without saying that Mycenae itself may have been one of the centres benefiting from increased centralisation.[20] To conclude, Mee and Cavanagh demonstrate in their studies that the distribution of tombs shows both regional and chronological variations. There is no clear distinction between large and small or between rich and poor tholos tombs, nor is a clear line drawn between poor tholos tombs and rich chamber tombs. The picture that emerges from the analysis is one of a society relatively simple in its social organisation and not rigidly hierarchical. Mee and Cavanagh further suggest that the population lived in scattered villages of mostly a small-farming-community character, with both rich and poor landowners and tenants present.[21]

Mortuary practices and their significance in a wider social and political perspective in the Mycenaean world has also been the subject of the work of Voutsaki.[22] Her conclusions concerning tomb evidence representing the LH III period are of considerable relevance here and in some important respects they differ from those presented by Mee and Cavanagh and Dickinson. Contrary to the conclusions presented by the latter, in which the possibility that chamber tombs were used for the burials of a large part of the population including the persons at the palaces is advocated. Voutsaki excludes the possibility that they were used as élite places of burial. Her results rather indicate an increase in the proportion of poorer and smaller chamber tombs and an impoverishment of chamber tombs in the LH IIIB period. Contrary to the conclusions drawn by Mee and Cavanagh, the decline in the wealth deposited in the tombs is to be explained as an indication of the emergence of a more hierarchical social structure with more wealth channelled toward the palaces. Furthermore, Voutsaki interprets the change in the pattern of wealth distribution as an indication of pressure on local élites, with a widening gap between this group and the palatial élite, buried in the now exclusive tholoi. The groups buried in the chamber tombs include not only poorer members of society and the children, but also the members of the local (as opposed to regional) élites, previously buried in tholos tombs. Interestingly, it seems as if children were buried in chamber tombs from LH IIIA onwards. Voutsaki interprets this mixture of children, the poorer members of society and the local élites as a further indication of the growing difference between the group buried in chamber tombs and the palatial élites.[23] Regarding the tholos tombs Voutsaki points out that the few of them in use are now exclusively restricted to the palatial centres and illustrates the growing distance between the palatial élites and the rest of the population. Her interpretation of the mortuary evidence therefore, and in contradiction to the view presented by Dickinson, posits the emergence of a stricter hierarchical order and the appearance of rigid classes, a process that was initiated in LH IIIA and culminated in the LH IIIB period. Voutsaki underlines the symbolic meaning and importance of the tholos in the LH IIIB, when the tomb type was restricted to the palatial élites. Indeed, mortuary display was an important strategy in social and political competition. Especially the tholos is recognised as having been the most conspicuous and most permanent symbol of wealth and prestige and, according to Voutsaki, this is made manifest from LH IIIA onwards by the confinement of tholoi to the palatial centres. She also remarks that the settlement evidence points to an unstable situation represented by destructions and fortifications. Meanwhile, the restrictive mortuary display and evidence in LH IIIA-B are interpreted as a strategy for the establishment and consolidation not only of palatial control but also of a successful centralised system, in which amongst other things wealth and labour were channelled exclusively to these centres.[24]

The third category, consisting of what in the following pages will be called "simpler tombs", that is, cist and pit graves, has so far been rather neglected. A possible reason for such a state of affairs may be that the tombs are not always properly reported, mostly owing to the lack of elaborate design and objects deposited. The cist burials are simple and often furnished with only a few

[18] Mee & Cavanagh 1984, 57.
[19] Ucko 1969, 273.
[20] Mee & Cavanagh 1984, 51-53, figs. 1-4.
[21] Mee & Cavanagh 1984, 62; 1990, 242.
[22] Voutsaki 1992; 1995a, 56.
[23] Voutsaki 1992, 7.6; 1995a, 62; 1998, 48, 55-56.
[24] Voutsaki 1995a, 57-57, 62-63.

objects. In addition, they may be in poor condition and are therefore not always easy to recognise in the landscape. According to Dickinson, this type of tomb, except for children's, are relatively rare after LH II. These tombs are found in connection with tholos and chamber tombs and close to chamber-tomb cemeteries. Dickinson further points to the change in tomb type in the final Mycenaean phases, LH IIIC and Submycenaean, when we again find a larger number of simpler graves. However, the change does not imply an abandonment of chamber tombs, as these, still, are in use in the LH IIIC period. Dickinson also considers the changing cultural features, for example burial customs where the rite of cremation appears, an interesting aspect which is recognised during the LH IIIC. Further, he regards the end of the Mycenaean period as a time of decline. The growing popularity of simpler burial types is understood as a sign of changing economic patterns with a tendency to decline. Simple graves can be constructed anywhere, even close to settlements where they are, perhaps, not as easy to rob, and they require little skill to construct. In fact, Dickinson asserts, local variations continued during the latest phase of the Bronze Age and were even intensified during the following period.[25] Lewartowski also notes the general change in frequency in the LH IIIC and the Submycenaean periods. The periods are characterised by a very small number of burials in chamber tombs and a larger number of interments in simple graves. Lewartowski interprets the burial evidence as a display of a hierarchically structured society. The two groups buried in chamber tombs or simpler tombs belonged to the same society and the same culture, but the simpler graves represent people belonging to a group characterised by lower levels of wealth and a low social status.[26]

To summarise, we may observe that tomb material has been used in several studies with the expressed purpose of analysing and evaluating the possibility of defining both social and economic status among Late Helladic populations. As the results have, more or less explicitly, been adopted in analyses of settlement models, the discussions on status are important in their own right. Tomb material has been regarded as a homogeneous group of archaeological finds. As such, it has been utilised as a test of similarity between the different regions of the Late Helladic world. But, as demonstrated by Dickinson, Voutsaki and Cavanagh and Mee, it is clear that such a homogeneous character is not self-evident. Instead, regional diversity as well as development and frequency change in the mortuary data is to be noted.

These observations harmonise with the premise proposed earlier for this study, namely that the Late Helladic world should not be regarded as a totally homogeneous unit. Instead we should avail ourselves of the opportunity to assess differentiation across the regions. By not simply assuming homogeneity, independent regional development can be detected. It should be possible, at least in theory, to see and understand such regionally differentiated patterns of development, if any, in the archaeological material. By the same token, judging by the goods found in the different tomb types, it is likely that the amount and type of goods differed within the tomb types. As has been demonstrated quite clearly in previous studies, Late Helladic tombs cannot be regarded as homogeneous and as exclusively representing one social group or other. This insight represents an important input to the following analysis. Differences between individual tombs, and not merely between types of tombs, allow for the possibility that status, whether economic, political or social, is expressed by size and richness. On the other hand, it makes a more detailed analysis of existing tombs necessary. We cannot afford to formulate generalisations of the type that underpins the models of Bintliff and Killian unless the underlying material has been thoroughly analysed.

6.3 THE PURPOSE OF THE TOMB STUDY

The purpose of the present study is to use tomb material to shed light on complex status positions in which social status and economic status are combined. Late Helladic mortuary practices and their significance in the economic perspective will therefore constitute a part of this discussion. The study will investigate whether it is possible to analyse the relationship between the preserved tomb material from the Late Helladic period and different modes of economic transaction. Specifically, the aim is to probe the issue of whether tombs can enlighten us on the predominant modes of exchange, that is, as exponents of reciprocal or non-reciprocal modes of transaction. It is of some interest to see whether the tomb remains can help to answer the question of whether any of these modes of transaction were practised during the LH III period. The tombs will be analysed in a local and intra-regional context.

6.4 MEASURING SOCIO-ECONOMIC STATUS IN LATE HELLADIC MORTUARY CONTEXTS

The methodological problems in the study of prehistoric burial material are complex and Late Helladic society is no exception in this regard. Beyond the obvious problem of looted tombs, the available material suffers from a quantitative bias, as some settlements are well represented by excavated and published, burial material, whereas others have been given less attention and have perhaps gone unrecorded. The resulting discrepancies in the volume of material remains create an archaeological problem quite distinct from the parallel, interpretative problem, which issues from our choice of approach to the burial evidence. In the following sections, these shortcomings will be noted and to the best of my ability

[25] Dickinson 1983, 62-63, 67.
[26] Lewartowski 1995, 107, 110.

will be addressed, as and when required. The main purpose of the remainder of this chapter, however, is to extend the preceding discussion and to provide more empirical detail that will allow me to put my generalisations on a sounder footing.

It goes without saying that the study of Late Helladic tomb material as an exponent of status and wealth is a complex problem; the literature referred to above makes this abundantly clear. Yet this is no excuse for not making use of the relatively rich material made available by the body of distinguished archaeologists who have worked on the prehistory of this particular region. The problems connected with the interpretation of the social significance of various tomb types cannot, of course, be avoided, but I believe that a comprehensive study will put the interpretations on a firmer footing. Such an analysis, however, should be preceded by a detailed discussion of the different types of tombs and their significance in a local and regional perspective.

Studies of mortuary data representing the Late Helladic period often raise problems connected with the real or imagined character of tombs as mirrors of social and political structures. The tombs as architectural phenomena have also attracted attention and the size, construction quality, energy expenditure and labour input have been discussed.[27] Wright has pointed out the possibilities of analysing burial facilities and proposed that a possible method is to measure the effort expended on the preparation of an individual burial.[28] The possibility of employing a method based on measures of labour and energy expenditure has more recently been discussed also by Voutsaki who argues against the usefulness of such a method in a prehistoric and premonetary society As we saw above, her study does not question the importance of the tholos as a symbol of power and prestige.[29]

In addition to the above, tombs have also attracted attention as expressions of spatial phenomena. Several studies have analysed their locations in the prehistoric landscape and it has been proposed that the clustering of tombs reflect social groups.[30] Furthermore, the monumental appearance of the tholoi and their spatial separation from chamber tombs has been interpreted as an expression of the higher status of the leaders buried in them. Wells interpreted the tholos as a territorial marker and symbol, which manifested the ownership of the land. The leaders in such a society are regarded as having been symbols of stability and continuity, but they also needed to legitimise their power and status through burial type.[31] Also according to Wright, the locations of tholoi are a conscious action and important in the strategy of symbolising power. The tombs at Mycenae were purposely placed to be viewed together with other monuments constructed of the same masonry at the same time; these monuments included the Lion Gate, the bridge and other outstanding constructions.[32] The tholos as a symbol of royal propaganda has also been discussed by Santillo Frizell in several articles.[33] Cavanagh and Mee have analysed the geographical clustering and distribution of tombs, but, as will be detailed later, they present a somewhat different pattern.[34]

As pointed out earlier, work in the area has predominantly been empirical in character, measuring both the quantity and the diversity of goods found in tomb contexts or employing a more impressionistic and subjective, qualitative method of interpretation. A qualitative approach need not imply lack of stringency, especially if it is used more explicitly, as by Dickinson. He argues that items such as weapons, jewellery and objects of precious or unusual material are indicators of high or special status. He admits that this is an imprecise method but feels that such an approach still has its value.[35] Cavanagh and Mee suggest otherwise and are of the opinion that it is dangerous to associate all burials with possible status symbols. Instead, they test the absence or presence of 46 categories of finds in the chamber tombs from Mycenae, Prosymna and Dendra. The categories include vessels, weapons, jewellery, tools, figurines, furnishing etc. Pottery is, however, omitted altogether as they are of the opinion that it is found so generally in tombs and is therefore unlikely to give any information about rich or poor burials. Chronologically, the analysis includes the periods LH I-LH IIIB, whereas LH IIIC is excluded. The results of their analysis indicated four clusters, based on the grounds of deposited grave goods, ranging from 1 to 4, which should be understood as a continuum from richest to poorest. The analysis shows that the three settlements are represented in all clusters, except in the fourth, in which there are no tombs from Dendra. It is also worthy of note that the clusters are not chronologically homogeneous, as tombs from all periods are found in each group. An interesting consideration is that it seems that there is no proof of the assumption that particular symbols, i.e. objects, were restricted to specific levels in the society. For example, weapons, although rare, were found in group 4, whereas they were less frequent in group 3. Also sealstones, objects which, it has been suggested, were associated with office, are most common in group 2 and even occur in groups 3 and 4.[36]

Four classes were also distinguished in the analysis based on architectural design. The classes based on size do not correspond exactly with those based on artefacts, but it can be seen that there is a high degree of

[27] Santillo Frizell 1997-1998; 1998; Wright 1987.
[28] Wright 1987, 172-174.
[29] Voutsaki 1992, 6.2.2, 7.6.1; 1995a, 56, 62-63.
[30] Blegen 1937, 231.
[31] Wells 1990, 128.
[32] Wright 1987, 180-184.
[33] Santillo Frizell 1997-1998; 1998.
[34] Cavanagh & Mee 1990, 58-63.
[35] Dickinson 1983, 56.
[36] Cavanagh & Mee 1990.

correspondence between the results of the two cluster analyses.[37] The analyses based on attributes and on geographical groups show that the chamber tombs at Mycenae and Prosymna are randomly scattered across the landscape. Their locations can be explained neither by reference to a horizontal, chronological stratigraphy nor to a distribution based on wealth and social status. Distribution maps show that social status did not coincide with the locations of the tombs, as, for example rich tombs are not invariably located close to the acropolis, with the poorer tombs at a distance. Nor does there seem to have been any correlation between date and distribution, as it can be demonstrated that early burials were located on the periphery of the cemetery. The analysis also provides evidence to the effect that each cluster comprises tombs of differing sizes, wealth and dates. In conclusion it is asserted that the location of tombs was not determined by status. Instead, Mee and Cavanagh propose that status was reflected by the sizes and contents of tombs, not by a distinctive type of tomb.[38]

Another analysis, by Voutsaki, similarly takes as its point of departure an attempt to measure the diversity of grave goods; also this study is based on the absence or presence of goods in tombs. The diversity index contained in her analysis lists 106 categories of valuable goods, classified by material, function and degree of elaboration. But also here pottery is excluded as a useful category. Chronologically, the study is extended to include the LH IIIC period, although no tables or figures for that specific period are available. The study encompasses all Argive settlements represented by tomb material and in this respect it differs from the study conducted by Cavanagh and Mee.[39] The results obtained by Voutsaki correspond quite well to the results of Cavanagh and Mee. Also Voutsaki notices a concentration of rich tombs to the earlier periods. The tholoi represented at several sites in the LH IIA period are interpreted as a tomb type more or less replacing the shaft graves. She postulates an overall increase in the deposition of wealth during the LH II period, with Mycenae retaining its pre-eminence, but other settlements are also emerging, with tholoi and rich chamber tombs represented also at Prosymna, Berbati and Dendra and at peripheral sites, such as Kokla and Kazarma. The increase continues in the following period, LH IIB, also with an obvious clustering of cist and pit tombs in the poorest categories. Wealth is concentrated to Mycenae, possibly with several tholoi in use, but rich chamber tombs now appear in Prosymna, Dendra, Asine and Argos. In LH IIIA1 the number of richer tombs remains quite stable, but also Voutsaki notes the increase in the number of poorer tombs. Rich chamber tombs are still found at several sites: Mycenae, Prosymna, Dendra and Asine. In LH IIIA2, there is an increase in the number of poorer tombs and stability in the number of richer tombs, and the dramatic abandonment of tholoi in use as the tomb type is now restricted to Mycenae, Dendra and perhaps Tiryns. The phenomenon with a trend towards an increase in the number of poorer tombs continues in the LH IIIB period. Furthermore, according to Voutsaki, the tholos is represented only at Mycenae and possibly at Tiryns. Generally the period shows a decline except at Mycenae and perhaps Tiryns. There is a decrease in the quality of the chamber tombs and also a decline in the level of wealth deposited in the tombs also for this period. The succeeding LH IIIC period is not analysed in the same detail, as it is outside the scope of the study conducted by Voutsaki. However, she registers a decrease in the level of wealth devoted to the tombs. Several of the larger settlements continue to be in use but are now represented by only a few chamber tombs. The Argos tombs are poor, whereas Asine has fairly rich chamber tombs.[40]

On the bases on this analysis, Voutsaki argues that the LH I period witnessed the rise of Mycenae, possible at the expense of Lerna, Argos and Asine, and an attendant re-organisation of the political landscape. In the subsequent period, LH II, the spread of the tholos is observed, as is the existence of rich chamber tombs. Voutsaki is not convinced, however, that there was a political centralisation towards Mycenae during these periods. Instead, she interprets the mortuary display as an important strategy of social and political competition between local elites who were still resisting the rise of Mycenae. During the following period, LH IIIA, the restriction of tholoi to the palatial centres, the impoverishment of the chamber tombs and the decline of simpler graves are significant. As has been mentioned earlier, Voutsaki interprets this information as the emergence of a stricter hierarchical order and the appearance of rigid classes. The process of concentration continued in the LH IIIB period and the mortuary display was concentrated to the palace élites. Owing to the fact that this was restricted to the palaces, the power and independence of the local leaders was limited. As we have already seen, despite these occurrences, Voutsaki argues that the mortuary data allow her to conclude that there existed a centralised, palatial system with wealth and labour channelled exclusively towards these centres and that the mortuary display played an important part in this process.[41]

6.5 PROBLEMS CONCERNING DEFINITION OF WEALTH AND STATUS

As confirmed both by anthropological and archaeological studies, it is obvious that there need not

[37] Cavanagh 1987, 163-169; Cavanagh & Mee 1990, 57; Mee & Cavanagh 1990, 233.

[38] Cavanagh & Mee 1990, 58-59, figs. 2-3; Mee & Cavanagh 1984, 56.

[39] Voutsaki 1992. 6.2.2; 1995a, 55-57.

[40] Voutsaki 1992, 7.5.3; 1995a; 1998.

[41] Voutsaki 1995a, 61-63.

be a correlation between the status of the deceased and the social position or wealth of the person when alive. It might, for example, have been of importance for the relatives to display wealth in death, and there are also examples when the paucity of burial goods need not imply low level of material wealth.[42] Anthropological research reveals that secondary burial ceremonies may have several functions. They may be important as a manifestation of conspicuous consumption, but also the communal symbolic meaning of the tombs may be the most important aspect. For example, to Merina, Madagascar, it is important to stress the link between the family and the land, and the regrouping of people and the land leads to fertility and power for the whole group. Obviously the most important duty is to ensure that the members of the group are together in the tombs.[43] I would suggest that the socio-economic aspect of secondary burial was of importance also in Late Helladic society. The display of wealth in connection with the burial ceremonies was important for the family, in order to ensure their status in the community. I would not exclude the importance of ceremonies performed in connection with the burial and reburial. As shown in ethnographic evidence such rituals have seldom left any traces,[44] perhaps only pottery sherds. The absence of deposits of goods in the LH IIIB period may indicate that such rituals were used as manifestations of status.

The survey of previous studies that discussed status clearly shows the difficulties involved in working with prehistoric data, when our knowledge has to be based on often fragmentary material remains. Much of these discussions have been concentrated on tombs as indicators of status and wealth. The concepts are not easy to define and in the following study, the earlier presented concept and definition of prestige goods, as indicators of socio-economic status will be used. It is here proposed that even if it is difficult or perhaps even impossible, to estimate the value of objects the presence of foreign goods and objects of high technical quality is an indicator of the wealth and perhaps status. Furthermore, the discrepancy in the burial remains will be emphasised and it is hypothesised, in line with other scholars, that the individual chamber tombs exhibit individual status. But this is defined not only as the status of the person buried, but also as the status of the family lineage. The assumption is based on the analysis of skeletons, which supports the conclusion that families were reunited in death, and it is believed, and has also been proposed by others, that the question of descent was important to the Mycenaeans.[45] As has been pointed out by, for example, Voutsaki, there are problems in attaching particular grave goods to individuals and the status of the specific individual buried will therefore not be discussed in detail. The possibility of discussing burial groups has also extended to the chamber tombs at Asine and it is generally agreed that it is difficult to isolate individual groups, owing to disturbances of the material. Despite these problems, an attempt will be made, using the material from Asine, to discuss isolated groups of objects, and their possible value in illuminating different periods will be tested. Tomb variation will be tested as a possible variable in discussing the socio-economic status and wealth of the individual settlement later expanded to a comparison with the tomb material from other settlements on the Argive Plain.

Any survey of the existing tomb material represented on the Argive Plain during the Late Helladic period, such as that reported in this study, would do well to emulate at least parts of previous studies. The analysis of wealth in the tomb context will partly be based on the analyses already presented by Mee and Cavanagh and Voutsaki. It is conceivable that a study of the absence or presence of different categories will be of interest in even a small tomb context, such as Asine. Important are also the wealth groups defined for Mycenae, Prosymna and Dendra as they will be used in the following discussion concerning tombs as exponents not only of individual status, but also the prevailing exchange systems.

Beside the categories used by Cavanagh and Mee, the present study will also include pottery, as it is believed that its significance is of importance. We have, for example, imported goods, decorated pottery – although, as has been recently stated, the amount of undecorated pottery is comparatively larger – and also the tinned vessels deposited in chamber tombs. As we already have the analyses made by Cavanagh and Mee and Voutsaki, the following discussion will be based on the general absence or presence, of different categories of finds.

It is important to establish such characteristics as status and wealth. But there is also a need to find a method that will help to uncover how economic transactions may have been organised. A study by W.E. Precourt presents a way forward here.[46] Precourt devised a model in which the relationship between mortuary practices and the predominant modes of transaction was tested. The study focused on the disposal of the deceased's movable property as a possible indicator of the predominant mode, or modes, of economic transaction. He holds in the article that the pattern differs between societies with a predominantly reciprocal mode of transaction and those with a predominantly redistributive or market mode of transaction. It should be noted, however, as does Precourt and as is also emphasised in this study, that the predominance of one mode of transactional does not exclude the existence of other modes. Yet, following Precourt, the two modes of transaction display different

[42] Ucko 1969, 265-268; Hodder 1982, 152.

[43] Bloch 1981, 137-147; Miles 1965, 168.

[44] Ucko 1969, 267-268.

[45] Cavanagh & Mee 1998, 131; Voutsaki 1995a, 60, 62; 1998, 47.

[46] Precourt 1984.

patterns in the social system. A predominantly reciprocal society has a social system emphasising symmetry. That implies a society with little distinction between its members, except differences based on age and sex. Concentration of wealth is not to be excluded, but it is not institutionalised.

This is in contradistinction to the non-reciprocal society (redistributive or market mode of transaction), which is characterised by an unequal distribution of wealth. Economic inequality is prominent and wealth concentration is institutionalised.[47] The definitions follow the ideas of Polanyi, who defined reciprocity and redistribution by the two concepts of symmetry and centricity. Reciprocity is defined by the pattern of symmetry, whereas the institutional pattern of centricity is to be associated with the provision for storage and redistribution of both goods and services and the collection and organisation are mainly administered by a central authority.[48] The concept of asymmetry, here defined as a pattern of predominantly non-reciprocal transactions, that is, redistribution or market exchange, where the distribution of wealth is unequal among the members of the society, will be used as a opposite to the pattern of symmetry. These concepts have recently been used by also Voutsaki in her study on Late Helladic tombs. She defined the pattern of wealth, prevailing in LH II, as more even compared to the previous period. A noticeable change is observed in the LH IIIA period, as the distribution of wealth became more asymmetrical. The change, according to Voutsaki, was the result of an increase in the number of poorer chamber tombs and a decline in the number of tholoi, as they were restricted to the palace sites. The pattern of asymmetry was then accentuated during the LH IIIB period, as no tholoi were in use outside Mycenae and Tiryns and, according to her, no rich chamber tombs were used outside Mycenae.[49]

The results presented by Voutsaki are interesting. In the following analysis, I shall therefore test whether the material remains from the Late Helladic chamber tombs can possibly be used as indicators of wealth and status and verify the commonly accepted view of Mycenaean society as predominantly redistributive or whether the pattern emerging can be interpreted in other ways. The discussion on the possibility of tracing the relationship between mortuary practices and the predominant mode of economic transaction will be based on published empirical evidence from the tombs of Asine and the published tomb material from other Argive settlements. Furthermore, the wealth-group analyses presented by Cavanagh and Mee and in the study by Voutsaki will be used as the point of departure for the discussion. The individual Late Helladic periods and the chamber tombs in use will be discussed in more detail and here I accept the proposal by Cavanagh and Mee that status is reflected by the sizes and contents of tombs and not by a distinctive type of tomb.[50] Their analyses and division of tombs into different wealth groups will therefore constitute an important background for the following discussion. The interpretation of the tholos as a symbol of status is accepted, but it is here argued that the essential symbolic meaning was restricted to the ceremonials conducted before, or at the time of the burial. It is believed that the significance of the tholos as a symbolic marker in the landscape faded with time as it was not visible after the tomb was closed and covered.

The obstacles

The general picture of the tomb material on the Argive Plain during the Late Helladic period is various and uncomfortably dependent on hitherto published material. The following study will focus in more detail on the chamber tomb material as a category. The tholos in the Late Helladic landscape has been of importance in earlier presented studies and may not be excluded in a study concerning wealth and status. The tomb type will, however, not be presented in detail as the tholoi on the Argive Plain are well known and studied and the earlier presented results will therefore be used in the following study. In this study is therefore no detailed study of the content of tholoi presented, but the tomb type will be used as an important architectural category in the following discussion.

One of the main problems associated with tomb remains is the dating and this is the case especially with the tholos tomb, as the material evidence is often very poor, owing to earlier disturbances of the tombs. That the dating of individual tholoi is uncertain may be exemplified by the tholoi at Prosymna, Tiryns and Mycenae, where especially the Tomb of the Genii, the Tomb of Clytaemnestra and the Treasury of Atreus seem to be difficult to date with any degree of precision. At seven settlements from the Late Helladic period have, so far, one or several tholoi been found: Mycenae, Prosymna, Berbati, Dendra, Tiryns, Kazarma and Kokla.[51] The tholos as a burial type has been much discussed, not only due to its significance in the prehistoric landscape, but also concerning the date of construction and use. Especially tholoi at Mycenae have since their discovery been studied in considerable detail and it is obvious that a more precise dating than that already achieved is difficult to arrive at.[52]

The first tholoi in the Argolid seem to have been constructed at Mycenae, Kazarma, Kokla and Prosymna

[47] Precourt 1984, 163.

[48] Halperin 1994, 95-97; Polanyi, 1944 (1957), 48-49, 51-52.

[49] Voutsaki 1998, 48.

[50] Cavanagh & Mee 1990, 58-59, figs. 2-3; Mee & Cavanagh 1984, 56.

[51] As for the tholoi in the Argolid, I have accepted the datings presented by Demakopoulou 1990b; Mylonas 1966a; Pelon 1976; Santillo Frizell 1984.

[52] Wace 1921-1923, 283-402.

during the LH II period.[53] Mycenae held a dominating position, with six tholoi dated as belonging to this period. Prosymna is of interest as here was not only a tholos, but also larger number of chamber tombs in parallel use.[54] The pattern of distribution changed during the early LH III period as the tomb type ceased to be in use at Prosymna and Kazarma. At Mycenae was a dramatic decrease of the number of tholoi in use observed. Probably the previously used tombs at Mycenae were all abandoned and replaced by a new tholos, the Tomb of the Genii, in use during the LH IIIA1 period. The tholos at Kokla was still in use during the LH IIIA1 period.[55] Tholoi were also represented at Berbati and Dendra during the LH IIIA1 period.[56] The LH IIIA2 period do not show evidence of tholoi at any site. Finally, the following period LH IIIB is characterised by change in the distribution of tombs. The tholos was in use at Mycenae, Treasury of Atreus middle of 1250 B.C. (beginning of LH IIIB2), and Tomb of Clytaemnestra probably somewhat later in LH IIIB2.[57] At Tiryns possibly two were used.[58]

Unlike the tholos material, chamber tombs are often better preserved and as stated by Alden, are probably therefore also better represented in numerical terms.[59] Cavanagh and Mee rightly point out the imbalance in the samples and also the lack of excavation reports.[60] Nevertheless, it is of importance to keep in mind that, as is the case with other categories of archaeological material, we do not know the total number of tombs. We are therefore dealing with a wide range of publications representing those well published, but unfortunately also those in the opposite case, in which excavation reports describe only a minor part of all the chamber tombs reported to have been found.[61]

Large chamber tomb cemeteries have been excavated or reported at Mycenae, Prosymna, Tiryns and Berbati,[62] Asine,[63] Argos, Nauplion and recently also Kokla.[64]

But at several of these sites only a small part of the tombs has been excavated and published. For example, at Dendra only fourteen or fifteen were reported and excavated, which seems very few for a settlement with a tholos tomb and large architectural remains.[65] The second problem of importance is the problem to associate specific finds to specific burials. It is not unusual that the find context in a tomb is highly disturbed owing to looting, but also owing to secondary burial ceremonials. The problem created by the disturbances is the difficulty of associating finds with pottery and therefore getting a more exact dating of other find categories, and also burial groups. Of course objects may have been used s heirlooms but still a more precise dating of, for example exotic trade items and other valuable goods would, of course, be of interest in discussing the socio-economic status of tombs in different periods.

The third category represented by simpler graves has attracted less attention, most probably on account of the fact that they have not been exposed in a similar way to the other categories of tombs. These tombs seem to have been treated as quite marginal until the studies presented by amongst others Dickinson and Lewartowski.[66] According to Dickinson, cist and pit graves for adult interments are relatively rare after LH II, whereas we find children buried in these tombs. They can be located to chamber tombs and tholos tombs, or in their dromoi, but are not found as cemeteries consisting entirely of cist and pit tombs.[67] A noticeable change in the frequency seems to take place during the LH IIIC period as these tombs are now more frequently found. The purpose of the following discussion is not to present a survey of cist and pit tombs in the Argolid, but to register the presence of child burials.

[53] Pelon 1976, 482-483.
[54] Alden 1981, 322.
[55] Demakopoulou 1990b, 113. LH IIB-LH IIIA1.
[56] Pelon 1976, 482-483; Santillo Frizell 1984, 32; Schallin 1996, 167, fig. 32.
[57] Mylonas 1966a, 122-123; Pelon 1976, 482- 483; Wace 1921-1923 for finds, 353-357, 363-374.
[58] Dragendorff 1913, 347-345; Janzen 1975, 213; Müller 1930, 18; Müller 1975, 4. Traces of a second tholos have been found, but unfortunately all information seems to have been lost during the Second World War.
[59] Alden 1981, 7.
[60] Cavanagh & Mee 1990, 56.
[61] Alden 1981, 122.
[62] Alden 1981, 230, 280.
[63] Frödin & Persson 1938, 151-192. For chamber tomb I:1 see, Gillis 1996; Hughes-Brock 1996; Mountjoy 1996. Some chamber tombs were relocated during the 1970s but have not been published.
[64] Alden 1981, 295-299; Demakopoulou 1993, 57-75.
[65] Alden 1981, 266.
[66] Dickinson 1983; Lewartowski 1995.
[67] Dickinson 1983, 62.

CHAPTER 7
THE CHAMBER TOMBS: THE CASE OF ASINE

7.1 INTRODUCTION

The excavations conducted during the 1920s located two chamber-tomb cemeteries and approximately 50 tombs were discovered, but unfortunately only a very limited number of these tombs have, so far, been excavated.[1] There are also reports that additional finds of chamber tombs were made during the 1970s.[2] The lack of published material in the case of Asine constitutes a serious restriction and the hitherto published chamber tombs and simpler graves make up the rather limited empirical material at my disposal for use here.

A mere eight of the chamber tombs at Asine have in fact been published. The 1938 publication, *Asine, results of the Swedish excavations 1922-1930*, by Frödin and Persson is very detailed and follows quite carefully the reports in the diaries. Objects excavated have been documented on photographs of good quality. The diaries describe in detail the excavations of most tombs and especially the bone material is well documented, with even smalle bones noted. Regrettably, this is not true for all categories of finds. For instance, a complete documentation of the pottery and other objects is often missing. Still more serious are the circumstances that surround the documentation of chamber tomb I:1. The tomb was primarily excavated in 1922, but the diaries contain no documentation at all of this work; indeed, the tomb is only mentioned briefly in *Diary* no. 2 from 1924, where the final work in the second dromos is recorded. Fortunately, recent work on the pottery material and the small finds that accrued from this particular tomb has, now that it has been published by more recent generations of archaeologists, added considerably to our knowledge of the site.[3]

Most of the tombs have detailed original plans that for the most part, but not invariably, indicate the find spots of whole vessels and also other objects found in the chamber tombs. An exception is the plan of chamber tomb I:2, as even though the finds from this tomb are amply documented by Frödin and Persson, the recording does not include information of objects found. No original plan of chamber tomb I:4 has been found. Most of the excavation plans have notes on measurements of find spots and find levels, although a systematic comparison with the diaries is in most cases impossible, as we very seldom have information concerning small finds and their find levels. In *Diary* 6, in which the excavation of chamber tomb I:7, is documented, the abbreviation "ö.g." (*över golvet*, that is, above the floor) is simply used. As concerns the other tombs, it is assumed in this study that, if nothing else is specified, the levels are measured from the floor level. For reasons of a poor state of preservation, it has not been possible to include copies of the original plans here.[4]

As will become apparent in the detailed analysis of the respective tombs, there are some lacunae and question marks as concerns the recording of finds. One of the main problems is the difficulty of reading the notes, but, generally speaking we have to be satisfied with the documentation preserved. We have to remember that not only the archaeological methods used but also the technology was of a different standard, compared with today. In fact, it is rather amazing that the field documentation is of such a high standard. A more serious problem, not least from the point of view of representativity, is that the tomb material from Asine is, of course, not very reliable, owing to the small amount of tombs published. This caveat aside, it is believed that a reasoned assessment of the available material will be of considerable help in trying to reconstruct the socio-economic situation at this settlement during the Late Bronze Age.

Some of the vases found in the tombs are today stored in the Museum at Nauplion and the Medelhavsmuseet in Stockholm and can therefore be studied in more detail. Most of the dating of the pottery has been based on the analyses made by Furumark[5] and Mountjoy,[6] but my own observations of the preserved objects will add something to the assessments made in the following pages.

The common complaint by archaeologists that it is difficult to associate a certain individual buried with certain objects is also valid in the case of the chamber-tomb material from Asine. The diaries and Frödin and Persson reveal that the tombs had been disturbed, owing to reburials, collapsed ceilings and perhaps for other reasons. It is therefore frequently the case that is not possible to establish a correlation between bone material

---

[1] Frödin & Persson 1938.
[2] Gillis 1996, 93.
[3] Hughes-Brock 1996, 69-80; Montjoy 1996, 47-67.
[4] The original plans are stored at the University of Uppsala.
[5] Furumark 1944; 1972a; 1972b, 1992.
[6] Mountjoy 1986; 1996.

and other finds in any obvious fashion. However, in those cases in which we have information on find levels and similar information the possibility of distinguishing burial groups will be discussed. Such a scenario will allow us to discuss with some confidence the status of a specific period.

A hypothesis presented here and applied to the analysis of the tomb contents is the specific and important meaning of objects deposited in tombs already at an early stage and later re-arrangement, as new burials took place. I assume that rich finds deposited in an earlier period need not have lost their value as symbols of status and wealth even when used in later burial contexts.[7] This assumption argues the importance of the lineage in the Late Helladic, further emphasised by the fact that also women and children, and, as it seems even infants, were buried in chamber tombs.[8]

In the following study, each tomb will presented with a short catalogue showing periods of use and find categories. Then follows a detailed analysis of the tomb contents, in which objects and skeletal remains are discussed. Detailed information concerning the vessels referred to will be found in Frödin and Persson. Although very difficult owing to the disturbed character of tombs the possibility of discerning burial groups within the frameworks of the known material will also be examined. Each analysis will discuss the grave finds in a holistic perspective and assess their possible value as symbols of the status of those buried and their possible economic significance.

7.2 CHAMBER TOMB I:1

Introduction

Diary: No. 2, 1924. The excavation started in 1922, but no diary from this part of it is known.
Original plan: Yes.
Silhouette: Irregularly rounded chamber with two niches and two dromoi.

Table 7.1: Chamber tomb I:1, finds by period of use

Periods of use	Number of vessels
LH IIB	3
LH IIIA1	16 (12 tinned)
LH IIIA2	24 (18 tinned)
LH IIIB	1 (1 tinned)
LH IIIC:M/L	10/14
Submycenaean/ Protogeometric	1/1

Pottery:[9] Total number 80; dated 70, decorated 45, undecorated 35, tinned 33 (2 undated).[10]
Other find categories: Metals: gold, tin, silver, bronze, lead, iron; amber; ivory; faience; steatite; wild boar's tusk; clay
Finds:[11] Fragment of silver vase, 2 gold rings, 1 toggle pin, pin head, beads, pendants, rosettes, leaves), amber beads, iron ring, faience beads, gems and one amulet of semi-precious stones, steatite buttons, ivory: pin, small column, fragment of large rosette, triangle, pieces of bone and boar's tusks.
Skeletal remains: Yes.

Analysis

The pottery found in the tomb indicates continuity of use from LH IIB to the Protogeometric period, except for the LH IIIC Early period to which no vessels can be assigned. The use of the tomb in the LH IIIB period is suggested only by one tinned vessel and the tomb follows the pattern that can be detected at other chamber-tomb cemeteries. The pottery found is concentrated to the LH IIIA1/2 periods and the Middle and Late LH IIIC periods.

The excavators identified three burial groups.[12] The proposed groupings were later discussed also by Furumark who isolated a penultimate burial belonging to the LH IIIC Middle period.[13] Later the tomb was also discussed by others. Cavanagh and Mee discussed in an article the re-use of tombs in LH IIIC and Mountjoy has analysed not only the pottery, but also the burial groups and the use of the tomb.[14]

Unfortunately, we have no more detailed information concerning the excavation of the tomb in 1922, and the *Diary* no. 2 from 1924 gives only very brief information, mostly about the excavation in the second dromos. But we have the original excavation plan, in which miscellaneous finds and also some whole vessels are plotted on the grid and listed square by square.[15] Moreover, the original plan records some vessels not drawn on the plan in Frödin and Persson. These are in square A1: 1 stirrup jar, A2: 1 bowl, A5: 1 bowl, 1 stirrup jar, B1: 1 kylix, B3: 1 stirrup jar, X2: 1 stirrup jar, X4: 1 bowl. As concerns other objects found in the tomb, the documentation is detailed although sometimes difficult to read. Obviously objects are mentioned on the plan, but not in Frödin and Persson, such as rod-like objects, a "bronsknif" (bronze knife?) etc.[16] The tomb was

[7] I would like to thank Dr. C. Gillis for her suggestion that objects may also have been considered as impure and untouchable.
[8] Nordquist 1990, 38.

[9] 75 vases are listed in Frödin & Persson 1938, 4 more vases in Mountjoy 1996, 66. The datings are based on Mountjoy 1996.
[10] Gillis 1991-1992, 26, table 2; 1996, 69.
[11] For detailed accounts of objects other than pottery, Frödin & Persson 1938, 371-377; Hughes-Brock 1996, 71-80.
[12] Frödin & Persson 1938, 377.
[13] Furumark 1944, 210.
[14] Cavanagh & Mee 1978; Mountjoy 1996.
[15] Although, only a small part of those vases is listed in Frödin & Persson 1938.
[16] Hughes-Brock 1996, 69-80.

excavated carefully and on the section drawing in the Asine volume the zero point is marked.[17]

The total amount of pottery from chamber tomb I:1 is large, but both on the plan in Frödin and Persson and on the original excavation plan only a small part is drawn, making the identification of eventual burial groups complicated. Fortunately, other objects are plotted on the original plan and since the find levels are recorded, a discussion of the conceivable relation between other finds and pottery is possible.

On the published plan of the chamber, some vessels, according to the excavators, constitute burial groups. The group composed by vessels nos. 1, 4, 21, 25 and 26 was identified as one of the earliest.[18] The vessels were either smashed or removed into one of the niches on the occasions of later burials or deposited in the niche.[19] A more detailed dating of this pottery shows that only nos. 1, 25 and 26 belong to the LH IIB period, whereas nos. 4 and 21 are later, LH IIIC Middle, respectively LH IIIA2.[20] The vessels are not marked on the original plan and therefore cannot be verified and associated with other finds.

Vessels nos. 29, 30, and 31 were grouped by the excavators in the latest burial. This was later verified by Furumark and, according to him, the vases belonged to the Late LH IIIC period.[21] To this group we may perhaps also add no. 11, an LH IIIC stirrup jar, located close to the other vessels and with a date matching the rest of the group.[22] The cluster of vessels is spread out and covers approximately squares B2 and C2 and parts of B1 and C1. On the original plan is noted in square B1 the finding of a gaming board, probably made of ivory and not mentioned in Frödin and Persson.[23] The last object is regarded as unusual and is dated by Krzyszkowska to the early LH IIIA.[24] The date is interesting as, so far, no evidence of regional production in ivory have been located in the Argolid. Square B2 was empty of other objects than vessels and sherds and the same situation was documented in C1 and C2.

Furumark identified a burial group C, consisting of vessels nos. 3, 33, 34, 36, 12, 19 and 15 (or 10) and probably also 2 and 4.[25] All the vessels belong to the Middle LH IIIC period, except no. 19, which is Late LH IIIC and not located close to the others. Also no. 12 was found a little further away from the assemblage. The published plan and the original excavation plan reveal that the cluster of pottery and the bones covered approximately squares E2-4. Only E2 has a larger number of finds registered on the plan, mostly conical buttons, but also a bead and possibly a pendant, which, according to Hughes-Brock, may be the Egyptian carnelian amulet no. 5.[26] The objects were located in the eastern part of the square and there were no bones or vessels in this corner to be directly associated with them. However, these objects, found at a level of between c. 155 and 175, are on much the same level, c. 160, as the bone material and the pottery documented in E2 and 3. Therefore it is possible that they should be connected with the late burial. But, we may speculate whether the objects may instead be connected with the burial in the southern part of the chamber, close to the wall in squares F2 and 3. This well-preserved skeleton was found on a level of c. 150-160 and on an equivalent distance from the objects. Unfortunately no pottery finds from this part of the chamber are plotted on the original plan, making dating difficult.[27] A cut, semi-precious stone is mentioned in connection with the skeleton and the only such object is registered in square F2 on level 178, i.e. somewhat lower than the bone assemblage. The skeleton is interpreted in the final publication as one of the last burials.[28] If the assemblage of vessels discussed above is associated with the skeleton the date may be plausible.

Furthermore, in square E1, the excavators registered a group composed of several vessels, nos. 23, 27, 7, 52, 53, 55, 56 and 64, as also part of one of the last burials.[29] A more detailed analysis of the pottery dates shows that these vessels are much earlier, as they are all of LH IIIA2 date, except no. 7 which is LH IIIA1. In this group, we may quite surely also include the tinned cup, no. 68 (LH IIIA2) owing to its location in the same cluster of vessels. Moreover, although not exactly at the same find spot or on the same level, the two vessels, nos. 62 and 22, both of LH IIIA2 date, and the tinned vessel no. 71 (LH IIIA1) may possibly, on account of their date be associated with this group. Perhaps the vessels were removed due to some unknown reason. A tinned LH IIIA1 kylix, no. 49, was also located a little further to the north in C1. Vase no. 19 was located close to no. 22 in square D2 but has, owing to its date, been assigned to another burial group, see above. The vessels were spread out in squares D1, D2 and E1 and, according to the original plan, they were found at levels between approximately 159 and 168. In square D1 no grave goods, except the tinned vessel no. 71 were found. D2 was richer in finds and the registered objects include, for example, buttons, a gold rosette and some finds made of silver and also of gold. All the finds in square D2 were plotted on a lower level, ranging between 188 and 205. Square E1 has only three objects registered and, as the original text is difficult to read, it has not been possible to identify them, but the recorded levels are between 183 and 202. In contrast to other parts

[17] Frödin & Persson 1938, fig. 134.
[18] Frödin & Persson 1938, 377.
[19] Frödin & Persson 1938, the former opinion to be connected with Persson, 311, and the latter with Frödin, 166.
[20] Nos: 1, FS 22; 4, FS 59; 21, FS 178; 25, FS 82; 26, FS 82.
[21] Nos: 29, FS 59; 30, FS 137; 31, FS 137.
[22] Frödin & Persson 1938, fig. 135, FS 175.
[23] Hughes-Brock 1996, 70.
[24] Krzyszkowska 1996, 86-88.
[25] Furumark 1944, 210.
[26] Hughes-Brock 1996, 70.
[27] See original plan.
[28] Frödin & Persson 1938, 160.
[29] Frödin & Persson 1938, 377.

of the chamber no bone material has been registered here, either owing to the fact that no bones were found, or because the bone material was too fragmentary to be registered. Also Mountjoy registered the early pottery groups and she regards this assemblage in front of the dromos as mixed LH IIIA1 and LH IIIA2.[30] However, this assumption may be slightly questioned, as the group of pottery is homogeneous, belonging, with the exception of three vessels, to the LH IIIA2 period. I would therefore suggest that this may be a pure LH IIIA2 burial group. The question is whether the other finds should be associated with the pottery and bone assemblage even though they were found on a quite different level? If the pottery is correctly dated, it may be suggested that the other objects found in the same location, but on a lower level, were deposited in connection with the earlier burial and not removed in connection with later ceremonies, either because they were covered by earth and not visible or because that their value as heirlooms was of importance to the next generation to be buried and their relatives.

Another early cluster seems to be formed by the vessel nos. 15, 16, 41, 43, 45 and 65. A more detailed examination shows a mixed chronology as no. 65 is of LH IIB-LH IIIA2 date, no. 41 of LH IIIA1, no. 45 of LH IIIA2 (tinned) and nos. 15 and 16 of LH IIIC Late.[31] These vessels cover approximately squares B3 and B4 and C3 and C4. In squares B3 and B4, there were finds of pottery, a bronze nail, an amber bead and a button. C3 and C4 were more rewarding, as the majority of the vessels and artefacts were precious objects made of amber, amongst other things a disc of amber, gold rosettes, silver fragments, ivory, steatite buttons and also an oval iron object, which according to Hughes-Brock is probably the gold and bronze ring no. 1.[32] The objects found in squares B3 and 4 were found on approximately levels 190 and 205, equivalent to the levels registered for the pottery and the bone material. Earlier vessels moved from their original locations in connection with new burials may perhaps explain the mixed nature of this assemblage. May we even assume that the lack of LH IIIA1 vessels in association with square D2, discussed above, can be explained in terms of LH IIIA1 vases swept away and mixed with this group?

Finally, although void of registered pottery, square D3 had to be mentioned owing to the number of precious finds. On the original plan and on a level between approximately 190 and 205, we find, amongst other things, gold rosettes, bronze, silver and amber.

Chamber tomb I:1 was furnished with two side niches that contained comparatively few bones. The chronology of these niches is difficult to determine, as on the original plan only some sherds are noted.[33] In niche 1, besides some sherds, a bronze buckle and some gold leaf were found, but the bronze buckle is not mentioned in the final publication.[34] Niche 2 was empty of other finds than bones, as on the original plan only one sherd is recorded. The suggestion in the final report that the earliest burials belonging to the LH IIB period may have been deposited in the niches seems plausible. Chamber tombs were often in use for long periods and obviously in connection with new burials the old interments were swept away. I would like to suggest that this is plausible also in this case.

The stratigraphical picture is partly confusing as the LH IIIA assemblages were not found on the same level. A similar situation prevailed for the LH IIIC burial groups. The LH IIIC group in C1-2 is on a level corresponding to the LH IIIA burial in C3-4, approximately at 200 cm. The other LH IIIA assemblage, in squares E1-2 in front of the southern dromos, was found on a higher level like the LH IIIC Middle vessels in E2 and E4, c. 160-170 cm. If the zero point is valid, then the situation may be explained by Mountjoy's suggestion that the layer in front of the southern dromos was increased because of fumigation in LH IIIA.[35] The habit of cleaning and burning inside tombs may also explain why the LH IIIC assemblage was found on a level corresponding to the earlier pottery. Earth, ashes etc. were probably swept aside towards the southern part of the tomb. The sweeping in turn emptied the central part of the chamber. Perhaps this explains why the LH IIIA assemblage in the central part of the chamber, C2-3 and the LH IIIC group, slightly to the left and closer to the northern dromos, are found on the lower level of c. 200.

As is exemplified above the correspondence between the burial groups and the levels is necessarily unclear and it is not always possible to discuss an association between objects and bone material. Hughes-Brock comments on the disorder among the objects and her opinion is that findspots may just occasionally hint at a useful association. She obviously regards the objects as out of context if not found with suitable pottery. An example is the fragment of a amber disc in square C4, which was found in connection with LH IIIA pottery but would probably better harmonise with the earlier material, as these imports are not found after the LH II period.[36] However, as is the case with the objects found in square D3, one may observe that they were recorded on approximately the same level as the finds of pottery, bones and other objects in square C3. Also, the hypothesis that objects may be heirlooms in tombs may explain what seems to be disorder in the tomb. The amber objects found not in connection with LH II pottery but with later pottery, as in squares B3-4, C3-4 and also D3-5 in the central part of the chamber, may exemplify this. If the amber was deposited in the two niches in connection

[30] Mountjoy 1996, 63.
[31] Nos. 15, FS 175; 41, FS 272; 43, FS 265; 45, FS 265.
[32] Hughes-Brock 1996, 70.
[33] Frödin & Persson 1938, 161; Original plan.
[34] Original plan, the bronze buckle is no. III in niche 1.
[35] Mountjoy 1996, 63.
[36] Harding & Hughes-Brock 1974, 156-157; Hughes-Brock 1996, 70.

with the LH II burial(s),[37] should we not expect to find some objects left *in situ*? Probably, as proposed by Persson, the earliest corpses were first deposited in the chamber and later, during a secondary treatment, removed into the niches [38] Amber objects were then deposited in the chamber in connection with the first burial(s). Either the cleaning in connection with a later ceremony did not succeed in sweeping these objects out of the chamber and we therefore find them still in their original location or they were deliberately left as heirlooms.

Another example of a possible heirloom is the Egyptian carnelian amulet found in square E2, where Middle and Late LH IIIC vessels were discovered. The ivory game-board found in square B1 may also be regarded as a heirloom. In the tomb were found two gold/bronze rings that are unusual and these and the seals found may have been deposited already in LH IIB but also a later date is possible as seals made of semi-precious stones seems to have been produced at Mycenae until end of LH IIIB2 or even late as LH IIIC.[39] It is therefore proposed that this treatment of objects in connection with burials may show the importance of the objects as heirlooms in burial contexts. Even if the objects were first placed generations ago, they may still have retained their value for the family now using the tomb. We cannot exclude the possibility that these objects were symbols of status that survived the LH IIIB period. The presence of objects in the "wrong" context may be an indication of the continuity not only between the LH IIIA and LH IIIB periods, but also the LH IIIB and LH IIIC periods.

Chamber tomb I:1 also had some highly interesting, small objects. Several objects made of gold were found and, according to Hughes-Brock, a gold ring, no. 1, lay in the densest cluster of the chamber[40] among mixed pottery dating from LH IIB to LH IIIC Late. Another gold ring, from the northern niche, is probably, like that previously mentioned, of Minoan origin, although the find context indicates an LH II burial Other finds were several fragments of silver, some bronze fragments, ivory, steatite conuli, beads of amber and something labelled "bärnstensbricka" (amber disc/spacer-plate?).[41] According to Hughes-Brock, the presence of amber indicates an earlier date of deposit also for ring no. 1, as amber was not found after LH II.[42] This chronological disorder represented in the context of ring no.1 may indicate a high value for the amber objects. The same family may have owned them for several generations, and kept them in the tomb from the very first burials, dated to LH II, or deposited them with later burials. Also interesting is a gold-plated toggle, no. 3, dated by Hughes-Brock not later than LH IIIA.[43] Parallels have been found at Mycenae, tomb no. 102 and Dendra, tomb no. 12, used in LH II to the LH IIIA1 period.[44] In addition, a toggle made of bone, or ivory, has been found in the settlement context of Asine. Hughes-Brocke has suggested that toggles continued to be produced in a cheaper and perishable material, perhaps couted with paint or gold for the purpose of embellishing the object.[45] A pinhead is also of interest, as it seems to be an exclusive find without any parallels.[46]

As usual, the dates of the metal objects are difficult to determine and at Asine pottery found in association with them represents a wide span of time covering LH IIB to LH IIIC Late.[47] Moreover, it is difficult to reconstruct exchange routes as the sources of different metals are much discussed.[48] Silver is reported to have been found only as small bits or flakes in tomb I:1 and the find context indicates LH IIIA. The date is interesting, as silver finds from LH IIIA have been reported from Kokla. Samples have been analysed and some of them are consistent with the Laurion field and one within the Chalkidiki. According to Z.A. Stos-Gale and C.F. Macdonald, may be expected that lead was a by-product of silver extraction and Laurion is possible as a source.[49] Lead has not been found in any large quantities in tomb I:1, a rivet or clamp was found in the (northern?) niche[50], and may be a piece of lead. The sources of lead ores are much debated. Lead is not found in the Argolid and one of the nearest deposits is Laurion which was probably also the main source for lead-mining during the Late Bronze Age.[51] The results of examinations of samples from Mycenae, Tiryns and Prosymna, the majority dating to LH IIIB and LH IIIC, confirm this picture.[52]

The origin of the raw material for making bronze objects is much discussed, but according to R. Laffineur, it seems plausible on logistical grounds to accept Laurion as the main source as the Argolid is geographically close. This may have been the case during the whole of the Late Bronze Age, although it seems that the eastern sources,

[37] Frödin & Persson 1938, 161. Frödin proposes that the earliest burials took place in the niches.
[38] Frödin & Persson 1938, 377.
[39] Tamvaki 1974, 260, 292.
[40] Hughes-Brock 1996, 70. According to her the "ovalt järnföremål" (oval iron object) mentioned on the original plan is probably the gold and bronze ring no.1, 71.
[41] On the original plan, square C4, nos. XV = amber sheet and XXIII = iron object. Hughes-Brock 1996, 70.
[42] Hughes-Brock 1996, 70.
[43] Hughes-Brock 1966, 71.
[44] Mycenae tomb no. 102, LH IIA; 323 Xenaki-Sakellariou 1985, no. 4916, pl. 139; Dendra tomb no. 12, LH IIB-LH IIIA1, Åström 1977, 12, 18, fig. 4.
[45] Frödin & Persson 1938, 255, fig. 180 the one on the right. Hughes-Brock 1996, 71-72.
[46] Hughes-Brock 1996, 72, no. 4.
[47] Original plan squares C2-C5.
[48] The number of articles dealing with metal sources is enormous and it seems that the discussions are sometimes quite intensive: Gale & Stos-Gale1981, 169-224; Stos-Gale 1982, 467-485; Stos-Gale & Macdonald 1991 249-287.
[49] Stos-Gale & Macdonald 1991, 271-272.
[50] Hughes-Brock 1996, 74.
[51] Mossman 1991-1993, 270.
[52] Stos-Gale & Macdonald 1991, 268-269.

for example, Cyprus, increased in importance.[53] Remains of bronze slag are attested only at Tiryns in the LH IIIB1 period, whereas in LH IIIB2 the remains of production have been found also at Mycenae. We may therefore assume that bronze production was evident on the Argive Plain in the LH IIIB period. The finds of bronze, silver and gold in LH IIIA contexts, see above, are interesting in this perspective as the finds indicate intra-regional contacts when metal was distributed between the Argive settlements or exchange was conducted directly with other regions. Objects made of iron are rare in Late Bronze Age contexts and if the iron fragments, perhaps a ring, are not to be associated with the single Protogeometric vessel, then, as suggested by Hughes-Brock, we indeed have a rarity.[54]

Tin is represented in the tomb. Possible sources have been discussed and Laffineur gives a good summary of the various sources under discussion. Tin is interesting, as it is an excellent example of a long-distance, tradable commodity and no sources are known in the Aegean region. Sources in the Anatolian region have been recorded, but even more interesting are the deposits in Afghanistan as that region is also the most probable source of lapis lazuli and perhaps gold. These observations are of interest, as these exotic and valuable materials are represented in the archaeological context in the Argolid. Other suggested sources are the Iberian Peninsula, Brittany, Cornwall, Tuscany and Sardinia and even north-western Europe, although the latter region probably in more indirect ways.[55] For the time being we do not know the specific geographical origin of the tin represented in the chamber tombs at Asine.[56]

On the original plan a large number of amber objects was registered but not listed in the final publication and the number of items on the plan does not correspond to those mentioned in Frödin and Persson. Most objects were found in the central part of the chamber where there was a jumble of finds. In Frödin and Persson five beads of black, resinous composition are mentioned.[57] A recent analysis has shown that these beads are of Baltic amber and are further evidence on external contacts.[58] The amber finds have earlier been dated to the LH IIIA period, but this has recently been revised and deposition with the earliest burials is suggested.[59] Therefore, the context in which the amber beads were found is interesting, as the Argolid was one of the two main centres for amber in this period, the other being Pylos. The distribution of amber seems to have diminished in LH IIIA/B and the number of pieces decreased.[60] Their chronological context may be logical if we accept the idea suggested by Persson that the earliest burials were carried out in the chamber and later removed to the lateral part of the chamber.[61] The question is why such a large amount of beads and also the fragment of the amber plate/disc were left in their original positions and not removed to the far end of the chamber? The most plausible explanation may be that these were deliberately deposited with the later burials. As has also been suggested by others, I would agree that their foreign origin qualifies them as heirlooms and objects of high status.

The semi-precious stones are interesting, as the motifs indicate contacts with other regions. The Agate (onyx) lentoid, no.1, may have been produced at a workshop near Thebes and no. 2 could have been produced at Thebes or Knossos. Another seal, no. 4, may have originated in India and a carnelian moon amulet may have been an import from Egypt.[62] Glass and faience beads were also found and Hughes-Brock has identified another four beads, apart from the objects listed in Frödin and Persson. The dating of these small objects is difficult owing to the lack of pottery references. A couple of parallels have been found in tombs at Mycenae, but unfortunately the problem of the lack of datable pottery is predominant also here.[63] The material used in these beads is of an exotic origin and the question is whether the glass and faience beads were produced at workshops in the eastern part of the Mediterranean or the raw material was imported to the mainland and workshops of a more local character engaged in the final production? Halstead argues for case for the palatial manufacture of glass, for example, at Mycenae and Thebes.[64] In the case of Mycenae production in LH IIIB2 may perhaps be confirmed in the Artists' Workshop and the Citadel Area.[65] Evidence of jewellery production in LH IIIB1 has been confirmed at Thebes and on the Argive Plain both Midea and Mycenae had jewellery production in the LH IIIB2 period. It may therefore be plausible to suggest contact and exchange outside the Argive region in the periods preceding LH IIIB2, whereas objects produced later were obtained by intra-regional exchange.

Some ivory objects were found and, according to Hughes-Brock, there are no parallels to nos. 1, 2 and 5. She believes that the ivory objects mentioned in Frödin and Persson do not account for all the objects found during the excavations.[66] This assumption is verified as on the original plan objects that are probably made of ivory are listed.

[53] Laffineur 1990-1991, 263-265.
[54] Hughes-Brock 1966, 74.
[55] Laffineur 1990-1991, 265-268.
[56] Personal communication Dr. Gillis.
[57] Frödin & Persson 1938, 376.
[58] Beck 1996, 91.
[59] Hughes-Brock 1996, 70, 78. She also rules out the late burial, LH IIIC.
[60] Harding & Hughes-Brock, 1974, 147-150, table 1.
[61] Frödin & Persson 1938, 377.
[62] Hughes-Brocks 1996, 75-77.
[63] Xenaki-Sakellariou 1985, 69-71, pl. 39.
[64] Halstead 1992a, 63.
[65] Iakovidis 1983, 64.
[66] Hughes-Brock 1996, 77.

Summary

It is proposed here that continuity in tomb context indicates not only the importance of ancestry, but also of those buried in this specific tomb context. An excellent example is chamber tomb I:1, in use for a long period, with its content of exotic and we may assume, valuable goods, left as heirlooms and illustrations of the status of the kin. However, as the objects became dirty and difficult to recognise, their value as heirlooms may have diminished with time. Regional and long-distance/ imported goods show that the tomb belonged to the members of a social group with contacts outside the local sphere. The tomb is represented by highly valuable goods that probably needed considerable labour input and technical skill or were of exotic origin. These objects are therefore assumed to have had a high value and importance for individuals. The large amount of objects of foreign character and of valuable character indicates that the status of those buried was important, and the reason for their prosperity and status could have been the location of the settlement by the coast and close to a fertile plain. As has been pointed out earlier, exclusive objects such as metal artefacts, tin-coated vessels, ivory, amber and so forth, point to a situation in which we may assume that those using the tomb were of the same family.[67] It is also believed that the members of this particular family were highly conscious of the value of these objects, which displayed their worldly status as part of the local élite and their rank in the social hierarchy. The objects deposited are comparable to the tomb contents at other sites and their outstanding quality points not only to external contacts but also the possession of the financial and social means to acquire these objects. It is believed that the position of these kinsmen was important and not only in the local context, their position in the regional social sphere may also have been of significance.

As has been pointed out earlier, we have *lacunae* as concerns grave goods representing the LH IIIB period. Amongst others, Mee and Cavanagh have suggested that changes in tomb content in LH IIIA and LH IIIB may be explained by their use by a new section of society that had previously followed other customs.[68] The observed lack of pottery may be an expression of the change proposed by Cavanagh and Mee. But I would not exclude the possibility that changes in belief patterns may have occurred and the deposit of worldly goods with the dead persons was no longer regarded as important. Also the possibility that objects deposited earlier functioned as heirlooms also in this period cannot be excluded. Furthermore, it is possible that other categories of objects were deposited in the tombs in connection with LH IIIB burials, as several tombs contained beads or seals made of semi-precious stones, gold leaf etc. Another observation, not studied in more detail here, is the presence of idols in LH IIIB contexts; perhaps this was also an expression of change in the belief pattern?[69] The deposit of goods made of perishable materials, such as food and drink should not be forgotten. Finally, I would like to emphasise the importance of ceremonies conducted in connection with the burial or reburial. Rituals may have changed and it should not be excluded that in the LH IIIB period ceremonies were more important than the objects displayed.

The social affiliation of those buried in chamber tomb I:1 has been discussed by Hughes-Brock. She interprets the material as a clear representation of a family of high standing, close relations to those buried in the tholoi. The presence of a bronze arrowhead and the “razor” or “cleaver” has been interpreted as an indication of a warrior burial. It is also of interest to observe the presence of conuli, which were probably garment weights, and the rosettes, which had holes for sewing. These may indicate a woman's garment and therefore a female burial.[70] If so, these objects suggest in turn that women may have been buried in rich chamber tombs, an observation from which we may conclude that women were not only significant in specific social situations, but were also important for the lineage as a symbol of continuity. It is also tempting to read the burial of children and infants in chamber tombs as a symbol for social continuity and the importance of ancestry and heritage. The same kind of pattern has also been recognised and proposed for Middle Helladic society.[71] The significance of the tomb is further emphasised by finds such as rings, seals and jewellery, as they are valuable finds and may have also functioned as heirlooms.[72]

In several articles, C. Gillis has argued that tin-coated vessels should be regarded as indicators of the importance of those buried.[73] Their chronological range is interesting as tin-covered vessels are represented already in the LH IIIA1 period, one in LH IIIB, though the majority belong to the LH IIIA2 period.[74]

Seals are associated with administrative functions connected with palaces and major sites. As they imply status, the findings of seals outside a palace context are interesting. The individuals linked with these finds may be assumed to have had a high status. I would hold that the positions of the individual families reflected the status of the settlement in the regional perspective.

---

[67] Gillis 1991-1992, 4.
[68] Mee & Cavanagh 1990, 234.
[69] Blegen 1937, 255-256, has suggested that idols were deposited in connection with child burials. It would be interesting to study the presence of idols in Late Helladic tomb contexts in more detail.
[70] Hughes-Brock 1996, 70, 73.
[71] Nordquist 1990, 38.
[72] Hughes-Brock 1996, 70; Tamvaki 1974, 292.
[73] Gillis 1996, 93-100. Bibliography for earlier references to tin-coated vessels. I would also like to thank Dr. Gillis for giving me all the information concerning tinned vessels.
[74] For catalogue numbers, Mountjoy 1996, 64-66.

7.3 CHAMBER TOMB I:2

Introduction

Diary: No diary information 1924.
Original plan: Yes.
Silhouette: The largest, excavated tomb. Chamber rectangular with a grave pit close to the north-western wall, gabled vault.

Table 7.2: Chamber tomb I:2, finds by period of use

Periods of use	Number of vessels
LH IIB	2
LH IIIA1	4
LH IIIA2	7
LH IIIB	1 (1 tinned)
LH IIIC:E/M/L	5/1/5

Pottery: Total number 53; dated 24, decorated 21, undecorated 3, tinned 2.[75]
Other find categories: Metals: gold, bronze; ivory; bone; stone: porphyry, steatite, red stone (so-called lapis lacedemonicus);semi-precious stone: alabaster, rock crystal, agate, black stone; amber; glass paste; faience.
Finds: Fragments of stone vessels (one bowl of Egyptian origin), one rhyton with parallels from Crete and from Mycenae. One steatite lamp with decoration similar to lamps found in chamber tomb I:7 and also at Mycenae and Dendra, fragments of three alabaster bowls and the rim of small vase of black stone of the same kind as was found in chamber tomb III at Dendra. Plenty of gold objects were also found, such as rosettes, pendants, beads, discs edged with filigree work, all of with parallels at Dendra. One small bead shaped like a bud, two large pendants representing sprays of papyrus, of the same shape as at Knossos, eight gold mounts for the heads of bronze rivets. four flower-buds, a large quantity of thin shapeless pieces of gold leaf; eight ivory flower-buds, fragments of the lid of a pyxis, the head of a duck or Nile goose, probably of Egyptian origin or influence, ivory staffs, buttons and a large quantity of ivory plaques; one bone pin, ten bone plaques, 18 worked pieces of boar's tusks, horn handle; rosettes, beads, ornaments, flower-buds made of glass paste; three beads made of agate, nine small hemispheres of rock crystal, five beads of amber, one steatite button; one bronze mirror, a large number of arrow-heads, a large quantity of bronze pieces.
Skeletal remains: Yes

Analysis

Continuity in pottery from LH IIB to LH IIIC:L, excepting the LH IIIB period. The published plan of the chamber has not vessels marked on it, as in the case with chamber tomb I:1, but instead the pottery list in Frödin and Persson mentions the squares in which vessels were found. From information provided in the final publication, it has been possible to plot most of the pottery, but it is also obvious that the majority of vessels were found as sherds, spread out over the chamber. Unfortunately, the original plan gives little information concerning pottery, as only vases nos. 16 and 17 are indicated. Neither do we have, as in the case of chamber tomb I:1, small finds plotted square by square on the original plan. According to the excavators pottery had been accumulated and we therefore find a mixture of periods. Also here the deposition of pottery is assumed to have been a consequence of burial ceremonials.

The identification of clusters and possible burial groups is difficult and complicated owing to the large amount of undated pottery. According to the excavators it was possible to identify some clusters, consisting of pottery.[76] They proposed that probably vases nos. 16, 17, 18, 19 and also 7, 10 and 12 belonged to the latest burial, in LH IIIC.[77] Some of the vessels verify this assumption; nos. 16, 17, 18 and 19 are LH IIIC Early, except no. 17, which is LH IIIC Late,[78] whereas, nos. 7, 10 and 12 are all LH IIIA.[79] The group in this part of the chamber may be supplemented by no. 20, LH IIIA2, together with a group of undated vessels. To the earlier burial, some other vessels may perhaps also be associated, no. 4 and probably also nos. 9 and 10, all LH IIB-LH IIIA1 vessels.[80] No measurements of levels, except for vases nos. 16 and 17, are available. But I assume that these burials represented the earlier phase, LH IIB-LH IIIA, and the later, LH IIIC. Another accumulation identified in Frödin and Persson is the pottery in squares B2, 3, C3, 4 and D5.[81] A survey of the pottery listed shows that probably seven vessels were found, nos. 5, 22, 23, 26, 37, 42 and 46. A discussion of the date of this group is complicated as only two vessels, nos. 5 and 37, are dated and both belong to the LH IIIA2 period. Owing to the unclear situation, we must be careful about accepting this as an LH IIIA burial. A third group of vases, nos. 6, 8 and probably also nos. 9, 24, 33, 35 and 40 were deposited in squares D2 and 3 and E2 and E3.[82] Of these it has been possible to date. nos. 6 and 8, LH IIIA, and no. 9 is LH IIB-LH IIIA1, whereas no. 35 belongs to the LH IIIC:L period.[83] The vessels representing the earlier periods may indicate that this was another LH IIB-LH IIIA burial.

[75] Gillis 1996, 96. Tin-coverered sherds from kylix and conical cup, not dated, personal communication from Dr. Gillis.

[76] Cavanagh & Mee 1978, 34; Frödin & Persson 1938, 162-170, 391.

[77] The grid referencies stated for each vessel in Frödin & Persson 1938, 391 do not correspond to those referred to in the find list, 383.

[78] Nos. 16, LH IIIC:L; 17, LH IIIC:L; 18, LH IIIC:E; 19, LH IIIC:E.

[79] Nos. 7, LH IIIA1; 10, LH IIIA1, or LH IIB; 12, LH IIIA2.

[80] Frödin & Persson 1938, 378, 381, figs. 248.1, 249.2, 3. Nos. 4, FS 17; 9, FS 23; 10, FS 23.

[81] Frödin & Persson 1938 391.

[82] Frödin & Persson 1938, 391, where nos. 6 and 8 are mentioned. The other vessels are plotted out according to the pottery list in Frödin & Persson 1938.

[83] Nos. 6, LH IIIA1, FS 19; 8, LH IIIA2, FS 34; 9, LH IIB-LH IIIA1, FS 23; 35, LH IIIC:L, FS 301.

The tomb also contained vessels from the LH IIIC period. A stirrup jar, no. 15 LH IIIC Middle, was found in square G6 and another vase, no. 35, LH IIIC Late, in the centre of the chamber. Of the pottery in the dromos, nos. 50 and 51 have been dated to LH IIIC Early and LH IIIC Late respectively. According to Frödin and Persson vases nos. 11, 15 and 48 inside the stomion were among the latest burial gifts.[84] However, the references are a little confusing as according to the find list no. 11, LH IIIC Middle, was located in the stomion, whereas no. 15 was in square G6. Also no. 48, a tripod cooking vessel, seems to have been found in the chamber.[85] A cluster of LH IIIC Early vessels, nos. 16, 17, 18 and 19, located in squares A3 and 4 probably indicates a later burial. To summarise the observations made, we can identify only a couple of more or less pure groups. With more dated pottery, the situation would be much clearer.

Among the exotic materials found in chamber tomb I:2, two tin-coated vessels have been identified.[86] Several other objects of foreign origin were found and gold, for example, is represented by rosettes, spiral pendants, beads and discs edged with filigree work with parallels found at Dendra. Also, large quantities of gold leaf, flower-buds, mounts for the heads of bronze rivets and two large pendants representing sprays of papyrus were found; according to the excavators a similar shape has been found on Crete.[87] Interesting is also the imported Canaanite jar of LH IIIA date.[88] The ivory objects are highly interesting, as several have no direct comparanda. According to Krzyszkowska, the uniqueness of the objects points to an early date in the LH IIIA1 or LH IIIA2 period. It seems more problematic to detect the place of production as we have no workshop material from the settlement.[89] Whether locally produced or imported the originality of the ivories indicates that that those who ordered them were interested in their unique design and, we may assume, also had the economic means to order them. The ivory material may indicate contacts with either the eastern part of the Mediterranean or settlements on the Argive Plain, although, probably only during LH IIIB workshops were in operation there. Glass paste was also found and two large rosettes were of the same shape as those on a necklace found in the tholos at Dendra, of LH IIIA1 date.[90] Furthermore, large beads with a double Argonaut design were found, as well as beads in the shape of a Mycenaean altar and a large number of other types of beads. Glass was obviously imported from the eastern part of the Mediterranean but in the LH IIIB period was possibly worked at, example, Mycenae and Thebes. Beads of agate have been found which may indicate contacts with Thebes, whereas rock crystal was worked at both Thebes and Mycenae.[91] Also in tomb I:2, some beads of amber have been found, further indicating external contacts or relations with other settlements or individuals in possession of these exotic items. Only one steatite button has been found. Amongst the bronze items listed, there are one mirror and a large number of arrow-heads. Obviously, also a large quantity of shapeless pieces of bronze was found.[92]

Summary

This tomb is without doubt compatible with chamber tomb I:1. Vessels of high quality and exotic origin were found here, for example, a bowl made of porphyry probably of Egyptian origin. Furthermore, there was a rhyton, obviously a quite exclusive object, and a lamp of steatite, parallels to which have been found in the Argolid, but we may suspect that the origin of these lamps was Crete. A three-handled jar, no. 4, of so-called Palace style also indicates early external contacts. The tomb was in use for a long period, as was the case with chamber tomb I:1.

The large number of arrowheads, the bronze mirror, the ivory objects, the semi-precious stones and the gold objects indicate the high status of both the individuals and the family in the LH IIIA period. Although there is no evidence of use in LH IIIB, it is proposed that some of the valuable items deposited in the tomb were later regarded as heirlooms. The tomb was in use in the LH IIIC period and I would like to suggest that it was the same family who used the tomb for the entire period. The importance of lineage and continuity is further strengthened by the presence of a woman buried in a pit. The use of a single tomb for such a long time may also have been important as a status symbol. The large number of objects made of exotic materials indicates that those who used the tomb had the contacts and economic means to acquire these objects. The importance of lineage and continuity is strengthened by the burial of a woman.

7.4 CHAMBER TOMB I:3

Introduction

Diary: No. 6, 1924-26.
Original plan: Yes.
Silhouette: The irregular chamber is set slightly obliquely in relation to the dromos. There is a niche in the dromos.

Table 7.3: Chamber tomb I:3, finds by period of use

Periods of use	Number of vessels
LH IIIA1	3

Pottery: Total number 3; dated 3, decorated 2, undecorated 1.

[84] Frödin & Persson 1938, 391.
[85] Frödin & Persson 1938, 378-391.
[86] Gillis 1996, 93-100.
[87] Frödin & Persson 1938, 386-391.
[88] Åkerström 1975, 185.
[89] Frödin & Persson 1938, 88; Krzyszkowska 1996.
[90] Persson 1931, 40.
[91] Halstead 1992a, 63.
[92] Frödin & Persson 1938, 389-390.

Other find categories; Clay; glass.
Finds: LH sherds. 1 glass bead.
Skeletal remains: Yes.

Analysis

Probably the tomb was in use for only a short period. Very decayed bones and three LH IIIA1 vases were found in the niche. In the dromos and the doorway were found some Late Geometric sherds. The poor status of this tomb is further emphasised by the only other reported object, a glass bead found with the three vases. According to the excavators the chamber was probably not robbed, as, if it had, traces of less valuable finds would have been left. They propose that the burial found in the niche may have taken place in the chamber, but later removed to the niche. Probably the tomb was not re-used owing to the bad condition of the chamber construction.[93]

Summary

We may conclude that this tomb was not one of the richest at Asine. The tomb contained only three vases, some sherds and one glass-bead. Although poorly equipped, the bead may be a symbol or a heirloom of the person(s) buried. With the acceptance of chamber tombs as burial grounds for the family and the lineage we may assume that this tomb belonged to a small family group. After LH IIIA1, they either moved their burials to another tomb, or the family ceased to exist after this period.

7.5 CHAMBER TOMB I:4

Introduction

Diary:No. 6, 1924-26.
Oroginal plan: None.
Silhouette: No chamber was cut. Dromos with two niches.

Table 7.4: Chamber tomb I:4, finds by period of use

Periods of use	Number of vessels
LH IIIC:M/L	1

Pottery: Total 1. Decorated 1.
Other find categories: Clay.
Finds: One vessel.
Skeletal remains: Yes.

Analysis

The tomb was in use in the latter part of the LH period as indicated by the single stirrup jar from the LH IIIC Middle or Late period. The diary mentions that quite a lot of Mycenaean sherds were found, but unfortunately the material seems to have been lost. The tomb was empty of other finds categories.

Summary

Probably the tomb was used only in the LH IIIC period as attested by the single vessel. Furthermore, only three poorly preserved bones were registered indicating one burial event.

7.6 CHAMBER TOMB I:5

Introduction

Diary: No. 6, 1924-26.
Original plan: Yes.
Silhouette: Dromos with niche. Symmetrical chamber.

Table 7.5: Chamber tomb I:5, finds by period of use

Periods of use	Number of vessels
LH IIIA2	1+8 (bronze)
LH IIIC:E/M/L	3/8/5

Pottery: Total 17; dated 17, decorated 15, undecorated 2.
Other vessels: 8 bronze vessels.
Other find categories: Metals: gold, bronze; glass-paste; ivory; bone.
Finds: Necklace of gold rosettes, necklace of gold and glass-paste, necklace of gold and glass, eight bronze vessels, pottery.
Skeletal remains: Yes.

Analysis

The tomb was in use in LH IIIA2, when also the bronze vessels with their content of three necklaces were deposited. Then followed the usual absence of LH IIIB vessels. The tomb was re-used from LH IIIC Early until the end of the period.

The plans in Frödin and Persson 1938 follow the original drawings, in which the vessels and the eight bronzes are illustrated. The only exception is the stirrup jar no. 6, mentioned in the *Dairy* and on the original drawing but not indicated on the published plan. The descriptive part of Frödin and Persson's work mentions small finds found in the chamber, but these are not listed in the catalogue part. For example, one glass bead, a decorated ivory ornament, a small and crushed gold ring and a decorated ivory ornament.[94] These finds are also registered in the *Diary* no. 6.

The original plan shows that the small, crushed gold ring and an ivory ornament were found in the western part of the chamber and immediately inside the door was found another ivory ornament and a glass bead. All these finds appeared in the same context as the pottery representing different phases of the LH IIIC period. Here were also found plenty of disordered bones which indicate that they may have been subject to re-burials. The disarrangement of the bones is also the reason why we should be careful

[93] Frödin & Persson 1938, 171-173.

[94] Frödin & Persson 1938, 393-400.

about accepting these items as burial goods to be associated with only the LH IIIC pottery and the bones. They may have been deposited earlier and later re-used, owing to their value as heirlooms. In the western part was found an undisturbed skeleton which could also be associated with the LH IIIC pottery.

The eight LH IIIA2 bronze vessels are the most spectacular finds from the tomb. In one of the jugs were found hundreds of beads of gold and glass paste. These necklaces were probably dedicated to the burial in the LH IIIA2 period.

The excavators identified three burials. To number I belonged the bronze vessels and also the vessels nos. 2, 7 and 13. The three clay vases are, however, all of Early and Late LH IIIC date. To burial II belonged vases nos. 1, 3, 4, 8, 9 and 10 and the last burial included vases nos. 5, 6 and 12.[95] All these are also of a mixed LH IIIC character.

Summary

Also this tomb is to be included amongst those without any indication of burials in the LH IIIB period. Here, the preceding LH IIIA2 period and also the LH IIIC period are represented. The finds from the tomb, the bronze vessels, the gold jewellery and the ivory, indicate that this also was a burial place for a family with the financial means to acquire precious goods. The objects show the high status of the persons and the family in the LH IIIA2 period and correspond to the status shown in other tombs. Interesting are the necklaces associated with the LH IIIA2 burial. It is tempting to propose that they may be evidence of a female burial and the importance of the lineage. Also in the case of tomb I:5 we should not exclude the value of the objects as heirlooms in the following periods.

7.7 CHAMBER TOMB I:6

Introduction

Diary: No. 1, 1924.
Original plan: Yes.
Silhouette: In relation to the stomion and dromos and an asymmetrically placed chamber.

Table 7.6: Chamber tomb I:6, finds by period of use

Periods of use	Number of vessels
LH IIIA1	1
LH IIIA2	1
LH IIIC:E/M/L	1/8/4

Pottery: Total 18; dated 15, decorated 17, undecorated 1.
Other find categories: Metal: gold; steatite; glass paste; faience; terracotta.

Finds: Beads of gold, beads of glass paste, pottery, fragments of silver and bronze.[96]
Skeletal remains: Yes.

Analysis

Also this tomb was in use in the LH IIIA1 and LH IIIA2 periods and was re-used in the LH IIIC period. In the final publication 18 vessels are recorded but on the plan only a couple.[97] The original plan and the diary have only nine vases documented. All these vases belong to the LH IIIC period.[98] Of the nine vases mentioned in Frödin and Persson, two belong to the LH IIIA period, two cannot be dated and the rest belong to the LH IIIC period.[99] The original plan is detailed when it comes to bone material and small finds made in the tomb. This is valuable and the publication gives a detailed analysis of the find contexts. The two LH IIIA vases indicate that also this tomb was in use for a long period and this could be confirmed by the distribution of the bones as they seem to have been assembled to form smaller collections.

Again the question is whether the small finds of gold objects, glass beads and so forth were deposited in the tombs in connection with the earlier burials or if they were placed here with the LH IIIC burials. According to the information provided in the diary and the analysis published in the final publication, it seems that the valuable objects were found in connection with bone material and vases interpreted as representing the LH IIIC period. It is interesting that, of those vases listed together with the bone collections, all, except vase nos. 4, 7 and perhaps 11 belong to the LH IIIC Late phase. Nos. 4 and 7 are both LH IIIC Middle material and according to the excavators they should be connected with bone collection I. Altogether five burial groups were identified and they all represent the Middle or Later part of the LH IIIC period.[100]

Summary

As is the case of chamber tomb I:5, the number of vessels from the LH IIIA period is small. In contrast to I:5, the other types of objects are also poor, although the 31 glass-paste beads indicate a necklace. I would like to suggest that the poor finds show that the tomb belonged to a family that was not associated with the local élite. Interesting is the use of the tomb throughout the LH IIIC periods. If we accept the deposits as LH IIIC burial groups we may observe that the more valuable objects

[95] Frödin & Persson 1938, 400.

[96] Frödin & Persson 1938, 181, the fragments of silver and bronze only mentioned in the description, not in the find list.
[97] Frödin & Persson 1938, 400-406.
[98] Nos. 4, LH IIIC:M, FS 175; 7, LH IIIC:M, FS 175; 11, LH IIIC:M/L, FS 175; 14, LH IIC:L, FS291; 15, LH IIIC:L, FS 70; 5, LH IIIC:M, FS 175; 2, LH IIIC:E, FS 43; 12, LH IIIC:L, FS 115; 1, LH IIIC:L, FS 137.
[99] Nos. 3, LH IIIA1, FS 150; 6, LH IIIC:M, FS 175; 8, LH IIIC:M, FS 175; 9, LH IIIC:M, FS 175; 10, LH IIIC:M, FS 175; 13, LH IIIA2, FS 264; 16, LH IIIC:M; nos.17 and 18 not dated.
[100] Frödin & Persson 1938, 182.

were deposited later. The association between the non-pottery objects and the later burials validates the importance of expressing lineage, but it is also possible that the status of the family changed with time. It is tempting to interpret the presence of the small gold beads and the necklace made of glass-paste as indicating the burial of a female member of the family.

7.8 CHAMBER TOMB I:7

Introduction

Diary: No. 6, 1926.
Original plan: Yes.
Silhouette: Dromos and an irregular chamber.

Table 7.7: Chamber tomb I:7, finds by period of use

Periods of use	Number of vessels
LH IIA	5
LH IIB	12 (3 tinned)
LH IIIA1	8
LH IIIA2	9 (5 tinned)
LH IIIB	4
LH IIIC:E/M/L	3/4/5

Pottery: Total 54. Dated 50, decorated 37, undecorated 17, tinned 8.[101]
Other find categories: metals, gold, bronze, lead, tin; ivory; bone; glass-paste; semi-precious stones: amethyst, steatite; clay.
Finds: Two small pieces of gold leaf, five ivory rosettes, fragments of ivory comb, four bone pins, one piece of boar's tusk, 82 beads of glass paste, three amethyst beads, 38 steatite buttons, fragment of bronze mirror, fragment of bronze ring, fragments of bronze nails, piece of bronze, large quantity of lead, large quantity of clay packing, eight tinned vases.
Skeletal remains: Yes.

Analysis

Obviously the tomb was used for a long period, as pottery from as early as LH IIA and LH IIB, followed by LH IIIA1 and LH IIIA2 and the LH IIIB period, was found. The last sequence is the LH IIIC period, in which pottery from the Early, Middle and Late phases is represented. The majority of vessels represent the LH II and LH IIIA periods.

The tomb was carefully excavated and the *Diary* 6 gives information not only on the quality and colour of the soil, but also very detailed data concerning the quality and provenience of the bone material. A third material group carefully recorded is the large quantities of clay packing. It seems that these were parts of wooden boxes or perhaps coffins.[102] Furthermore, the original plan has some interesting notes made in the margins, where the provenience of some of the miscellaneous finds is indicated and also large quantities of bones are recorded. The tomb is well described in the final publication and follows the original plan, as far as concerns the few intact or nearly intact vessels and the larger bones. However, a certain discrepancy in the amount of vessels listed in Frödin and Persson and those plotted on the plan can be recorded. The probable reason is that only a few whole vessels were found, but it was later possible to mend a large amount of sherds.[103] The *Diary*, with its very detailed information on bones and such like is, peculiarly enough, not very informative on other objects. The only objects mentioned in the diary are the so-called silver threads, a bone pin, button(s) and a fragment of a bronze mirror.

This lack of information is partly compensated, as already indicated, by the information provided by the original excavation. But, for some reason, several of the objects in the final publication are not mentioned either in the diary or on the original drawing. For example, the small pieces of gold leaf, the fragments of ivory combs, the piece of boar's tusk, the fragment of a bronze ring, the large quantity of lead in the shape of thick and thin wire and the 82 beads of glass paste are not mentioned. The lack of information on the glass paste beads is perhaps the most surprising, since the amount indicates that they might have formed a necklace. But the omission of the large quantities of lead is also peculiar. The silver finds recorded in the diary and on the original plan may be the lead wires mentioned in the publication. But, contrary to Frödin and Persson's work in which a large quantity of lead wire is mentioned, only two pieces of silver wire are recorded in the diary. Therefore, it is not to be excluded that silver threads were found, but for some unknown reason these were not documented in the final publication. Despite these *lacunae*, the diary and the original plan are valuable as sources of information and make it possible to reconstruct some kind of stratigraphical picture. The measurements are given as "above the floor" in the diary and these numbers are also indicated on the plan. This is a rather vague measuring point and to discuss and compare find levels is rather difficult, especially, as it seems obvious that the tomb was disturbed due to several burials.

Despite these problems the burial groups mentioned in Frödin and Persson will be discussed. According to the publication the last three burial groups were composed by 1) nos. 15, 16 and 20; 2) vases nos. 12, 17 and 19 and 3) vases nos. 6, 7 and 18.[104] If the groups are studied in detail we find that no. 15 is LH IIIC:L and no. 16 is LH IIIC:M, whereas no. 20 is LH IIIC:L. No. 20 was found 35 cm "above the floor", whereas, according to the *Diary*6 , no. 15 was found 50 cm "above the floor". Here it should be observed that this measurement was made on the upper part of the vessel whereas the plan shows 25 cm, and probably this is the correct measurement. In

[101] Gillis, 1996, 96.
[102] Frödin & Persson 1938, 186; Mårtensson 2002.
[103] Frödin & Persson 1938, 186.
[104] Frödin & Persson 1938, 421.

square C3, there was also a bronze nail on a level of 10 cm, a silver thread 20 cm "above the floor", and one bone rosett.[105] on a level of 5 cm. The second group was also made up of three vases (no.12, LH IIIC:M, no.17, LH IIIC:L and no.19, LH IIIB). The LH IIIB vase was measured 15 cm "above the floor" and this was also the estimated level for the LH IIIC:L vase, no. 17, whereas no. 12, LH IIIC:M, was found on a level of 20 cm. The third and, according to the excavators, the last burial is composed of vases nos. 6, 7 and 18, all of LH IIIC date.[106] The LH IIIC:M vase no. 18, was found 4 cm "above the floor" and the two LH IIIC Early vessels on 5 cm (no.7), respectively 6 cm (no.6).

These groups of vessels are only some examples of the difficulty of discussing stratigraphy in a burial context. It is most likely that the vases identified as a burial group by the excavators had been dislocated. We may also observe that the finds listed on the plan indicate quite different levels. The small objects found in square C3 were all, except the silver thread which was noticed on 20 cm, found on a notable lower level than the pottery. Unfortunately we cannot reconstruct any possible finds of pottery from the lower levels and therefore cannot combine the other finds with a certain pottery group.

On the original plan in square C4 on a level between 45 and 50 cm a bronze mirror, a steatite button and a silver-rod were marked, whereas no dated pottery was mentioned. The discrepancy in levels between the vessels and other objects may have been caused by material falling down, but it is more likely that the disturbed filling in the chamber was caused by re-burials, ranging from LH IIA to LH IIIC Late. The sherds later mended to form whole vessels could further attest the tradition of secondary burials.

Chamber tomb I:7 was furnished with several categories of exclusive goods which may be defined as objects of high value and status. Both gold and bronze objects and a large quantity of lead were found. Also this tomb contained tin-coated vessels that should be included in the category of status objects. However, the dates differ as compared with other tombs as three of the eight analysed vases may belong to the LH IIB period,[107] whereas the others are probably LH IIIA2.[108] The early use of tin-covered vessels is interesting as we may assume that the tomb already in this early period belonged to a family of a certain importance. Ivory was present in the form of some fragments of a comb. Further finds representing foreign material were beads made of amethyst and glass paste and 38 steatite buttons.

[105] Frödin & Persson 1938, 420.

[106] Nos. 6, LH IIIC:E; 7, LH IIIC:E; 18, LH IIIC:M.

[107] Nos. 35, 36, 37 FS 271, LH IIB.

[108] Nos. 39, 40, FS 264, LH IIIA2; nos. 42, 44, FS 267, LH IIIA2.

Summary

Obviously the tomb was in quite a disordered state and, according to the excavators, this was intentionally caused by those who used the chamber. Also here we find the same pattern as in other tombs, with bones that seem to have been intentionally moved for the purpose to make room for new burials. The excavators observed that no undisturbed skeleton was found, something which it would have been natural to expect at least in the case of the last burial. The excavators proposed that this was a sign of an infant burial, as the bones of infants are more fragile and should have decomposed and left no traces of the last burial. Some of the bones have been analysed and at least a couple of women were buried here and there was also evidence of children.[109] In my opinion, the presence of these bones strengthens the argument about the importance of women and children as symbols of lineage. The woman is the symbol of continuity as mother and child-bearer, and the infant is the link between the past and the future.

The tomb is well represented by pottery from the LH IIB and LH IIIA periods. Here it is proposed that the other categories of finds may have been, as in other tombs, deposited during these periods. The finds are numerous and the material exclusive and of exotic origin. Objects such as these may be associated with a family belonging to the local élite. It is argued, as it has been earlier, that the same chamber tomb being in use for such a long period indicates its importance as a place of ceremonial meaning, family identification and exponent of status.

7.9 CHAMBER TOMB II:1

Introduction

Diary: No. 6, 1926.
Original plan: Yes.
Silhouette: Dromos with asymmetrical chamber.

Table 7.8: Chamber tomb II:1, finds by period of use

Periods of use	Number of vessels
LH IIIA1	2

Pottery: Total number 2, out of which dated 2, decorated 1, undecorated 1.
Other find categories: Metal: iron.
Finds: Round iron belt buckle.
Skeletal remains: Yes.

Analysis

The tomb is poor as regards pottery and only two whole vessels dated by Furumark to LH IIIA1, were found.[110] The *Diary* no. 6 also mentions a broken amphora, but the sherds have not survived, making a dating impossible. It

[109] Frödin & Persson 1938, 188; Moberg 1986, 36.

[110] FS 109; FS 112.

is possible that the tomb was used only for one burial during the Late Helladic period, as the finds of bones that can be combined with the LH vessels are quite sparse and in disorder. One skeleton perhaps deposited later was found in the upper and outer part of the chamber and an iron belt buckle was discovered in association with it. There is nothing to indicate, however, that this is not a Late Helladic deposit, which makes the find interesting as finds of iron from the Late Bronze Age are few. As already noted, the excavators investigated only one chamber tomb from Necropolis II and therefore it is difficult to make any conclusions or ideas concerning the status of the burials.

Summary

We may conclude that the tomb was used for at least one burial in the LH IIIA1 period. For some reason, the tomb was not re-used for burials during the remaining part of the Late Helladic period and we may perhaps assume that it was abandoned or belonged to a family of such a low status that they could not re-use it. It is, of course, also possible that the lineage ceased to exist after LH IIIA.

7.10 THE CHAMBER TOMBS AT ASINE: DISCUSSION AND SUMMARY

It has been suggested earlier by Cavanagh and Mee that status may have been expressed by tomb content and size. The disparity in size and wealth is interpreted by Cavanagh and Mee as an indication of alliances between rich and poor family relations that were maintained after death. Against the background of the presented material from Asine we may conclude that their proposal is supported as deposits of finds fluctuate and differences in wealth and consequently status in different periods are obvious.

Three of the published tombs were in use in LH IIB. Tomb nos. I:1, I:2 and I:7 are outstanding, as they were in use for a very long period and especially I:1 and I:2 contain very exclusive and rich finds and also objects of a prestigious character. Although equipped with some precious objects the number of exclusive and foreign goods in I:7 is not comparable with the two other, but, on the other hand the number of vases is large. Chamber tomb I:7 contained pottery from LH IIA, some nice Palace-style vases and also tin-coated vessels. Owing to the large number of vessels and the tin-coated vases, I shall include the tomb in the same category of rich tombs as I:1 and I:2. The finds in these tombs follow the same pattern as was also observed by Voutskai, who noticed that the distribution of wealth was more even in the LH II period.[111] The Asine material illustrates a symmetrical pattern of wealth with equally rich deposits in the tombs and if we follow Precourt's model, the society could have been based on reciprocal exchange.

The following LH IIIA period shows asymmetry in the wealth of tombs, a pattern previously observed in the Argolid.[112] Chamber tombs: I:1, I:2, I:5 and I:7 are rich in finds, whereas other tombs are poor. Several tombs contained objects of exotic origin and with high labour input, recognised as prestige goods. For example tinned vessels were found and also deposits of exclusive objects made of ivory, obviously produced in the earlier part of LH IIIA. These highly interesting ivory objects can be interpreted as status symbols owing to their uniqueness. According to Krzyszkowska, the ivories have virtually no exact parallels and although it is difficult she argues for a date in early LH IIIA, before large-scale production came into effect. It is therefore possible that these objects were direct import. However, a pyxis lid in the shape of as a roundel found in chamber tomb 520, LH IIIA2, at Mycenae is a parallel. Krzyszkowska does not exclude the possibility that the ivory objects found in tomb I: 2 also served as heirlooms.[113] Ivory objects were found also in chamber tomb I:1 and some of these may also have been imported goods from other parts of the Mediterranean. A further sign of status was found in tomb I:5 where eight bronze vessels deposited in the LH IIIA2 period were found. Apparently one of the vessels also contained several necklaces. Tombs I:3, I:6 and II:1 were also in use in the LH IIIA period. The find status in these tombs is poor compared to the other.

The asymmetrical picture emerging for the LH IIIA period indicates that the socio-economic situation in Asine was not equal, as individuals and families had the opportunity of manifesting status through prestige objects, and also interest in doing so. In an article, R. Hägg observed two levels of Mycenaean cult, in which the official level was primarily connected with the palaces but was also practised by some inhabitants of the smaller centres. He suggested that these were the upper levels of society with the proper means of affording luxury items and also with the possibility of establishing contacts with foreign countries.[114] The two rings from Asine with Minoan motifs found in chamber tomb I:1 are interesting examples of objects that may be associated with this local group. It is tempting to interpret the presence of the rings in the tomb as symbols of the local élite who not only had the financial means but were also the interested in taking up these items as symbols of wealth and power. Although few tombs have been excavated, I would not exclude the possibility that the families using these tombs constituted part of the local élite.

The character of the finds from LH II and LH IIIA displays a society in which social relations were differentiated. The nature of the objects, made of precious material of exotic origin, show that individuals at Asine were able to acquire these commodities. The location of the site is fortunate and it is possible that Asine

[111] Voutsaki 1998, 48.

[112] Voutsaki 1998, 48.

[113] Krzyszkowska 1996, 84-88.

[114] Hägg 1981, 36.

functioned as a focal point for goods from other Argive settlements meant for distribution outside the region. At Berbati there was a pottery workshop established, probably in the LH II period, which continued in use until, perhaps, the beginning of the LH IIIB period. Research has located samples from a workshop labelled My/Be and vessels have been located within the region but also in the eastern part of the Mediterranean.[115] The pre-LH IIIB road m5 (*Fig. 5*) passing through the Berbati valley[116] may have been the route used for pottery vessels distributed to the south, to perhaps Asine and for further transport. The ivory finds, the metal objects and the tinned vessels may all be evidence of commodities traded directly with foreign trading partners. The asymmetrical pattern displayed in chamber tombs at Asine, following Precourt, should be interpreted as showing an economy based on redistribution or market exchange. Although it is most likely that the basic character of the economy was self-sufficiency, other modes of exchange were probably used for integrated exchange between individuals and settlements, both on the regional and the inter-regional level.

The following LH IIIB period is more difficult to evaluate. Voutsaki has observed that the period was even more asymmetrical as concerned wealth as tholoi were not used outside the palatial centres and there are no rich chamber tombs outside Mycenae.[117] The find situation at Asine is poor, as only tombs I:1 and I:7 had a few vessels dating from this period and the absence of pottery in LH IIIB is significant and cannot be neglected. Whether this phenomenon can be explained in terms of new groups of individuals using the tombs or changing burial traditions may be discussed. Changing burial traditions may be a plausible explanation, as perhaps it was not longer appropriate to exhibit worldly status. I would suggest that the burial tradition in Sweden, and also other countries, today might be seen as a parallel. Exclusive and monumental tombs are not considered appropriate and not even royal burials are manifested in large and more elaborate tombs. Instead, the ceremonies surrounding the burials of people of different social statuses may be different, but, as they leave no traces, these details will not be detectable in the future. The lack of LH IIIB pottery may perhaps also have its explanation in the fact that it was not important to deposit pottery and this therefore did not necessarily imply a break in the use of tombs.[118] Consequently, it is not excluded that the same lineage buried their dead relatives during this long span of time. Social and economic status may still have been important and earlier deposits of grave goods may have served as heirlooms. Few other finds of other categories can be connected with burials from this period. However, the tinned vessel in tomb I:1 is of interest and may be a symbol of the status of those buried in this tomb.

The tombs at Asine have a more symmetrical pattern, which implies change in the economic structure to a system based on reciprocity. Economic wealth should accordingly not primarily have been expressed by deposits of rich grave goods. Here, the value of heirlooms appears as interesting and it is believed that the same families may also in LH IIIB have represented the local élite, who still had the financial means to acquire expensive and exotic tradable goods and were interested in doing so. The difference in the number of goods and materials should, however, not be neglected and it is possible that the tombs reflect a situation in which the dominance of Asine as a transmitter of commodities between the region and the foreign partners had diminished.

The LH IIIC period is well represented in the chamber-tomb material, as all the tombs, except I:3, were in use. Not all the tombs seem to have been in continuous use through all the phases of LH IIIC, but it is not to be excluded that such lacunae may also be an error owing to the difficulty of dating LH IIIC pottery. The pattern of symmetry is valid for the LH IIIC period, as there are no such obvious fluctuations in tomb content as in the LH IIIA period. However, the presence of earlier deposits of goods and their symbolic meaning as symbols of status may not be neglected, although it is possible that their value had diminished as the knowledge of these objects now perhaps dirty and buried in the earth, faded. The symmetrical pattern points to a society based on symmetrical relations, in which no great discrepancies in wealth between individuals can be recognised. The tombs in use at Asine increased in this period which may indicate that the site resumed a more important status amongst the settlements still in use on the Argive Plain. The commodities found do not show that an extensive trade was conducted but, on the other hand, it is possible that there was no demand for more exclusive commodities. It is possible that the destruction that hit the Plain in the end of LH IIIB2 and especially later in LH IIIC had severe effects on the economy of individuals and also on the whole region.

Finally, a few words concerning simple earth cut tombs dated to the Late Helladic period, mentioned in Frödin and Persson. These tombs, except nos.10 and 12 found in dromoi in chamber tomb I:1, were located inside the settlement and contained the remains of children's skeletons.[119] The location of child burials in intra-mural contexts may be explained in terms of superstition or belief in an after-life. But I would also like to emphasise the meaning of the child as the important link of heritage for the lineage and also as a symbol of the continuity of the family. Moreover, it should not be forgotten that the child was important as an economic subject. In a society mostly based on self-sufficiency, and in which most likely the margins were tight, children were the resources needed to provide for the economic future, supplying

[115] Mommsen, Lewandowski, Weber & Podzuweit 1988; Mommsen & Maran 2000-2001.

[116] Lavery 1995.

[117] Voutsaki 1998, 48.

[118] Cavanagh & Mee 1978, 31.

[119] Frödin & Persson 1938, 128-129, figs. 43, 68.

their parents and elders with economic and labour support. I also propose that the presence of women buried in chamber tombs indicates a view of women as an intermediary of lineage and as a person with high social status.

CHAPTER 8
ARGIVE CHAMBER TOMBS

8.1 INTRODUCTION

This chapter is devoted to a more detailed study of Late Helladic tombs in space and time. The intention is to arrive at a more detailed picture of the settlement system as well as the economic situation of the Argolid during the Late Bronze Age. This is so since a close examination can be expected to provide information on the relative rank of settlements across the hierarchy of central places in the Argolid. In parallel, it may give us important clues as to the nature and extent of exchange in the area. To advance our knowledge on these scores, however, we need to be more careful than hitherto have been the case in distinguishing the various sub-periods of the Late Helladic era.

Methodological remarks

Several settlements have a large number of tombs, quite a few of which have been dated. Dating is not possible at all sites, however, as a closer examination of pottery has not always been done. For the present purposes detailed information concerning the number of vessels from each period is of considerable importance. The vessels have mainly been dated through analyses presented by A. Furumark, P. Mountjoy and of photos published. Recent work on the pottery from Prosymna by K. Shelton[1] provides an excellent possibility to date not only the chamber tombs from Prosymna in more detail, but also tombs from other sites. Despite these advances, it unfortunate that it has not always been possible to find more detailed dating for pottery from the LH IIIB and the LH IIIC periods.

During the initial stage of the Late Mycenaean period the chamber tomb was still an infrequent element in the landscape. Mycenae, Argos, Dendra, Schoinochori and perhaps Kokla[2] had a few tombs each of this type during the LH I period. Prosymna stands out as something of an exception in this regard, as nine chamber tombs were used at this site during the opening period of the Late Helladic era. The following period LH II is characterised by an increase in the use of chamber tombs. The type is now represented also at Tiryns, Asine, and possibly also at Nauplion where some of the tombs may be from the LH II, or even the LH I period.[3] The transition to the LH III period is signified by a general increase in the use of chamber tombs on the Argive plain and we may now also add Berbati to the list.[4] The general picture of tombs in use during the LH IIIA is one of variation and there are apparent fluctuations to be noted as we have a distinct increase of tombs in use from LH IIIA1 to LH IIIA2. The transition to the LH IIIB period shows a general decline in the number of tombs in use and the tomb now disappears at Schoinochori. In the chamber tomb material compiled by Alden the turn to the LH IIIC period is indicated by a general decrease with tombs in use only at Mycenae, Argos, Tiryns and Asine. At Asine, contrary to the other settlements, an increase is registered.[5] Some LH IIIC finds are reported also from Nauplion, although the provenience of the finds seems utterly vague [6]

8.2 MYCENAE

Compared to most other sites in the Argolid, our knowledge concerning the chamber tomb material from Mycenae is good. Wace[7] has published tomb material and these tombs also provide us with information concerning the date of the tombs. What is more, the enormous number of finds from the excavations conducted by Tsountas between 1887 and 1898 has now been published by Xenaki-Sakellariou.[8] These tombs seem to have been rich in finds, but unfortunately little pottery material is present, our at least accounted for, and the possibility of establishing the chronology of these chamber tombs is therefore quite limited.

The tombs follow the known pattern of little representation of other finds than pottery from the LH IIIB period.
Find categories: metals: gold, lead, silver, bronze; semi-precious stones: crystal, amethyst, agate, onyx, steatite; stone: flint, marble, porphyry; obsidian; shell; ivory; amber, bone; faience; glass.
Skeletal remains: Yes.

---

[1] Shelton 1996.
[2] Alden 1981, 153, 185, 209, 262, 289, table page 322a of tombs in use; Demakopoulou 1993, 57-75, pls.1-14.
[3] Alden 1981, 322a, 297.
[4] Alden 1981, 322a.
[5] Alden 1981, 322a.
[6] Alden 1981, 295-296.
[7] Wace 1932.
[8] Xenaki-Sakellariou 1985.

Table 8.1: Tombs in use/number of dated pottery[9] at Kalkani, south/north bank

Tomb No.	LH I	LH IIA	LH IIB	LH IIIA1	LH IIIA2	LH IIIB	LH IIIC
513 W G 2						2	
514 W G 3						1	
515W G 1			9	2	6 (4 tinned)		11
516 W G 4	2	3			3		
517 W G 2	11	7	5		1		1
518 W G 1	8	15	14	8			
519 W G 2					1	3	
525 W G 4					7		
526 W G 3							
527 W G 4					7	4	4
528 W G 4	Sherds						
529 W G 1		4	8		7		
530 W G 3		2		2	8		
532 W G 4		3	2	3	1		2
533 W G 4		3		3	1	5	1
520 W G 2					29	1	
521 W G 3					7		
522 W G 4	Disorder						
523 W G 3					9		
524 W G 3					12	2	5
531 W G 4					3		
Tombs/Vessels	3/21	7/37	5/38	5/18	15/102	7/18	6/24

Table 8.2: Tombs in use/number of dated pottery at Kalkani, Third Kilometer Cemetery

Tomb no.	LH I	LH IIA	LH IIB	LH IIIA1	LH IIIA2	LH IIIB	LH IIIC
102 W G 2		X					
502 W G 3				3 (1 tinned)		9	11(m/l)
504 W G 4				figurines	figurines	figurine	
505 W G 4					X		
Tombs/Vessels		Sherds		1/3		1/9	1/11

[9] Alden 1981, 141-153, 322, used the Kalkani material; Furumark 1972a, 585-643; 1992; Wace 1932.

Analysis

The tombs from Mycenae are similar to those found at other Late Helladic cemeteries in the region. They are often represented with several skeletons in disturbed positions. In some cases this might be due to ceilings and walls having fallen down, but most probably the disturbances result from reburials and the removal of older skeletons. This is not true of all tombs, however, and for instance tomb no. 526 has only one skeleton registered, whereas no. 528 has no traces of bones at all. No. 522 was obviously very disturbed, probably due to looting, and no bones were left. The chamber in no. 528 was empty of finds except some potsherds. No. 526 has no vessels allowing dating the tomb, but the only skeleton, obviously female, was by Wace dated to LH IIIA1 due to the three Egyptian scarabs representing Amenophis III.[10]

An analysis conducted by Cavanagh and Mee assigned tombs from Mycenae into four wealth groups.[11] In group one, the richest, we find 12 tombs. Unfortunately, only three have been possible to date as the other tombs belong to the group excavated by Tsountas from which not much pottery is recorded.[12] Tombs assigned to wealth group one are tombs nos. 515, 518, 529 and tombs nos. 2, 5, 25, 33, 78, 81, 82, 88 and 99 excavated by Tsountas. Tomb 515 contained a comparatively large number of vessels representing the periods LH IIA, LH IIIA2 and LH IIIC:m and also four tinned LH IIIA2 vessels.[13] Other finds were different bronze objects (tweezers, fragments and whole knifes, one scale pan, a pin, nails), silver fragments, silver pin, arrowheads, ivory, beads of glass, faience and several gold objects. Most of the pottery found in the dromos may be dated to LH IIB and we may assume that no. 515 was cleared and reused. Nos. 518 and 529 were both equipped with not only pottery, but also other finds of high quality. A more detailed study of the pottery reveals that these tombs were in use not later than LH IIIA2. These dates are of some consequence as two categories of finds are bronze and ivory. In tomb 515 were found for instance a fragmentary bronze knife, a scale pan, awl, beads and tweezers. Tomb 518 contained amongst others a bronze dagger and a broken knife, ivory combs, pyxides and inlays, several sealstones, beads made of amber, carnelian, glass and also finds of silver and gold. No. 529 contained a larger number of bronze items, including a dagger, a knife, scale pans and tweezers. To this could be added objects such as those made of ivory, amber, glass and faience. We have no evidence of ivory production at Mycenae before LH IIIB1 and either the objects arrived as part of external exchange or local production took place here earlier than the archaeological record currently allows us to verify.

[10] Wace 1932, 93.
[11] Cavanagh & Mee 1990, 58.
[12] Cavanagh & Mee 1990, 56.
[13] Nos. 48, FS 265; 49, FS 266; 51, FS 295; 52, FS 267.

Amber objects indicate external relations already in the LH I-IIIA2 period.[14] This may indicate that amber was imported in the LH I/II periods and its presence in tomb context later than this period could be explained by its importance as heirloom. Also, objects made of other exotic materials such as agate, amethyst, faience, carnelian, crystal and onyx were found. Glass is reported from several tombs and quite a few of these predate LH IIIB.[15] Again, these finds indicate that either these objects were imported to Mycenae, or produced at a local workshop in operation already prior to the possible LH IIIB2 workshops at Mycenae and Midea.

Finds of lead and silver are very rare. Lead was reported only from one tomb and silver in four.[16] These tombs were in use LH IIA until LH IIIA2 with the exception of tomb 514, wealth group 3, with one single vessel of probable LH IIIB date. The metal finds may indicate either external relation or local production. As concerns lead and silver working no indication of production is found in the settlement material from these earlier periods. It is interesting to note, however, that there are silver vessels with a regional shape found at Kokla; they indicate regional or local production in the LH IIIA1 period.[17] Objects made of bronze were found in 10 tombs and all, except nos. 533, 520 and 523, antedate the LH IIIB period.[18] Production of bronze is not documented at Mycenae before the LH IIIB2 period. Slag from bronze smelting has been found in the area labelled Artists' Workshop and the Citadel House Area in use LH IIIB2.[19] If the bronze items found in earlier chronological contexts are not import goods it may be assumed that bronze production occurred already in periods preceding LH IIIB.

Surprisingly few finds of gold objects are documented as only tomb nos. 513, 515, 517, 518, 520 and 502 contained such. These tombs are chronologically quite heterogeneous. As is the case with other materials the occurrence of gold in earlier tombs indicates either imports to Mycenae, or local production at an earlier stage than currently thought possible; after all, gold production is indicated only in a later context. The LH IIIB2 Artisans' Workshop area could also have been used for production of gold objects.[20] The lack of gold in the previously mentioned tombs stands in contrast to some tombs excavated in the 19th century by Tsountas.[21] As is the case with other categories of finds deposited in earlier

[14] Tomb nos. 515, 517, 518, 526, 529, 533.
[15] Tomb nos. 514, 515, 516, 517, 518, 519, 526, 529, 530, 520, 521, 523, 524, 502. Tomb, nos. 516, 518, 526, 521, 523, 529, 530 predate LH IIIB, 515 and 517 were in use before LH IIIB and reused in LH IIIC.
[16] Lead: no. 530; silver: nos. 514, 515, 518, 530.
[17] Demakopoulou 1990b, 117-119; 1993, 59.
[18] Bronze: nos. 515, 518, 525, 526, 529, 530, 532, 533, 520, 523.
[19] Iakovidis 1983, 64.
[20] Iakovidis 1983, 64.
[21] Xenaki-Sakellariou 1985, for example nos. 8,10, 55, 58, 68 77, 78, 84 and 91.

periods it is not far-fetched to propose that also gold objects could have functioned as heirlooms.

Ivory objects are found rather more frequently. A survey of the chronology associated with this category of finds shows that some objects have been found in pre-LH IIIB contexts.[22] As has been shown in Chapter 5 there is no indication of ivory production at Mycenae in the periods preceding LH IIIB1. Again, we are reduced to noting that either local production so far has gone undocumented, or that these objects were distributed from other sites.

Summary

The wealth group analysis made by Cavanagh and Mee is an important input to our understanding of the status of settlements on the Argive Plain. The tendency they document is that from LH IIIA1 to LH IIIA2 there is a clear increase in the number of tombs used, followed by a decrease in LH IIIB. The number continues to decrease and tombs in use in LH IIIC compares to the initial phases of the Late Helladic period. If the richness of tombs is considered, we will find, according to Cavanagh and Mee and also Voutsaki, richer and larger tombs in the earlier part and poorer coming into use later in the LH III period.[23]

The number of tombs assigned to wealth group 1 at Mycenae is similar to Prosymna and none of those dated was in use in LH IIIB. Wealth group 2 represents tombs from all periods except LH IIIA1.[24] There is, however, a question mark as concerns tomb no. 519. Finds of pottery are few, but still more notable are the few other categories of finds made. For example, no metal finds are reported. Tomb 513 is also quite empty, but the find of a gold ring is on record. No. 520 had on the other hand a larger number of vessels, although Cavanagh and Mee do not count this particular category of finds. Gold ornaments are reported, but otherwise the finds mostly seem to consist of the same group of finds found in many other tombs such as beads of glass and some ivory. Tomb no. 102, assigned to group 2, is something of a puzzle as no finds at all are reported and should better be assigned as a group 4 tomb. In group 4, tomb 505 contained a huge number of sherds, probably as many as about 500 vessels all of LH IIIA1 origin, but very few other finds. The large number of pottery finds suggests the tomb should better be assigned to a higher wealth group.

Voutsaki claims that in the LH II period the distribution of wealth was more even across the Argive sites than in the preceding LH I period, at which point Mycenae claimed the leading position. The pattern of wealth distribution changed in the LH IIIA period and became, according to Voutsaki, more asymmetrical due to the rise of the number of chamber tombs of which the majority were poor and the decline in number of tholoi which now were gradually concentrated to the palaces. According to Voutsaki, the asymmetrical distribution of wealth noticed in LH IIIA is accentuated in LH IIIB as no tholoi were in use outside the palatial sites and no rich chamber tombs were in use outside Mycenae.[25]

It can be observed that tombs classified as poorer (groups 3 and 4) are more numerous at Mycenae than the two other settlements analysed.[26] Considering that only part of the tombs are possible to date in more detail an overview indicates that there is a change to recognise in the number of wealth groups 1 and 2 from LH IIIA1 to LH IIIB. Tombs belonging to wealth group 1 are not in use in LH IIIB and group 2 tombs are in use in LH IIIB, but the number of deposited vessels is small. As concerns the two non-wealthy groups, 3 and 4, there is a distinct increase from LH IIIA1 to LH IIIA2. The figures indicate an asymmetrical social situation with different wealth groups represented in the LH I-LH IIIA2 periods. However, as concerns the LH IIIB period a more even distribution of tomb wealth is observed. No wealth group 1 tombs are in use and the number of tombs belonging to group 2 in decline. Still, and contrary to the view held by Voutsaki, it could be argued that the situation at Mycenae changed in the LH IIIB period, becoming more symmetrical as the pattern is now dominated by poorer tombs. The tholos is, of course, to be recognised, but in view of the possibility that the status associated with the richer offerings there was relevant only for a short period of time, that is in connection with the burial, and expressed status of a single person, or one family. Once the tomb was closed, its status could have changed and diminished over time.

The following period, LH IIIC, is characterised by a decrease in number of tombs in use; only two tombs each of wealth groups 1 and 2 have been identified. These tombs were in use already in the period preceding LH IIIB and it is proposed that either they were used also in LH IIIB, although without any material evidence, or were re-used by the same families. The general pattern is one of symmetry without any dramatic difference in the distribution of wealth.

8.3 TIRYNS

In 1973 W. Rudolph published the tombs excavated in the 1920s; originally approximately 50 tombs were located.[27]

---

[22] Tomb nos. 518, 525, 529 and 530.

[23] Cavanagh & Mee 1990, 62; Voutsaki 1995a, 58-59.

[24] Tomb nos. 513, 517, 519, 520. It can not be excluded that the representation and distribution of wealth groups was the same in the group of tombs excavated by Tsountas.

[25] Voutsaki 1998, 48.

[26] Cavanagh & Mee 1990, 58. Of 100 tombs at Mycenae 50% were classified as wealth group 3 and 4.

[27] Rudolph 1973, 23-126, taf. 8-56.

Table 8.3: Tombs in use/number of dated pottery at Tiryns[28]

Tomb No.	LH I	LH IIA	LH IIB	LH IIIA1	LH IIIA2	LH IIIB1	LH IIIB2	LH IIIC
I				2	7			
II				1+sherds	sherds	sherds		
III				6				
IV		1		1	5	1		
V					1	2	1	5
VI					1		5	4
VII			4	5	3			1
VIII				1	4	2		1
XI				Sherds	sherds			
XIII				Sherds	sherds			
XIV					1	7	1	
XV					3	1	4	2
XVI		1	7	6	11	2	1	sherds
XVII		1						
XVIII		3	2	1				
XIX	1		3	2	4			
XX		1						
XXII		1	3					
XXV				Sherds			sherds	
XXXVI		sherds	Sherds	1	sherds	sherds		
Tombs/Vessels	1/3	7/8	6/19	14/32	14/40	8/15	6/12	6/13

Table 8.4: Tombs in use /number of dated pottery at Dendra[29]

Tomb No.	LH I	LH IIA	LH IIB	LH IIIA1	LH IIIA2	LH IIIB	LH IIIC
1 W G 3					2	7	
2 W G 1					3	5	
3 W G 1						2	
6 W-G2		9					
7 W G 1			2			1 figurine	1
8 W G 1		2	1				
9 W G 2						1	
10 W G 2		7	9	9 (5 tinned)	2		
11 W G 2			1	1	4	2	1
12 W G 1 (Cuirass tomb)			2	2			
13		1	8	16	9	6	
14						9	
Tombs/Vessels		4/19	6/23	4/28	5/20	8/32	2/2

[28] Furumark 1972a, 585-643; Rudolph 1973, 23-126; Alden 1981, 233.
[29] Alden 1981, 262; Furumark 1972a, 585-643; Mountjoy 1986; Persson 1931; 1942.

Pottery is well represented in the tombs whereas other categories of finds are more infrequent. For example, figurines are found in four tombs only, nos. VI, XVI, XIV, XV, and also finds of metals are rare. Otherwise, according to Rudolph, these tombs do not diverge too much from other cemeteries in the Argolid.[30]

Find categories: metals: bronze, gold, silver, lead; semi-precious stones: steatite, amethyst, agate, carnelian; amber; glass; faience; and bone.[31]

Skeletal remains: yes.

Analysis

Compared to tombs at other Argive settlements, for example Asine, Mycenae and Dendra, the tombs on Prophitis Elias are not as well endowed (as assessed by the number of finds). A more detailed look at the objects points to some interesting details. As Rudolph noted, the number of objects made of precious metals is small, although he proposed that with more tomb material the situation might be rather different.[32] Several tombs are empty of other find categories than vessels and figurines.[33] Nos. XVII, XX and XXII were used only in the LH II period and contained only a few vessels. In nos. II, XI, XIII, XXV and XXXVI mostly sherds were found. The poor find status may here, as at other sites, be explained by looting.[34]

One stone lamp found in tomb XVI has parallels at Dendra, Asine and Mycenae.[35] The question whether it was produced locally, or imported to the Mainland, is not answered and also the date of the lamp remains elusive. Parallel finds at the other locations are of little help in this regard as tomb 2 at Dendra was used in LH IIIA2 and LH IIIB, and chamber tomb I:2 at Asine from LH IIB to LH IIIA2, as well as in the LH IIIC period and tomb I:7 in all periods.

Beads made of glass, glass paste and faience were found in tombs nos. III, VI, VII, VIII, XI, XV, XVI, XVIII, XIX.[36] The dates of these tombs differ, but together they cover the entire Late Helladic period. The presence of glass and faience beads in tomb no. III, not in use after LH IIIA1, supports the idea of non-local production in the periods preceding LH IIIB. Precious stones such as agate, amethyst and carnelian are also found. Rudolph made an attempt to establish the chronology, as their find contexts seem to have been quite clear. The beads from tomb no. III seems to be of LH IIIA1 vintage and the same applies to the amethyst beads in tombs VII, whereas the pearl in tomb no. VIII was found with a LH IIIB1 cup. In tomb VI was a larger number of beads found in the same context as an alabastron belonging to the earlier part of LH IIIA. Finds of amber were made in tomb no. VI, in use between LH IIIA1 and LH IIIC, no. VII in use in LH IIB to LH IIIA2 and perhaps also in LH IIIC, and no. XVI, in use through LH IIA until the LH IIIC period.[37] Perhaps we may assume that in the case of tombs VII and XVI the amber was deposited in the LH II period and in the case of tomb VI in a later period? As has been stated earlier amber was probably imported already in the LH II period and it cannot be ruled out that this was the case also with the amber found at Tiryns. Four gems were reported, but only one – from tomb no. XIX – seems to have been preserved. Thanks to the find context the gem is dated to the later part of LH IIIA2. It has some similarities with gems found at Prosymna and Midea.[38]

Objects made of metals were found, but most gold and silver finds are now lost and only a few objects made of gold were documented in tombs V, XVI and XIX and in tomb XVI also a ring of silver.[39] These tombs cover all periods. Of particular interest is no. XIX as deposits of vessels after LH IIIA2 have not been found. We may therefore be quite sure that the gold objects were deposited earlier than LH IIIB. Two tombs contained fragments of lead and the date of the tombs suggest a pre-LH IIIB deposit.[40] Also in the case of Tiryns it is observed that there is no evidence of local production in metals before the LH IIIB1 period. The source of origin may therefore have been external, but also local yet still not documented production remains a possibility. Silver is also found at other sites, such as at Kokla, Prosymna and Dendra and there we sometimes find it in contexts pre-dating LH IIIB. Bronze objects are more frequently reported and consist for the most part of small objects such as nails. Some tools made of bronze, including nails, tweezers and a tong were found in tombs V, VI and VII, and three scales pans in tomb XVI. The bronze objects have been found in contexts covering even the LH IIIC period. A fibula represents the latter period and the only parallel has been found at Argos, also from the same period.[41] It is similarly reported that a piece of iron was found in tomb V, a possible deposit of the LH IIC period[42] Finally, it can be observed that no finds of ivory are reported.

Summary

The find context is to some extent comparable to the situation at Argos: no larger variety, or quantity, in

[30] Rudolph 1973, 116-117.

[31] Rudolph 1973, 116-123.

[32] Rudolph 1973, 117.

[33] Rudolph 1973, 59, 87, 124, tomb nos. II, XIII, XIV, XVII, XX, XXII, XXV and XXXVI.

[34] Rudolph 1973, 23-126.

[35] Rudolph 1973, 77. For Asine and Dendra see Persson 1931, 101. A lamp with similar pattern was found in tomb I:2, Asine. The lamp referred to in tomb I:7 is not documented in the final publication. For Mycenae Bosanquet 1904, 324-329, pl. 15, no find context.

[36] Rudolph 1973, 39-32, 40-59, 63-85.

[37] Rudolph 1973, 118-119. The cup no. 5 in tomb VIII, has been dated to LH IIIB1 by Shelton 1996, 126, which gives another context for the find.

[38] Rudolph 1973, 120-121. Prosymna tomb XXXIV.

[39] Rudolph 1973, 36-40, 67-78, 81-85, 120.

[40] Rudolph 1973, 122-123, tomb nos. VII, XVIII.

[41] Rudolph 1973, 120-122. Argos tomb no. XXIX.

[42] Rudolph 1973, 40, 122.

objects made of precious metals or other categories of exotic materials. The number of vessels deposited is low, with the exceptions in tomb nos. V, and XVI and also the number of other finds is low. Tombs with more numerous finds include nos. V, VI, VIII, XVI and XIX.

As has been observed earlier, the occurrence of metals is poor and none of the tombs displayed collections on a par with those found, for example, at Asine, Mycenae and Dendra. However, the presence of bronze tools and scale pans, all probably deposited in the LH IIIA period or even earlier, are worthy of note. The scale pans indicate the need for measuring and could have been used in exchange transactions. The at times small size and quality could point towards use when small or not too heavy items needed to be measured. Silver and lead are found in tombs in use before LH IIIB. The scarcity of later deposits of lead is surprising, as lead production is documented at Tiryns in the LH IIIB2 period. Bronze is on the other hand found in tomb contexts covering nearly all periods and we may note that some tombs were also in use in the LH IIIB period, that is, simultaneously with the documented bronze production at Tiryns. The bronze fibula found at Tiryns, which has a parallel at Argos, is either a heirloom or evidence of relations between the two sites as late as LH IIIC. Ivory however, represented in tombs at several sites, is not found which is slightly puzzling as local production is documented in the LHIIIIB2 period. An interesting find is the gem in tomb XIX; gems of a much similar type have been found at Prosymna, indicating relations between the two occurring perhaps as late as in the LH IIIA2 period.[43]

Only six tombs have groups of finds that may be characterised as deviating from the others: tomb nos. V, VI, VII, VIII, XVI, XIX. For example, in no. VII an interesting assemblage of finds, amongst others tweezers, spindle whorls and possible hooks made of lead, as well as a tong made of bronze, was found. All these objects have been dated to the LH IIIA1 period. Also tomb no. XVI, where three scale pans and a legshield were found, is of interest. The tombs may have belonged to families that for some reason thought it important and appropriate to project their interests through the use of burial goods. It can not be excluded that the families may have belonged to the local élite. Of these tombs two ceased to be in use after LH IIIA2, namely tombs nos. VII and XIX. The other tombs were all in use before and after LH IIIB1. All tombs were used for more than a short period of time and it is believed that the same families held position of the tombs and the status embedded. The other tombs from Tiryns contained very few finds, or were nearly empty, and compared with the tombs analysed by Cavanagh and Mee these may be classified as wealth group 3 and 4.

To summarise, we may conclude that the tombs at Tiryns did not have deposits compatible with those found at several other sites. This can be explained, as Rudolph suggests, as a result of only a minority of tombs having been found, but also due to looting. Nevertheless, twenty tombs have been published and more than half of these are close to empty of other find categories than pottery and also this category is poorly represented. There is an increase of tombs in use from LH IIB to LH IIIA1 and in contrast to other Argive sites there is no increase in tombs in LH IIIA2. Some goods in the six tombs with richer finds may have been deposited in the periods preceding LH IIIB. Vessels were deposited in the LH IIIB and LH IIIC periods. The difference in total number of tombs in use between LH IIIA and LH IIIB is also at Tiryns significant whereas there is no change in the number of tombs in use in LH IIIC.

Although not as significant as at other sites, the LH IIIA period also at Tiryns is characterised by a discrepancy in tomb wealth and as such illustrates a more asymmetrical pattern. It can be observed that it is generally the chamber tombs with more deposits that are poorer than at other sites. Some finds, such as for example metals and the gem found, indicate extended relations with other settlements on the Argive Plain. The exchange that probably has been conducted in this period may also reflect the status of the local economy. Here, as elsewhere, the local economy was most probably based on a considerable degree of self-sufficiency. But, when other products than those produced locally were needed, either due to economic reasons or for socio-political motives, exchange took place. The number of tombs in use decreases in LH IIIB, but we may observe that four of the richer tombs were still in use. It is believed that also at Tiryns earlier deposits may have functioned as heirlooms. The chamber tombs indicate the emergence of a slightly symmetrical pattern, but the clear-cut symmetrical pattern found at other sites is not in evidence at Tiryns. The status of the settlement, as echoed by the chamber tombs, comes across as something of a surprise. This is especially so as the settlement saw considerably expansion in the LH IIIB period. As concerns the tholos, or tholoi, they may have been used in the latter part of the LH IIIB period. Here, as in the case with other tholoi, it seems plausible to emphasise the symbolic value of the tomb in connection with the actual burial ceremonies and, as is the case with Mycenae, it could therefore be interpreted as a symbol for a single event and a single family. As with other tombs, of course, the memory of those buried may have survived for a considerable time span.

Tiryns has been defined as one of the major sites on the Argive Plain, but compared to other sites the status, as reflected in the chamber tombs, is poorer in all periods. The tombs in use in the LH IIIA period correspond with the settlement evidence and may reflect the actual situation. However, the following LH IIIB period, especially LH IIIB2, is characterised by expansion as houses were constructed and the settlement area was extended. Production, especially in metals, is

[43] Rudolph 1973, 84, no. 15. Prosymna, tomb VI was in use in LH IIA and LH IIB2, XXXIV is pre-LH IIIB.

documented. Linear B material has been found and at least one tholos was in use. The settlement finds suggest a prospering community, which is not mirrored in the tomb material. In the LH IIIC period a more symmetrical pattern is observed. Only six tombs were in use and it is interesting to note that five of the richer tombs from the previous periods were still in use. It is possible that these tombs still had their value as burial for the local élite. The settlement evidence from LH IIIC contradicts the status of the settlement as mirrored in the tombs. The material suggests a site that expanded in LH IIIC and was apparently not in a dramatic decline.

8.4 DENDRA

The published tombs from Dendra are few and tomb nos. 4 and 5, excavated in the 1930s, remain unpublished.[44] The dating of the pottery in tombs 12, 13 and 14 has been made by P. Åström,[45] whereas the tombs published by A.W. Persson are dated with the help of published ceramic.[46] The number of tombs in use in different periods is not entirely consistent with the figures published by M.J. Alden;[47] this discrepancy arises from the attempt below to account for all pottery and figurines possible to date. Also at Dendra a tholos is found, dated to the LH IIIA1 period.[48]

The number of finds from some of the tombs is impressive; see, for example, tomb nos. 2, 10 and 12. Figurines were deposited in some tombs, namely nos. 1, 3 and 7.

Find categories: metal objects: bronze, gold, lead, silver; semi-precious stones: amethyst, agate, steatite, carnelian; amber; glass; ivory; faience; obsidian; bone; and wild-boars tusks.

Skeletal remains: yes.

Analysis

Cavanagh and Mee include the tombs from Dendra in their analysis. An interesting observation of theirs is that out of ten tombs all except one belong to wealth group 1 or 2. Tomb nos. 13 and 14 are not included in their investigation however. In tomb 13 the finds are limited to a large number of vessels, most of which belong to the periods LH IIIA1 and LH IIIA2. Tomb 14, for its part, is poor in LH IIIB1 remains with only a few vessels deposited.

The tombs are exceptionally well furnished with finds of other categories than pottery. Objects are made of metals such as bronze, gold, silver and large quantities of lead wire. Interestingly, the silver and lead found in tomb no. 8 was used only in the LH II period. Other categories of finds include semi-precious stones (agate, amethyst), glass, faience, amber and seal stones. Several of the rich tombs of Dendra were used already in the periods preceding LH IIIB. An exception is tomb no. 3, which apparently was used only in the LH IIIB period, but with a rich deposit of objects made of exclusive materials. Another rich tomb is no. 2, wealth group 2, also in use only in LH IIIB. Amber is documented in at least two tombs.[49] Tomb, no. 10, was in use in the periods preceding LH IIIB and the amber must have been an early deposit indicating exchange. Beads of precious stones are found in most tombs, whereas glass is more infrequent.[50] The glass found in tomb no. 6 is worthy of note, as it seems as this tomb was only used in LH IIA. Further finds include a bead of amethyst, perhaps of Egyptian origin. Ivory is seldom found and probably the objects are pre LH IIIB.[51]

The tombs are very rich in finds of metal objects and we may assume that in most cases they were deposited in the periods preceding LH IIIB. An amazingly large number of silver objects were registered in tomb 10, which also contained gold objects and several seal stones. Furthermore, a possible six tinned goblets were found in this tomb.[52] Yet Cavanagh and Mee defined the tomb as a category 2 tomb. Due to its rich finds, it would seem more natural to conceive of it as belonging to wealth group 1.[53] Bronze is found in most tombs and the deposits are sometimes impressive in size and quality. Suffice it to mention the scale pans found in tomb no. 10, which were, as is typically the case also at other sites, found in a pre LH IIIB context. Tomb no. 12, the so called Cuirass tomb, contained a most impressive array of finds of especially bronze objects. Also this tomb pre-dates LH IIIB; it was use in LH IIB-LH IIIA1. Here were also found fragments of silver vessels. Gold, finally, is found in several tombs, and in various chronological contexts.[54]

Summary

The tombs from Dendra differ from all other settlements in one important respect: here we have a very homogenous picture of wealth extending from LH II until the LH IIIC period, at which point only two tombs were apparently in use. The tombs are exceptional in their content, and especially the representation of objects made of metals is impressive. This is in contrast with other settlements as no observed decline in number of tombs in use between LH IIIA2 and LH IIIB is not found. Instead an increase in the number of tombs in use can be noticed.

The LH II period should be mentioned specifically as the tombs in use expose considerable wealth. Quite a few of the finds provide evidence for trade. For example, in tomb no. 8 silver and lead was found and these metals are

[44] Alden 1981, 260-261; Åström 1977; Persson 1931; 1942.
[45] Åström 1977.
[46] Åström 1977; Furumark 1972a, b; 1992; Mountjoy 1986; Persson 1931; 1942.
[47] Alden 1981, 262.
[48] Pelon 1976, 483-483.
[49] Tomb nos. 2, 10.
[50] Glass, tomb nos. 1, 2, 6.
[51] Tomb nos. 8, 12, 13. Tomb 13, however, used also in LH IIIB.
[52] Persson 1942, 59-101. Vessels nos. 41-45.
[53] Cavanagh & Mee 1990, 58.
[54] Tomb nos. 3, 7, 8, 9, 10, 11, 12.

not mined within the region. They must have been exchanged, either in the form of raw material or as finished objects. A seal was found in tomb no. 6, used only in LH IIA, and could indicate status of the owner.

Following Precourt, the symmetrical pattern observed in the LH IIIA1 period should indicate symmetrical economic relations based on reciprocity. The tholos in use in this period display wealth of a high level. Finds of exotic materials are numerous and find categories include objects such as semiprecious stones, glass, ostrich egg and faience, just to name a few. Interestingly, the large number of metal objects found in fact also includes iron. If it can be established beyond doubt that the rings are made of iron these finds are indeed unique.[55] The finds of metals such as bronze, silver, gold and tin and of other materials including amber and glass in earlier contexts attest to exchange having taken place already in the LH IIIA period. The LH IIA2 period follows the symmetrical pattern from the previous period. The tombs stand in contrast to the finds of the nearby settlement of Midea, with which we may assume that Dendra was associated, as there is no evidence there of prosperity in the periods preceding LH IIIB2. It has not been possible to verify that production took place at this site in the earlier periods and the exclusive objects found therefore were most probably obtained through exchange with other settlements. Scale-pans were found in tomb no. 10, in use before LH IIIB. This in turn indicates the need to measure something, in itself a further piece of evidence for exchange of items through trade or taxation. The strategic location of Dendra/Midea support the idea of the site as an early exchange node of goods distributed from the Berbati valley to Tiryns and Asine.

We may note that in contrast to other settlements the number of tombs increased in the LH IIIB period. The wealth displayed finds no parallel elsewhere in chamber tombs from this period; indeed, nearly all belong to wealth groups 1 or 2. What is more, wealth seems to have increased after the tholos ceased to be in use. This points towards the use of the chamber tomb as a symbol of importance for individuals and family groups. The pattern found at Dendra also stands in contrast to the conclusions drawn by Voutsaki, who regards the tholos a symbol for high status of persons and sites. The chamber tombs of Dendra shows that the tholos most probably did not have the single, exceptional extended symbolic meaning for the settlement. The increase of rich tombs in use at Dendra is paralleled in the pattern of economic prosperity observed in the rich settlement finds. The exchange relations established already in the LH II period continued into and extended throughout the LH IIIB period.

Only two tombs were used in the LH IIIC period and it is possible that other types of burial ceremonies were used as recent excavations at the settlement have exposed that also the LH IIIC period may have been well represented. It is assumed that the symmetrical pattern from the previous periods continued.

It must not be forgotten, however, that the number of tombs analysed is small. Yet the picture to emerge indicates a prosperous settlement where families displayed their status through exclusive finds in connection with burial ceremonies. Although limited in quantity because of the relative small number of tombs found and excavated, it cannot be ruled out that the prosperity extended to several families. However, it would be presumptuous to believe that the wealth displayed in the tombs comprised all individuals of the settlement. Quite possibly, most people were dependent on a household economy based on self-sufficiency.

To summarise, the chamber tombs at Dendra are few and from a statistical point of view not likely to yield significant results. Yet, by virtue of their character they are of considerable and general interest. Compared to other sites Dendra provides a more homogenous picture of affluence. It appears that all tombs, except nos. 1 and 14, were burials for families of higher social rank. If this is indeed indicative of the status of the settlement as a whole (even after allowing for the possibility that most of its inhabitants did not share into this affluence), Dendra/Midea was a site of importance from the LH II period until the end of the LH IIIC period.

8.5 ARGOS

Compared to other settlements, Argos is represented with a rather large number of chamber tombs and also pit and fossa graves. The following discussion is based on material published by W. Vollgraff and J. Deshayes.[56]

The chamber tombs reported mostly contained pottery; other finds are rare.

Find categories: metals: gold, bronze, lead; semi-precious stones: steatite; ivory; clay.

Skeletal remains: yes.

Analysis

The chamber tombs at Argos follow the pattern most prominently seen at Mycenae and Prosymna. That is, an increase in tombs in use between can be noticed from LH IIIA1 to LH IIIA2. This stands in contrast to the decrease of tombs in use observed at other settlements. Interestingly, vessels deposited in the LH IIIB period are nearly absent at Argos. As concerns the LH IIIC period, traces of burials have been found also in other areas at Argos.[57]

The tombs at Argos are quite empty of other find categories than pottery. A more detailed study of the tombs shows that three of them – Vollgraff nos. I, IV and

[55] Persson 1931, 33.

[56] Deshayes 1953, 59-89; 1966; 1969, 574-616; Vollgraff 1904, 364-399.

[57] Croissant 1972, 883-886.

Table 8.5: Tombs in use/number of dated pottery at Argos, Vollgraf[58]

Tomb No.	LH I	LH IIA	LH IIB	LH IIIA1	LH IIIA2	LH IIIB	LH IIIC
I						17	
II					10	14	
III			1	6	3		
IV					7	1	
VI			1	15	9	4	
VII			7	7	5	3	
VIII				4	13	5	
IX			7	13	6	2	2
Tombs/Vessels			4/16	5/45	7/53	7/46	1/2

Table 8.6: Tombs in use/number of dated pottery at Argos, Upper Town

Tomb No.	LH I	LH IIA	LH IIB	LH IIIA1	LH IIIA2	LH IIIB	LH IIIC
XXIV				5	4		
XXVI				1	1	3	
XXVII					3	1	
XXVIII						3	
XXVIIIA					2		
XXIX					4	2	1
XXX				1	sherds	1	2
XXXII					1		
XXXIII				2	6		1
XXXIV					sherds		
XXXV					2	14	
XXXVI						1	
Tombs/Vessels				4/7	10/17	7/25	3/3

Table 8.7: Tombs in use/number of dated pottery at Argos, Lower Town

Tomb No.	LH I	LH IIA	LH IIB	LH IIIA1	LH IIIA2	LH IIIB	LH IIIC
XI					5		
XII					4	9	
XIII					2		
XIV					1	10	4
XV						sherds	
XVI					4	2	6
XVII					1	2	4
XVIII							1
XIX					2	1	
XX							1
XXI					4	2	
XXII							3
XXIII						1	
XXXI							3
Tombs/Vessels					8/23	9/27	7/22

[58] Alden 1981, 185; Deshayes 1953; 1966; 1969; Furumark 1972a, 585-643.

VI – were empty as regards find categories other than pottery, and figurines dominated the others. The only exception is tomb III, were the single object found was a steatite button.[59] The pattern is repeated in other Deiras tombs.[60] The content of these tombs cannot be compared with other cemeteries and their pattern of richer tombs represented in the earlier periods. An exceptionally large number of vessels deposited in LH IIIB should perhaps balance the lack of other objects. However, a closer examination of tomb contents shows that only three tombs, I, II and XXXV, contained more than ten vessels and only the latter tomb had more exclusive categories of objects deposited.[61]The vessels deposited in the remaining tombs number between one and ten in each tomb. In other words, no large or exclusive deposits have been found.

We may note that the occurrence of exotic material is insubstantial. Ivory, for example, is registered only in tomb XXIV, in use LH IIIA1-LH IIIA2, and tomb XXX, in use from LH IIIA1 to LH IIIC. Amber is not found and precious metals such as gold and silver are very rare. One gold ring, flake of bronze and lead bands are mentioned in tomb XXXV (LH IIIA2/LH IIIB). Two bronze buckles were found in tomb XVI (LH IIIA2-Geom) and a bronze rivet in tomb XVII (LH IIIB/IIIC). Tomb XXX1 (LH IIIC) contained a metal object (knife?). Further objects made of metal were found in tomb XXIV (LH IIIA1/IIIA2) where a ring, a balance, knife, nails and a mirror were deposited. Also tomb XXIX (LH IIIA2-LH IIIC) had several small objects of metal such as nails, two finger rings and a fibula. Tomb XXXIII (LH IIIA1/IIIA2) contained a nail and a fragment of a finger ring. In grave 21a was a balance weight of LH IIIA1 date found.[62]

To the chamber tomb material in Argos we may also add the large number of published pit graves, some 30 of them, mainly in use in the LH IIIA1-LH IIIA2 periods. Also these tombs have unsubstantial finds as only nine of them had other objects than vessels deposited. The objects found are figurines, beads, buttons and fragment of metal.[63]

Summary

Argos, and the status of the finds made there, contrasts very much with the situation at other settlements. The rather few objects made of precious materials of exotic origin, or with high labour input, indicates a status of tombs at a considerable remove from those found, for example, at Mycenae and Asine. Furthermore, it may indicate that exchange between Argos and other settlements was insignificant. Of course, the imbalance may also be explained as a result of excavations conducted at the sites, but the number of known tombs is rather large and therefore useful. As a consequence, it cannot be ruled out – if anything, it seems rather plausible – that the situation at Argos was different due to the economic means of those who built the tombs. No tombs with exceptionally rich finds have been located and only tombs XXIV, XXIX, XXX and XXXV may be compared to those found in wealth group 1 and 2 at other sites. Interpreted in economic terms, the pattern indicates that people did not have the economic means to acquire these objects. The few registered exceptions, that is, exclusive finds, are marginal compared with other settlements. It is also possible that the large number of other types of graves in use mainly in LH IIIA could be a further indication of the status of the settlement.

A certain level of regional exchange is indicated in objects of similar type or similar material, such as bronze and ivory, found also at other sites in the Argive region. The status of infrastructure on the Argive Plain in the periods preceding LH IIIB is rather vague and as shown by Lavery no obvious communication routes connected Argos to other sites in LH IIIA.[64] Although quite few in number, the finds do however suggest that certain contacts were maintained with other sites and informal roads, that is paths, plausible served as communication routes. With respect to transport, apparently the situation changed in LH IIIB as a road connecting Argos and Mycenae has been documented.[65]

To conclude, the tombs indicate a symmetrical economic situation already in the LH IIIA period with no significant wealth distinction such as observed at other sites. No dramatic change in number of tombs in use is observable in the transition to LH IIIB and the pattern of symmetry is repeated across periods. In the LH IIIC period a decrease of tombs in use can be observed and the symmetrical pattern continued with poor tombs in use. The following Submycenaean period is represented at Argos, although our knowledge about it is limited. Even so, the presence of tombs is an indication of continuity also here.[66]

Limited external relations may explain the few objects made of exotic exclusive material found in the tombs. For example, ivory is documented only in two tombs, lead only in one and the same applies to gold.[67] Similarly, bronze is quite infrequently found in the tombs.[68] Interestingly, weights and balances have been found in contexts as early as LH IIIA1-LH IIIA2 and LH IIIB/C. Their presence indicates the need for measuring and also exchange already in LH IIIA1. Balances and weights have been found also at other sites and it is possible that these tombs may have been the burial grounds for merchants or other categories involved in trade. If so,

[59] Deshayes 1969, 574-616.
[60] Deshayes 1953, 59-89; 1966.
[61] Deshayes 1966, 104-110.
[62] Deshayes 1966, 82.
[63] Graves nos. 11, 12, 17, 18, 19, 21a, 23, 25 and 27.
[64] Lavery 1995, maps 1-2.
[65] Lavery 1995, maps 1-2.
[66] Hägg 1974, 23-27.
[67] Ivory: nos. XXIV, XXX; lead: XXXV; gold: XXXV.
[68] Tomb nos. XVI, XVII, XII, XXXI, XXIV, XXIX, XXXV, XXXVI, 21a.

these categories may have constituted a more affluent part of the population and also an elite within the local community.

Following Precourt, the symmetrical pattern displayed in the tombs material indicates that the local economy may have been based on reciprocal exchange of commodities. Yet, the low level of affluence may in itself suggest a high level of self-sufficiency. If and when non-local products were needed, or a surplus production of goods was possible, reciprocal exchange may have followed, based on supply and demand for goods of interest. It is quite possible of course that Argos through all periods has functioned as a node for exchange, although on different levels, conducted with villages and farmstead in the hinterland of the settlement. The presence of objects made of precious, non-local, materials is evidence of products flowing from external trade partners to the site, and may we assume, local products moving into the regional exchange system.

8.6 PROSYMNA

At Prosymna, the number of known chamber tombs is large. These have been published by C. Blegen.[69] At the time when the report was published the knowledge concerning the chronology of Mycenaean pottery was not fully developed. The tombs were later examined in more detail by Furumark and as a result we have published dates for the tombs at our disposal.[70] More recently still, Shelton conducted an analysis of vessel deposited and thanks to this study more detailed chronological information concerning each tomb is at hand.[71] During the present study it became clear that the pottery attributed to three tombs, XXXII, XXXVIII and XLIII, dated to LH IIIB, was nowhere to be seen. Instead, these tombs contained figurines. Although probably from the LH IIIB period, it makes dating less precise and secure. As for burial goods, Cavanagh and Mee grouped the tombs into four wealth groups. In view of the importance of their work to the present analysis, two small remarks are in order. Firstly, tomb no. XLII have been counted twice, with slightly different results.[72] Secondly, tomb no. IX was not analysed, but it is poorly equipped and is best thought of as belonging to group 4.

Pottery is well represented and the majority is decorated.[73]
Find categories: metals: gold, bronze, lead, silver; semi-precious stones: crystal, carnelian, amethyst, steatite; amber; glass; ivory; obsidian; stone; bone; shells; terracotta; figurines; seals.
Skeletal remains: yes.

Analysis

The analysis presented by Cavanagh and Mee of tombs within each wealth group is sometimes difficult to follow and a commentary concerning the division is necessary. It has already earlier been proposed that pottery, as a find group, should not have been excluded in the analysis. This is so on account of pottery not being a marginal deposit in tombs. An overview of tombs shows that pottery is well represented in most of them, including a majority of tombs in group 3.[74] These figures are unexpected as these tombs are counted as representing the poorer part of the population. By the same token, those thought of as belonging to wealth group 3 includes several tombs that have more objects deposited in the, than some of those included into groups 1 and 2.[75] In group 1 and 2 we find the reverse situation, as tombs X and L have few vases and the other finds which make them similar to tombs defined as group 3.

The second wealth group is represented by only three tombs. As has already been suggested, as the objects deposited are few tomb no. L may better be assigned to wealth group 3. Tombs XVIII and XLIX could also be candidates for reassignment as not only many vessels, but also several categories of finds such as silver, gold and amber, were found in them. The tombs are more similar to wealth group 1 tombs than the second one. Finally, while on the subject of fine tuning, tomb XIII, categorised as wealth group 4, should perhaps be better thought of as belonging to group 2. It did after all yield, amongst other things, a seal, a dagger and a knife.

The finds represent categories found also at other sites, including Mycenae, Asine, Midea and Tiryns. Objects made of bronze, especially daggers and knifes, are frequently found,[76] whereas gold objects are found in only five tombs chronologically covering LH IIIA to LH IIIB1.[77] Lead wire is found in tombs where a majority represents wealth group 1; also these cover nearly all Late Helladic periods except LH IIIC.[78] Silver is not limited to wealthier tombs or specific periods. At least one group 3 tomb contained traces of silver and chronologically these tombs extend over several periods.[79] Interestingly, there are reports of tinned vessels in tomb XXXVII, but perhaps also nos. XXXVIII, XLI, XV and II. The vessels in tomb XXXVIII are dated to LH IIIA1 and 2, and we may also conclude that if tinned vessels are found in

[69] Blegen 1937.
[70] Furumark 1972b, 129-131.
[71] Shelton 1996.
[72] Cavanagh & Mee 1992, 58.
[73] Shelton 1996, 294-295.

[74] Tomb nos. VIII, XVIII, XIX, XXI, XXIV, XXV, XXXIII, XXXVI, XXXVII, XLV, LI and W I, all have more than 15 vases deposited.
[75] Blegen 1937, 253. Tomb nos. VIII, XVII, XXI, XXIV, XXV and XXXVI.
[76] Blegen 1937. Tomb nos. XXVI, XIV, XXIX, XXXIV, XXXVIII, XLI, XLII, XLIII, XLIV, XLIX, W II, XIII, XXVII, XXXII, XXXV, LII, II, III, X, VII, XV, XVII, XVIII, XIX, XXI, XXIV, XXV, XXVIII, XXX, XXXIII, XXXVI, XXXVII, XLVI, LI,.
[77] Tomb nos. II, III XLI, XLIV = W G 1, XLIX = W G 2.
[78] Tomb nos. XXVI, XXIX, XLI, XLII, XLIV, X, VII, XXXIII.
[79] Tomb nos. XLIII, XLIV, XLIX, III, XXX.

Table 8.8: Tombs in use /number of dated pottery at Prosymna[80]

Tomb No.	LH I	LH IIA	LH IIB	LH IIIA1	LH IIIA2	LH IIIB1	LH IIIB2
I W G 3		4	1			7	
II W G 1		2	9	25			
III W G 1		1	3	7	14		1
IV W G 3					5		
V W G 3						3	
VI W G 3		1					3
VII W G 3		1			3	3	
VIII W G 3			3	3	23	2	
IX							1
X W G 1					3	10	1
XI W G 4		2	3	1	13		
XII W G 4					6	4	
XIII W G 4		2	5	3	4	1	
XIV W G 1		4	2		6	1	1
XV W G 4					4	1	2
XVI W G 4					5		
XVII W G 3		11	6	6	3	4	
XVIII W G 3		2	8	6	7	3	
XIX W G 3					3	3	2
XX W G 4						1	3
XXI W G 3				1	26	5	
XXII W G 4					5	8	1
XXIII W G 3							
XXIV W G 3				1	36	3	
XXV W G 3	9	4	1	3	15	1	
XXVI W G 1	11	1	5			7	
XXVII W G 4					11		
XXVIII W G 3		3	3		28	5	
XXIX W G 1			8	11	11		
XXX W G 3		6	3				
XXXII W G 4		1	2		8	figurine	
XXXIII W G 3				7	23	6	4
XXXIV W G 1		1	3	22	39		
XXXV W G 4					6	1	
XXXVI W G 3			6	10	7	3	1
XXXVII W G 3				13	5	4	
XXXVIII WG1				2 (tinned?)	16 (tinned?)	figurines	
XXXIX W G 4					4	1	
XL W G 4					1	7	
XLI W G 1					37	4	
XLII W G 1			3	11	15	3	
XLIII W G 2				16	28	figurine	
XLIV W G 1		12	1		27	10	
XLV W G 3			3	1	5	13	
XLVI W G 4		3	1		5		
XLVII W G 4					2		
XLVIII W G 4				1	10		
XLIX W G 2			3		11	3	
L W G 2			6		2	4	
LI W G 3				2	21		
LII W G 4	4			1			
WI			6	4	3		
WII	empty						
Tombs/Vessels	3/24	17/61	24/94	23/157	42/503	31/131	10/20

[80] Alden 1981 has a table based on the chronology in Furumark 1972a, 585-643; 1972b, 129-131; Shelton 1996.

tomb II they are not later than LH IIIA1.[81] Beads made of precious stones are found in a larger quantity and some may have originated outside the Argolid.[82] Thebes has plausibly been suggested as a possible locality for non-local production of these goods as evidence of jewellery production is documented there in LH IIIB1.[83] Glass was also found in large number and these objects are found in tombs covering all periods and all wealth groups.[84] Amber was found in nine tombs.[85] Faience was found in tombs covering most periods.[86]A majority of these are clustered in the two highest wealth groups and chronologically covers LH IIA to LH IIIB1. Ivory was found in at least 13 tombs.[87] As noted by Blegen, ivory was imported and then worked on the mainland. However, the ivory finds in tombs II, XI and XXIX, in use before the LH IIIB period, raises the possibility of imported finished goods as the production of ivory is not yet documented for the region at this early point in time.

Summary

Prosymna is valuable as a case study as the number of excavated and published tombs is large. In LH IIA to LH IIIA1 an asymmetrical pattern can be observed with approximately a third of the tombs classified as group 1 and 2. The following period, LH IIIA2, shows an increase in the number of poorer tombs and in the LH IIIB1 period even more tombs of categories 3 and 4 are to be found. The largest number of tombs in use is concentrated to the LH IIIA2 and LH IIIB1 periods. This pattern harmonises with the results presented by Shelton who suggests that the LH IIA period is best interpreted as the starting point for a long period of expansion, not only in population, but also in wealth. The process of improvement continues, according to Shelton, into the LH IIIA2, described as the wealthiest and most populated at the settlement.[88] The LH IIIB1 period is then seen as a period of slight decrease in the population; as such it is also reflected in the display of wealth.[89] The number of tombs in use decreased and amongst the tombs to disappear we find those included in the highest wealth group. Poorer tombs now predominate and wealth represented through tombs seems more symmetrical. The LH IIIC period is not represented in the tomb material and it is quite possible that the cemetery was located elsewhere. However, most probably the settlement was abandoned and not resettled.

Prosymna is also represented by several other categories of finds, such as amber, ivory and gold; these have been documented in tombs in use in periods preceding LH IIIB. The finds suggests that exchange occurred with other sites already in the earliest part of the Late Helladic period and continued throughout the period. So far, production of objects made of precious materials has not been documented in the Argolid in periods preceding LH IIIB1. Thebes is an interesting candidate as an exchange partner as early (i.e., up to LH IIIB1) production of gold, bronze, jewellery, ivory, glass and so on has been documented at that particular site.[90] The location of Prosymna at the end of road m4 (fig. 5) indicates that the site may have functioned as a market for goods exchanged with other sites already in the pre-LH IIIB periods.[91] The road appears to have connected Prosymna with Mycenae and it is quite possible that the northern site was the entry point for goods of a non-regional character. As is often the case, it cannot be ruled out that peasant goods were transferred via Prosymna to other settlements and in return commodities not obtainable locally were received in return. The asymmetrical pattern could be seen as characteristic for a redistributive economy, but it could also be interpreted as sign of market transactions. Even though the prehistoric economy may have been based for the most part on a considerable degree of self-sufficiency, this should not be thought of as excluding the possibility of different types of reciprocal exchange taking place.

The LH IIIB1 period show a decrease in number of tombs in use and it is noticeable that few tombs of wealth categories 1 and 2 are in use. A further decrease of tombs in use is observed during the LH IIIB2 period, when the symmetrical pattern identified for LH IIIB1 continues. The symmetrical pattern points in the direction an economy founded on reciprocity. We may suggest that the exchange pattern demonstrated for the LH IIIA period was valid also in LH IIIB. It is possible, of course, that the exchange relations may have changed character and trade diminished, but on the other hand the site was better linked to Tiryns in this period as road M4 passed Prosymna on its way south (*fig.* 5). Tiryns prospered in LH IIIB and it is quite possible that Prosymna did not go empty-handed.

At Prosymna, as at other Argive sites, finds indicate that certain families had the economic means to acquire objects traded long-distance. Tombs containing a large number of these objects are generally thought of as tombs belonging to wealthier groups. However, this does not stand up to closer scrutiny. If this was indeed the case, how should we then explain the presence of these objects in less wealthy tombs, where they have in fact also been found? Even for poorer families the symbolic and ritual meaning could have been of importance. As concerns deposits in tombs used also in LH IIIA and LH IIIB, it has been repeatedly proposed above that objects deposited earlier functioned as heirloom. It should be noted, though, and as originally proposed by Blegen, that it is also possible that heirlooms could have been

[81] Immerwahr 1966, only vessels for no. XXXVIII were registered in the article.
[82] Blegen 1937, 253, 287-296.
[83] Demakopoulou 1990a, 311.
[84] Blegen 1937, 296-306.
[85] Blegen 1937, 253, tomb nos. II, III, VII, XLI, XLII, XLIII, XLIV, XLIX, LI.
[86] Blegen 1937, 306-312.
[87] Blegen 1937, 281-285.
[88] Shelton 1996, 276-284.
[89] Shelton 1996, 291.
[90] Demakopoulou 1990a, 311-313.
[91] Lavery 1995, m-roads = pre-LH IIIB, M-roads = LH IIIB.

deposited with the dead.[92] If so, this could explain the presence of certain categories of finds produced in earlier periods, but found in later tomb contexts.

Child burials in chamber tombs are found also at Prosymna where probably nineteen tombs contained child bones.[93] The presence of children indicates the importance of status inheritance, be it thought of in economical, political or social terms. It can be argued that the presence of children in burials is an emerging conception and that the consciousness of the importance of lineage and symbol for continuity of the family group increases over time. This proposition is supported by the fact that simpler tomb types are relatively rare after LH II, with the exception for children's burials. Interestingly, these burials are dug within chamber and tholos tombs, or in dromoi.[94] In the case of Prosymna we may observe that child burials are not limited to tombs of wealth category 1; rather a majority were buried in tombs classified as poorer. Late Helladic figurines were found in several tombs and it was observed by Blegen that a majority of these contained children's bones.[95] Figurines are found in tombs of both the LH IIIA and LH IIIB period and a majority is found in tombs of wealth categories 3 and 4. I would not exclude the possibility that figurines indicate change in burial customs.

8.7 BERBATI

At Berbati, only eight chamber tombs, out of an unknown number, have been published. One tomb was excavated and later published by E. Holmberg.[96] During an excavation conducted by G. Säflund another seven chamber tombs were discovered and later published.[97] Both publications are detailed. As also the pottery is dated, a chronological discussion is facilitated. The limited number of tombs is, however, something to bear in mind when discussing the tombs. At Berbati a tholos has also been found and although robbed on a majority of finds the single burial is dated to LH IIIA1.[98]

The finds are dominated by pottery and only the chamber tomb excavated by Holmberg yielded a larger amount of other find categories than pottery. Similarly, compared to other chamber tomb cemeteries on the Argive Plain, the number of find categories is limited.

Find categories: metal; bronze, tin encrusted vessels, semi-precious stones; steatite, carnelian, terracotta; glass; figurines.

Skelatal remains: yes.

Analysis

The pottery material makes evident that tombs were in use in the period LH IIIA1 to LH IIIB. However, in the dromos of tomb I some sherds representing the LH II period were found together with two whorls of steatite, indicating earlier use of the tomb (even though Säflund did not interpret it this way).[99] The vessels found in the tombs belong mainly to the LH IIIA1 and LH IIIA2 periods, whereas LH IIIB is represented with only a few vessels. The number of vessels is comparatively small and amongst those excavated by Säflund only tomb no. XII has more than twenty vessels. The other exception is the tomb excavated by Holmberg; this contained 43 vessels of which 14 were tinned.

Pottery dominated the finds and a survey of the tombs shows that other find categories represented are rather poor. The tombs contained beads of glass paste, although not in any large number. The only exception is tomb V, where more than forty beads made of cornelian, whorls made of steatite and also figurines were found. In comparison with other cemeteries, the tombs at Berbati are quite empty of metal finds. A few objects made of bronze have been located in tomb nos. II, III, X, and XI. The tomb excavated by Holmberg displayed two leaf shaped daggers, fragments of a bronze bowl, six fragmentary or whole arrowheads, pieces of gold plate, several metres of lead wire and in addition the tomb contained 14 tin covered LH IIIA2 vessels.[100] The tomb compares with some of the rich tombs found at for example Mycenae, Dendra and Asine. The tin-covered vessels and other objects made of exotic and precious materials indicate external exchange relations. A category of finds quite frequently found at other cemeteries, but not registered at Berbati, is beads of amber. The tombs also differ from other as none of them had objects made of faience, ivory or silver.

Summary

Generally speaking, the tombs were poorly equipped with grave goods. The only exception is the tomb published by Holmberg as it is in both find categories and number of finds comparable to those more well-equipped at other cemeteries. The 14 tin-encrusted vessels are of particular interest as the metal is not very frequent in tomb contexts and, as a rare metal, indicative of high status. Tin-covered vessels in this period have also been found at Asine, Mycenae and Prosymna and their very presence suggest regional exchange relations. Other objects made of bronze, gold, glass paste and semi-precious stones are further evidence on external relations. The finds from the LH IIIA2 period may have been distributed via the road linking Berbati with Mycenae in the north and Dendra/Midea and Tiryns in the south. I would suggest that the presence of tin-covered vessels also at Asine point towards that settlement as a port of trade in this

[92] Blegen 1937, 261.
[93] Blegen 1937, 252.
[94] Dickinson 1983, 62; Voutsaki 1995a, 62.
[95] Blegen 1937, 255-256, tomb nos. VIII, XXVIII, XXXIII, XXXVI, XLV, WI, X, III, XXIX, XXXVIII, XLII, XLIII, XXVII, XXXII, XXXV.
[96] Holmberg 1983.
[97] Säflund 1965.
[98] Santillo Frizell 1984.
[99] Säflund 1965, 22-23, 81, table 6.
[100] Holmberg 1983, 34-41.

Table 8.9: Tombs in use/number of dated pottery at Berbati[101]

Tomb No.	LH I	LH IIA	LH IIB	LH IIIA1	LH IIIA2	LH IIIB	LH IIIC
I		sherds	sherds		12	5	
II				8	3		
III					18		
VIII					1		
X				8	4	7	
XI				11	4		
XII				14	9		
Holmberg					37 (14 tinned)	6	
Tombs/Vessels		1/sherds	1/sherds	4/41	8/88	3/18	

Table 8.10: Number of tombs in use at Schoinochori[102]

Tomb No.	LH I	LH IIA	LH IIB	LH IIIA1	LH IIIA2	LH IIIB	LH IIIC
A					X		
B					X		
G			X?		X		
D				X	X		
E	X	X		X	X		
Tombs/Vessels	1	1	1?	2	5		

[101] Alden 1981, 279; Furumark 1972a, 585-643; Holmberg 1983; Säflund 1965.
[102] Alden 1981, 289; Furumark 1972b, 41, 52-57.

period. The vessels produced at the workshop at Berbati may have been transported from here.

It may perhaps be expected that the position of Berbati as a producer and distributor of high quality pottery between LH IIB and LH IIIB1[103] should have been mirrored in tombs containing more numerous finds of exotic and valuable objects. Instead, the group of tombs analysed is small and suggests an socio-economic situation without extreme social differentiation. An exception is the tomb excavated by Holmberg. Its tinned vessels indicate that those using the tomb had the economic means to acquire these vessels. Tin was not obtained locally and is a sign of external relations. On the other hand, the metal may have been applied on the vases at the local workshop. The appearance of a tholos, probably not in use later than LH IIIA1, indicates social stratification, although not pronounced in this period. The tombs in use in LH IIIA reflect a slightly asymmetrical pattern of wealth. The number in use decreased to the point where only three poor tombs existed in LH IIIB. The pattern to emerge indicates symmetrical economic relations. No tombs could be connected to the LH IIIC period. The pattern associated with LH IIIB and LH IIIC may reflect the economy of the Berbati region after the workshop closed. The quite insubstantial number of objects indicating contacts with areas outside the locality could be interpreted as a local economy based on self-sufficiency. The exotic finds in a few tombs may have been exchanged in connection with pottery distributed for sale. It is possible that reciprocal exchange of commodities was the predominant model of trade.

8.8 SCHOINOCHORI

Few chamber tombs have been published and the information concerning finds is very poor.
Finds: pottery.
Skeletal remains: yes.

Analysis

The tombs have all been in use for a fairly short period of time. All have evidence of the LH IIIA2 period, but only two, possibly three, have been in use in any other period. Also, the number of burials in each tomb was small.[104] As already established by Alden, few tombs represent the Late Helladic period and we may assume that the number of persons living in this community was comparatively small.[105] Following the description of the published tombs they were fairly poor and no spectacular finds were registered.[106]

Summary

The total number of tombs found is small and it is difficult to estimate whether these tombs reflect the reality of the LH III period. If they do, we may assume that the community living here was quite small and the goods deposited in the excavated tombs do not expose a flourishing society. Rather, the tombs may be classified as of wealth groups 3 or 4.

8.9 OTHER SITES

These sites all have very few chamber tombs published, although in several cases the known number is higher.

The material

Aria, Kiveri, Kokla, Lerna, Monasteraki, Nauplion, Phychtia, Vreserka.[107]

Analysis

Very few chamber tombs have been found at respective site and the material is for most part too scanty for an analysis both of rank and of the possible connections between sites.[108] The site of Lerna is of special interest, as the area was inhabited for a long period. The importance in the MH period is made manifest through settlement installations and tombs documented, both at Lerna itself and in the surrounding area.[109] However, the material evidence for the Late Helladic period is scarce and very few tombs representing this period have been found. Two shaft graves from the early Mycenaean period have been documented and Wiencke, in a recent article, suggests that this may indicate a certain degree of independence for the site. The LHIIIA2 period is represented by few burials; Wiencke interprets this as representing a period of more centralised control, conducted by a larger neighbouring settlement that may have been Argos.[110]

At Kokla has recently been located one tholos and nine chamber tombs.[111] The tombs were not looted and therefore provide us with important information concerning their content. The tholos is dated to LH IIB-LH IIIA1 and the finds published show that the tomb was richly endowed. Most vases are LH IIA and LH IIB, some are LH IIIA1, LH IIIA2 and LH IIIB. Amongst other, four LH IIIA1 silver kylikes as well as three silver conical cups were found. Interestingly, the shapes are similar to LH IIIA1 clay types.[112] The chamber tombs were used from LH I to perhaps LH IIIB and according to Demakopoulou the cemetery could be compared with those at Dendra and Prosymna. The nine tombs found all had rich deposits of finds and the total number of vessels comprises 232 complete vases. Apparently most vases could have been produced in the Argolid and the closest parallels are found at Mycenae, Prosymna and Argos.[113]

[103] Schallin 1997, 77-78.
[104] Alden 1981, 289.
[105] Alden 1981, 289-290.
[106] Renaudin 1923, 190-240.

[107] Bibliography for each site, see Alden 1981; Cavanagh & Mee 1998.
[108] Alden 1981, 307-315.
[109] Dietz & Divari-Valakou 1990, 62.
[110] Wiencke 1998, 208.
[111] Demakopoulou 1990b 113-123, 1993, 57-75, Pl. 1-14.
[112] Demakopoulou 1990b, 119, figs. 8-12; 1993, 59, 70.
[113] Demakopoulou 1993 57-59, 70-71.

Unfortunately, so far only a few of the vases have been published.

The total number of chamber tombs at Nauplion, so far registered, is more than 50.[114] It is of particular interest to note that most of the latest discovered tombs seem to have been in use until the end of LH IIIA, whereas no information of deposited LH IIIB or LH IIIC pottery is provided. As observed by Alden, the chamber tomb cemetery is important due to the large number of tombs and their contents.[115] The other sites are not well documented and it is believed that they constituted small communities essentially based on self-sufficiency.

Summary

Information concerning chamber tombs found at these sites is too scanty for any detailed discussion concerning the local communities using these tombs to be made. Kokla of considerable interesting, though, as the rich tombs and the content of the tholos gives evidence of a prospering site – at least until the end of LH IIIA1, when apparently most tombs ceased to be in use. According to Demakopoulou, the richly furnished chamber tombs strengthen the picture of a rich community that must have been an important centre in its own right.[116] As concerns Nauplion not much can be said about the local community. The apparently large number of chamber tombs identified indicates that this may have been a settlement of importance, at least in the periods preceding LH IIIB, perhaps deriving its status from its location by the sea. The lack of material from the LH IIIB and LH IIIC periods indicates a change to a less important site. This may have been so due to the expansion of Tiryns in LH IIIB, as well as LH IIIC.

8.10 THE REGIONAL PERSPECTIVE AS REFLECTED IN THE TOMB MATERIAL

As has been shown earlier, most scholars have rejected the idea of chamber tombs as symbols for a specific social group. Rather, this particular type is generally regarded as interments for the larger part of the Late Helladic population. There is little reason to object to the view that chamber tombs represented the larger part of the population and that, as a consequence, social and economic ranking should be looked for in the differences between individual tombs. But before turning to an extended discussion on these matters, a brief survey and analysis of the tholos would be useful. This is so in light of prevailing view that this type of tomb, and unlike the chamber tombs, has been regarded as an important symbol for status.

The view of the tholos tomb as a pre-eminent symbol of an élite and as an expression of their power is so common so as to constitute the archaeological equivalent of a truism. The symbolic value need therefore be considered in detail before a discussion concerning settlement relations as displayed in the chamber tomb material is embarked upon. The question is whether the tholos should be regarded as an expression of a high status burial and, if so, whether the symbolic meaning is restricted to one burial event, or is there a chronologically extended symbolic meaning?

Recently Voutsaki discussed the problem, claiming that the tholos probably had different symbolic meanings in different regions. She tries to demonstrate that the situation in the Argolid and Messenia may not have been equivalent. Whereas in the Argolid the tholos carried the weight of a symbol of status under political and economic centralisation, the Messenian tholos, although important, had few of these connotations. The difference is deduced from the fact that, in the former case, the use of the tomb was the restricted to the LH IIIA2-LH IIIB period, that is, the very period during which economic and political centralisation took place.[117]

Also Wright, who sees a major change from the Shaft Grave period to the following palatial periods, favours the idea of a political territorial symbolic significance where the tholos was used as part of a larger statement of power. The change should, accordingly, be seen as change in the political complexity of Mycenae with the tholos tomb as a symbol for political control extending over a wider territory and with the efficiency as a symbol for the leader within the period of rule.[118]

This is a stance also adapted by Wells, who regards the tholos as a burial form which, through its monumentality and spatial separation from other types of tombs, expressed the higher status of the leaders buried there or else associated with it. The leaders were important as they symbolised stability and continuity and their status might have been legitimised through ancestral remains. Wells thus considers the tholos as a symbolic territorial marker of ownership, not merely a border marker.[119]

The role of the tholos in royal propaganda has been discussed at some length by Santillo Frizell. She is convinced that the propaganda was not directed only towards an audience in the local and regional realm but also towards a much wider sphere and the target of the message was the Eastern Mediterranean and the Near East.[120] Bennet in a recent article on the palatial centres in Messenia puts forth the equally interesting idea that the symbolic meaning of the tholos may have changed over time. Perhaps, at some point, the tholos was no longer a symbol intended for display to a wider community. The symbolic value may instead have been associated with the ruling elite and also with the historical roots. Instead, the display of elite status may in

[114] For bibliography see, Alden 1981, 292-299; Cavanagh & Mee 1998, 83.
[115] Alden 1981, 297-298.
[116] Demakopoulou 1990, 113; 1993, 71.
[117] Voutsaki 1998, 55-56.
[118] Wright 1987, 176, 183-184.
[119] Wells 1990, 128, note 24.
[120] Santillo Frizell 1998, 183.

the later phases have been expressed through festivals, feasting and other ceremonies and rituals.[121]

While it is easy to go along with the proposition that the tholos carried symbolic content, it is more difficult to establish, and hence to accept without the availability of further supporting evidence, that its role extended beyond the period of actual use. Similarly, instead of encompassing or extending to the polity as such, any symbolic value could have been limited to the individual or a family connected with it. At the very least, in the absence of additional evidence, we should be careful not to extend it beyond the time of the burial and the ceremonials connected therewith. Thus, as the sealing of the dromos and stomion was obviously an accepted burial custom during the Mycenaean period,[122] the custom to close the tomb and also cover it with earth can be interpreted as a highly symbolic action that not only closed the tomb and prevented it from being robbed, but also affected the presence and nearness of the deceased. With the disappearance of the monumentality – it was after all covered – also the symbolic meaning, such as high status and power, connected with an individual ruler can be assumed to have faded away. Especially, this can be assumed to have been the case in those instances where the tomb was not reused for further burials. The meaning of the tomb then changed with time, as pointed out by Bennet.

The acceptance of the opposite view, where the tholos as a strong symbol of power survives for extended periods of time, should logically lead to the conclusion that a very different set of relationship between and relative of settlements must be taken into account. This is so, as several other sites used the tholos in earlier periods. With such a scenario the obvious conclusion would be that also other settlements with tholoi in use in the pre-LH IIIB periods should have been honoured with a high rank also subsequently, that is, in the periods after closing the tomb. Such examples include Dendra and Kokla, where rich tholos tombs were in use in LH IIIIA1, but not later. The hitherto accepted view of Mycenae as the supercentre during the mature Mycenaean period would thus be challenged by virtue of the extended symbolic meaning of tholoi elsewhere. The tholos as a long term manifestation of settlement power and status therefore does not comes across as particularly plausible. Instead the symbolic value should be seen as connected to those using the tomb rather than the physical structure per se.

More generally, Cavanagh and Mee have suggested that status may have been expressed through tomb content and size. The obvious disparity in size and wealth, Cavanagh and Mee maintain, can be interpreted as an indication of alliances between rich and poor families maintained after death. Against the background of the material from Asine and the other settlements presented above, we find that their proposal receives some support.

[121] Bennet 1999, 16.

[122] Wright 1987, 183.

The depositing of finds fluctuates and difference in wealth, and consequently status, in different periods is rather marked. I would like to propose that the observed variation in artefacts and also quantity of objects suggest the possibility that some families had the economic means to acquire commodities of exotic origin, made of precious materials, with high technical skill and high labour input. Although already used extensively in the description and analysis of tomb material, in the following the two concepts symmetry and asymmetry as mirrored in the tomb material will be applied more systematically with a view to establishing economic integration or disintegration in the region.

During the LH II period, the chamber tombs is represented at several sites; it can also be observed that the wealth as displayed in tombs fluctuate between tombs and sites. The symmetrical pattern, as found by Voutsaki,[123] is difficult to uphold. Instead, the general pattern displayed is one of asymmetrical relations, that is, pronounced variations in wealth and status.

As for LH IIIA, Voutsaki alerts us to the emerging asymmetrical picture.[124] The pattern implies an asymmetrical, and therefore non-reciprocal, society, characterised by an unequal distribution of wealth. Economic inequality is made manifest and the concentration of wealth may have been institutionalised. The pattern emerging can be characterised as predominantly redistributive or based on market modes of transactions. Yet, the existence or non-existence (as may be the case) of symmetrical or asymmetrical relations cannot be taken to imply a given mode of exchange to the exclusion of others.[125]

If the tomb material is analysed from a narrower angle we may observe that the number of tholos tombs decreased in the LH IIIA1 period. At Mycenae one tholos was in use and also at Kokla, Berbati and Dendra a similar situation prevailed. As observed earlier, the chamber tomb material shows marked fluctuations in wealth also within the local cemeteries. The general pattern indicates asymmetrical distribution of wealth within the Argolid. A general increase in number of tombs in use may be observed in the LH IIIA2 period and the results presented by Cavanagh and Mee suggest, for Mycenae, a marginal increase of tombs of wealth group 1 and 2. By contrast, at Prosymna the change is easier seen.[126] Another observation is that most probably the tholos tomb is not represented in this period at any site. Despite the lack of this symbol of status, the asymmetrical distribution of wealth observed by Voutsaki seems valid also for this period. The pattern is, following Polanyi and Precourt, connected to an economy based on redistribution or market exchange.

[123] Voutsaki 1998, 48.

[124] Voutsaki 1998, 48.

[125] Precourt 1984, 163.

[126] Cavanagh & Mee 1990, 58.

For the LH IIIB period the pattern found, or so Voutsaki characterises it, more accentuated with no more tholoi in use outside the palatial centres and no rich tombs in use outside Mycenae.[127] Unfortunately, it is not possible to connect to the two periods for analytical ends, as we do not have the detailed chronological observations of pottery needed for all sites. We should note however that the study by Cavanagh and Mee, and contrary to Voutsaki who claims that rich tombs were found only at Mycenae in this period, shows that at Mycenae no dated tombs of wealth group 1 were in use and only three of the second group. This is in contrast to Dendra, where an increase of tombs belonging to group 1 and 2 can be found. Something similar can be said of Prosymna where, despite a slight decrease in overall numbers, still ten tombs of the two richest categories were observed. Generally speaking, however, the number of tombs in use decreases at this point in time and also the wealth displayed is not as pronounced as in the earlier periods. Interestingly, these observations suggest that we should not be as categorical as regards the status of Mycenae during this period.

If we accept the tholos as a major symbol for status, it should also be noted that the tomb type was in use at Mycenae during the LH IIIB2 period as were also, perhaps, two tholoi used at Tiryns. There is no denying that the tholoi was used for burials of an elite or upper strata of the society, but as argued previously, for want of evidence suggesting otherwise the value of the tomb as a symbol of status is best restricted to the time of the burial. Nor is the wealth in chamber tombs referred to by Voutsaki possible to verify. This reveals a picture, as far as the tomb material is concerned, where the pre-eminent status of Mycenae may be questioned. Although local differences in tomb content may be observed wealth difference is not as distinctive as during the preceding periods. We may, of course, not exclude the possibility of earlier deposits of goods functioning as heirlooms and as symbols of status, but still a gradual process of change may have started, as most tombs did apparently not survive into the following LH IIIC period. Due to the information provided in the tomb material, and contrary to the observation made by Voutsaki, I would therefore propose that the LH IIIB period displayed a generally more symmetrical pattern of wealth. The emerging pattern of symmetry implies, following Polanyi, a predominantly reciprocal society where egalitarianism is central and concentration of wealth not encouraged.[128] It is appropriate, however, to point out that the lack of exposed material in tombs and the indicated change in economic structure towards a system more based on reciprocity need not be interpreted as a general decline in wealth.

Finally, it is recognised that at some sites on the Argive Plain chamber tombs were still in use in LH IIIC. Perhaps we may suggest that in those cases where tombs were used in also proceeding periods, most probably the same family controlled the grave. The LH IIIC period is also characterised by a considerable number of simple graves. This is the case, for example, at Tiryns and Mycenae. Apparently these graves show variation in number of grave goods deposited, as the simpler graves at Tiryns were poorly equipped whereas grave goods accompanied those at Mycenae.[129] Perhaps the stepwise appearance of cremation can be associated to a gradual change in burial customs and traditions as suggested by Dickinson.[130]

The pattern of symmetry emerging in LH IIIB continues in LH IIIC. This can be taken as an indication of relatively small social and economic variation across society and its members. If the earlier applied logic has anything going for it, this is also indicative of predominantly reciprocal transactions. However, some local deviation is to be observed. At Asine, four richly equipped tombs used in earlier periods continued to be in use. At Tiryns, three tombs deposited with valuable objects can be noted and at Dendra two. At Mycenae seven tombs remain in use in LH IIIC, although only one can be categorised as well equipped.[131]

By and large, the number of pottery deposited in tombs is low although Asine is something of an exception with its larger number of vessels. Of special interest is tomb I:1. Here no vessels from LH IIIC:e have been registered, but a full two dozen from LH IIIC middle and late. The tombs from the Argive settlements imply that social status was no longer displayed in the manner and to the extent as was the case during the earlier part of the Late Helladic period. Asine is an exception in this regard as a substantial amount of pottery from the LH IIIC middle and late tombs have been found. In turn, this may imply that the status of Asine in a regional perspective had changed. Cavanagh and Mee recently suggested that Asine was almost abandoned in LH IIIB. A re-settlement then followed in the LH IIIC period and the people moving to the site re-used the old chamber tombs.[132] But, as has been argued elsewhere in this study, the tombs were most probably used by the same lineage and family

[127] Voutsaki 1992, 10.2.2; 1995a, 58-59; 1998, 48.

[128] Polanyi 1944 (1957), 48-50; Precourt 1984, 163.

[129] Cavanagh & Mee 1998, 90-91.

[130] Dickinson 1983, 67.

[131] Asine: ChT. I:1, I:2, I:5 and I:7. Compared to the others, tomb I:6 was not particularly well equipped. Dendra: tomb 7 is wealth group 1 and tomb 11 wealth group 2. Tiryns: V, VI, VII, VIII, XV. Although not classified, a comparison of the objects deposited in these tombs with those at Dendra, Prosymna and Mycenae show that they are of equal status to those of wealth group 1 and 2. Mycenae has evidence of seven chamber tombs in use in this period, but only T.515 belongs to wealth group 1. It is to be observed that tombs of wealth group 1 were excavated by Tsountas, but these are not dated. It is possible that some contained LH IIIC pottery. Argos: eleven tombs have been found with evidence of LH IIIC pottery. However, compared with Asine, Tiryns and Dendra these are fairly poor. The exceptions are tombs XXIX and XXX. A couple of chamber tombs may have been identified at Monasteraki and perhaps also at Nauplion; Cavanagh & Mee 1998, 99.

[132] Cavanagh & Mee 1998, 89-90.

during the whole period without any disruption in LH IIIB. The archaeological material from the settlement is therefore best thought of as demonstrating continuity.

Finally, the Submycenaean period need to be mentioned. At several sites burials have continued into this period and in some cases also traces of settlement activity can be traced. At Argos, for example, continuity is clearly documented as is also the case at Asine, although no tombs possible to connect to this period have been located at the latter site. At Mycenae scattered evidence for activity during the period exists and at Nauplion some tombs have been found.[133] This material indicates continuity between the Late Bronze Age and the Iron Age as the tombs were used by those living in the area.

[133] Hägg 1974, 23-27, 51, 65-66, 72, 79-82; Styrenius 1967, 127-136.

PART IV

HIERARCHY AND CENTRALISATION?

Chapter 9
FINAL DISCUSSION

9.1 FINDINGS

Time has now come to step back and see what the detailed analysis of previous archaeological findings from Late Helladic Argolid has yielded. The main objective of the analysis conducted in chapters 4 to 8 was to try to assess the relative strengths of two dominant, yet contrasting frameworks of interpretation as regards the economy of the north-eastern Peloponnese in the Late Bronze Age. These two frameworks, the one being Polanyian in outlook and emphasising the redistributive nature of the economy under the control and dominance of the palaces (primarily Mycenae, possibly also Tiryns), the other is a more loosely structured grouping of dissenters arguing that economic transactions to a greater extent than implied by the received view had the character of market based exchange. Although the latter typically do not deny the possibility of redistribution taking place, they would put greater trust in market allocation and economic rationality. The respective positions can be seen as an outgrowth of the at times rather stale debate between substantivists and formalists that put its mark on economic anthropology in the not so distant past.

Yet it would be unfair to characterise the Aegean debate as a mere recycling of old and outdated ideas. The various propositions put forth over the past two decades have shown an increasing awareness of the need to overcome simple dichotomies and entrenched positions. Even so, the main problem remains a lack of a systematic gathering of archaeological evidence conducted with a view to sorting out the facts from mere assumptions. The analysis presented up to this point represents a first step towards this particular end.

In order to do so, a number of research questions were formulated. What type of material is at our disposal? Can the material at hand be used to shed light on the economic issues in focus in the Aegean debate? If so, what does it tell us about the economic system in operation? Is the resulting picture in line with any of the main positions of the Aegean debate? Indeed, does the material at hand allow us the privilege of discriminating between the various suggested interpretations implied by the two main schools of thought (or variants thereof)? The outcome of an exercise of this nature, at least if reasonably successful, can be put to a variety of uses, but given the focus of the region-wide economy it was suggested that this might here be used to refine the models of the Argive settlement hierarchy as formulated by Bintliff and Kilian in their attempts to capture some of the essential features of Mycenaean society.

With that in mind, this chapter will present an alternative model to those already available in the research literature. In order to do so the outcome of the analysis must be summarised. Since Chapters 4 through 8 have described and analysed a large amount of material in considerable detail (if admittedly by the use of secondary sources), there is a need to draw together the various threads. This is the objective of the first section of this chapter; some of the resulting propositions will be developed as we move on to the subsequent sections, which will focus on an alternative model of the Argive hierarchy of settlements and point to some further issues that would be most worthwhile to address.

At its most fundamental, the findings can be summarised in four propositions. The first one concerns the support for the favoured framework, the redistributive model of economic organisation. On closer inspection it appears that there is precious little by way of evidence that can be drawn upon as direct support for that model. This may come as a surprise to those knowledgeable about the research literature on the Argolid. After all, the picture to emerge from earlier research is one of great coherence and effectiveness. However, and this constitutes the second proposition, these desirable traits stem from the model being imposed on fragmentary data. It works as an interpretative framework of considerable strength within which individual pieces can be fitted to good effect. The existence of the reality reflected in the model is assumed, not proven. As a consequence, it would be next to impossible to arrive at the redistributive model if one was to work one's way up from the material evidence alone.

In part the strength of the evidence put forth derives from the fact that material that reflects different conditions has been put into a common mould without due regard for the different contexts within which they should ideally be assessed. Put differently, proposition three suggests that support for the redistributive model as put forth in previous research often has joined several periods into one, generalising across several of the phases distinguishable in the material. In effect, evidence has been accumulated by pooling finds that strictly speaking are not to be added together.

This is not to imply, however, that the alternative framework finds much greater support in the material made available over more than a century of excavations in the region. There is considerable evidence to suggest that exchange did take place and that pure self-sufficiency was not practised throughout the Argolid. High levels of self-sufficiency there might have existed and it is not entirely unlikely that many or even most households were basically outside the scope of whatever exchange that took place. There is simply no way of telling whether or to what extent markets or other modes of exchange made an imprint on the livelihoods of the Argive population. What can be said is that there are clear signs of a division of labour and that, as we would therefore expect, exchange did indeed take place. In the absence of a currency or any standard medium of exchange, it is more likely to have been in the form of market based barter or centrally directed redistribution than anything else. From this observation does not follow, however, that we can pass judgement on whether it was at arm's length or socially embedded. The fourth proposition, therefore, is that it is not possible to tell to what extent any of the three modes of exchange identified by Polanyi were practised, only that exchange as such was present. If anything, the situation is closer to that implied by the emerging critique than that of the received view. This is so on account of a lack of evidence also for the basic infrastructure needed for large-scale redistribution.

9.2 IMPLICATIONS: HIERARCHY AND INTRA-REGIONAL EXCHANGE IN THE LATE HELLADIC PERIOD

As was mentioned already in Chapter 2, irrespective of the outcome of our discussion of the two dominant positions on the Mycenaean economy, both existing models of the Argive hierarchy of settlements need to be amended on one important score: both pool material collected from distinct and quite possibly very different chronological settings. While the tendency to treat a long time span as a single period may seem to increase the range of evidence at hand for the construction of these models, it actually serves to hide variation that may in itself prove helpful in understanding developments. There is thus a need to differentiate the models of Bintliff and Kilian with respect to time and period. The first task of the remainder of this chapter, therefore, will be to try to take change over time into account. As was outlined at some length in Chapter 3, the empirical part (or rather re-examination of previously published empirical data) of the present thesis, as well as trying to locate information on the nature of exchange in the economy, also set out with a view to collect and collate information on the position of the various settlements. In addition to this basic task we also need to integrate the findings summarised in the opening section of the present chapter.

In the following, this information will be assembled in a more systematic fashion, sub-period by sub-period of the Late Bronze Age, allowing for the two strands to be integrated into one model. For each sub-period, the discussion will be conducted in two steps. Firstly, an attempt will be made to rank settlements on account of indicators of relative wealth and status. Secondly, information on contacts between settlements will be assessed. Together this should result in a model which, although not necessarily complete in the sense of having all actually existing links included, should allow us to trace the shifting fortunes of the various settlements while at the same time remaining true to the possibilities in interpretation that exist. As such it will be inspired both by the pioneering work by Bintliff and Kilian, yet will seriously consider the possibilities of lateral links being deployed and developed.

LH II (Fig.6)

The opening period of Late Helladic Argolid has left a rich crop of finds, as displayed in the shaft graves at Mycenae, but architectural remains are few. Also the LH II period has left us little by way of settlement material. This is unfortunate for a variety of reasons, including the resulting difficulty in constructing a baseline for the task at hand here. This is in part compensated for, however, by the tomb material. At several sites we now find chamber tombs in use and some are rich in finds. At Prosymna, for example, a large number of tombs were in use and the tombs from Dendra are rich in finds. Also the tholos was in use at four sites, namely Kazarma, Kokla, Mycenae and Prosymna. With respect to the latter, although Mycenae with six tholoi in use retained its eminent position, Voutsaki observed in her examination of tombs that the distribution of wealth was more even during LH II than would later be the case as several sites had similar tombs in use.[1] However, the results compiled by Cavanagh and Mee show that it may not be characterised as even as sites had both poor and rich tombs in use; on the basis of these findings it would be more natural to characterise it as a pattern of asymmetry. The tholoi in use are evenly spread out and the number found at Mycenae point towards a situation where several families had both the desire and possibilities to display wealth and status.

With respect to categories of settlement material, such as houses, workshops and so forth, few remains have been documented. As a consequence, our ability to assess not only the general level of wealth of individual sites but also economic activities as such is diminished. What we may say is that the wealth status as reflected in tombs suggests a society where at least some individuals had the means to acquire products made of exotic materials, possibly also of foreign workmanship. If this single category of wealth is used as a measurer of status we may conclude that at Mycenae generously furnished chamber tombs and the six tholoi suggest a high status for the settlement. Another site of emerging importance is Dendra where rich tombs similarly indicate high status. Kokla may fall into the same category, its tholos and also

[1] Voutsaki 1998, 48.

rich chamber tombs indicating wealth on part of the settlement. Also Asine is of interest as the tombs in use display a measure of wealth over the ordinary, the tinned vessels in tomb I:7 dated to LH IIB being a case in point.

It can be observed that in tombs are found evidence of exchange relations with regions also beyond the Argolid. Of an exclusive character are finds such as tinned vessels, amber and also gold/bronze rings and perhaps a seal as found at Asine. At Dendra gold, silver, lead and ivory have been found in a pure LH II context. Furthermore, to the LH IIA period exotic objects such as glass and a bead made of amethyst could be assigned.[2] Also at Tiryns finds of bronze, silver, ivory and glass have been made.[3] Similarly, metal of non-local origin was found in the tholos tomb at Kokla. These finds of objects made of exotic materials, distributed across a set of rather different sites, are not only evidence of long-distance exchange. Although our knowledge concerning physical links is limited and formal roads have not been documented – more impermanent and possibly informal transportation routes (such as paths)[4] must have been employed – the very fact that some of these settlements do not enjoy direct access to the sea or natural overland routes suggests the existence of some form of intra-regional exchange.

The limited range of material remains does not award us the privilege of establishing the rank of individual sites in more detail (*Fig. 6*). Already in LH II the strategic location of Mycenae may however have been an important factor determining the relation to and hence possibly status of, the other settlements in the region. The location as a gateway to the north favours the site as an intermediate node for exchange of products from the north to the central and southern part of the Argive Plain. If the location is regarded as a prime factor for the rank and status of a site in an hierarchical system of settlements, the location of Asine as a coastal site and port of trade may similarly have determined its status as an intermediary through which goods produced on the Argive Plain were distributed to markets or other recipients outside the region. The objects found in chamber tombs, as many are not only made of exotic materials but also unique attest that this could be the case.

At Prosymna the large number of tombs and the tholos in use indicates the presence of a nearby settlement. The objects found here and at other sites such as at Dendra, show that even they had interest in exchange of not only locally produced goods but also more exotic objects. The status and relation to other sites in a regional perspective is not possible to determine, but the exchange displayed may have functioned through vertical links and both sites may have functioned as standard markets for locally produced goods distributed upward and imported goods transferred downward the hierarchy. The status of Kokla is also difficult to evaluate, but the tholos and chamber tombs with their rich finds of exotic and presumably valuable materials suggest an above average wealth of the local community. The riches may have been obtained through the position of the site as a distribution and collection point, on the same level as Dendra and Prosymna, for an extended hinterland. The sites represented with rich chamber tombs and also tholoi may point towards the upward mobilisation of groups of inhabitants and emerging élite groups. This was people who had the economic means to obtain valuable goods but, as has been discussed earlier in this work, the socially embedded exchange is also of importance. The prime purpose of such relations may have been to create alliance between kin groups, through marriage, political relations and so forth. These alliances should have been of importance throughout the Late Helladic period and I would propose that the chamber tomb burials are a further sign of the importance of the social group.

Evidence of horizontal links is difficult to find as products produced locally, such as agricultural goods, rarely leave traces behind. Pottery produced locally may as well have been exchanged on a local minor market level, but to prove exchange needs analyses of the material. Also, some of the exotic items distributed to the lower levels of the hierarchy, the equivalent of Skinner's standard market, may later have been exchanged locally within a lateral system. Despite lack of evidence to this effect, it is conceivable that such a minor market could have been the basic and necessary point of exchange for products needed daily within the household; at the very least this represents a testable proposition that future research may help verify or reject.

The fact that no apparent medium of exchange has been found for this (or, for that matter, any later) period does not imply that the favoured mechanism of exchange in this early period is easy to identify. What can be said is that the basic features of redistribution, large storage areas and other centralised functions, are yet to be found within this region. Nor can we beyond reasonable doubt establish that pure market exchange occurred. What can be said is that evidence for both lateral and vertical exchange is present.

LH IIIA1 (Fig. 7)

Compared with the preceding period, the LH IIIA1 is somewhat more rewarding as far as material remains are concerned. Settlement activity is indicated in LH IIIA1, but only as far as pottery and a few architectural remains allow. At Mycenae and Tiryns the citadel areas were at their initial stage of development and few dwelling remains have been secured for this period. In contrast to other sites, an increase of chamber tombs in use is observed at Tiryns. The wealth of these tombs is not outstanding, but rather compares unfavourably with those at for example Dendra. At Mycenae, no similar increase in chamber tombs in use is to be observed and as at other sites those tombs that were in use belonged to different

[2] Dendra, tomb nos. 6, 8.

[3] Tiryns tomb no. XXX.

[4] Trombold 1991, 3.

wealth groups indicating asymmetrical social relations. The imbalance in social structure is further observed in the presence of a tholos in use.

The published results of the Berbati survey have extended our knowledge concerning this area in the Late Helladic period. Evidence for a LH IIIA1 settlement was not forthcoming as only activities at a few findspots were registered and all except one are tombs.[5] However, the presence of a tholos, four chamber tombs and a pottery kiln indicates activity at the Mastos in this period.[6] The kiln may have functioned through LH IIIA1, when it was moved and only wasters have been found from the later kiln.[7] At Dendra/Midea activity in this period is documented through a tholos and a few chamber tombs in use. The tholos is very rich in finds and the few tombs published are also well furnished with exclusive objects of exotic materials. The tomb pattern at Dendra indicates a symmetrical wealth pattern for the site. The tomb contents document that those using these tombs had the economic and social means to acquire objects made of an exotic and precious character.

The wealth displayed at Kokla in the preceding period continues and is indicative of a community prospering also in LH IIIA1. Our knowledge concerning other architectural features is meagre, but possibly a settlement was located close by. Prosymna had an extensive chamber tomb cemetery in use already in LH IIIA1. Several tombs have been assigned as wealthy but also in this case lack of settlement evidence is an irritating circumstance. The content of the tombs indicates a prospering local community. The previously utilised tholos tombs apparently ceased to be in use. At Argos, archaeological evidence is limited to one house with a documented storage room and a number of chamber tombs in use; finds of more exotic character are few. Finally, at Asine continued use of chamber tombs has been documented and those found are asymmetrical in wealth as some display rich finds, whereas others are poorer. Other categories of installations have been possible to associate with this period, although as at other sites no large constructions. Also pottery remains indicate use of the settlement. Finds of pottery moreover show that the area inhabited extended outside the settlement, at least in the earlier part of the LH III period.[8]

Traces of production have been possible to associate with this period only at one locality, at Berbati where pottery production is in evidence during this period. Nor does the meagre archaeological evidence provide traces of other facilities such as storage areas, houses and so forth. This general lack of signs of production may have several plausible explanations, such as workshops located outside the settlement, or objects produced by itinerant workmen, or that objects were still imported as finished goods.

We may thus establish that also in LH IIIA1 tombs are the major category of archaeological remains that allows us the possibility of discussing status and wealth. At Mycenae, wealth is displayed in some tombs and also a tholos is found. Also some other sites, for example Asine, have rich tombs assigned to this period and at Berbati a tholos is also in use; the latter, however, and unlike the chamber tombs, is characterised by the meagre finds. The presence of rich tombs at Dendra and Kokla with contents not found at other sites and also richly furnished tholoi could be noted. The tombs and their contents attest to the fact that individuals had the economic, and social, means to acquire valuable goods.

Evidence for exchange was documented already in the LH II period and finds of different categories of objects and materials can also in LH IIIA1 be used as indicators of exchange relations. This is true both of intra-regional and long-distance exchange. Objects made of foreign material make the assumption of Asine as a port of trade and intermediary of exchange of goods equally plausible for this period as was the case for LH II. Goods have been found that probably were traded directly with external trade partners; the Palace style vases found in chamber tomb 1:2 can serve as an illustration of this point. Objects made of ivory in chamber tombs I:1 and I:2 are not found at other settlements on the Argive Plain and these unusual objects may have been purchased directly by members of the local élite. Indication of intra-regional exchange in LH II-LH IIIA1 is found in an ivory mirror handle found in chamber tomb I, excavated in 1978. It has a butterfly motif, similar to the motif on a gold plaque found at Mycenae and a parallel in type is found at Dendra. The typological development should have taken place between LH I and LH IIIA1.[9] Furthermore, the gold toggle found in chamber tomb I:1 has parallels at Mycenae and Dendra (silver) and some examples have been found also at Knossos and Thorikos. The chronological contexts of the geographically closest finds are in the case of Mycenae LH IIA, whereas in the case of Dendra it is LH IIB-IIIA1.[10] We may assume that the toggles were produced in the earliest part of the Late Helladic period and exchanged intra-regionally. The Minoan gold rings deposited in chamber tomb I:1 in the earlier part of the Late Helladic period were probably also acquired in exchange for tradable goods in the possession of a tradesmen, or group, at Asine. Also tinned vessels have been found and a survey of the material shows that tinned vessels were deposited in tombs at Mycenae, Dendra and probably also at Prosymna. More detailed studies concerning the place of production of these vessels is needed as tin covered vessels are also to be found outside the region. Hence, it cannot be ruled out that the vessels were traded long-distance during the LH IIIA period.[11] It is possible, however, that these vessels

---

[5] Schallin 1996, 165-166, fig. 32.
[6] Åkerström 1940, 296-298; Schallin 1996, 170.
[7] Mountjoy 1999, 65.
[8] Sjöberg 1996, 101-106.
[9] Patrianakou-Iliaki, 1996, 1273-1280. Tomb no. 102, LH IIA. Dendra tomb no. 2, LH IIIA2-LH IIIB. The Dendra deposit may belong to the LH IIIA2 burial.
[10] Mycenae tomb no. 102; Dendra, Åström 1977, 12, 18, fig. 4.
[11] Immerwahr 1966, sites in appendix 1, 394-395.

were distributed from one and the same Argive workshop and therefore a further indication of intra-regional lateral contacts between sites of equal rank.

Tomb finds at Midea/Dendra similarly indicate that people conducted external exchange relations and enjoyed a high level of wealth. Finds of metals such as silver, gold and bronze are numerous here and, as at several other sites, we also find objects made of glass, faience and precious stone. The tholos exposed rich finds of metals and for example the silver finds are of considerable interest in this context as silver is also found in the tholos at Kokla. Apparently the silver finds from Kokla are of a regional shape and the possibility that these vessels are evidence for a regional workshop would be well worth further investigation. Be this as it may, the silver finds do serve as further evidence of the possibility of intra-regional lateral exchange between communities of similar rank. The finds displayed indicate that the élite group that obviously emerged in the previous period still had the interest and possibility to express status and wealth. Interestingly, although limited in number, at Kokla also chamber tombs display wealth. This is a further indication of a prospering community where individual family groups had the possibility to acquire valuable and exotic objects.

In view of the lack of settlement remains, it is of more than passing interest to note that Dendra/Midea thanks to its location at road m5 – linking the site with Berbati and Tiryns – fulfils all the requirements of an hypothetical node of intermediate exchange for the eastern part of the Argive Plain (*Fig.* 5). Again, this could form the basis for further efforts to find support for, or to conclusively reject, the idea of this site as one of above average prominence. Be that as it may, the map in *(Fig.7)* represents an attempt to capture exchange relations as made evident by tomb and settlement remains. Compared to both the previous and, as we shall see, the subsequent period, LH IIIA1, comes across as integrated. Links are dense and, in particular as compared to LH IIIA2, more settlements appear to take part in exchange activities.

The finds from chamber tombs at Mycenae indicate external relations as, for example, objects made of bronze, lead, silver, faience, amber and ivory have been found. Faience found at Dendra, Tiryns, Prosymna and Asine are also of LH II-LH IIIA origin. Yet, it seems as if production of faience diminished drastically on the Mainland in these periods. Finds from a LH IIIB1 context, viz. The House of Shields at Mycenae, indicates a brief revival of interest for this manufacture, which may have been caused by fashion or wealth.[12] Similar categories of finds have also been found at Asine, Dendra and Tiryns with the added proviso that ivory has not been located at the latter site.

[12] Foster Polinger 1979, 156-158.

While on the subject of missing types of objects, it is worth noting that at Argos and Berbati no amber has been found, nor do these two sites display outstanding wealth in their tomb contents. Lack of evidence of a high level of external contacts is in fact noticeable. In fact, the find pattern from Berbati is somewhat unexpected, as the production of pottery did evidently not generate – or could at least not support – demand for exotic and exclusive objects. The wealth displayed in the tombs is not outstanding. However, the tholos indicates that the local community was not based on equal status. After all, at least some people had the possibility and interest to project status – social, economic or a combination of the two – through the building of a tholos tomb. It is mere speculation, of course, but the family group responsible for the pottery production may have been the group with the means not only to acquire valuable exotic objects, but also to make status manifest through the building of a tholos tomb.

This raises the issue of whether, and if so to what extent, those living at Berbati took part in the regional division of labour and if the site served as a focal point for the surrounding countryside. Although there is precious little evidence in the survey material to that effect, it is conceivable that Berbati served the hinterland, and those living there, as a site for lateral exchange of locally produced standard goods and a potential location for exchange of more exotic items found outside the Berbati-Limnes area, that is, as node in a system of vertical exchange. The site served as a starting point for the upward flow of not only pottery produced at the kiln, but it easy to see that the same could be true also of other goods of local character produced by, for example, local farmers. Some support for such a contention already exists. The location of the site close to the pre-LH IIIB road m5 (*Fig. 5*) connecting it and the surrounding valley not only with the northern part of the Argive plain and with Mycenae, but by way of Midea/Dendra also to the southern part of the plain points in this direction.[13] The distribution pattern of pottery from the Berbati kiln is obviously now secured,[14] as analyses made on fine ware sherds from Mycenae are from the LH IIIA/B, and distribution outside the region is documented in the LH IIIA/B periods.[15] It would seem natural that Asine could have served as the gateway for distribution to these distant recipients. Indeed, if this was the beaten track for one type of goods, why not others?

[13] Lavery 1990, 168, fig 1; 1995, 264, maps 1-2.

[14] I would like to express my gratitude to Professor H. Mommsen for this information. See also Mommsen, Beier & Hein 2002, 621-622.

[15] Mommsen, Lewandowski, Weber & Podzuweit 1988, 166, table 1; Mommsen & Maran 2000-2001; Mommsen, Beier & Hein 2002. As some of the results reported are partly at odds with earlier findings – and which the latter study attributes to e.g. sample selection effects – further analyses would be most welcome. As far as Asine is concerned, such analyses are underway as part of a co-operation between Prof. Mommsen and the present author.

As is the case with other sites in this period the position of Tiryns within the Argive settlement system is not easy to establish. Although its location close by the sea is often seen as a major advantage, at this point in time it is assumed not to have been of particular importance. It is possible that élite groups, such as those that obviously had established themselves at several sites, such as Dendra, Mycenae, Prosymna, Kokla and Asine, was close to absent at Tiryns. This is so on account of the size of the settled area (which is small) and also the lack of obvious prosperity in the chamber tomb material. Road m5 (from the Berbati valley and Dendra/Midea) terminated here and the presence of the road and exotic objects indicates that the site functioned as a node for the flow of goods to and from the surrounding hinterland. If Tiryns indeed served any distribution function as suggested by the finds mentioned above, this is more likely to have been in a format reminiscent of Skinner's standard market.

Another similar site was located at Kokla where finds made of precious materials, such as silver, are evidence of external exchange and the tombs attest the presence of a local élite. Yet another one could have been located at Prosymna. In this case, the location at the pre LH IIIB road m4 (*Fig.* 5), which may have originated at Mycenae, suggests as much. The finds at Argos indicate sparse exchange relations with other people on the plain and there is no notable wealth displayed in the few tombs in use. The lack of wealth indicates that the local community did not have the need, or possibility, to establish exchange relation with people outside the settlement. Evidence of a road is not documented in the LH IIIA period and the position of the site is difficult to determine. The site may have been of a minor importance only and functioned as a local focal point of exchange, if at all.

To summarise, the asymmetrical pattern of wealth as displayed in tomb offerings reflects a society where the economy was based on some form of exchange, either in the form of market exchange or redistribution. As for traces of the latter, no large storage facilities have been located; whether by accident or as a natural and logical result of the fact that there never were any cannot be established. After all, to the extent that they did exist in the past, these facilities may have disappeared or left traces that we fail to interpret correctly. However, as we do not find wealth centralised to one or two settlements, the case for a redistributive system seems rather weak. We find, for instance, that the tholos – by several scholars regarded as a symbol for high rank and associated with a centralised and redistributive society – is still found at several sites and the concentration and restricted use to a few palatial centres, as argued by Voutsaki, is not to be seen in the LH IIIA1 period.[16] Voutsaki observes that the number of chamber tombs increase and most of these are poor.[17] If the results presented by Cavanagh and Mee[18] are anything to go by, an increase of poorer tombs can indeed find support. However, the pattern of finds shows that commodities made of precious material are not concentrated to Mycenae only, but finds of a more exclusive character have been found at several sites. In short, at least as far as the LH IIIA period is concerned, the archaeological material does not support the theory of an emerging economy based on redistribution and wealth centralised to one single site, i.e. Mycenae. What we do observe is that high levels of wealth, as displayed in tombs, are characteristic not only of Mycenae, but are also true of Dendra, Asine and Kokla. This is so as especially Dendra and Kokla provide not only rich chamber tombs but also tholoi with impressive finds. The wealth displayed at all these sites show that the people living not only had the economic means, but also the social and perhaps political wherewithal, to acquire objects of high value. Furthermore, they may not only have had intra-regional contacts but also exchange relations with individuals representing or middlemen conducting trade with regions outside the Argolid Plain.

The finds suggest a pattern where similar types of commodities are found at several sites. If this pattern of distribution could be linked to sources of production much would be gained. To the extent that widely spread goods could be linked to one or a few sources, a geographical division of labour can be established. This in turn presupposes exchange. The emerging road network would fulfil a natural role in such a system. As the roads, whether formal or informal, would allow for both vertical links between intermediate sites and lateral links between settlements at the same hierarchical rank, elaborate systems of exchange are a distinct likelihood; at the very least they cannot be ruled out. Whether these in turn would be based on redistribution, barter or reciprocal exchange between trade partners (or any combination thereof) cannot be established at this point.

LH IIIA2 (Fig. 8)

By the LH IIIA2 period it is possible to detect a change in habitation at Mycenae and several houses have been assigned to this period. The building activity includes houses of a domestic character, although the contents of the House of the Wine Merchant and the Petsa's House indicate a commercial function. Indeed, all houses assigned to this period had storage facilities for domestic and, as is commonly asserted, commercial purposes. At Tiryns as well as most other sites evidence of habitation is still limited. Neither storage areas, nor workshops are typically found. In the Berbati-Limnes area the LH IIIA2 period is associated with an increase in number of farmsteads and of the area cultivated.[19] A re-examination of the figures published show that we may assume that the settlement patterns in LH IIIA2 and LH IIIB1 were

[16] Voutsaki 1998, 48.

[17] Voutsaki 1998, 48.

[18] Cavanagh & Mee 1990b.

[19] Schallin 1996, fig. 32.

more nucleated than was the case during the earlier periods.[20]

The tomb pattern indicates a significant increase in the number of tombs in use, while at most sites differences in wealth in the chamber tombs are clearly to be seen. The wealth displayed varies between the sites as both poor and rich tombs were in use. At Dendra and Asine the wealth displayed in the few tombs in use indicates a high status for those who used the chamber tombs. At Kokla only chamber tombs were now in use, but as publications as exist do not allow for a more detailed view of the material it is difficult to estimate the status of the site. The change in use may have several reasons. Burial traditions may have changed and the tholos was not favoured as a symbol of status, or the family who used the tomb earlier was no longer in the position of local power. It is also possible that the population moved and tombs were built elsewhere. As concerns Argos, it remained marginal also during this period. In short, we find that sites are still for the most part void of other architectural categories than tombs. An exception is the houses at Mycenae, which may point towards a positioning of the settlement although the status and wealth of the site need not have changed dramatically from the previous period.

Tomb contents make evident that precious goods of categories found in LH IIIA1 were continued to be deposited in this period. These finds, which include tinned vessels at Mycenae, Prosymna, Berbati and Asine, bear witness to intra-regional exchange and long-distance relations. Immerwahr in an early article proposed that the tinned vessels distributed came from local and palatial workshops and mentions Mycenae as the distribution centre for the Argolid.[21] The idea has considerable merit as many tin covered vessels are from the LH IIIA period, but, so far, no evidence for metal production has been traced. Moreover, it has previously been observed that the deposition of bronze objects in tombs is mainly concentrated to LH IIIA. Yet, as is the case with tin production, no bronze working areas have been identified in the LH IIIA period. The lack of workshops may of course be due to locations not identified or that these products were finished import goods. There is also the possibility that objects were initially produced outside the region, but with increased demand – and the local acquisition of the skills required – production was taken up within the region itself.

Once this was done, however, we must not assume that production had to be or actually was stationary. Just as we should be weary of explanations that take it for granted that merchants were stationary and supported with elaborate installations (storage areas, market places in the most physical form of that word), the idea of the itinerant craftsman should not be rejected out of hand. They could have been regular or occasional visitors to the local market, availing themselves of superior mobility (as compared to the sedentary agricultural population) to round up whatever demand there might have existed. Such an idea incidentally fits well with a model of exchange where markets are local and periodical, and where each locale was insufficient to provide for the survival of the full or even part time specialist.[22] In other words, Late Helladic Argive society may not have been able to muster the demand for the skills of professional workmen on a scale that could support permanent workshops.

As mentioned above several roads passed close to Mycenae already in periods preceding LH IIIB. A road labelled m3 stretched north from Mycenae, road m4 and m4W to the south and m5 to the southeast (*Fig.* 5).[23] Particularly, as was noted above, the road pattern illustrates that Mycenae as an early economic node cannot be ignored. Furthermore, the presence of roads is of critical importance as they reflect the need of connecting certain points with each other and they are also evidence of intra-regional contacts. As striking, however, is the eastward shift of activities made evident by *Fig. 8*. As Kokla is reduced to insignificance – and Argos remains at the lowest tier – most activities follow the eastern edge of the Argive Plain. Mycenae, Dendra and Asine form a chain of high level centres, apparently capable of dominating whatever exchange activities that we have been able to associate with this particular sub-period of the Late Helladic Argolid.

Berbati, the probable location of the so called Myc/Be workshop from which fragments of pictorial pottery have been identified as far away as Cyprus, is a case in point. That this is not simply coincidence is shown by other well travelled products of this workshop, such as a sample from a krater assigned to the Myc/Be group, LH IIIA2/B1, found at Tell Dan.[24] Until LH IIIA2 Berbati was, or so Schallin asserts, independent, at which point the production of pottery at Berbati came in the hands of Mycenae. Yet the very presence of road m5 is important evidence of a trade route connecting Berbati with the southern part of the region. Probably no well-built roads existed in this period as scholars specialised in this field interpret the Argive main roads as constructions of the LH IIIB period.[25] Thus, rather than simply assuming that Mycenae was the logical point of distribution of Myc/Be output, are we not equally warranted in this case to suggest that Asine could have served as the export gateway? Although pottery produced at Berbati could have been the main commodity exchanged, once the

[20] The definitions used by Schallin are in contrast to those in Roberts 1996, 19, 24, 88, who defines nucleation as a situation where three farmsteads are closely located and form either a row or a triangle. The definitions of nucelation is possible to adapt to the LH IIIA2 period, and partly to LH IIIB1, if also the find spots with only tombs are used.

[21] Immerwahr 1966, 392.

[22] Skinner 1964, 10.

[23] Lavery 1990, 168, fig 1; 1995, map 1.

[24] Mommsen & Maran 2000-2001.

[25] Jansen 2002, 14; Lavery 1995, map 1; Mylonas 1966a, 87.

channels were in place could they not with equal ease have been used for trade in, say, agricultural produce.

The position of Asine did probably not change and the settlement functioned also in LH IIIA2 as an intermediate market for import of long-distance exotic goods and export hub of regional products, such as pottery. The information available for Tiryns in LH IIIA2 is limited and there is little to indicate that it should have achieved a higher rank in the settlement hierarchy than it did in the previous period. Like Prosymna, Tiryns barely made the ranks of the Argive equivalent of Skinner's standard market, that is, the next lowest level of the implied hierarchy of central places.

The settlement material is meagre although a few houses have been found at Mycenae and one at Argos. Nor have any large-scale storage facilities been located. We therefore have to fall back on the evidence provided by the tombs excavated. As was the case in the previous period, also the LH IIIA2 period is characterised by a pattern of wealth best described as asymmetrical; both very rich tombs and those very poor are found. Tombs display rank amongst those who used them and the absence of tholoi apparently did little to reduce the differences in status across settlements. Yet this must not be taken to imply that wealth is concentrated to but one site, that is, Mycenae. On the contrary, there are still rich tombs in use at Dendra and at Prosymna we may even notice an increase of rich tombs. It could be assumed that the groups that previously used these tombs were still part of the local élite and the asymmetrical economic pattern is displayed in non-equal social relations. What the pattern shows is that Mycenae is to be found at the rich end of the spectrum but also that other sites held a high (if not necessarily equally high) rank primarily due to strategic location. Asine, for instance, by virtue of its location and the riches found in some tombs could be included at an intermediate level.

The asymmetrical pattern of the tomb should, following the concepts of symmetry and asymmetry, indicate an economy based on market exchange or redistribution. Neither pure market exchange nor redistribution is easily deduced from the material, however, as the desirable traits, such as large storage areas and other categories of finds associated to centralisation, are not found. If anything, evidence as exist challenges the view that economic power was concentrated to one or two settlements. Furthermore, the objects found in mainly tombs do show that exchange relations existed across a wide range of settlements. It may therefore be more natural to conclude that the regional economic system, while still likely hierarchical, was integrated and economic activities dispersed rather than centralised. The implications of this situation for the mix of modes of exchange are not entirely straightforward, but it is not unlikely that both lateral and vertical exchange may have taken place in parallel, the former in particular being more conducive to reciprocal or market exchange than redistributive activities of the sort proposed by Polanyi.

LH IIIB1 (Fig. 9)

At Mycenae, the LH IIIB1 period is represented by several houses located outside the citadel area. Remains indicate that some buildings have probably been used for small-scale production and storage. The material remains indicate specialisation towards jewellery, ivory and oil/perfume production, if indeed any production as such has taken place (and not merely storage). If, on the other hand Mycenae did see production of these categories of goods, it is quite probable that objects were produced at or beyond the perimeter of the settlement; else, supplies must have been secured through imports.

Several factors are important for the status and function of a settlement. I would suggest that due to its location, the growth of the settlement area, the existence of specialised production and the evidence of written documentation, Mycenae changed from an intermediate to a top level centre. The settlement was now an economic node of importance. The Linear B material indicates need of documentation already in the LH IIIB1 period. For example, those dealing with production probably needed documentation of personnel when a specialised work force was needed. The tablets document locally produced commodities, but not the allocation or distribution of products of a more exotic origin such as ivory, faience and so forth which may point towards private entrepreneurs rather than a central or palatial administration dealing with these activities. The actual physical concentration to a palatial site does not necessarily imply that a central authority carried out the production; it is equally, if not more, plausible that the palace generated a substantial portion of whatever effective demand there was for these products. Indeed, the lack of mention of ivory in the tablets lends itself to an interpretation favouring non-palatial control. This is in contrast to textiles and wool, which are explicitly mentioned. The latter are goods that we know were widely produced and being mentioned in this context may imply that such commodities served as a convenient means of taxation or perhaps even being used as a medium of exchange within the Mycenaean realms.

The citadel area at Tiryns was also expanding at this point. Several houses were in use and finds indicate production in old metals and bronze, whereas large-scale storage facilities have not been identified. The archaeological information shows that Dendra in this period, and in contrast to other sites, displays an increase both in number of tombs in use and in the number of rich tombs. This is in marked contrast to the Acropolis of Midea, where no signs of dwelling have been found. Yet the tombs bear witness to a prosperous society, which raises the question whether the population in this period was dispersed over the surrounding area or, perhaps, that we are yet to reach the excavation levels where the period is found. Whatever the reasons, we may conclude that for a considerable period of time Dendra/Midea remained a site of high rank within the realms of the Late Helladic Argolid. The location and the plain surrounding the site were important for the accumulation of wealth. The position held in LH IIIA, as an intermediate centre should not have been challenged.

This is in contrast to the Berbati-Limnes area, where the LH IIIB1 period sees a decrease in the number of findspots; the relation to Mycenae has been characterised as close and dependent.[26] However, it can be argued that Berbati need not to have been totally dependent of Mycenae. Jansen has recently shown that the orientation of highways near Mycenae, constructed in the LH IIIB period, seems to have been most likely for local circulation, serving the immediate hinterland of the citadel. Jensen additionally notes that the main roads could serve to show the extent of the territory dominated by a certain settlement, that is, as a kind of territorial markers. As concern Mycenae, Jansen argues that the power of the citadel seems to have been based on the fertile upland region to its north-east. The roads thus served agriculture by facilitating transports within the area, but also enabling the distribution of agricultural products to the citadel and the settlement near it. The fact that the two main roads are oriented not towards the Argive Plain could be seen as lending support to this interpretation. The remains of other highways in the LH IIIB period are, according to Jansen, more oriented toward Tiryns.[27]

Recently analysed samples of pictorial pottery suggest the existence two different workshops on the Argive Plain. On the one hand, we find a northern Myc/Be group located at Berbati and in use from LH II until probably LH IIIB 1 and, on the other, a southern Tir/As group located close to Asine and Tiryns in the LH IIIB period. Several samples from this latter group represent the LH IIIB1 period. Some are from the Levant, but according to Mommsen and Maran samples have also been found locally at Midea.[28] The road connecting southward from Berbati to Midea and Tiryns could certainly have been used for this purpose. Of course, it is possible that Mycenae received part of the vessels produced, but it could also be argued that the vessels found at the other sites are evidence of direct exchange between Berbati and these settlements. In the case of trade outside the region, to the Levant and Cyprus, Tiryns is as likely a gateway for exports during this period as any. As concern Asine, pottery evidence and some scattered architectural remains indicate that the site was in use. The previously documented wealth in tombs is no longer to be seen and the material evidence suggests a settlement that was past its prime.

[26] Schallin 1996, 171-173.

[27] Jansen 2002, 15, 130-133.

[28] Mommsen, Lewandoski, Weber & Podzuweit 1988, 165-171; Mommsen & Maran 2000-2001.

Like previous periods, Voutsaki interpreted the LH IIIB period as asymmetrical with wealth concentrated to Mycenae; it is only at this site richer tombs and tholoi have been found.[29] In contrast to this, it was argued in Chapter 8 above that the LH IIIB period is characterised by a symmetrical pattern with no large differences in wealth as reflected in the tomb material. Unfortunately, it has not been possible to divide the period into more detailed sequences as we still lack detailed information for the pottery from most sites. The information provided through the analysis presented by Cavanagh and Mee has, however, shown some interesting local variation. At Mycenae a few rich tombs may still be observed to be in use, although none of category 1. In contrast to the pattern found at other sites, at Dendra there is an increase of rich tombs and at Prosymna the figures are nearly the same as in the preceding period. Generally speaking, the contrast in wealth is not as pronounced as in previous periods and the tombs show a more symmetrical pattern. It cannot be ruled out that the poorer wealth pattern reflected in the tombs from this period could be explained in terms of a change in burial traditions, due change in belief pattern or any such event. Of course, earlier deposits of objects may have functioned as heirlooms while other categories of goods may have been deposited. Some conceivable examples of the latter – food and drink spring to mind – are unlikely to have left any traces in the tombs. Nor may it be excluded that the ceremonials performed at each burial were more important as messages of status of the individual or family, than objects deposited. It has not been possible to verify that tholoi were in use during the first half of the LH IIIB period and probably the tomb type, at both Mycenae and Tiryns, came in use again in the middle or second half of the period.

The poor status displayed in tombs is in contrast to developments visible at several settlements. The strategic location of Tiryns close to the sea may have been utilised from LH IIIB1 and onwards. The increase of import goods, the expansion of the settlement area and the presence of metal production and, finally, road M4 that linked Tiryns with Mycenae can be interpreted in terms of a change in the distribution network. If so, the settlement may from the LH IIIB1 period have functioned as an intermediate market or distribution point. It is possible that the growth of Tiryns as a harbour site affected Asine in a negative manner and it cannot be ruled out that the settlement was not of the same importance as a hub for exchange of long-distance goods as it had been in the past. The established regional production of ivory, metals and so on may have affected the demand for imported goods of exotic character previously sourced via Asine. The rank of the settlements is believed to have been affected by the changes at other settlements and the site ceased to function as an intermediate node for locally produced goods.

[29] Voutsaki 1998, 48.

The road system developed during this period and settlements such as Argos and Prosymna could, thanks to their location close to roads M4 and M7, conceivably have found their position elevated to a higher tier. Both roads ran close to Mycenae and M7 seems to have terminated at Argos, whereas M4 continued to Tiryns by way of Prosymna.[30] In *Fig. 9*, this translates into an intermediate level for Argos, while Prosymna retains its position at the next lowest level.

The resulting map (*Fig. 9*) is one of rather dense links across the Argive Plain. A striking feature, however, is the lack of evidence for contacts between proximate sites. In particular, a look at the map easily suggests that it would have been natural for Berbati and Prosymna to develop or retain links with Mycenae. In the former case, this is indeed suggested by the discussion, referred to above, regarding Berbati's alleged dependence on Mycenae.

To summarise, during the LH IIIB1 period we find that the only site with storage areas was Mycenae. The limited size of these facilities makes it doubtful whether they could be accepted as storage facilities for a centralised and redistributive economy. If we regard, as suggested by Jansen, the road system surrounding Mycenae as primarily local, more easily serving the citadel with agricultural product from the hinterland, the pattern of transactions indicate a diversified economic structure with the surrounding agricultural areas as support for the citadel. However, to argue for large scale, regional, redistribution does not seem fully appropriate. Their size and content indicate that they probably were used for products originating locally, that is, quite possibly within some of the houses at the site itself. Ivory and jewellery production (faience, precious stones, etc.) was concentrated to Mycenae, whereas at Tiryns metals were found.

The pattern to emerge is indicative of development of the region in LH IIIB. Change is manifested in growing settlements and improved infrastructure. The decline in wealth in the chamber tombs is not reflected in the settlement activities and instead the changes indicate an economically prosperous society. Following the model of Precourt, the symmetrical pattern displayed in the tomb material should reflect an economy based on reciprocity or at least equal access to wealth and the processes that generated affluence. Again, the alternative interpretation, that of symmetry resulting from redistribution, is not immediately borne out: large-scale storage areas are not found. Linear B material, which has long been regarded a major source of information on central control of production, could possibly fill this void. Critically, these changes may have been purely ideological, that is change in belief matters and new burial traditions rather than the outcome of changes in the economic system as such. The tablets found at Mycenae, however, are all from locations outside the citadel and there is as yet no evidence that would allow us the privilege of confidently associating the written material with a centralised administration rather than with individual entrepreneurs.

Specialisation and a division of labour are also often associated to a centralised polity. The reasons for the specialisation observed between Mycenae and Tiryns can of course not be established with certainty, but the cost involved in procuring the raw material would favour few production locales. Also, access to natural resources, such as water and wood, is important as concerns production, and these resources might be localised rather than ubiquitous. Moreover, in case demand was low, due to the character of luxury objects and therefore expensive, or the palace had assumed control over the use and consumption, use being the right of the ruling élite, the outcome is likely to have favoured production at only one location. The level of demand, or the size of the market, not only sets the limits to specialisation and the division of labour; it is also likely to favour locales with an initially relatively high level of demand over other conceivable locations.

Material remains show that at both Mycenae and Tiryns palatial development was in progress. We may assume that those investing in these arrangements were part of the local élite who had the economic means not only to support such building programmes, but also to acquire precious goods. The specialisation between sites as exposed in the material implies exchange between these settlements. The scenario described above involves the local élites but as shown there is no evidence that exchange has been of a redistributive character.

LH IIIB2 (Fig. 10)

On the destruction at the end of LH IIIB1 follows an increase in dwelling activity at several sites. Destruction hit Mycenae and the houses outside the citadel, where production of ivory, oil and jewellery had previously taken place, were destroyed and not rebuilt. Panagia House II and III were, however, used also in this period and the latter may have been connected to production. The increased building activity within the citadel area is worthy of note. Here houses of mainly multifunctional character are found. In LH IIIB2 evidence of workshop activity was documented in some houses with production of objects with ivory, jewellery and bronze as major inputs. Tiryns is also characterised by expansion of the inhabited area with several new buildings in use. The multifunctional character of houses found at Mycenae is not evident as buildings show diversified function divided into industrial and domestic and a few multifunctional. There is evidence for production and specialisation in metals, bronze, gold, lead, and also iron, although it is possible that the latter belongs to a LH IIIC context. At Tiryns a pottery workshop is identified in samples assigned to the LH IIIB2 and LH IIIB2 final[31]

[30] Lavery 1990, 165; 1995, 264, maps 1 & 2.

[31] Mommsen & Maran 2000-2001.

and also kiln wasters from the Unterburg at Tiryns have been analysed, the latter indicating a pottery workshop in or near Tiryns.[32] Linear B material has been found at Tiryns although their contexts are often not clear. Midea is in this period of major interest as a remarkable expansion of the occupied domain is documented and the buildings excavated have mostly, as at Mycenae, a multifunctional character. Production of jewellery, textiles and metals is confirmed. Linear B signs and seals attest to the need of documentation.

The Berbati-Limnes area is during the LH IIIB2 period characterised by a decrease in number of findspots; overall, the period is not well represented in the material. The valley was, according to Schallin, still exploited by Mycenae and needed for the production of goods such as wool and food. The production of pottery was probably in decline or had ceased, and with that the economic status of the settlement plummeted. Possibly the area had only limited contacts with other parts of the region and exchange based on lateral links.[33] Also in this period the position of Asine in the regional exchange system is difficult to evaluate, as both tomb and settlement material is meagre. It has been shown that the site was inhabited in this period, but we do not know to what extent. It cannot be excluded that the settlement still served as a minor exchange node for goods distributed. The difficulties in assessing the role and status of Asine also at this point are compounded by our limited knowledge of roads in this part of the region. The equivalent to Skinner's standard market could also now be applied to sites such as Asine and Prosymna, in the latter case thanks to its location close to main roads. Argos, meanwhile, retained its previously achieved rank.

Storage facilities from this period have been identified at Mycenae, Tiryns and Midea. The capacity of those found at Mycenae is not large and they could have been used for storage of items produced at the workshops, or acquired from other places, and only for local use. At Tiryns it has been proposed that the capacity may have been more extended as the galleries have been interpreted as storage areas. As already observed in this study this hypothesis can be questioned, however, on the grounds that no secure evidence for stored goods has been found and they may instead have been used for defence as suggested by Janzen.[34] As for Midea, Demakopoulou has connected the storage facilities in the West gate area to a centralised economy with collection and distribution of agricultural products.[35] Certainly such products were stored in the area but there is not much support for the large-scale storage presumably needed for a larger population. Also here the stored products may have been used for the consumption of those living in the citadel.

[32] Mommsen, Lewandowsky, Weber & Podzuweit 1988, 165.
[33] Schallin 1996, 170-173, fig. 32, 35.
[34] Janzen, 1975, 22.
[35] Demakopoulou 1995, 151-152, 161.

The three settlements, Midea, Mycenae and Tiryns, all show evidence of economic activity as reflected in extensive and impressive building programmes, specialised production and exchange of goods of exotic origin such as ivory and metals. This pattern, however, is in marked contrast to the chamber tomb material as tombs in use continue to decrease in number. What is more, the wealth displayed is symmetrical with tombs of the poorer categories dominating at all sites. The tholos was probably used for burial(s) at both Mycenae and Tiryns in this period and they have unquestionable been used as monuments for display of wealth and status of the person buried. But, as argued earlier, the most important point as status marker might have been in connection with the ceremonials conducted in association with the burial and when the impressive construction still was exposed. As concern the chamber tombs it is possible that the tradition of heirlooms and also change in burial ceremonies affected the data in this period (perhaps objects of other categories than pottery may have been deposited in LH IIIB but have not been identified as LH IIIB products?).What this might imply is that tombs as a single category of data for display of status of a settlement is not enough. Instead the use of several categories of material is needed to arrive at a more secure conclusion. It is possible that the socio-economic situation as displayed in the LHIIIA period was prevalent also now, although we do not find it represented in the chamber tomb material.

It is assumed that pictorial pottery had a high exchange value as it was one of the trade goods used in exchange transactions with other regions. The samples from the Tir/As group found in the eastern part of the Mediterranean are a case in point.[36] Material from the Tir/As pottery group has been identified at Midea, probably from LH IIIB2. The information provided by the archaeological remains indicate specialisation and that the division of craft specialisation between the settlements registered already in the preceding period developed further. The specialisation in LH IIIB1 changed in LH IIIB2 as evidence of production of metals is found at Midea, Mycenae and Tiryns, although it seems as the latter had the most diversified production of metals. Jewellery production has been documented at Mycenae and Midea. Mycenae and Tiryns both had production of ivory objects although the archaeological evidence indicates a higher level of production at Mycenae.

As shown for LH IIIB1 the road system on the central plain developed and integrated the settlements in a regional network. The strategical location of Mycenae and Tiryns determines their function as central market places (*Fig. 10*). Mycenae may have functioned as a hub for distribution of goods from the northern part of the Peloponnese. The status of Tiryns as a central place of high order may have been connected to the location close

[36] Mommsen & Maran 2000-2001.

by the sea. Along with probable harbour facilities the presence of roads M4 and m5 should have played an important part. Goods traded long-distance had the possibility to reach the regional market through this port and roads M4 and m5 as the inland channels of distribution. The finds of raw metal at Tiryns and Midea point towards such a function, as does the ivory found at Mycenae. Road m5 that connected the Berbati-Limnes area with Midea and the coast at Tiryns indicates no need for the exclusive distribution of goods via Mycenae in this period. Instead we may propose that Midea in the LH IIIB2 period functioned as a central place of intermediate rank connected both to higher ranked Mycenae and Tiryns.

The resulting hierarchy of settlements, shown in *Fig. 10*, is one of restraint. Links are fewer, they tend to underline the role of the two predominant centres, Mycenae and Tiryns, as focal points. At the same time Berbati retreats into insignificance. As was true during the previous period, however, it would seem natural to suggest that the settlements closest to Mycenae should have developed direct links with that particular centre. Yet, while plausible, no evidence to this effect has been located.

As was developed at some length in Chapter 1 above, the LH IIIB period is of particular interest as it is associated with a redistributive economic system. Even so, it should be underlined that the material at hand does not provide for irrevocable proof of palatial involvement and domination of all sectors of production and economy. The establishment and presence of specialisation and large-scale storage facilities have traditionally been interpreted in terms of centralised and redistributive palatial economic activity. As shown above, however, production of certain commodities could have been centralised due to several other factors than redistribution. Both land and sea transport, and especially long-distance trade, must have been a both risky and costly investment. For example, the possibility to use only part of the year for sea transports must have been a cost. The supply of foreign exotic materials and goods must have been low, with the commensurate high prices that scarce goods would fetch. The expenses had to be covered which implies that tradable goods had a minimum price when they arrived at the final destination. Yet, the demand for objects made of exotic materials was high as the finds from the settlements show. The costs involved in acquisition and production may have further limited the number of buyers of the raw material. The specialisation indicated in the settlement material from the LH IIIB2 period might be a sign of these limitations. Furthermore, specialised production, such as metal-working and ivory-carving, needed skilled craftsmen and artisans and certain investments must have been necessary. Nor can the use of storage areas for redistributive purposes be verified, as the facilities known at sites on the Argive Plain do not have the capacity to store large quantities of products. The Linear B tablets are few and, so far, no evidence of a more developed administrative level has been discovered. Instead the material indicates that at least three sites in the LH IIIB2 period had the need of documentation and also individuals who mastered the skill of writing.

As has been shown, distribution of goods may have been conducted at several levels. The high rank central places composed by Mycenae and Tiryns were in all likelihood the nodes for distribution and exchange of exotic goods. Due to its location, Midea may have had the status of the intermediate centre whereas the standard market is found at Argos, Asine and Prosymna. For most small sites lateral exchange relations were probably more important, dominated by exchange of peasants' produce. In the rural society most people were dependent on the annual cycle of the agricultural year.[37] If food or daily items were missing, the local market was the node for exchange. It is to be remembered that different cycles regulate daily life in traditional agrarian societies and the marketing week is one such.[38]

LH IIIC (*Fig. 11*)

The LH IIIB2 period ends with destruction, probably an earthquake. We find that some settlements are not rebuilt and at others life continued. The symmetrical pattern of wealth for tombs in the LH IIIB period continued and a sharp decline in use of tombs at all sites, except Asine where earlier used tombs were re-used, is also observed. It has been remarked that the LH IIIC period lacked the traits characteristic of the previous complex administrative system, such as Linear B tablets.[39] The preceding LH IIIB period has also, if perhaps not entirely warranted, been associated with large-scale storage facilities and the assumed lack of these in LH IIIC has been seen as a further evidence of change in economic structure. Be that as it may, changes need not to have been as radical as previously proposed.[40] As is shown by the archaeological remains, sites such as Mycenae, Midea and Tiryns did not initially fall back. At Mycenae a rebuilding of houses destroyed can be observed, but also the construction of new houses. Remains of production are not documented, but it cannot be excluded that some of the activities conducted in the LH IIIB2 period were resumed. Storage areas seem to have been extended in LH IIIC and possibly indicate storage of agricultural produce, not needed in LH IIIB2. At Mycenae, as elsewhere, few objects indicate exchange within, or outside the region. An exception is the presence of LH IIIC Middle pottery (Close and Granary Style) at Asine and Tiryns, in both cases perhaps originating at Mycenae.[41] It is assumed that the status of Mycenae as a market or redistribution site diminished due to the low level of demand (availablility?) of products.

---

37 Roberts, 1996, 12

38 Skinner 1964, 10-11.

39 Eder 1998, 53.

40 Eder 1998, 53-55.

41 On Asine, Gullög Nordqvist, personal communication.

At Tiryns continuity is observed throughout the LH IIIC periods. The inhabited area of Tiryns was impressive in this period, some 25 ha,[42] and attests to the status of the site at this point. The construction of the dam, after an flash flood at the end of LH IIIB2, or possibly periodic flooding between LH IIIB1 and beginning of LH IIIC, indicates that the settlement had the economic means but also the organisation to build such a construction. The date of the dam is therefore interesting, as it is not an early LH IIIB construction, but probably built in the end of LH IIIB, or even early LH IIIC. The construction of large-scale water works could be associated with control by a political unit, as proposed by Balcer,[43] and indicates the capacity of Tiryns. It has recently been suggested that the construction of the dam should not exclusively be sought in an idea of protection but also in a wish by the inhabitants to extend and develop the area. Possibly this was done by families belonging to a new upper social group.[44] Work areas, although not always with defined products, have been identified. Remains of melted lead indicate that the tradition of production of lead objects continued until the end of LH IIIC:M, although probably on a reduced scale. Of particular interest are the finds of iron in Bau VI/VIa as this may indicate production already in the LH IIIC Early or Middle period. In the same building also ivory has been found in a LH IIIC Early context. A pottery kiln has similarly been identified and was probably in use in LH IIIC:E. Samples of Tir/As pottery found at Midea and Mycenae show that intra-regional exchange occurred at least in the earliest part of LH IIIC and probably in the middle.[45]

Recent excavations at Midea show that the site was occupied also in the LH IIIC period. It is possible that some of the functions observed in LH IIIB2 continued. It is proposed that Midea and Tiryns held positions at an intermediate level at least in the earlier and middle part of the LH IIIC period. It is not excluded that the publication of more material from these two sites will reveal further information concerning the following part of the period. At least as concerns sites other than Tiryns and Asine, a gradual change may instead have occurred after the middle of the LH IIIC period. During the LH IIIC:E period Asine is not represented with any house structures. Remains from the following LH IIIC:M and LH IIIC:L periods attest to a larger settled area. The houses and the chamber tombs indicate a flourishing site and it is can perhaps be assumed that the location was the prime factor for the resumed position. Evidence of production is limited to two possible pottery kilns while a large number of bobbins could indicate textile production. The kilns are small and most probably the vessels produced were meant for local, household consumption. Also textiles produced were probably for household use. It is here proposed that the size of buildings, the extension and continuity of the settlement indicate that Asine not only resumed its position as an intermediate centre in the LH III Middle and Late periods but also a certain level of prosperity, as well as differentiated, was found amongst the people who lived in the houses and used the chamber tombs.

The initial phase of LH IIIC shows evidence of activity also at Argos and Iria. These sites are, however, not inhabited in the following periods and it is assumed that most people moved out and lived on small farmsteads dispersed on the countryside. The results from the Berbati-Limnes survey suggest a similar pattern also for that area.[46] All in all, therefore, LH IIIC is characterised by low levels of activity and, as can be seen in *Fig. 11*, the pronounced focus on the eastern reaches of the Argive Plain makes this period similar to LH IIIA2. The intensity in contacts and exchange is lower than at any point previously. On the other hand, the major centres appear to be more equal to each other during LH IIIC than was the case during earlier periods.

Pottery evidence from the Lower Town has established that Asine was inhabited in the Submycenaean period. Evidence of small-scale habitation on the Argive Plain in this period has also been found at Mycenae, Tiryns and at Argos. Theories concerning the decline of the Mycenaean world are many and varied,[47] and the invasion theory is still applied as has recently been shown.[48] B. Eder argues for a short break between LH IIIC:L and the Submycenaean period. She interprets changes, such as a break with the Mycenaean burial tradition, the use of settlement areas for burials and change in settlement pattern, as evidence for new groups of people arriving.[49] As shown in this study the quantitative gap with respect to archaeological material between the LH IIIC and the Submycenaean period is wide at all sites. The reason for the decline need not be explained in terms of invasion of foreign groups of people and so forth. Instead, it seems more plausible to assume that the succession of earthquakes hitting the area from the end of LH IIIB1 and on must have had an adverse impact on the social and economic fabric of the area. In this perspective, the earthquakes that hit the Argolid Plain in the LH IIIC period, are notable mainly on account of being the last of a long series of disasters to strike. Whether this in fact served to interrupt all dwelling activity is however questionable. Pottery finds from Asine indicate possible re-use of later LH IIIC structures and it is believed that more detailed research concerning pottery will reveal a situation of even more explicit continuity. It is proposed that the Submycenaean period may have been very short and a link between the Late Bronze Age and the Early Iron Age.

[42] Kilian 1988b, 135.
[43] Balcer 1974, 141.
[44] Maran 2002-2003, 223-224.
[45] Mommsen, Lewandowski, Weber & Podzuweit 1988; Mommsen & Maran 2000-2001.
[46] Schallin 1996, fig. 32.
[47] For example, Lewartowski 1989; Rystedt 1997, 147-154; Seymour, Mazara & Stern 1998.
[48] Eder 1998.
[49] Eder 1998, 87.

☼ ☼ ☼

To summarise the economic pattern prevailing in the Late Helladic society I would yet again like to suggest that a controlled and centralised economy based on redistribution could not be confirmed. The centralised settlement patterns arrived at by Bintliff and Kilian are open to challenge if the chronology is taken into account. It is not possible, for example, to establish beyond reasonable doubt that Mycenae was the dominant centre on the Argive Plain throughout this period. The model by Kilian similarly suggests that Tiryns was a major and important settlement, its prominent role strongly tied to redistribution. Set against this view, the sequence of models presented here suggests that no single centre dominated until the end of LH IIIC period. Instead, spatial differentiation was built around local nodes rather than a fully integrated settlement system covering the entire region under the influence of Mycenae. Settlements functioned as centres of exchange at various levels, either laterally and locally or vertically and across the region as the case might be. Especially the LH IIIB period indicates a diversified and decentralised exchange pattern where Mycenae, Tiryns and Midea were the major markets for vertical flow of goods and minor settlements functioned as distributors of goods exchanged at lower levels, that is, at a level equivalent to Skinner's standard market. It is here proposed that this level was important not only for distribution of precious goods to the minor settlements, but also as a market for locally produced agricultural products.

The larger settlements may have been dependent on the surplus of agricultural produce for their everyday needs, and perhaps as the mainstay of their economy. As has been shown, however, an approach that identifies storage areas as indicators of a centralised and redistributive economy is not possible to apply on the Argive Plain. Neither Mycenae nor Tiryns are in possession of any large capacity facilities for storage in any period. The model of redistribution suggested by Halstead, focusing on subsistence relief, is more plausible in view of the limited storage space provided.[50] Indeed, if the storage rooms in LH IIIB in fact contained agricultural products these may primarily have been stored for distribution to the palace household. To be noted is the case of the Panagia Houses, located outside the citadel area in LH IIIB and where foodstuffs may have been stored. Here storage probably was for the household and not the palace. Nor is it possible to verify that production *per se* was concentrated to the palace as only a few specialised workshops have been identified. The question is if these workshops had the possibility to produce to meet anything other than local demand? These objects most probably held an élite status value and were used as such in transactions conducted within the region.[51] It is easy to go along with W.A. Parkinson, who suggests that the élite status goods could have been exchanged with local-regional élites and also used in inter-palatial exchange to secure alliances and so on.[52]

At this juncture it is appropriate to take a closer look at the physical infrastructure for the distribution of goods in exchange. The Argive Plain was served by a set of formal roads that 'provided the land-locked but rich plains of Phlious, Nemea, Kleonai, Tenea and Berbati with access to the sea and the market'.[53] In addition to these formal roads of the LH IIIB period, most of which converged at or ran nearby Mycenae, a network of informal roads supplemented the major ones.[54] Jansen draws the conclusion that the roads near Mycenae were likely for local circulation and the other roads in the Argolid appear to have been oriented more towards Tiryns.[55] Together, they gave considerable scope for contacts between settlements and favoured agricultural areas of the region but may also have been associated with the economic development of the region. According to Jansen these activities indicate civil rather than strict military reasons for developing roads.[56] Although his work also refers to the situation during LH IIIB, it is plain to see that the hierarchical nature serves to afford Mycenae a dominant position. The issue whether this was because Mycenae derived its status from it geographical position, that is, as a gateway, or, because of Mycenae's dominance in political and economical matters, roads were laid out to reflect its needs, can perhaps not be resolved, but the prominent position of Mycenae is plain to see. Yet, the difference between being a gateway for contacts further north and that of being the unchallenged centre and focal point of the region is not trivial one.

In addition to identifying the links with producing regions, with the outside world and underlining the role of Mycenae, the road pattern affords us the privilege of deducing further insights. Although hierarchical in nature, it still allows for local contacts and then not only of the vertical variety. Also horizontal links could support, or be fostered by, the roads identified to date. This opens up for the possibility of local exchange systems that extended well beyond everyday exchange with immediate neighbours; it allows for local nodes deployed for local trade or collection of produce for redistributive ends. What is more, an emerging road network of this character and magnitude is precisely the sort of infrastructure needed for the periodic markets, common throughout much of the world, which first became well known through the work on China by Skinner. As detailed in the introduction chapter, such markets were highly useful in a traditional agrarian context, where a considerable degree of self-sufficiency

[50] See also Parkinson 1999, 82, for a discussion on the relevance of redistribution.

[51] Parkinson 1999, 83, in his analysis of Pylos, makes the same assumption.

[52] Parkinson 1999, 81-82.

[53] Lavery 1995, 265.

[54] Lavery 1990, 165. fig. 1: 1995, 264, maps 1-2; Jansen 2002, 12-14, map 1.

[55] Jansen 2002, 14-15.

[56] Jansen 2002, 128-133.

probably characterised most economic pursuits. Yet to the extent that needs could be better met by a division of labour (or not met at all through domestic production), the periodic market makes it possible for peasants to visit markets close by when needed. These markets could in turn be linked to higher order nodes of exchange, such as the standard market mentioned by Skinner, thereby ensuring that also other types of goods could come in local circulation. To the extent that such a nested and layered system of exchange was developed, it was perhaps rather members of the local élite that availed themselves of the opportunities of the latter type that it presented; the presence of tholoi and chamber tombs decked out with objects of exotic character or superior craftsmanship suggests as much. Yet, markets as may have existed should not only be seen as nodes for exchange of goods but are also likely to have functioned as social nodes: markets provide the possibility to meet and establish relations of different kinds and purpose. Markets allow one to meet people of equal rank and establish further contracts, for example, marriage. It was also possible to secure alliances of political character.

BIBLIOGRAPHY

UNPUBLISHED SOURCES

The documentation used in this study, that is original plans for the excavation and the diaries from the excavations conducted in the 1920s, are deposited in the storage rooms of the Department of Archaeology and Ancient History, University of Uppsala, Uppsala, Sweden.

Diary 1. Kjellberg, E. 1924. Barbouna: Grave 2, chamber tomb VI, Barbouna top terrace, terrace below the graves; Astros 1926. Säflund, G. & Sjöqvist, E., Barbouna top terrace.

Diary 2. Nilsson, N. 1924. Barbouna: chamber tomb I, grave 1; 1924-26. Svensson, N. et.al., Mycenaean terrace.

Diary 5. Nilsson, N. 1926. Lower Town.

Diary 6. Arbman, H., Erlandson, S., Knutzon. J.E. & Hanell. K. 1924-1926. Barbouna, chamber tombs III-VII.

Diary 7. Hanell, K. 1926. Lower Town.

Diary 8. Svensson, N. 1926. Lower Town.

PUBLISHED SOURCES

Åkerström, Å. 1940, 'Das Mykenische Töpferviertel in Berbati in der Argolis', in *Bericht über den VI Internationalen Kongress für Archäologie, Berlin 21-21 August 1939*, Berlin, 296-298.

Åkerström, Å. 1968, 'A Mycenaean potter's factory at Berbati near Mycenae', in *Atti e memorie del 1° Congresso internazionale di micenologia, Roma 27 settembre-3 ottobre, Roma*, Rome, 47-53.

Åkertröm, Å. 1975, 'More Canaanite jars from Greece', *OpAth* 11, 185-192.

Alden, M.J. 1981, *Bronze Age population fluctuations in the Argolid from the evidence of Mycenaean tombs* (SIMA-PB, 15), Göteborg.

Ålin, P. 1968, 'Unpublished Mycenaean sherds from Asine', *OpAth* 8, 87-105.

Åström, P. 1968, 'The destruction of Midea', in *Atti e memorie del 1° Congresso internazionale di micenologia, Roma 27 settembre-3 ottobre*, Roma, 54-57.

Åström, P. 1977. *The cuirass tomb and other finds from Dendra*. Part 1: *The chamber tombs* (SIMA, 4:1), Göteborg.

Åström, P. & Demakopoulou, K. 1986, 'New excavations in the citadel of Midea 1983-84', *OpAth* 16, 19-25.

Åström, P., Demakopoulou, K., Divari-Valakou, N. & Fischer, P. 1992, 'Excavations in Midea, 1989-1990', *OpAth* 19, 11-22.

Åström, P., Demakopoulou, K., Divari-Valakou, N., Fischer, P. & Walberg, G. 1990, 'Excavations in Midea 1987', *OpAth* 18, 9-22.

Avila, R., Grossmann, P. 1980, Grabungen in bereich des Bauses 2' in *Tiryns. Forschungen und Berichte* IX, Mainz, 1-87.

Balcer, J.M. 1974, 'The Mycenaean dam at Tiryns', *AJA* 78, 141-149.

Bech Gregersen, M.L. 2000, 'Acquisition and distribution: *ta-ra-si-ja* in the Mycenaean textile industry' *Trade and production in premonetary Greece: acquisition and distribution of raw materials and finished products. Proceedings of the 6th international workshop, Athens 1996* (SIMA-PB, 154), eds. C. Gillis, C. Risberg & B. Sjöberg, Jonsered, 42-61.

Beck, C.W. 1996, 'Spectroscopic identification of "amber" and "black resin" from Asine', in *Asine* III. *Supplementary studies on the Swedish excavations 1922-1930I*, fasc. 1 (ActaAth-4°, 45:1), eds. R. Hägg, G.C. Nordquist & B. Wells, Stockholm, 91-92.

Bennet, J. 1988a, 'Approaches to the problem of combining Linear B textual data and archaeological data in the Late Bronze Age Aegean', in *Problems in Greek prehistory. Papers presented at the Centenary conference of the British School of Archaeology at Athens, Manchester April 1986*, eds. E.B. French & K.A. Wardle, Bristol, 509-518.

Bennet, J. 1988b, 'Outside in the distance', in *Text, tablets and scribes. Studies in Mycenaean epigraphy and economy offered to Emmett L. Bennett, Jr.*, eds. J.-P. Olivier & T.G. Palaima (Minos Suppl., 10), Salamanca, 19-41.

Bennet, J. 1999, 'Pylos. The expansion of a Mycenaean palatial centre', in *Rethinking Mycenaean palaces. New interpretations of an old idea* (The Cotsen Institute of Archaeology, University of California, Los Angeles, Monograph 41), eds. M.L. Galaty & W.A. Parkinson, 9-18.

Bennett, E.L., Jr. 1958, 'Catalogue of the Mycenaean (Linear B) inscriptions from Mycenae', in *The Mycenae tablets* II (= *TAPS* 48:1), ed. E.L. Bennett, Jr., Philadelphia, 45-75.

Betts, J.H. & Younger, J.G. 1982, 'Aegean seals of the Late Bronze Age: masters and workshops', *Kadmos* 21:2, 104-121.

Bintliff, J.L. 1977, *Natural environment and human settlement in Prehistoric Greece* (BAR-SS, 28), Oxford.

Blanton, R.E, 1994, *Houses and households. A comparative study*, London.

Blegen, C. 1937, *Prosymmna. The Helladic settlement preceding the Argive Heraeum*, vols. 1-2, Cambridge.

Bloch, M. 1981, 'Tombs and state', in *Mortality and immortality: the anthropology and archaeology of death*, eds. S.C. Humphreys & H. King, London, 137-147.

Bosanquet, R.C. 1904, 'Some "Late Minoan" vases found in Greece', *JHS* 24, 615-329.

Carsten, J. & Hugh-Jones, S., eds., 1995, *About the house. Levi-Strauss and beyond*, Cambridge.

Caskey, J.L. 1954, 'Excavations at Lerna, 1952-1953', *Hesperia* 23, 3-29.

Caskey, J.L. 1955, 'Excavations at Lerna, 1954', *Hesperia* 24, 25-49.

Caskey, J.L. & Amandry, P. 1952, 'Investigations at the Heraion of Argos, 1949', *Hesperia* 21, 165-221.

Cavanagh, W.G. 1987, 'Cluster analysis of Mycenaean chamber tombs', in *Thanatos. Les coutumes funeraires en Egée à l'âge du bronze. Actes du colloque de Liège (21-23 avril 1986)* (= *Aegaeum* 1), ed. R. Laffineur, 161-169.

Cavanagh, W. & Mee, C. 1978, 'The re-use of earlier tombs in the LH IIIC period', *BSA* 73, 31-44.

Cavanagh, W.G. & Mee, C. 1990, 'The location of Mycenaean chamber tombs in the Argolid', in *Celebrations of death and divinity in the Bronze Age Argolid. Proceedings of the Sixth International Symposium at the Swedish Institute at Athens, 11-13 June, 1988* (ActaAth-4°, 40), eds R. Hägg & G.C. Nordquist, Stockholm, 55-64.

Cavanagh. W. & Mee, C. 1998, *A private place: death in prehistoric Greece* (SIMA, 125), Jonsered.

Chadwick, J., ed., 1963, *The Mycenae tablets* III (= *TAPS* 52:7), Philadelphia 1963, 54-67.

Chadwick, J. 1976, *The Mycenaean world*, Cambridge.

Clark, G. 1986, *Symbols of excellence: precious materials as expression of status*, Stockbridge.

Cook, S. 1966, 'The obsolete "anti-market" mentality: a critique of substantive approach to economic anthropology', *American Anthropologist* 68:2, 323-345.

Croissant, F. 1972, 'Rapport sur les travaux de l'École française en 1971. Argos', *BCH* 96, 883-886.

Crouwel, J.H. 1991, *Well Built Mycenae. The Helleno-British excavations within the Citadel at Mycenae, 1959-1969*, 21. *The Mycenaean pictorial pottery*, eds. W.D. Taylor, E.B. French & K.A. Wardle, Oxford.

D'Agata, A.-L. 1996, 'The "Lord" of Asine reconsidered: technique, type and chronology', in *Asine* III. *Supplementary studies on the Swedish excavations 1922-1930*, fasc. 1 (ActaAth-4°, 45:1), eds. R. Hägg, G.C. Nordquist & B. Wells, Stockholm, 39-46.

D'Altroy, T.N. & Earle, T.K. 1985, 'Staple finance, wealth finance, and storage in the Inka political economy', *Current Anthropology* 26, 187-206.

Dalton, G. 1965, 'Primitive, archaic and modern economies: Karl Polanyi's contribution to economic anthropology and comparative economy', in *Essays in economic anthropology dedicated to the memory of Karl Polanyi. Proceedings of the 1965 annual spring meeting of the American ethnological society*, ed. J. Helm, Seattle, 1-24.

Dalton, G. 1975, 'Karl Polanyi's analysis of long-distance trade and his wider paradigm', in *Ancient civilization and trade*, eds. J.A. Sabloff & C.C. Lamberg-Karlovsky, Albuquerque, 63-131.

Darcque, P. 1987, 'Le tholoi et d'organisation socio-politique du monde mycenien', in *Thanatos. Les coutumes funeraires en Egée à l'âge du bronze. Actes du colloque de Liège (21-23 avril 1986)* (= *Aegaeum* 1), ed. R. Laffineur, 185-205.

Deger-Jalkotzy, S. 1977, *Fremde Zuwanderer in spätmykenischen Griechenland. Zur eine Gruppe handgemachter Keramik aus den Myk. III C Siedlungsschichten von Aigeira* (SBWien, 326), Wien.

Demakopoulou, K. 1990a, 'Palatial and domestic architecture in Mycenaean Thebes', in *L'habitat égéen préhistorique. Actes de la table ronde internationale organisée par le Centre National de la Recherche Scientifique, l'Université de Paris I et École française d' Athènes (Athènes, 23-25 juin 1987)* (BSA Suppl., 19), eds. P. Darcque & R. Treuil, Athènes, 307-317.

Demakopoulou, K. 1990b, 'The burial ritual in the tholos tomb at Kokla, Argolis', in *Celebrations of death and divinity in the Bronze Age Argolid. Proceedings of the Sixth International Symposium at the Swedish Institute at Athens, 11-13 june, 1988* (ActaAth-4°, 40), eds. R. Hägg & G.C. Nordquist, Stockholm, 113-123.

Demakopoulou, K. 1993, 'Argive Mycenaean pottery: evidence from the necropolis at Kokla', in P*roceedings of the international conference Wace and Blegen. Pottery as evidence for trade in the Aegean Bronze Age 1939-1989*, eds. C. Zerner, P. Zerner & J. Winder, Amsterdam, 57-75.

Demakopoulou, K. 1995, 'Mycenaean citadels: recent excavations on the Acropolis of Midea in the Argolid', *BICS* 40, 151-176.

Demakopoulou, K. 2001, 'The Mycenaean Acropolis of Midea: a third palatial centre in the Argolid', *BICS* 45, 180-181.

Demakopoulou, K. & Divari-Valakou, N. 1992-1993, 'A Linear B inscribed stirrup jar from Midea (MI Z2)', *Minos* 27-28, 303-305.

Demakopoulou, K. & Divari-Valakou, N. 1994-1995, 'New finds with Linear B inscriptions from Midea (MI Z 2, Wv 3, Z 4)', *Minos*, 29-30, 323-328.

Demakopoulou, K. & Divari-Valakou, N. 1999, 'The fortifications of the Mycenaean Acropolis of Midea', in *Polemos, Le contexte guerrier en Égée à l'âge du bronze* (= *Aegaeum* 19), ed. R. Laffineur, Liège, 205-215.

Demakopoulou, K., Divari-Valakou, N., Åström, P. & Walberg, G. 1996, 'Excavations in Midea 1994', *OpAth* 21, 13-32.

Demakopoulou, K., Divari-Valakou, N., Åström, P. & Walberg, G. 1997-1998, 'Excavations in Midea 1995-1996', *OpAth* 22-23, 57-90.

Demakopoulou,K., Divari-Valakou, N. & Walberg, G. 1994, 'Excavations and restoration work in Midea 1990-1992', *OpAth* 20, 19-41.

Desborough, V.R.d'A. 1964, *The last Mycenaeans and their successors: an archaeological survey c. 1200-c. 1000 B.C.*, Oxford.

Desborough. V.R.d'A. 1973, 'Late burials from Mycenae', *BSA* 68, 87-101.

Deshayes, J. 1953, 'Les vases mycéniens de la Deiras (Argos)', *BCH* 77, 59-89.

Deshayes, J. 1966, *Argos: les fouilles de la Deiras* (Études Péloponnésiennes, 4), Paris.

Deshayes, J. 1969, 'Les vases Vollgraff de la Deiras', *BCH* 93, 574-616.

Dickinson, O.T.P.K. 1982, 'Parallels and contrasts in the BA of the Peloponnese', *OJA* 1(2), 1982, 125-137.

Dickinsson, O.T.P.K. 1983, 'Cist graves and chamber tombs', *BSA* 78, 55-67.

Dietz, S. 1980, *Asine* II. *Results of the excavations east of the Acropolis 1970-1974*, fasc.2. *The Middle Helladic cemetery, the Middle Helladic and Early Mycenaean deposits* (ActaAth-4°, 24:2), Stockholm.

Dietz, S 1982, Asine II. *Results of the excavations east of the Acropolis 1970-1974*, fasc.1. *General stratigraphical analysis and architectural reamins* (ActaAth-4°, 24:1), Stockholm.

Dietz, S. 1984, 'Kontinuität und Kulturwende in der Argolis von 2000-700 v.Chr. Ergebnisse der neuen schwedisch-dänishen Ausgrabungen in Asine', in *Zur ägäischen Frühzeit* (Kleine Schriften aus dem Vorgeschichtlichen Seminar Marburg, 17), 23-52.

Dietz, S. & Divari-Valakou, N. 1990, 'A Middle Helladic III/Late Helladic I grave group from Myloi in the Argolid (Oikopedon Manti)', *OpAth* 18, 45-61.

Döhl, H. 1973, 'Iria: Die Ergebnisse der Ausgrabungen 1939', in *Tiryns. Forschungen und Berichte* VI, Mainz, 127-194.

Douglas, M. & Isherwood, B., eds., 1980, *The world of goods: towards an anthropology of consumption*, Harmondsworth.

Dragendorff, H. 1913, 'Tiryns', *AM* 38, 329-356.

Dragendorff, H. 1914, 'Archäologische Funde im Jahre 1913, Griechenland', *AA*, 133-136.

Drews, R. 1993, *The end of the Bronze Age: changes in warfare and the catastrophe ca. 1200 B.C.*, Princeton.

Earle, T.K. 1977, 'A reappraisal of redistribution: complex Hawaiian chiefdoms', in *Exchange systems in prehistory*, eds. T.K. Earle & J.E. Ericson, London, 213-229.

Earle, T. 1985, 'Prehistoric economics and the evolution of social complexity: a commentary', in *Prehistoric production and exchange: the Aegean and eastern Mediterranean* (Institute of Archaeology, University of California, Los Angeles, Monograph, 25), eds. A.B. Knapp & T. Stech, Los Angeles, 106-111.

Earle, T.K. & D'Altroy, T.N. 1982, 'Storage facilities and state finance in the Upper Mantaro Valley, Peru', in *Contexts for prehistoric exchange*, eds. T.K. Earle & J.E. Ericson, New York, 265-290.

Eder, B. 1998, *Argolis, Lakonien, Messenien. Vom Ende der mykenischen Palastzeit bis zur Einwanderung der Dorier* (Mykenische Studien, 17), Wien.

Finke, E.A.W. 1988, *Landscape evolution of the Argive Plain, Greece: paleoecology, Holocene depositional history, and coastline changes* (unpublished Ph.D. dissertation, University of Stanford).

Finley, M.I. 1957-58, 'The Mycenaean tablets and economic history', *Economic History Review* 10, 128-141.

Foster Polinger, K. 1979, *Aegean faience of the Bronze Age*, New Haven.

French, E. 1961, 'Mycenaean occupation near the Cyclopean terrace building at Mycenae', *BSA* 56, 81-87.

French, E. 1963, 'Pottery groups from Mycenae: a summary', *BSA* 58, 44-52.

French, E. 1965, 'Late Helladic IIIA2 pottery from Mycenae', *BSA* 60, 139-202.

French, E. 1967, 'Pottery from Late Helladic IIIB1 destruction contexts at Mycenae', *BSA* 62, 151-193.

French, E. 1969, 'A group of Late Helladic IIIB2 pottery from Mycenae', *BSA*.64, 71-93.

French, E. 1977, 'Mycenaean problems 1400-1200 B.C.' *BICS* 24, 136-138.

French, E. 1981, 'Cult places at Mycenae', in *Sanctuaries and cults in the Aegean Bronze Age. Proceedings of the First International Symposium at the Swedish Institute in Athens, 12-13 May, 1980* (ActaAth-4°, 28), eds. R Hägg & N. Marinatos, Stockholm, 41-48.

French, E. 1991, 'Trading exports of Mycenaean pottery: the Manchester contribution', in *Bronze Age trade in the Mediterranean. Papers presented at the conference held at Rewley House, Oxford, in December 1989* (SIMA, 90), ed. N.H. Gale, Jonsered, 121-125.

French, E. 1998, 'The ups and downs of Mycenae: 1250-1150 BCE', in *Mediterranean peoples in transition, thirteenth to early tenth centuries BCE,* eds. S. Gitin, A. Mazar & E. Stern, Jerusalem, 2-5.

French, E.B. 1999, 'The post-palatial levels at Mycenae: an update', *BICS* 43, 222-223.

Frizell, B. 1978, 'Finds of the Late Helladic Period', in *Excavations in the Barbouna Area at Asine* 2 (Boreas. Uppsala Studies in Ancient Mediterranean and Near Eastern civilizations, 4:2), eds. I. & R. Hägg, Uppsala, 63-91.

Frödin, O. & Persson, A.W. 1938, *Asine* [I]. *Results of the Swedish excavations 1922-1930*, ed. A. Westholm, Stockholm.

Furumark, A., 1944, 'The Mycenaean IIIC pottery and its relation to Cypriote fabrics', *OpArch* 3, 194-265.

Furumark, A. 1972a, *Mycenaean pottery* 1 (ActaAth-4°, 20:1), Stockholm.

Furumark, A. 1972b, *Mycenaean pottery* 2 (ActaAth-4°, 20:2), Stockholm.

Furumark, A. 1992, *Mycenaean pottery* 3 (ActaAth-4°, 20:3), Stockholm, eds. P. Åström, R.Hägg & G. Walberg, Stockholm.

Galaty, M.L. & Parkinson, A.A. 1999, 'Putting Mycenaean palaces in their place: an introduction', in *Rethinking Mycenaean palaces. New interpretations of an old idea* (The Cotsen Institute of Archaeology, University of California, Los Angeles, Monograph, 41), eds. M.L. Galaty & W.A. Parkinson, Los Angeles, 1-8.

Gale, N.H. ed., 1991, *Bronze Age trade in the Mediterranean. Papers presented at the conference held at Rewley House, Oxford, in December 1989* (SIMA, 90), Jonsered.

Gale. N.H. & Stos-Gale, Z.A. 1981, 'Cycladic lead and silver metallurgy', *BSA* 76, 169-224.

Gates, C. 1995, 'The Mycenaeans and their Anatolian frontier', in *Politeia. Society and state in the Aegean Bronze Age* (= *Aegaeum* 12), eds. R. Laffineur & W.-D. Niemeier, Liège & Austin, 296-297.

Gercke, P. & Hiesel, G. 1971, 'Grabungen in der Unterstadt von Tiryns von 1889 bis 1929', in *Tiryns. Forschungen und Berichte* V, Mainz, 1-19.

Gercke, P., Gercke, W. & Hiesel, G. 1975, 'Tiryns-Stadt 1971: Graben H', in *Tiryns. Forschungen und Berichte* VIII, Mainz, 7-36.

Gillis, C. 1991-1992, 'All that glitters is not gold', *MedMusB* 26-27, 24-32.

Gillis, C. 1996, 'Tin at Asine', in *Asine* III. *Supplementary studies on the Swedish excavations 1922-1930*, fasc. 1 (ActaAth-4°, 45:1), eds. R. Hägg, G.C. Nordquist & B. Wells, Stockholm, 93-100.

Gillis, C. 1997, 'The smith in the Late Bronze Age: state employee, independent artisan, or both?', in *Techne. Craftsmen, craftswoman and craftsmanship in the Aegean Bronze Age. Proceedings of the 6th international Aegean conference, Philadelphia, Temple University, 18-21 April 1996* (= *Aegaeum* 16), 505-513.

Godart, L. & Olivier, J.-P. 1975, 'Nouveaux textes en Linéaire B de Tirynthe', in *Tiryns. Forschungen und Berichte* VII, Mainz, 37-53.

Godart, L., Killen, J.T. & Olivier, J.-P. 1979, 'Un sixième fragment de tablette en Linéaire B de Tirynthe', *AA*, 450-458.

Godart, L., Killen, J.T. & Olivier, J.-P. 1983, 'Eighteen more fragments of Linear B tablets from Tiryns', *AA*, 413-426.

Grannovetter, M. 1985, 'Economic action and social structure: the problem of embeddedness', *American Journal of Sociology*, 91, 481-510.

Graziadio, G. 1991, 'The process of social stratification at Mycenae in the shaft grave period: a comparative examination of the evidence', *AJA* 95, 403-440.

Gregory, C.A. 1994, 'Exchange and reciprocity', in *Companion encyclopedia of anthropology*, ed. T. Gold, 911-939.

Grossmann, P. 1980, 'Beschreibung der Baureste', in *Tiryns. Forschungen und Berichte* IX, Mainz, 155-170.

Grossman, P. & Schäfer, J. 1971, 'Tiryns Unterburg, Grabungen 1965', in *Tiryns. Forschungen und Berichte* V, Mainz, 41-75.

Grossman, P. & Schäfer, J. 1975, 'Tiryns: Unterburg 1968. Grabungen im Bereich der Bauten 3 und 4', in *Tiryns. Forschungen und Berichte* VIII, Mainz, 55-96.

Hägg, I. 1973, 'Report on the field-work in the Levendis sector, 1970-72', in *Excavations in the Barbouna Area at Asine* 1 (Boreas. Uppsala Studies in Ancient Mediterranean and Near Eastern civilizations, 4:1), eds. I. & R. Hägg, Uppsala, 22-82.

Hägg, R. 1962, 'Research at Dendra', *OpAth* 4, 79-89.

Hägg, R. 1968, 'Mykenische Kultstätten im archäologischen Material', *OpAth* 8, 39-60.

Hägg, R. 1974, *Die Gräber der Argolis in submykenischer, protogeometrischer und geometrischer Zeit, 1. Lage und Form der Gräber* (Boreas. Uppsala Studies in Ancient Mediterranean and Near Eastern Civilizations, 7:1), Uppsala.

Hägg, R. 1981, 'Official and popular cults in Mycenaean Greece', in *Sanctuaries and cults in the Aegean Bronze Age. Proceedings of the First International Symposium at the Swedish Institute in Athens, 12-13 May, 1980* (ActaAth-4°, 28), eds. R. Hägg & N. Marinatos, Stockholm, 35-40.

Hägg, R. & Nordquist, C.G. 1992, 'Excavations in the Levendis sector at Asine, 1989', *OpAth* 19, 59-60.

Halperin, R.H. 1985, 'The concept of the formal in economic anthropology', *Research in Economic Anthropology*, vol. 7, ed. B.I. Isaac, London, 339-368.

Halperin, R.H. 1994, *Cultural economies. Past and present*, Austin.

Halstead, P. 1988, 'On redistribution and the origin of Minoan-Mycenaean palatial economics', in *Problems in Greek prehistory. Papers presented at the Centenary conference of the British School of Archaeology at Athens, Manchester April 1986*, eds. E.B. French & K.A. Wardle, Bristol, 519-530.

Halstead, P. 1992a, 'The Mycenaean palatial economy: making the most of the gaps in the evidence', *PCPS* 38, 1992, 57-86.

Halstead, P. 1992b, 'Towards a model of Bronze Age palatial economy', in *Agriculture in ancient Greece. Proceedings of the Seventh International Symposium at the Swedish Institute at Athens, 16-17 May, 1990* (ActaAth-4°, 42), ed. B. Wells, Stockholm, 105-117.

Halstead, P. 1996, 'Pastoralism or household herding? Problems of scale and specialization in early Greek animal husbandry', *WorldArch* 28, 20-42.

Hamilakis, Y. 1999, 'The anthropology of food and drink consumption and Aegean archaeology', in *Paleodiet in the Aegean. Papers from a colloquium held at the 1993 meeting of the Archaeological Institute of America in Washington D.C.* (Wiener Laboratory Monograph, 1), eds. S.J. Vaughan & W.D.E. Coulson, Oxford, 55-63.

Harding, A. & Hughes-Brock, H. 1974, 'Amber in the Mycenaean world', *BSA* 69, 145-172.

Haskell, H. 1997, 'Trade and production in "Mycenaean" Crete', in *Trade and production in premonetary Greece: production and the craftsman. Proceedings of the 4th and 5th international workshops, Athens 1995 and 1995* (SIMA-PB, 143), eds. C. Gillis, C. Risberg & B. Sjöberg, Jonsered, 101-111.

Hazelgrove, C. 1982, 'Wealth, prestige and power: the dynamics of late Iron Age political centralisation in south-east England', in *Ranking, resource and exchange: aspects of the archaeology of early European society,* eds. C. Renfrew & S. Shennan, Cambridge, 79-88.

Hiesel, G. 1989, *Späthelladische Hausarchitektur*, Mainz am Rhein.

Hodder, I. 1982, 'The identification and interpretation of ranking in prehistory: a contextual perspective', in *Ranking, resource and exchange: aspects of the archaeology of early European society*, eds. C. Renfrew & S. Shennan, Cambridge, 150-154.

Holmberg, E. 1983, *A Mycenaean chamber tomb near Berbati in Argolis* (Acta Regiae Societatis Scientiarum et Litterarum Gothoburgensis. Humaniora, 21), Göteborg.

Hooker, J.T. 1976, *Mycenaean Greece*, London.

Hope Simpson, H. & Dickinson, O.T.P.K. 1979, *A gazetteer of Aegean civilization in the Bronze Age: the mainland and islands*, 1 (SIMA, 52), Göteborg.

Hughes-Brock, H. 1996, 'Asine chamber tomb I:1: the small finds', in *Asine* III. *Supplementary studies on the Swedish excavations 1922-1930*, fasc. 1 (ActaAth-4°, 45:1), eds. R. Hägg, G.C. Nordquist & B. Wells, Stockholm, 69-80.

Iakovidis, S. 1983, *Late Helladic citadels of mainland Greece*, Leiden.

Immerwahr, S.A. 1966, 'The use of tin on Mycenaean vases', *Hesperia* 35, 381-396.

Jansen, A.G. 2002, *A study of the remains of Mycenaeaen roads and stations of Bronze-Age Greece*, (Mellen Studies in Archaeology, 1), New York.

Jantzen, U., ed., 1975, *Führer durch Tiryns*, Athen.

Kardulias, P.N. 1999, 'Multiple levels in the Aegean Bronze Age world-system', in *World-systems theory in practice: leadership, production, and exchange*, ed. P.N. Kardulias, Oxford, 179-201.

Kilian, K. 1978, 'Ausgrabungen in Tiryns, 1976', *AA*, 449-470.

Kilian, K. 1979, 'Ausgrabungen in Tiryns, 1977', *AA*, 379-411.

Kilian, K. 1980, 'Zum Ende der mykenischen Epoche in der Argolis', *RGZM* 27, 1980, 166-195.

Kilian, K. 1981, 'Ausgrabungen in Tiryns, 1978, 1979', *AA*, 149-193.

Kilian, K. 1982. 'Ausgrabungen in Tiryns, 1980', *AA*, 383-439.

Kilian, K. 1983, 'Ausgrabungen in Tiryns 1981', *AA*, 276-328.

Kilian, K. 1987a, 'Der Hauptpalast von Mykene', *AM* 102, 99-113.

Kilian, K. 1987b, 'Zur Funktion der mykenischen Residenzen auf dem griechischen Festland', in *The function of the Minoan palaces. Proceedings of the Fourth International Symposium at the Swedish Institute in Athens, 1-6 June, 1984* (ActaAth-4°, 35), eds. R. Hägg & N. Marinatos, Stockholm, 21-38.

Kilian, K. 1988a, 'The emergence of *wanax* ideology in the Mycenaean palaces', *OJA* 7:3, 291-302.

Kilian, K. 1988b, 'Mycenaeans up to date, trends and changes in recent research', in *Problems in Greek prehistory. Papers presented at the Centenary conference of the British School of Archaeology at Athens, Manchester April 1986*, eds. E.B. French & K.A. Wardle, Bristol, 115-152.

Kilian, K. 1988c, 'Ausgrabungen in Tiryns, 1982/83', *AA*, 105-151.

Killen, J.T. 1985, 'The Linear B tablets and the Mycenaean economy', in *Linear B: a 1984 survey. Proceedings of the Mycenaean Colloquium of the VIIIth Congress of the International Federation of the Societies of Classical Studies (Dublin, 27 August – 1st September 1984)* (Bibl. des cahiers de l'Institut de linguistique de Louvain, 26), eds. A. Morpurgo Davies & Y. Duhoux, Louvain-la-Neuve, 241-305.

Killen, J.T. 1988, 'Knossos woman and cloth records', in *Text, tablets and scribes. Studies in Mycenaean epigraphy and economy offered to Emmett L. Bennett, Jr.*, eds. J.-P. Olivier & T.G. Palaima (Minos Suppl., 10), Salamanca, 167-183.

Knapp, A.B. 1985, 'Production and exchange in the Aegean and eastern Mediterranean: an overview', in *Prehistoric production and exchange: the Aegean and eastern Mediterranean* (Institute of Archaeology, University of California, Los Angeles, Monograph, 25), eds. A.B. Knapp & T. Stech, Los Angeles, 1-11.

Knapp, A.B. & Stech, T. 1985, eds., *Prehistoric production and exchange: the Aegean and eastern Mediterranean* (Institute of Archaeology University of California, Los Angeles, Monograph, 25), Los Angeles.

Kopcke, G. 1995, 'The Argolid in 1400 – what happened?', in *Politeia. Society and state in the Aegean Bronze Age* (= *Aegaeum* 12), eds. R. Laffineur & W.-D. Niemeier, Liège & Austin, 89-93.

Krzyszkowska, O.H. 1996, 'Asine chamber tomb I:2: the ivories', in *Asine* III. *Supplementary studies on the Swedish excavations 1922-1930*, fasc. 1 (ActaAth-4°, 45:1), eds. R. Hägg, G.C. Nordquist & B. Wells, Stockholm, 81-90.

Laffineur, R. 1990-1991, 'Material and craftsmanship in the Mycenae shaft graves', *Minos* 25-26, 245-295.

Landenius Enegren, H. 2000, 'Craft production at Knossos–raw materials and finished goods – the Linear B evidence' in *Trade and production in premonetary Greece: Acquisition and distribution of raw materials and finished products. Proceedings of the 6th international workshop, Athens 1996* (SIMA-PB, 154), eds. C. Gillis, C. Risberg & B. Sjöberg, Jonsered, 29-42.

Lavery, J. 1990, 'Some aspects of Mycenaean topography', *BICS* 37, 165-171.

Lavery, J. 1995, 'Some "new" Mycenaean roads at Mycenae', *BICS* 40, 264-267.

Lewartowski, K. 1989, *The decline of the Mycenaean civilization. An archaeological study of events in the Greek mainland*, Warsaw 1989.

Lewartowski, K. 1995, 'Mycenaean social structure: A view from simple graves', in *Politeia. Society and state in the Aegean Bronze Age* (= *Aegaeum* 12), eds. R. Laffineur & W.-D. Niemeier, Liège & Austin, 103-113

Maran, J. 2002-2003, 'The town of Tiryns after the fall of the palace: some new insight', *BICS* 46, 223-224.

Mårtensson, L. 2002, 'Traces of boxes: linings of boxes in Helladic tombs', in *New research on old material from Asine and Berbat in* celebration *of the fiftieth anniversary of the Swedish Institute at Athens* (ActaAth-8°, 27), ed. B. Wells, Stockholm, 43-48.

Mee, C.B. & Cavanagh, W.G. 1984, 'Mycenaean tombs as evidence for social and political organisation', *OJA* 3(3), 45-64.

Mee, C.B. & Cavanagh, W.G. 1990, 'The spatial distribution of Mycenaean tombs', *BSA* 85, 225-243.

Miles, D. 1965, 'Socio-economic aspects of secondary burial', *Oceania* 35(3), 161-174.

Moberg, K. 1986, *En analys av animalt och humant skelettmaterial i Asine* (unpublished B.A. thesis Uppsala University).

Moberg, K.N. 1996, 'Animal bones from terrace III in the Lower Town of Asine', in *Asine* III. *Supplementary studies on the Swedish excavations 1922-1930*, fasc. 1 (ActaAth-4°, 45:1), eds. R. Hägg, G.C. Nordquist & B. Wells, Stockholm, 111-115.

Mommsen, H., Beier, Th. & Hein, A. 2002, 'A complete chemical grouping of the Berkeley Neutron Activation Analysis data on Mycenaean Pottery', *Journal of Archaeological Science*, 29, 613-637.

Mommsen, H., Lewandowski, E., Weber, J. & Podzuweit, Ch. 1988, 'Neutron activation analysis of Mycenaean pottery from the Argolid: the search for reference groups', in *Proceedings of the 26th international archaeometry symposium*, eds. R.M. Farquhar, R.G.V. Hancock & L.A. Pavlish, Toronto, 165-171.

Mommsen. H. & Maran, J. 2000-2001, 'Production places of some Mycenaean pictorial vessels: the contribution of chemical analysis', *OpAth* 25-26, 95-106.

Moody, J. 1987, 'The Minoan palace as a prestige artifact', in *The function of the Minoan palaces. Proceedings of the Fourth International Symposium at the Swedish Institute in Athens, 1-6 June, 1984* (ActaAth-4°, 35), eds. R. Hägg & N. Marinatos, Stockholm, 235-241.

Morris, H.J. 1986, *An economic model of the Late Mycenaean kingdom of Pylos* (unpublished Ph.D. dissertation, University of Minnesota).

Mossman, S. 1991-1993, 'Mycenaean lead', *BICS* 38, 270.

Mossman, S. 1998, 'The lead finds', in G. Walberg, *Excavations on the Acropolis of Midea. Results of the Greek-Swedish excavations* I. *The excavations on the Lower Terraces 1985-1991* (ActaAth-4°, 49:1:1), Stockholm, 271-276.

Mossman, S. 2000, 'Mycenaean Age lead: a fresh look at an old material' in *Trade and production in premonetary Greece: acquisition and distribution of raw materials and finished products. Proceedings of the 6th international workshop, Athens 1996* (SIMA-PB, 154), eds. C. Gillis, C. Risberg & B. Sjöberg, Jonsered, 85-119.

Mountjoy, P.A. 1976, 'Late Helladic IIIB pottery dating the construction of the South house at Mycenae', *BSA* 71, 77-111.

Mountjoy, P. 1986, *Mycenaean decorated pottery* (SIMA, 73), Göteborg.

Mountjoy, P.A. 1996, 'Asine chamber tomb I:1: the pottery', in *Asine* III. *Supplementary studies on the Swedish excavations 1922-1930*, fasc. 1 (ActaAth-4°, 45:1), eds. R. Hägg, G.C. Nordquist & B. Wells, Stockholm, 47-67.

Mountjoy, P. 1999, *Regional Mycenaean decorated pottery*, vol. 1, Rahden.

Müller, K. 1930, *Tiryns. Die Ergebnisse der Ausgrabungen des Instituts* III. *Die Architektur der Burg und des Palastes*, Augsburg.

Müller, K. 1975, 'Das Kuppelgrab von Tiryns', in *Tiryns: Forschungen und Berichte* VIII, Mainz, 1-6.

Mylonas, G.E. 1966a, *Mycenae and the Mycenean Age*, Princeton.

Mylonas, G.E. 1966b, 'The east wing of the palace of Mycenae', *Hesperia* 35, 419-426.

Naumann, U., Godart, L. & Olivier, J.-P. 1977, 'Un cinquiéme fragment de tablette en Linéaire B de Tirynthe', *BCH* 101, 229-234.

Nordquist, G.C. 1990, 'Middle Helladic burial rites: some speculations' , in *Celebrations of death and divinity in the Bronze Age Argolid. Proceedings of the Sixth International Symposium at the Swedish Institute at Athens, 11-13 June, 1988* (ActaAth-4°, 40), eds. R. Hägg & G.C. Nordquist, Stockholm, 33-43.

North, D.C. 1981, *Structure and change in economic history*, New York.

O'Shea, J. 1981, 'Social configurations and the archaeological study of mortuary practices', in *The archaeology of death*, eds. R. Chapman, I. Kinnes & K. Randsborg, 39-52.

Palaima, T.G. 1987, 'Mycenaean seals and sealings in their economic and administrative contexts', in *Tractata Mycenaea. Proceedings of the Eighth international colloquium on Mycenaean studies, held in Ohrid, 15-20 September 1985*, Skopje, 249-266.

Palaima, T.G. 1990, 'Origin, development, transition and transformation: the purposes and techniques of administration in Minoan and Mycenaean society', in *Aegean seals, sealings and administration. Proceedings of the NEH-Dickson conference of the program in Aegean scripts and prehistory of the department of classics, university of Texas at Austin, january 11-13, 1989* (=Aegaeum 5), ed. T.G. Palaima, 83-104.

Palaima, T.G. 1991, 'Maritime matters in the Linear B tablets', in *Thalassa. L'Egée prehistorique et la mer. Actes de la troisème Rencontre égéenne internationale de l'Université de Liège, Station de recherches sous-marines et océanographiques (StaReSo), Calvi, Corse, 23-25 avril 1990* (=Aegeum 7), eds. R. Laffineur & L. Basch, 273-310.

Palmer, R. 1994, *Wine in the Mycenaean palace economy* (=Aegeum 10), Liège.

Palmer, L.R. 1965, *Mycenaeans and Minoans*, London.

Papadimitriou, A. 1988, 'Bericht zur früheisenzeitlichen Keramik aus der Unterburg von Tiryns', *AA*, 227-243.

Parkinson, W.A. 1999, 'Chipping away at a Mycenaean economy: obsdian exchange, Linear B and palatial control in Late Bronze Age Messenia', in *Rethinking Mycenaean palaces. New interpretations of an old idea* (The Cotsen Institute of Archaeology, University of California, Los Angeles, Monograph, 41), eds. M.L. Galaty & W.A. Parkinson, 73-85.

Patrianakou-Iliaki, A. 1996, 'An ivory mirror handle from Asine', in *Atti e memorie del Secondo congresso internazionale di micenologia, Roma-Napoli, 14-20 ottobre 1991*, vol. 3, eds. E. de Miro, L. Godart & A. Sacconi, 1273-1280.

Pearson, M. Parker 1999, *The archaeology of death and burial*, Stroud Sutton.

Pelon, O. 1976, *Tholoi, tumuli et cercle funéraires, recherches sur les monuments funéraires de plan circulaire dans l'Égée de l'âge du bronze (IIIe et IIe millénaires av. J.-C.)* (BEFAR, 229), Paris.

Pelon, O. 1990, 'Les tombes à tholos d'Argolide: architecture et ritual funéraire', in *Celebrations of death and divinity in the Bronze Age Argolid. Proceedings of the Sixth International Symposium at the Swedish Institute at Athens, 11-13 June, 1988* (ActaAth-4°, 40), eds. R. Hägg & G.C. Nordquist, Stockholm, 107-112.

Penttinen, A. 1996, 'Excavations on the Acropolis of Asine 1990', *OpAth* 21, 149-167.

Perry, D. 2000, 'Rural weekly markets and the dynamics of time, space and community in Senegal', *Journal of Modern African Studies* 38(3), 461-468.

Persson, A.W. 1931, *The royal tombs at Dendra near Midea* (Skrifter utg. av Kungl. Humanistiska vetenskaps-samfundet i Lund, 15), Lund.

Persson, A.W. 1942, *New tombs at Dendra near Midea* (Skrifter utg. av Kungl. Humanistiska vetenskapssamfundet i Lund, 34), Lund.

Persson, A.W. & Åkerström, Å. 1937-38, 'Zwei mykenische Hausaltäre in Berbati', *BLund* 3, 59-63.

Podzuweit, C. 1977, 'Ein mykenischer Kieselmosaikfussboden aus Tiryns: die Fundsituation und Datierung des Mosaiks', *AA*, 124-134.

Podzuweit, C. 1978, 'Bericht zur Spätmykenischen Keramik', *AA*, 471-498.

Podzuweit, C. 1979, 'Bericht zur Spätmykenischen Keramik', *AA*, 412-440.

Podzuweit, C. 1981, 'Bericht zur Spätmykenischen Keramik', *AA*, 194-220.

Podzuweit, C. 1983, 'Bericht zur Spätmykenischen Keramik', *AA*, 359-402.

Podzuweit, C. 1988, 'Keramik der Phase SH III C-Spät aus der Unterburg von Tiryns', *AA*, 213-225.

Polanyi, K. 1944 (1957), *The great transformation: the political and economic origins of our time*, Boston.

Polanyi, K. 1957, 'The economy as instituted process', in *Trade and market in the early empires*, eds. K. Polanyi, C.A. Arenberg & H.W. Pearson, New York, 243-270.

Polanyi, K. 1968a, 'Societies and economic systems', in *Primitive, archaic and modern economies: essays of Karl Polanyi*, ed. G. Dalton, New York, 3-26.

Polanyi, K. 1968b,'On the comparative treatment of economic institutions in antiquity with illustrations from Athens, Mycenae and Alalakh', in *Primitive, archaic and modern economies: essays of Karl Polanyi*, ed. G. Dalton, New York, 306-334.

Precourt, W.E. 1984, 'Mortuary practices and economic transactions. A hologeistic study', in *Research in economic anthropology*, ed. B.L. Isaac, vol. 6, London, 161-170.

Renard, J. 1995, *Le Péloponnèse au Bronze Ancien* (=Aegeum 13), Liège.

Renaudin, L.R. 1923, 'La necropole "mycénienne" de Skhinokhori-Lyrkeia (?)', *BCH* 47, 190-240.

Renfrew, C. 1972, *The emergence of civilisation. The Cyclades and the Aegean in the third millennium BC*, London.

Roberts, B.K. 1996, *Landscapes of settlement: prehistory to the present*, London.

Rudolph, W. 1973, 'Die Nekropole am Prophitis Elias bei Tiryns', in *Tiryns. Forschungen und Berichte* VI, Mainz, 23-126,

Rystedt, E. 1997, 'Approaching the question of Bronze-to-Iron Age continuity in ancient Greece', *Current Swedish Archaeology* 5, 147-154.

Säflund, G. 1965, *Excavations at Berbati 1936-1937* (Stockholm Studies in Classical Archaeology, 4), Uppsala.

Sahlins, M. 1972, *Stone Age economics*, New York.

Santillo Frizell, B. 1980, *An Early Mycenaean settlement at Asine* (Ph. D dissertation, University of Göteborg).

Santillo Frizell, B. 1984, 'The tholos tomb at Berbati', *OpAth* 15, 25-44.

Santillo Frizell, B. 1986, *Asine* II. *Results of the excavations east of the Acropolis 1970-1974*, fasc. 3. *The Late and Final Mycenaean periods* (ActaAth-4°, 24:3), Stockholm.

Santillo Frizell, B. 1997-1998, 'Monumental building at Mycenae: its function and audience', *OpAth* 22-23, 103-116.

Santillo Frizell, B. 1998, 'Giants or geniuses? Monumental building at Mycenae', *Current Swedish Archaeology* 6, 1998, 167-184.

Schaar, K. 1979, *An interpretation of the palace plans at Mycenae* (unpublished Ph.D. dissertation, Cornell University).

Schallin, A.-L. 1993, *Islands under influence. The Cyclades in the Late Bronze Age and the nature of Mycenaean presence* (SIMA, 111), Jonsered.

Schallin, A.-L. 1996, 'The Berbati-Limnes archaeological survey. The Late Helladic period', in *The Berbati-Limnes archaeological survey 1988-1990* (ActaAth-4 °, 44).

Schallin, A.-L. 1997, 'The Late Bronze Age potter's workshop at Mastos in the Berbati Valley', in *Trade and production in premonetary Greece: production and the craftsman. Proceedings of the 4th and 5th international workshops, Athens 1994 and 1995* (SIMA-PB, 143), eds. C. Gillis, C. Risberg & B. Sjöberg, Jonsered, 73-88.

Scoufopoulos, N.C. 1971, *Mycenaean citadels* (SIMA, 22), Göteborg.

Seymour, G., Mazar, A. & Stern, E., eds. 1998, *Mediterranean peoples in transition. Thirteenth to early tenth centuries BCE*, Jerusalem.

Shear Mylonas, M. 1968, *Mycenaean domestic architecture* (unpublished Ph.D. dissertation, Bryn Mawr), vols. 1-3.

Shear Mylonas, M. 1987, *The Panagia Houses at Mycenae* (University Museum Monograph University of Pennsylvania, 68), Philadelphia.

Shelmerdine, C.W. 1987, 'Architectural change and economic decline at Pylos', *Minos* 20-22, 559, 565-568.

Shelmerdine, C.W. 1997, 'Review of Aegean prehistory VI: the palatial Bronze Age of the southern and central Greek Mainland', *AJA* 101, 537-585.

Shelton, K.S. 1996, *The Late Helladic pottery from Prosymna* (SIMA-PB, 138), Jonsered.

Shennan, S. 1982, 'Exchange and ranking: the role of amber in the earlier Bronze Age of Europe', *Ranking, resource and exchange: aspects of the archaeology of early European society*, eds. C. Renfrew & S. Shennan, Cambridge, 33-45.

Sherratt, A. 1994, 'Core, periphery and margin: perspective on the Bronze Age', in *Development and decline in the Mediterranean Bronze Age* (Sheffield Archaeological Monographs, 8), eds. C. Mathers & S. Stoddart, 335-345.

Sherratt, A. & Sherratt, S. 1991, 'From luxuries to commodities: the nature of Mediterranean Bronze Age trading systems', in *Bronze Age trade in the Mediterranean. Papers presented at the conference held at Rewley House, Oxford, in December 1989* (SIMA, 90), ed. N.H. Gale, Jonsered, 351-384.

Sjöberg, B. 1995, 'The Mycenaean economy: theoretical frameworks', in *Trade and production in premonetary Greece: aspects of trade. Proceedings of the Third international workshop, Athens 1993* (SIMA-PB, 134), eds. C. Gillis, C. Risberg & B. Sjöberg, Jonsered, 1995, 19-32.

Sjöberg, B.L. 1996, 'Five Mycenaean vases from Zafer Aga, 1924', in *Asine* III. *Supplementary studies on the Swedish excavations 1922-1930*, fasc. 1 (ActaAth-4°, 45:1), eds. R. Hägg, G.C. Nordquist & B. Wells, Stockholm, 101-110.

Sjöberg, B. 1997, 'Two possible Late Helladic kilns at Asine: a research note', in *Trade and production in premonetary Greece: production and the craftsman. Proceedings of the 4th and 5th international workshops, Athens 1995 and 1995* (SIMA-PB, 143), eds. C. Gillis, C. Risberg & B. Sjöberg, 89-100.

Sjöberg, B.L. 2001, *Asine and the Argolid in the Late Helladic III period: a socio-economic study* (unpublished Ph.D. dissertation, Uppsala University).

Sjöberg, B.L 2002, 'Economic interaction on the Argive Plain: a research note on Late Helladic Asine', in *New research on old material from Asine and Berbat in celebration of the fiftieth anniversary of the Swedish Institute at Athens* (ActaAth-8°, 27), ed. B. Wells, Stockholm, 57-69.

Skinner, G.W. 1964, 'Marketing and social structure in rural China, part 1', *Journal of Asian Studies* 24, 3-43.

Skinner, G.W. 1976, 'Mobility strategies in late imperial China: a regional systems analysis', in *Regional analysis: economic systems*, vol. 1, ed. C.A. Smith, New York, 327-364.

Slenczka, E. 1974, 'Zur Chronologie der Burg von Tiryns', in *Tiryns. Forschungen und Berichte* VII, Mainz, 153-159.

Smith, A. 1776 (1999), *The wealth of the nations*, books I-III, St Ives.

Smith, C.A. 1985, 'Methods for analysing periodic marketplaces as elements in regional trading systems', *Research in Economic Anthropology* 7, ed. B.L. Isaac, 291-335.

Smith, M.E. 1987, 'Household possessions and wealth in agrarian states: implications for archaeology', *Journal of Anthropological Archaeology* 6, 297-335.

Smith Kirkpatrick, S. 1999, 'Skeletal and dental evidence for social status in Late Bronze Age Athens', in *Paleodiet in the Aegean. Papers from a colloquium held at the 1993 meeting of the Archaeological Institute of America in Washington D.C.* (Wiener Laboratory Monograph, 1), eds. S.J. Vaughan & W.D.E. Coulson, Oxford, 105-113.

Snodgrass, A.M. 1991, 'Bronze Age exchange: a minimalist position', in *Bronze Age trade in the Mediterranean. Papers presented at the conference held at Rewley House, Oxford, in December 1989* (SIMA, 90), ed. N.H. Gale, Jonsered, 15-20

Stos-Gale, Z.A. 1982, 'The sources of Mycenaean silver and lead', *JFA* 9, 467-485.

Stos-Gale, Z.A. & Macdonald, C.F. 1991, 'Sources of metals and trade in the Bronze Age Aegean', in *Bronze Age trade in the Mediterranean. Papers presented at the conference held at Rewley House, Oxford, in December 1989* (SIMA, 90), ed. N.H. Gale, Jonsered, 249-287.

Styrenius, C.-G. 1967, *Submycenaean studies* (ActaAth-8°,7), Lund.

Styrenius, C.-G. 1975, 'Some notes on the new excavations at Asine', *OpAth* 11, 175-183.

Taffinder, J. 1998, *The allure of the exotic. The social use of non-local raw materials during the Stone Age in Sweden* (Aun, 25), Uppsala.

Tamvaki, A. 1974, 'The seals and sealings from the Citadel House Area: a study in Mycenaean glyptic and iconography', *BSA* 69, 259-293.

Taylour, W.D. 1963, 'The Citadel House', in *The Mycenae tablets* III, ed. J. Chadwick (= *TAPS* 52:7), Philadelphia, 35-46.

Taylour, W.D. 1969, 'Mycenae, 1968', *Antiquity* 43, 91-97.

Taylour, W.D. 1971, 'The House with the idols, Mycenae, and its chronological implications', *AJA* 75, 266-268.

Taylour, W.D. 1981, *Well Built Mycenae, The Helleno-British excavations within the Citadel at Mycenae, 1959-1969*, 1, *The Excavations*, eds. W.D. Taylour, E.B. French & K.A. Wardle, Oxford.

Tegyey, I. 1988, 'Some problems of the status of the working groups on the Linear B tablets', *Acta classica univ. scient. Debrecen* 25, 3-8.

Thomas, C.G. 1970, 'A Mycenaean hegemony? A reconsideration', *JHS* 90, 184-192.

Thomas, C.G, 1995, 'The components of political identity in Mycenaean Greece', in *Politeia. Society and state in the Aegean Bronze Age* (= *Aegaeum* 12), eds. R. Laffineur & W.-D. Niemeier, Liège & Austin, 349-355.

Tournavitou, I. 1995, *The Ivory Houses at Mycenae* (BSA Suppl., 24), 1995.

Tournavitou, I. 1997, 'Jewellers' moulds and jewellers' workshops in Mycenaean Greece: an archaeological utopia', in *Trade and production in premonetary Greece: production and the craftsman. Proceedings of the 4th and 5th international workshops, Athens 1994 and 1995* (SIMA-PB, 143), eds. C. Gillis, C. Risberg & B. Sjöberg, Jonsered, 209-256.

Trombold, C.D., ed. 1991, *Ancient road networks and settlement hierarchies in the New World*, Avon.

Tzonou, I. 1998, 'The architectural remains', in G. Walberg, *Excavations on the Acropolis of Midea. Results of the Greek-Swedish excavations* I. *The excavations on the Lower Terraces* (ActaAth-4°, 49:1:1), Stockholm, 87-94.

Ucko, P.J. 1969, 'Ethnography and archaeological interpretation of funerary remains', *WorldArch* 1(2), 262-280.

van Andel, T.H. & Zangger, E. 1990, 'Landscape stability and destabilisation in the prehistory of Greece', in *Man's role in the shaping of the Eastern Mediterranean landscape. Proceedings of the INQUA/BAI Symposium on the impact of ancient man on the landscape of the Eastern Mediterranean and the Near East, Groningen, Netherlands, 6-9 March 1989*, eds. S. Bottema, G. Entjes-Nieborg & W. van Zeist, Rotterdam, 139-157.

van Wees, H. 1998, 'The law of gratitude: reciprocity in anthropological theory', in *Reciprocity in ancient Greece*, eds. C. Gill, N. Postlethwaite & R. Seaford, Oxford, 13-49.

van Wijngaarden, G.-J. 1999, 'An archaeological approach to the concepts of value: Mycenaean pottery at Ugarit', *Archaeological Dialogues* 6(1), 2-46.

Varas, C. 1994-1995, 'A tentative analysis of dialectical differences in the Linear B texts from Mycenae', *Minos* 29-30, 134-157.

Ventris, M. & Chadwick, J. 1973, *Documents in Mycenaean Greek*, 2nd ed., Cambridge.

Verdelis, N.M. 1963, 'The West House', in *The Mycenae tablets* III (= *TAPS* 52:7), ed. J. Chadwick, Philadelphia, 13-29.

Vermeule, E. 1964, *Greece in the Bronze Age*, Chicago.

Voigtländer, V. 1973, 'Zur Chronologie der Spät-mykenischen Burgen in Tiryns', *Tiryns. Forschungen und Berichte* VI, Mainz, 241-266.

Vollgraff, W. 1904, 'Fouilles d'Argos', *BCH* 28, 1904, 364-399.

von den Driesch, A. & Boessneck, J. 1990, 'Die Tierreste von der mykenischen Burg Tiryns bei Nauplion/ Peloponnes', in *Tiryns. Forschungen und Berichte* XI, Mainz, 87-164.

von Reden, S. 1995, *Exchange in ancient Greece*, London.

Voutsaki, S. 1992, *Society and culture in the Mycenaean world: an analysis of mortuary practices in the Argolid, Thessaly and the Dodecanese* (unpublished Ph.D. dissertation, University of Cambridge).

Voutsaki, S. 1995a, 'Social and political processes in the Mycenaean Argolid', in *Politeia. Society and state in the Aegean Bronze Age* (= *Aegaeum* 12), eds. R. Laffineur & W.-D. Niemeier, Liège & Austin, 55-66.

Voutsaki, S. 1995b, 'Value and exchange in premonetary societies: anthropological debates and Aegean archaeology', in *Trade and production in premonetary Greece: aspects of trade. Proceedings of the Third international workshop, Athens 1993* (SIMA-PB, 134), eds. C. Gillis, C. Risberg & B. Sjöberg, Jonsered, 1995, 7-17.

Voutsaki, S. 1997, 'Value and prestige in Late Bronze Age', *Journal of European Archaeology* 5:2, 34-51.

Voutsaki, S. 1998, 'Mortuary evidence, symbolic meanings and social change: a comparison between Messenia and the Argolid in the Mycenaean period', *Sheffield Studies in Aegean Archaeology* 1, 41-58.

Waarsenburg, D.J. 1995, *The Northwest Necropolis of Satricum. An Iron Age cemetery in Latium Vetus* (*Satricum* 3; Scrinium, 8), Amsterdam.

Wace, A.J.B. 1921-1923, 'Excavations at Mycenae', *BSA* 25.

Wace, A.J.B. 1932, *Chamber tombs at Mycenae* (= *Archaeologia* 82), Oxford.

Wace, A.J.B. 1953, 'Preliminary Report on the Excavations of 1952', *BSA* 48, 2-18.

Wace, A.J.B. 1954a, 'Preliminary report on the excavations of 1953', *BSA* 49, 231-243.

Wace, A.J.B. 1955, 'Mycenae 1939-1954. Part 1. Preliminary report on the excavations of 1954', *BSA* 50, 175-189.

Wace, A.J.B. 1956, 'Mycenae 1939-1955. Part I. Preliminary Report on the Excavations of 1955', *BSA* 51, 103-127.

Wace, A.J.B. & Rowe, K.R. 1954, 'Mycenae 1939-1953. Part IV. The "Gallery" in the north wall', *BSA* 49, 254-257.

Wace, A.J.B. & Wace, E.B. 1958, 'Introduction', in *The Mycenae tablets* II (= *TAPS* 48:1), ed. E.L. Bennett, Jr., 1958, 3-44.

Wace, E.B. 1954b, 'The Cyclopean Terrace Building and the deposit of pottery beneath it', *BSA* 49, 267-291.

Walberg, G. 1992a, 'A Linear B inscription from Midea', *Kadmos* 31(1), 93.

Walberg, G. 1992b, 'Excavations on the Lower Terrace at Midea', *OpAth* 19, 23-39.

Walberg, G. 1996-1997, 'Two new nodules from the Lower Terraces at Midea', *Minos* 31-32, 133-134.

Walberg, G. 1998a, *Excavations on the Acropolis of Midea* I. *Results of the Greek-Swedish excavations. The excavations on the Lower Terraces* (ActaAth-4°, 49:1:1), Stockholm.

Walberg, G. 1998b, 'The stratigraphy', in *eadem, Excavations on the Acropolis of Midea. Results of the Greek-Swedish excavations* I. *The excavations on the Lower Terraces* (ActaAth-4°, 49:1:1), Stockholm, 18-53.

Walberg, G. 1998c, 'The summary', in *eadem, Excavations on the Acropolis of Midea. Results of the Greek-Swedish excavations* I. *The excavations on the Lower Terraces* (ActaAth-4 °, 49:1:1), Stockholm, 175-178.

Walberg, G. 1999, 'The end of the Late Bronze Age at Midea', in *Polemos. Le contexte guerrier en Égée à l'âge du bronze* (= *Aegaeum* 19), ed. R. Laffineur, Liège, 157-160.

Walberg, G. & Giering, K.L. 1998, 'Roman and Bronze age rooms', in G. Walberg, *Excavations on the Acropolis of Midea. Results of the Greek-Swedish excavations* I. *The excavations on the Lower Terraces* (ActaAth-4°, 49:1:1), Stockholm, 77-86.

Walløe, L. 1999, 'Was the disruption of the Mycenaean world caused by repeated epidemics of bubonic plague?', *OpAth* 24, 121-126.

Waterson, R. 1995, 'Houses and hierarchies in Island Southeast Asia', in *About the house. Levi-Strauss and beyond*, eds. J. Carsten & S. Hugh-Jones, Cambridge, 47-68.

Wells, B. 1983, *Asine* II. *Results of the excavations east of the Acropolis 1970-1974*, fasc. 4. *The Protogeometric period.* Part 2. *An analysis of the settlement* (ActaAth-4°, 24:4:2), Stockholm.

Wells, B. 1990, 'Death at Dendra. On mortuary practices in a Mycenaean community', in *Celebrations of death and divinity in the Bronze Age Argolid. Proceedings of the Sixth International Symposium at the Swedish Institute at Athens, 11-13 June, 1988* (ActaAth-4°, 40), eds. R. Hägg & G.C. Nordquist, Stockholm, 125-140.

Wells, B., Runnels, C. & Zangger, E. 1990, 'The Berbati-Limnes archaeological survey. The 1988 season', *OpAth* 18, 207-238.

Wells, B., Runnels, C. & Zangger, E. 1993, 'In the shadow of Mycenae', *Archaeology* 46(1), 54-58, 63.

Wiencke, M.H. 1998, 'Mycenaean Lerna', *Hesperia* 67(2), 125-214.

Wright, J, 1987, 'Death and power at Mycenae: changing symbols in mortuary practice' in *Thanatos. Les coutumes funeraires en Egée a l'âge du bronze. Actes du colloque de Liège (21-23 avril 1986)* (= *Aegaeum* 1), ed. R. Laffineur, 171-184.

Wright, J. 1984, 'Changes in form and function of the palace at Pylos', in *Pylos comes alive: industry+ administration in a Mycenaean palace*, eds. C.W. Shelmerdine & T.G. Palaima, New York, 19-29.

Xenaki-Sakellariou, A. 1985, *Les tombes a chambre de Mycènes. Fouilles de Chr. Tsountas (1887-1898)*, Paris.

Zangger, E. 1993, *Argolis* II. *The geoarchaeology of the Argolid*, Berlin.

Zangger, E. 1994, 'Landscape changes around Tiryns during the Bronze Age', *AJA* 98, 189-212.

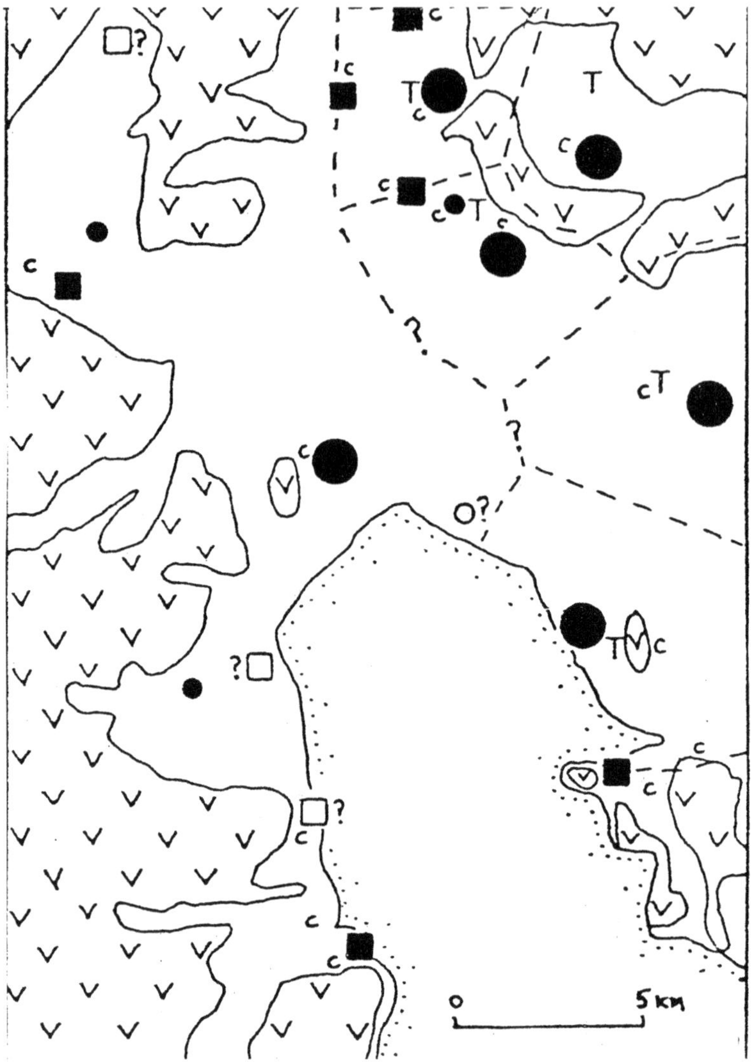

Fig. 1. The Argive hierarchy of settlements according to J.L. Bintliff. Originating from J.L. Bintliff *Natural environment and human settlement in Prehistoric Greece*, (BAR-SS, 28), map. 7, Oxford 1977.

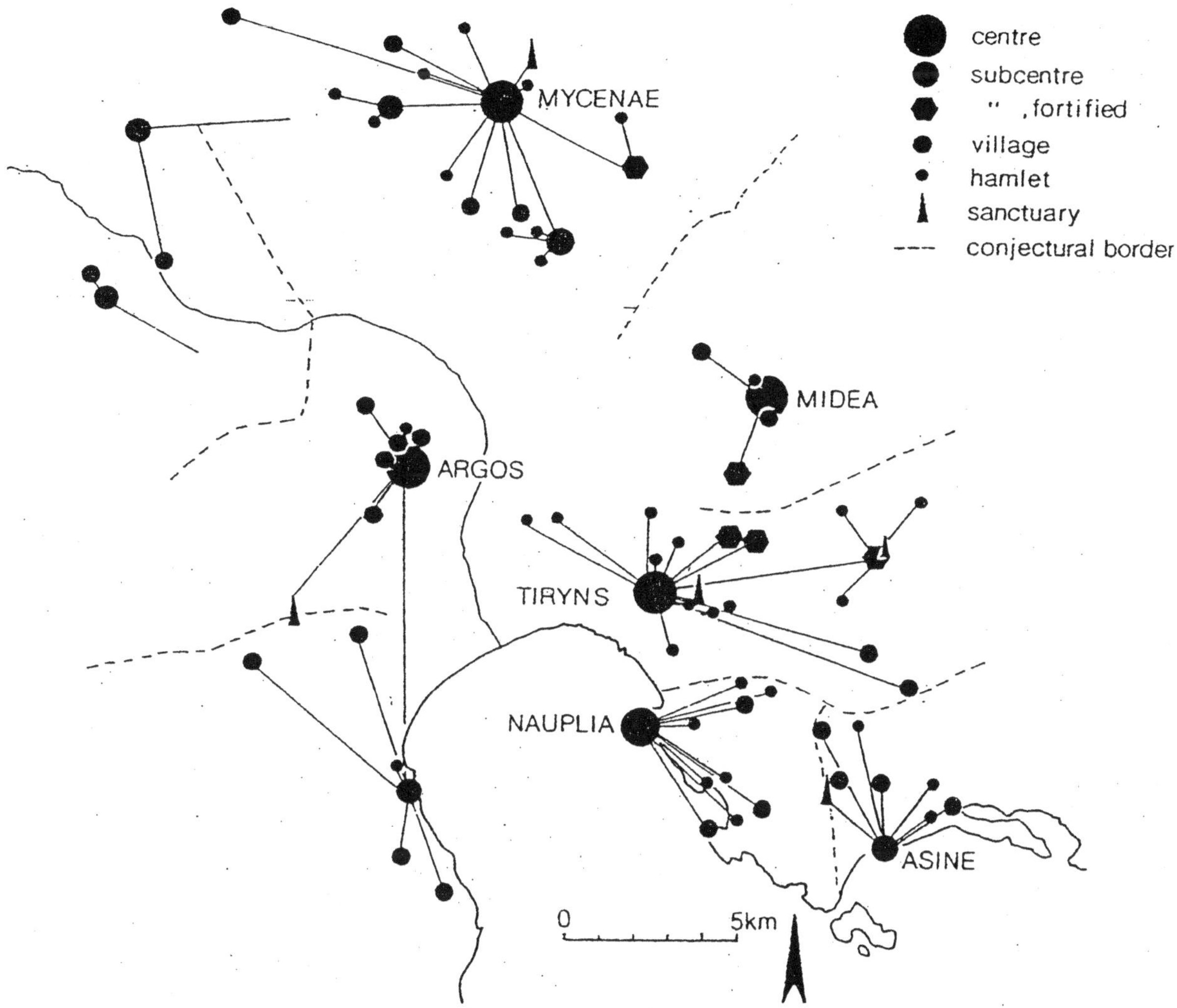

Fig. 2. The Argive hierarchy of settlements according to K. Kilian. Originating from K. Kilian, 'The emergence of *wanax* ideology in the Mycenaean palaces', *OJA*, vol. 7:3, 291-302, fig. 3, 1988. Has been included with the permission of Blackwell Publishing Ltd.

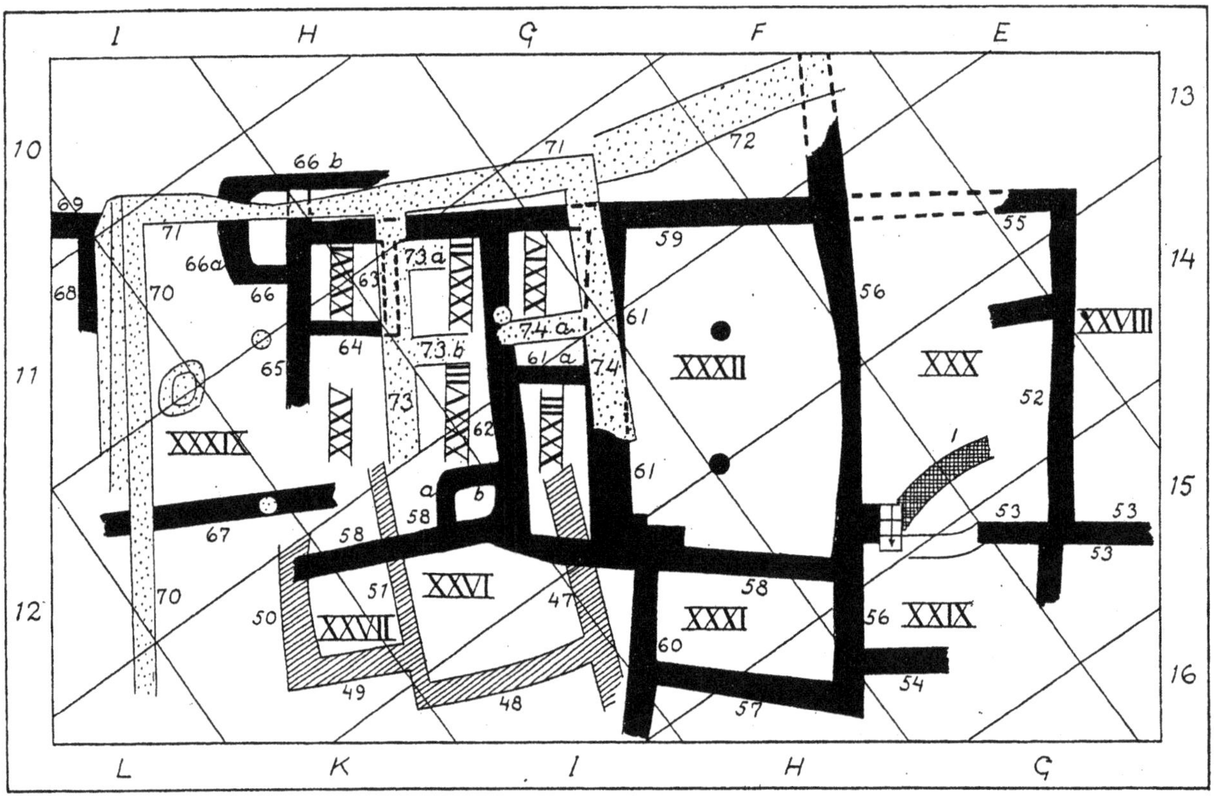

Analytical plan of Houses F—H (Latticed walls = House F; black walls = House G; punctated walls = House H; the hatched wall in Squares F—G 14 belongs to an E.H. house).

Fig. 3. Asine. Houses F-H. Originating from O. Frödin and A.W. Persson, *Asine. Results of the Swedish excavations 1922-1930*, fig. 53, Stockholm 1938.

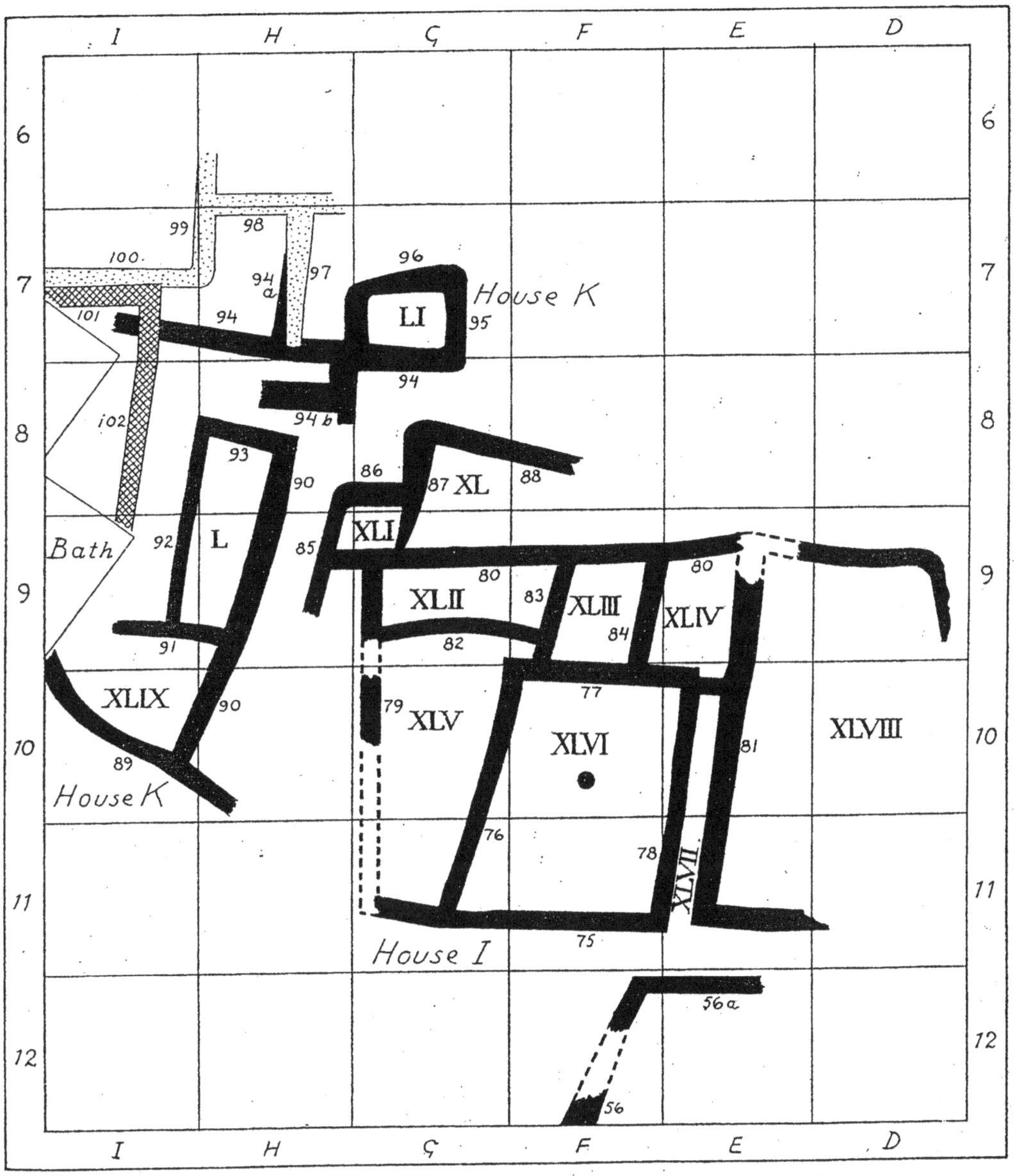

Fig. 4. Asine. Houses I-K. Originating from O. Frödin and A.W. Persson, *Asine. Results of the Swedish excavations 1922-1930*, fig. 58, Stockholm 1938.

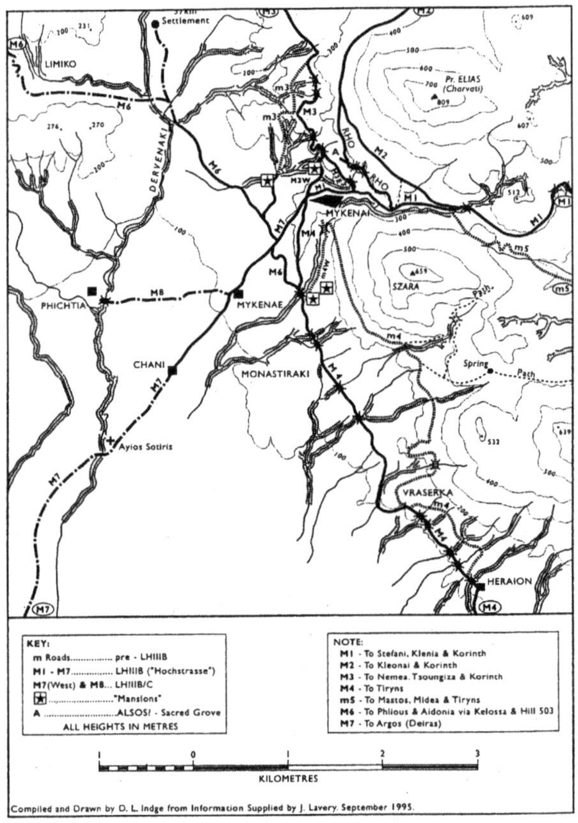

MAP 1

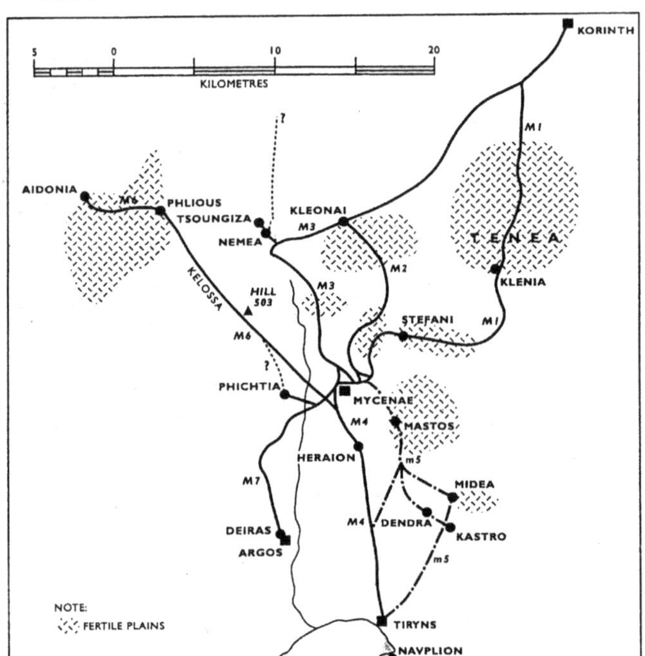

MAP 2

Fig. 5. The road system of the Argolid according to J. Lavery. Originating from J. Lavery, 'Some "new" Mycenaean roads at Mycenae', *BICS* 40, 264-267, maps 1-2, 1995. The first of the two maps in fig. 5 was originally compiled and drawn by D.L. Indge from information supplied by J. Lavery. The permission granted by the '©Institute of Classical Studies, School of Advanced Study, University of London: published by courtesy of the Institute of Classical Studies', to reproduce these maps.

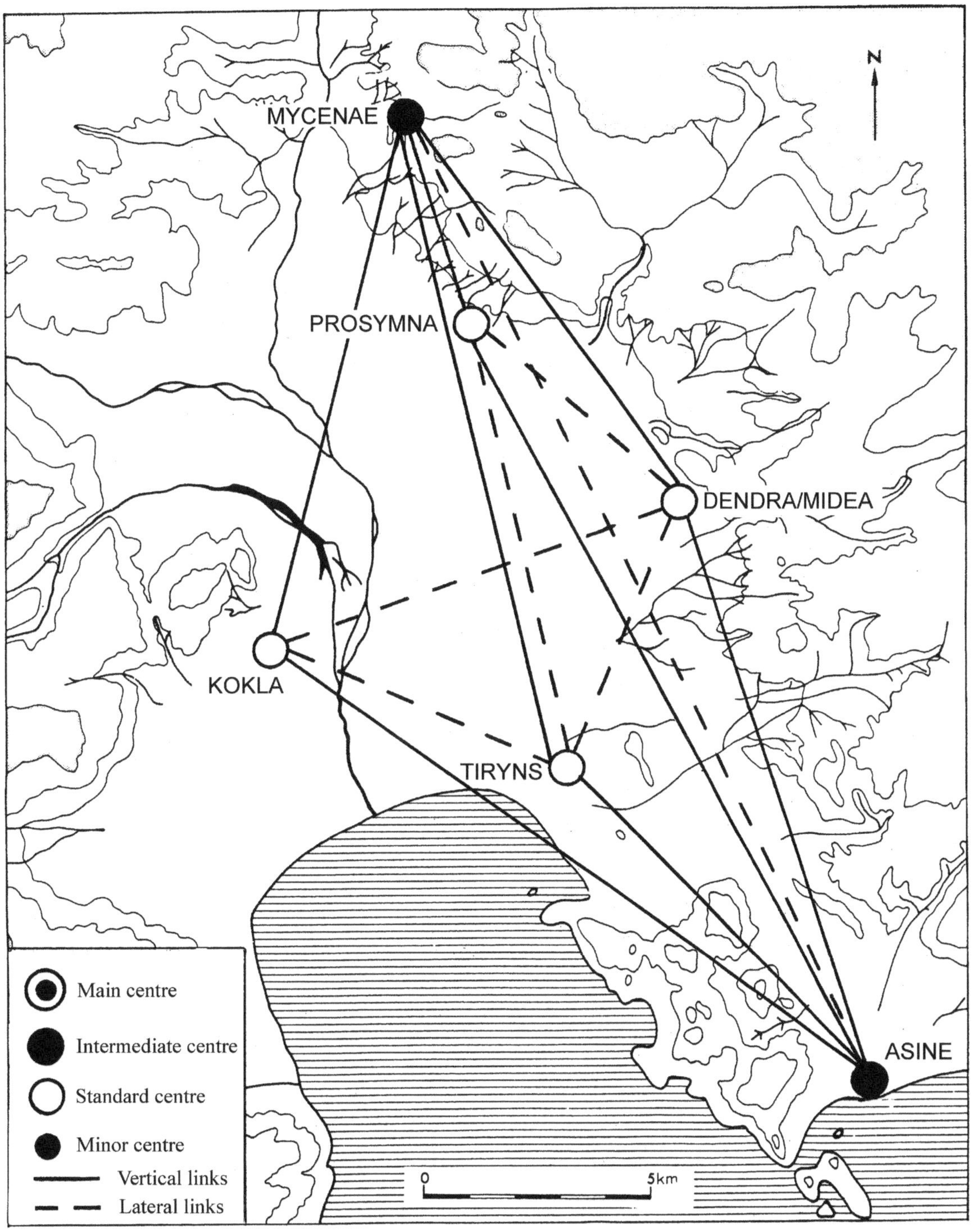

Fig. 6. The Argive settlement system: LH II. Drawn by Dr. A. Klynne on information compiled by B.L. Sjöberg. Map based on a base map originally published by R. Hägg in *Die Gräber der Argolis in submykenischer, protogeometrischer und geometrischer Zeit*, 1. *Lage und Form der Gräber* (Boreas. Uppsala Studies in Ancient Mediterranean and Near Eastern Civilizations, 7:1), fig. 1, Uppsala 1974.

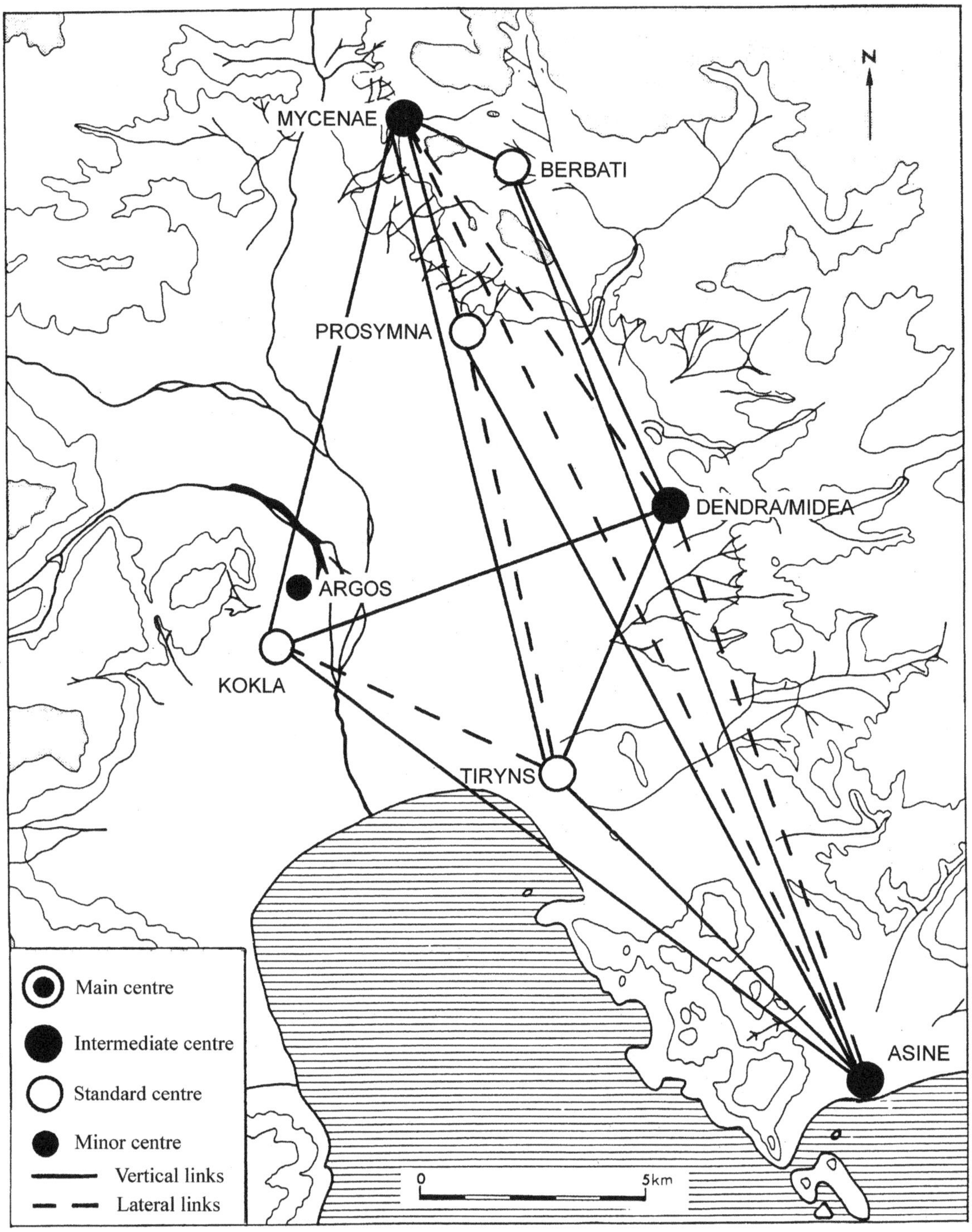

Fig. 7. The Argive settlement system: LH IIIA1. Drawn by Dr. A. Klynne on information compiled by B.L. Sjöberg. Map based on a base map originally published by R. Hägg in *Die Gräber der Argolis in submykenischer, protogeometrischer und geometrischer Zeit*, 1. *Lage und Form der Gräber* (Boreas. Uppsala Studies in Ancient Mediterranean and Near Eastern Civilizations, 7:1), fig. 1, Uppsala 1974.

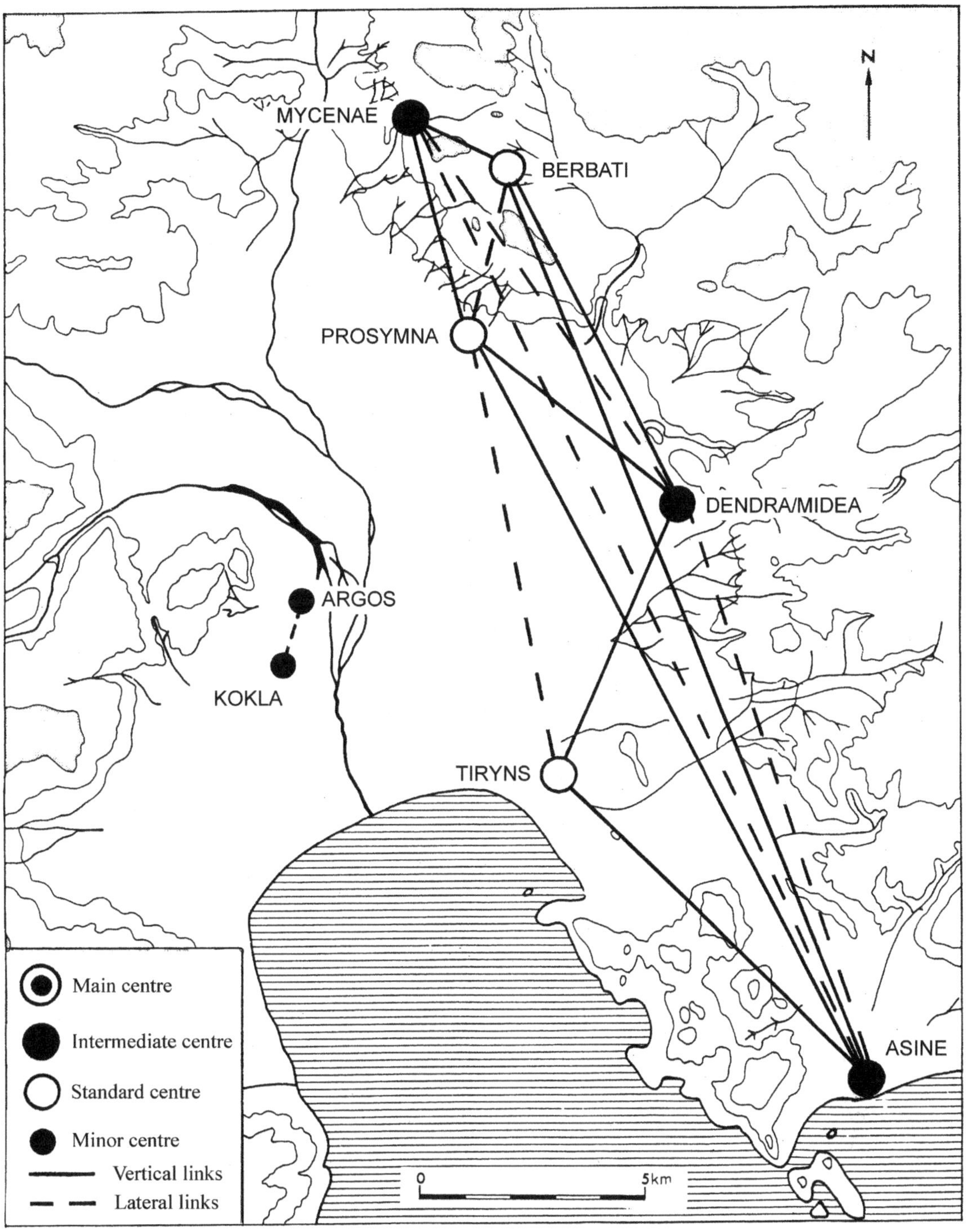

Fig. 8. The Argive settlement system: LH IIIA2. Drawn by Dr. A. Klynne on information compiled by B.L. Sjöberg. Map based on a base map originally published by R. Hägg in *Die Gräber der Argolis in submykenischer, protogeometrischer und geometrischer Zeit*, 1. *Lage und Form der Gräber* (Boreas. Uppsala Studies in Ancient Mediterranean and Near Eastern Civilizations, 7:1), fig. 1, Uppsala 1974.

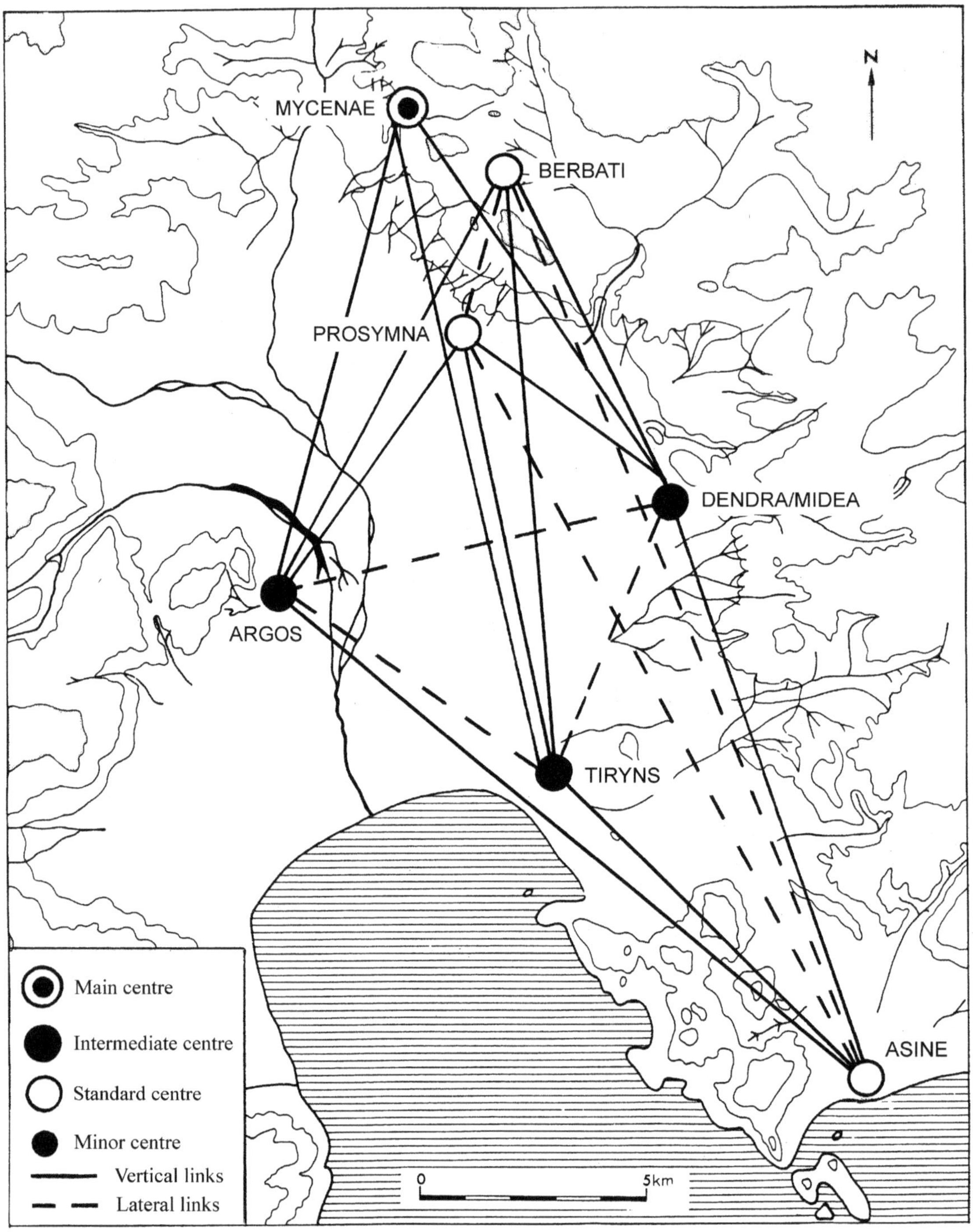

Fig. 9. The Argive settlement system: LH IIIB1. Drawn by Dr. A. Klynne on information compiled by B.L. Sjöberg. Map based on a base map originally published by R. Hägg in *Die Gräber der Argolis in submykenischer, protogeometrischer und geometrischer Zeit*, 1. *Lage und Form der Gräber* (Boreas. Uppsala Studies in Ancient Mediterranean and Near Eastern Civilizations, 7:1), fig. 1, Uppsala 1974.

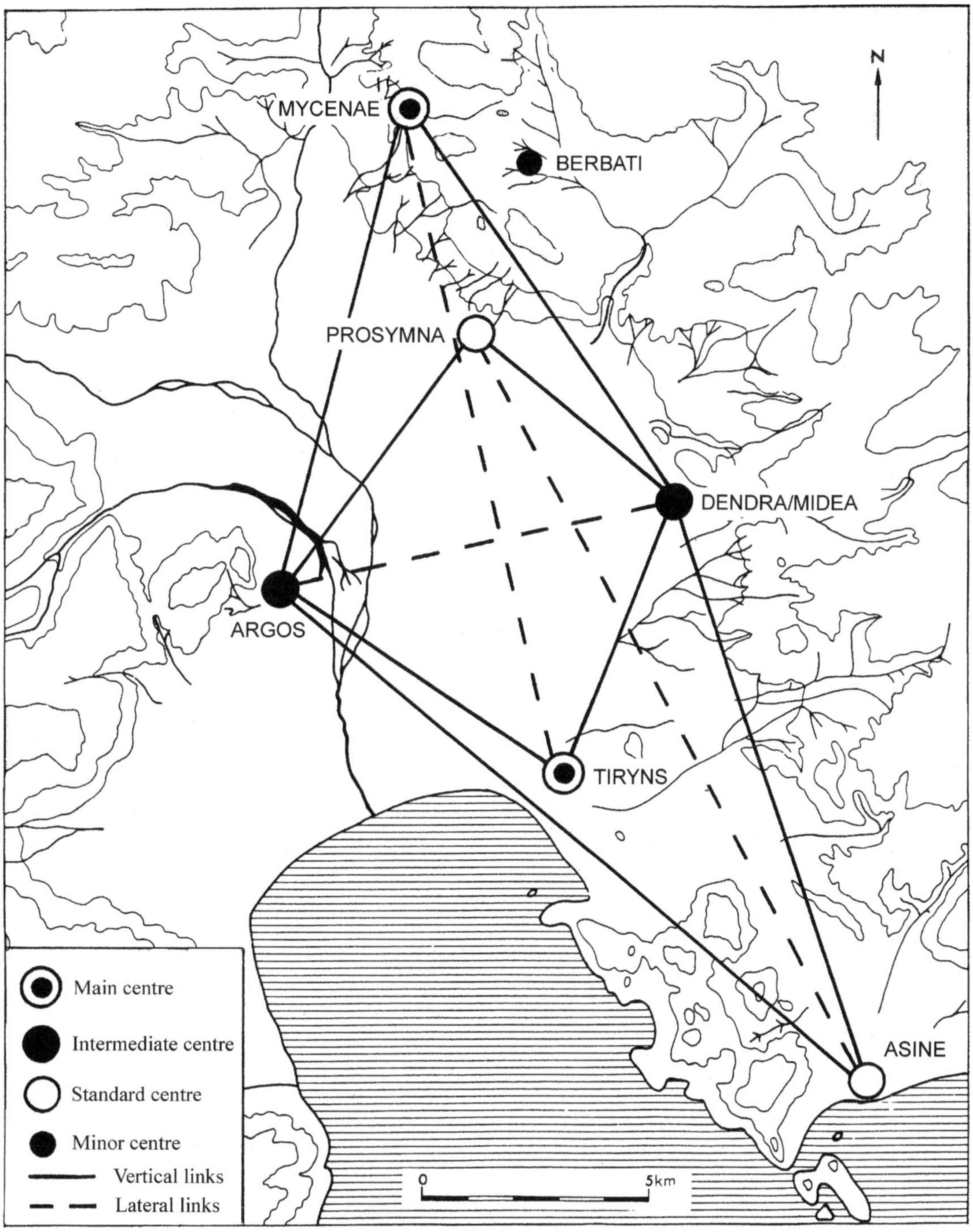

Fig. 10. The Argive settlement system: LH IIIB2. Drawn by Dr. A. Klynne on information compiled by B.L. Sjöberg. Map based on a base map originally published by R. Hägg in *Die Gräber der Argolis in submykenischer, protogeometrischer und geometrischer Zeit*, 1. *Lage und Form der Gräber* (Boreas. Uppsala Studies in Ancient Mediterranean and Near Eastern Civilizations, 7:1), fig. 1, Uppsala 1974.

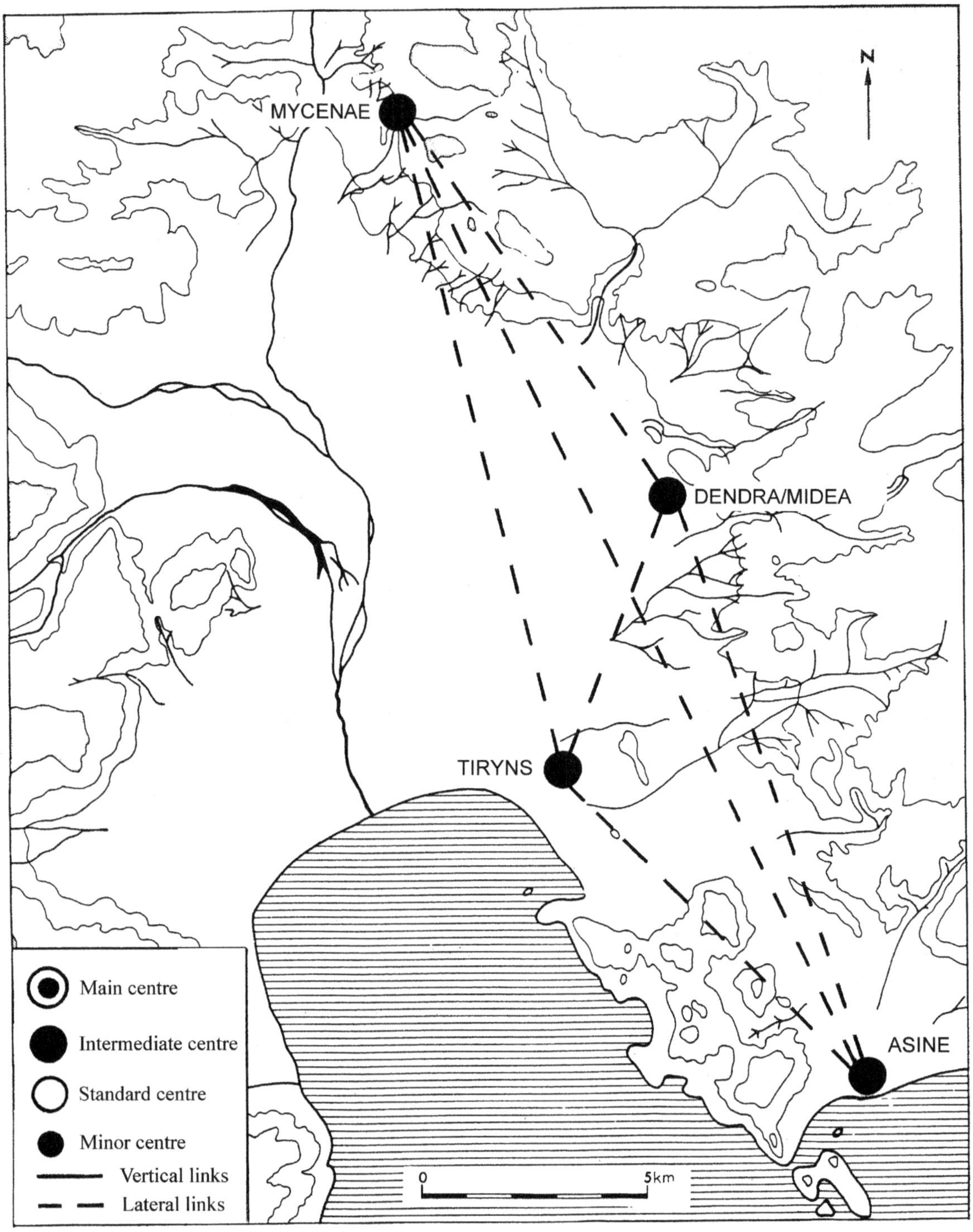

Fig. 11. The Argive settlement system: LH IIIC. Drawn by Dr. A. Klynne on information compiled by B.L. Sjöberg. Map based on a base map originally published by R. Hägg in *Die Gräber der Argolis in submykenischer, protogeometrischer und geometrischer Zeit*, 1. *Lage und Form der Gräber* (Boreas. Uppsala Studies in Ancient Mediterranean and Near Eastern Civilizations, 7:1), fig. 1, Uppsala 1974.

www.ingramcontent.com/pod-product-compliance
Lightning Source LLC
LaVergne TN
LVHW071212210926
848482LV00015B/789